Women Warriors and Wartime Spies of China

In this compelling new study, Louise Edwards explores the lives of some of China's most famous women warriors and wartime spies through history. Focusing on key figures including Hua Mulan, Zheng Pingru and Liu Hulan, this book examines the ways in which these extraordinary women have been commemorated through a range of cultural mediums including film, theatre, museums and textbooks. Whether these women are perceived as heroes or anti-heroes, Edwards shows that both the popular and official presentations of them and of their accomplishments have evolved in line with China's shifting political values and military aspirations over the past 100 years. In lively and accessible style, with illustrations throughout, this book sheds new light on the relationship between gender and militarisation and the ways that women have been exploited to glamorise war both historically and in China today.

LOUISE EDWARDS is Professor of Chinese History and Asian Studies Convener at UNSW, Australia.

Women Warriors and Wartime Spies of China

Louise Edwards
UNSW Australia

CAMBRIDGE
UNIVERSITY PRESS

University Printing House, Cambridge CB2 8BS, United Kingdom

Cambridge University Press is part of the University of Cambridge.

It furthers the University's mission by disseminating knowledge in the pursuit of education, learning and research at the highest international levels of excellence.

www.cambridge.org
Information on this title: www.cambridge.org/9781316509340

© Louise Edwards 2016

This publication is in copyright. Subject to statutory exception and to the provisions of relevant collective licensing agreements, no reproduction of any part may take place without the written permission of Cambridge University Press.

First published 2016

Printed in the United States of America by Sheridan Books, Inc.

A catalogue record for this publication is available from the British Library

ISBN 978-1-107-14603-7 Hardback
ISBN 978-1-316-50934-0 Paperback

Cambridge University Press has no responsibility for the persistence or accuracy of URLs for external or third-party internet websites referred to in this publication, and does not guarantee that any content on such websites is, or will remain, accurate or appropriate.

For my sisters
Debbie, Kate and Nicola
He ao-mārama rangimārie, he taonga pounamu

Contents

Figures

Acknowledgements

This book had its genesis in my experience as a student in the late 1970s at Canada's Lester B. Pearson College of the Pacific – part of the United World College (UWC) network. I spent two challenging years with young people from all around the world pondering the problems of war and peace in all manner of geographic and historical contexts. A generous scholarship provided by the New Zealand UWC Committee enabled me to attend the college, and the experience was nothing short of life changing. My interest in understanding the failure of leadership that produces war and conflict continues to this day. And it was at Pearson that I began my studies of China.

China's experience of war and the miseries it produced from the mid-1800s is etched as an indelible scar on the consciousness of all its citizens. As those who experienced the trauma of war pass on, the government teaches the history of China's suffering to new generations. Presenting opportunities for us to learn lessons from past mistakes is surely one of history's greatest powers, yet we see equally commonly narratives of the past being used to perpetuate hatred, distrust and fear as global elites seek to turn citizens into soldiers. This book explores the ways that ideas of women and gender are used to create an environment conducive to militarised violence within deep-seated but immensely malleable cultures of war. Understanding this malleability is central to building cultures of peace.

Many people have helped in the researching and writing of this book and deserve my heartfelt thanks. Darrell Dorrington, Miwa Hirono, Samantha Hauw, Stephen Su, Chen Minglu, Franchesca Marron, Amanda Kunafi, Narelle Ng and Mike Dennison helped gather material and read draft chapters. Colleagues at Australian National University, University of Technology Sydney, Hong Kong University and UNSW Australia provided generous critiques on early drafts, as have participants in many conferences and workshops over the years. The friendship of Johanna Hood, Lauren Gorfinkel, Lili Zhou, Zhang Yun, Selena Orly, Cui Tao and Anna Costa has been invaluable in spurring me to finish the book. To Tim Wright, Nick Knight and Mary Farquhar, thank you for your guidance and generosity over many decades on all manner of personal and professional matters. I would also like to express my gratitude to the referees at Cambridge University Press who provided incredibly useful advice and a detailed reading of the manuscript. Lucy Rhymer has been an assiduous editor – thank you for your support throughout. And thanks also to the production team who turn manuscript pages into the final crafted book and to Sherrey Quinn for the indexing.

Finally, to Kam, Chris and Alex, you give meaning to everything.

Louise Edwards
Sydney 2015

The Australian Research Council provided funding for this project.

Earlier versions of two chapters have appeared in journals and are reprinted with permission.

Chapter 2 appeared as 'Transformations of the Woman Warrior Hua Mulan: From Defender of the Family to Servant of the State', *Nan Nü: Men, Women and Gender in China* 12 (2010), 175–214.

Chapter 8 appeared as 'Women Sex-Spies: Chastity, National Dignity, Legitimate Government and Ding Ling's "When I Was in Xia Village"', *China Quarterly* 212 (2012), 1059–78.

Chronology

1900:	Boxer War – Eight foreign nations combine to defeat the Qing and Boxer forces, leaving Beijing ransacked
1911:	Qing Dynasty collapses under pressure from anti-Manchu republicans
1912:	Republic of China (ROC) established
1912:	Sun Yat-sen's Revolutionary Alliance merges with other parties to form the Nationalist Party
1915:	Progressive intellectuals launch the New Culture Movement designed to modernise China's social, political and intellectual structures – including prominent calls for sex equality
1919:	Paris Peace Conference, Versailles, denies China the return of German-held territory, prompting mass student-worker protests called the May Fourth Movement
1921:	Chinese Communist Party (CCP) established
1924:	Chinese Nationalist Party reforms and aligns itself with the Soviet Union
1923–1927:	First United Front between the Nationalist Party and the CCP
1926–1928:	Northern Expedition to unite China – a combined Nationalists and Communist venture
1927:	Collapse of the United Front with the right wing of the Nationalist Party attempting to eradicate its left-wing members and the CCP
1928:	Nationalist Party government established with its capital in Nanjing, led by Chiang Kai-shek
1931:	Japan invades North East China
1932–1945:	Manchukuo established under Japanese control
1936–1945:	Second United Front between Nationalist Party and CCP
1937–1945:	Sino–Japanese War, aka War of Resistance against Japan – Nationalist and CCP forces battle Japan's invasion
1938:	Chiang Kai-shek moves his Nationalist Government capital inland to Chongqing as Japanese occupy Beijing, Shanghai and Nanjing

1940–1945:	'Reorganized National Government of China' formed under Wang Jingwei's leadership – collaborating with the Japanese
1942:	Yan'an Talks on Literature and Art held in Communist Base area – Mao's Socialist Realist Principles for all creative works formulated
1945:	Japan defeated and her troops depart China
1946–1949:	Civil War between Chiang Kai-shek's Nationalist Party forces and Mao Zedong's CCP forces
1949:	CCP claims victory in the Civil War and forms the People's Republic of China (PRC). The Nationalist Party retreats to the island of Taiwan to continue the ROC
1950–1953:	Korean War – PRC troops fight in support of the North Koreans
1957:	Mao launches the Hundred Flowers Movement and the Anti-Rightist Movement to suppress dissent
1957–1958:	Great Leap Forward: formation of People's Communes in rural China
1966–1976:	Great Proletarian Cultural Revolution propels the country into constant revolution, intra-party purges and criticism of authority figures
1978:	'Opening-up and Reform' era of political and economic liberalisation commences, led by Deng Xiaoping
1989:	Tiananmen student and worker protests suppressed
1991:	Patriotic Education Campaign commences to build nationalism among youth
2006:	CCP promotes the 'Harmonious Society' ideal to build social stability and a 'Moderately Prosperous Society' to manage growing inequality

1 Soldiering, war and gender in China

Women soldiers and wartime spies challenge foundational gender norms in their daring deeds and dramatic actions – so it is little wonder that stories about women's involvement in wartime action attract instant popular interest all around the world. The vision of a woman killing another human being affronts long-held views about women as life-givers rather than harbingers of death. Envisioning female bodies in military uniforms challenges normative ideas about feminine beauty and grace. Contemplating women risking their lives undermines the notion that such courage is primarily a manly attribute. Imagining the adventures of the beautiful and sexy undercover agent thrills audiences as they see conventional sexual morays crumble in the face of service to the nation. How can a woman kill? How can she lead in battle? Will she have the courage to fight? How can she sacrifice her virtue to trade sex for secrets?

In China the popular fascination with women who go to war has existed for centuries. They filled the pages of classical novels, frequently appeared in operas and plays, and in our current-era populate movies, television series, propaganda posters, computer games and schoolbooks. Interest in women warriors and wartime spies shows no sign of abating in the twenty-first century despite the dramatic changes in gender norms that have occurred during the last 100 years. All around the world, including China, women have become politicians, bankers, lawyers, teachers, landowners and scientists – roles previously prohibited to them. But none of these roles generates as much fascination as women's participation in warfare and espionage. In many countries, the armed forces remain one of the few professions where biological sex can still determine the nature of duties assigned – women are frequently prohibited from front-line combat. The People's Republic of China (PRC) is one such nation that limits women's combat roles – despite the extensive promotion of women as active war fighters in public narratives. This phenomenon tells us that war fighting continues to be intimately linked to notions of maleness and masculinity in ways that teaching, banking or administering are not. The symbolic power of the woman war fighter reveals that war and militarised violence continues to be structured around gender norms – indeed war *needs* gender norms to continue its logic.[1] Conventional, some would say outdated, gender norms help governments and armed groups present war as an attractive option for conflict resolution to ordinary citizens.

This book reveals the ways that women and men, femininity and masculinity have been used to advocate for war, to promote militarised violence and to perpetuate the seeming logic of the inevitability of war through the public commemoration of woman warriors and wartime spies. Such thought structures are integral to militarisation. Jacklyn Cock explains that 'Militarization is a social process that involves the mobilization of resources for war on political, economic and ideological levels.'[2] Anuradha Chenoy's work on South Asia shows that 'militarization is a larger phenomenon than war' that needs to be challenged at an ideological level in order to promote peace.[3] And, as Cynthia Enloe has argued, militarisation continues during peacetime because governments argue that it maintains military preparedness and enhances national security.[4] Militarisation is more than the expenditure of money on weapons; it involves creation of a militarised consciousness among citizens and a culture of war throughout society – in schools and workplaces and through all forms of media.[5] The militarisation of society requires rituals, memorials, movies and school texts to give war legitimacy – despite its evident and well-documented horror and futility. Enloe explains its pervasive nature – 'Militarization is never simply about joining a military. It is a far more subtle process. And it sprawls over far more of the gendered social landscape than merely those peaks clearly painted a telltale khaki.'[6] She warns us against only seeing militarisation in the men and women of the armed forces and to recognise its form in food, fashion and film stars.[7] But the stories told about the men and women in the armed forces are among the most evident and sustained forms of militarisation because they popularise war by personalising it. Accordingly, this book explores the narratives of women warriors and wartime spies and reveals their significant role in the militarisation of Chinese society. Women war fighters become powerful icons to proclaim the urgency of war, of its demands that *all* patriots make some sort of sacrifice. They help hide its dirty, calculated nastiness beneath a deceit of eroticised glamour, or a promise of the 'opportunity' to break free of ordinary-life restrictions. The continued promotion of women warriors and wartime spies across all forms of media reveals their centrality to the militarisation of peacetime societies as well as their utility during wartime battles.

All the women featured in this book are household names in the PRC, yet few, with the exception of Hua Mulan (Chapter 2) and perhaps Qiu Jin (Chapter 3), are known beyond China's borders. Most studies of women war fighters ignore the Chinese instances or give them cursory attention.[8] Scholars of China have provided us with important studies of some key women and their experiences of war – usually within a rubric of women's increasing penetration of the male-dominated public sphere or in a narrative celebrating 'exceptional women of China's past'.[9] My purpose here is to address Nicole Dombrowski's challenge to consider the complicity of women in the 'atrocities or war crimes committed in part in their name'.[10] Through this study of the woman warrior and wartime spy as iconic phenomena created and mobilised in twentieth-century China, I explore how womanhood, femininity and masculinity are useful as militarisation strategies. The real women, their actual stories and their motivations are significant but even more powerful are the ways that their stories are used in political and social contexts through their many subsequent renditions and remakings. Where other scholars have focused on the lives and social roles of the women warrior or spy, I delve deeper to explore the many uses to which they have been put in public narratives. Some of the women included in this book have become more important in their commemorative afterlife than they were during their lifetimes because of the immense volume of materials discussing them in the public realm and the considerable investment by governments in promoting particular versions of their histories. For many of the women, their 'reality' has been entirely eclipsed by the narratives constructed around them. Even the two fictional women included in the book, Hua Mulan (Chapter 2) and Zhenzhen (Chapter 8), are frequently debated *as if they were real* and narratives of both play important roles in gendering militarisation and perpetuating the war system, even when recognised as fiction.[11]

The stories we tell and are told about war, regardless of our actual experience, are central to the promotion of war as a necessary or even desirable option for conflict resolution. We are frequently told that our nations were forged through the mass violence of war, and the *way* that these events are commemorated reveals a great deal about the society that emerges from those wars. During the twentieth century, China faced a series of militarised conflicts that drew artists, writers, filmmakers and journalists into close cooperation with governments and military leaders in their joint efforts to secure victory or legitimise control over territory. As we will see throughout this book, they produced material replete with information about the gendered nature of war through their frequently romanticised invocations of women's particular roles. Marketing war to the masses could not be achieved without the invocation of long-held ideas about gender or the symbolic functions 'women' perform within societies.

War fighting is among the most gendered arenas of human activity – its conceptualisation, promotion, execution and retreat. Effective rehabilitation of affected societies often relies heavily on gender norms. So intimate are war's links with gender that Joshua Goldstein alerts us to the 'mutuality of gender and war', declaring that 'Causality runs both ways between war and gender. Gender roles adapt individuals for war roles, and war roles provide the context within which individuals are socialised into gender roles'.[12] Stories of war, combat films, memorial sites, news reports, school history curricula and war art depend upon the mutuality of gender roles and war roles for their efficacy – consumers of these products are socialised into the war system regardless of the presence or absence of actual militarised violence and are trained in their appropriate gender roles simultaneously. The materials explored in this book reveal how this process of militarisation operates in China today and the way that it was built from sophisticated patterns of earlier war systems. In this respect, my project is not about the detailed operations of war or espionage as they occurred in China but, rather, about how they are narrated and specifically how they narrate the connection between gender and the war system.[13]

By the mid-twentieth century, the establishment of the PRC meant that all cultural production came under the control of the Chinese Communist Party (CCP) who recognised the power of cultural products to deliver ideological messages and took direct interest in managing their nature, form and style. Women warriors and wartime spies would be harnessed by the CCP as the party consolidated its rule of the country, and almost all chapters of this book address the CCP's preferred perspectives on the contributions and significance of the women. Dead and martyred women warriors are the preferred objects of commemoration – they cannot contradict the messages the state seeks to deliver. All forms of state-controlled media herald the heroism and sacrificial glory of the woman warrior as she fought for her country (e.g. mother-guerrilla Zhao Yiman of Chapter 6 and girl-guerrilla Liu Hulan of Chapter 9). The book also reveals the CCP's post-conflict anxiety about what to do with women who challenged ideals about the sexual virtue of women patriots (e.g. the Shanghai cover girl Zheng Pingru of Chapter 7 and the fictional peasant 'comfort woman' Zhenzhen of Chapter 8). It reveals the CCP's sometime difficulty in managing the outliers such as women of competing national and ideological loyalties (e.g. the Taiwan and American-based writer-soldier, Xie Bingying of Chapter 4 and the Manchu Princess Aisin Gioro Xianyu of Chapter 5). The current book, then, is a discussion of the ways women warriors and wartime spies have been put to work by those who would recreate them for their own purposes. It reveals the ideology of those who recreated them as much as it does the women's own motivations for joining up to fight.

Women Warriors and Wartime Spies of China is organised largely chronologically. This structure enables readers to trace the changing nature of these iconic women as they are mobilised by various types of governments and respond to different types of media and consumer demand. The major conflicts of the twentieth century are represented as well as their continued significances as active, cultivated historical memories in the twenty-first century. However, the next chapter narrates the ideological journey of the grandmother of all women war fighters, Hua Mulan. If she existed, her war was centuries before the twentieth century but her relevance to this book and to all later women warriors cannot be underestimated. Mulan's evolution sets the template from which all others are judged and in exploring her changing story over centuries we see the ideological power of the Chinese woman warrior in the marketing of war and the selling of militarised violence to generations of Chinese people. Chapter 3 discusses Qiu Jin, a member of Sun Yat-sen's underground group that prompted the 1911 revolution and established Asia's first, albeit shaky, republic. Soldier-journalist Xie Bingying appears in Chapter 4 as a major commentator on the 1926–1928 Northern Expedition in which the CCP and the Nationalist Party joined together for a time to unify the country under one government. Her *War Diaries* are some of the few extant personal documents written by a serving soldier from that time. The Japanese invasion of North East China in 1931 and their establishment of a new nation state, Manchukuo, provide the backdrop for the colourful Manchu Princess Aisin Gioro Xianyu. Fighting against the Chinese and in defence of her ethnic homeland, Xianyu was tried and (perhaps) executed at the end of the eight-year-long War of Resistance against Japan. Communist guerrilla fighter Zhao Yiman was among the 'red' forces that plagued Xianyu's short-lived nation. Zheng Pingru, the cover girl, honey-trap spy, also operated at this time but in Japanese-occupied Shanghai – working against the security and espionage forces of a collaborationist Chinese government. The latter half of the Sino–Japanese war dovetailed with the Second European 'World' War of 1939–1945. Ding Ling's fictional 'comfort woman' spy, Zhenzhen, was created during this struggle against the Japanese invasion, although her afterlife in post-1949 peacetime PRC would generate her more fame than she won during the war. The conflicting ambitions of the CCP and the Nationalist Party saw China descend into civil war in 1946, providing a platform for the girl underground fighter, Liu Hulan. Captured and executed by a guillotine-like hay-cutter, Liu Hulan was a loyal communist child whose story would appear in children's textbooks for decades as the CCP promoted patriotism and sacrifice among youngsters in the PRC.

The following sections of this introduction explain the core challenges that women warriors and wartime spies pose for the war system in its traditional-gendered form and the ways that they are co-opted and tamed by it. I turn first to explore how they disrupt the logic in which enemies are feminised in official and popular stories. I then move to examine how women's presence outside the space of 'hearth and home' as warriors and spies upsets the idealised vision of men's protection of women's virtue. From here I discuss the ways that women's fighting skills intersected with feminist aspirations for new roles for women citizens in China. I close the introduction with a discussion of the role that women warriors played in elevating the social status of the soldier generally in the modernisation of China's military during the first half of the twentieth century. These themes reappear in different parts of the book as they manifest in the particular women warriors or wartime spies themselves.

Disrupting the logic of feminised enemies

The use of gender in militarised thinking is often horrifically explicit – as in the statement below explaining why Japan needed to take over China in the 1930s. Business leader Ishihara Koichiro, President of the Ishihara Trading and Navigation Company, explained his position in 1935 as follows: 'An old saying has it that there is nothing more uncontrollable than a woman. China is like an unchaste woman. She is a sycophant before the stronger, and a braggart before the weaker. In dealing with such a nation, it is necessary for Japan to strike her first, and then caress and coddle her.'[14] Such comments are found the world over during war and point to the commonplace feminisation of the enemy in propaganda or media reports. Goldstein points out that this feminisation of the enemy frequently involves 'enacting rape symbolically (and sometimes literally), thereby using gender to symbolise domination'.[15] Ideals of manhood, martial prowess and the right to discipline a feminised China were central to Japan's projection of the war that Japan waged against China. Ishihara's images of paired beatings and caresses of a cringing female China presaged the systematic rape and sexual enslavement of real women that would emerge as the most brutal manifestations of this gendered logic of war. How then do women warriors and wartime spies, as icons, work within this rubric?

Part of the ongoing popular fascination with their form emerges because women warriors and wartime spies intersect with the logic that feminises the enemy and presumes a link between femininity and weakness. Women warriors are frequently heralded for their exceptional courage and strength – and while this is sometimes explained as manifesting their 'unfeminine' behaviour or 'masculine tendencies' it nonetheless exposes the fraudulence of the long-held 'truth' that positions women as essentially vulnerable. The presence of strong and effective women war fighters disrupts this logic of a feminine and, thereby, weaker 'enemy other' that can be easily overcome and even sexually dominated as part of the spoils of victory. Some of the women discussed in this book explicitly present themselves as directly fighting against male dominance over women through their participation in warfare, for example Qiu Jin (Chapter 3) and Xie Bingying (Chapter 4). They undermine, by their deeds and words, the gendered logic of Ishihara's war system by refusing to be the cringing feminine form waiting to be beaten and then caressed. They destabilise this taken-for-granted pattern that presents femininity as weak and women, the presumed 'more feminine' sex, as victims. Women warriors and wartime spies make the normal gendering of militarisation a 'problem' to be picked over.

Yet within the same gendered logic of militarisation, women warriors and wartime spies present contradictory possibilities about the capabilities of 'our side'. On the one hand, they intimate that *even* our women are capable of manifesting (masculine) strength – presenting the whole national population as possessing increased strength. On the other, they risk trivialising the armed forces they join, diminishing its masculinity with the contamination of woman's (feminine) weakness. Lu Xun, China's greatest twentieth-century writer, exposed this latter aspect of the woman warrior in his satirical piece 'New "women generals"' from 1931. The scare quotes around the noun mark his doubts about the generals' efficacy. He argues that women soldiers are merely the wartime manifestation of a common, colourful diversionary role that women have long performed in popular theatre. He describes Shanghai newspapers' enthusiasm for including pictures of beautiful women – variously called Madam A, Madam B, Madam C – depicting their fashion choices as the seasons progressed. In spring they wore tight-fitting clothes, while in the summer heat their sleeves and trousers shortened as they engaged in that ever-so diverting pastime of 'sea-bathing'. Lu Xun caustically continues, 'As we entered the autumn and the temperatures dropped the Japanese unexpectedly invaded the North Eastern provinces, so the pictorials immediately featured nurses in long white medical gowns, or young educated women dressed in military uniforms carrying guns. These images elicit readers' approval since they are rich with drama.' He then makes a direct comparison between the Chinese enthusiasm for diverting visions of women's wartime participation and the absence of these in the Japanese enemy. 'Let's look at some facts for evidence: (1) Nobody has ever seen pictures of nurses from the Japanese "Punish China Troops"; (2) There are no women generals in the Japanese army. But they are the ones that attacked. This is because when the Japanese take action they really take action and when they are playacting they really playact. They don't muddle the two together.'[16] No doubt Lu Xun was not alone in his view that the presence of women soldiers, and even women nurses, revealed China's vulnerability rather than its strength. But, within the gendered logic of war women warriors tweak a central point – the state's desire to mobilise *everyone* for the war effort. The challenge is to make women useful when the logic of the war system depends so much on femininity being equated with weakness (and women being construed as its corporeal form) and masculinity as strength (and men being construed as its corporeal form).

Protecting our girls' virtue

Dombrowksi and Goldstein, among many others, have identified the gendered coding of the hearth and home that is to be protected in militarisation narratives. Men are encouraged to go to war to protect the feminine domestic space. In this logic, women wave men off to war from the doorstep of the family home, wait in chaste quietude and welcome them back once victory is secured. Protecting women and their sexual virtue is central to the masculinity of the war project soldiers are invited to join. The location of women in the 'to-be-defended home' isolates femininity in a discreet social space and therein increases the masculine world of the soldiers' barracks. Women warriors and wartime spies confound this neat dichotomy because they trouble the boundary between war space (masculine and morally ambiguous) and home space (feminine and virtuous). Women's participation in war fighting demonstrates that some women do not perceive of themselves as passive or potential victims to be rescued. Their active roles in non-domestic space destabilises the gendered principle that war enhances the masculine power of men by granting them, by dint of their sex, the role of protector of women and their virtue.

Women warriors and wartime spies reject the system that would reduce them to symbols of sexual integrity by wilfully disregarding its value to patriarchal lineages and honour when they go to war. Men are encouraged to go to war to prevent the contamination of 'our' women's sexual virtue. Women going to war risk that very same feminine virtue. The challenge women warriors pose to men's masculine roles as protectors of a sexually chaste, feminine space is managed within the war system through the narratives that present 'our side' of the war terrain as largely asexual. Not only do 'our men' *not* rape and pillage, neither do they harass or abuse 'our female comrades-in-arms' – that kind of immoral behaviour is always credited to 'the enemy'. Xie Bingying (Chapter 4) devotes considerable time explaining to readers of her newspaper diaries the importance, for her peer women recruits, of suppressing romantic notions about male recruits. Zhao Yiman (Chapter 6) is depicted in early post-1949 propaganda as living the life of communist guerrilla alongside male troops without the slightest hint of sexual attraction. Her connections with men are comradely and professional as are theirs with her. Through stories of the high moral standards and asexual environment of 'our troops', women soldiers facilitate the glorification of the virtue of 'our boys'. This de-sexualisation of the 'our side' front lines is also achieved by constructing a hypersexual 'enemy side' space – and sex spies are central to establishing this vision.[17]

The notoriety of the Manchu spy, Princess Aisin Gioro Xianyu (Chapter 5), reveals the fascination with unbridled enemy-side sexual desire. Xianyu's story is infused with inferences of multiple sexual deviance that confirm the Japanese military's immorality. The princess used sexual identities throughout her life – masquerading as a taxi dancer and socialite she was linked to a series of Japanese officers while also dressing as a man, commanding an army and operating a nightclub. Similarly, Ding Mocun, the collaborator whose failed assassination led to the execution of the Nationalist spy Zheng Pingru (Chapter 7), is routinely described in the popular press and later histories as a sex-fiend. His weakness for alluring young women enabled Zheng to penetrate his security apparatus. Debates about her actions as a spy revolve around her 'sacrifice' (i.e. of her feminine virtue) or her 'purity'. Zheng Pingru is no longer discussed as suffering from warped or excessive sexual desires – her work was all sacrifice. Ding Ling's fictional spy, Zhenzhen (Chapter 8), is described as a victim of unbridled Japanese sexual appetites as she provides sexual services in Japanese barracks while gathering intelligence. In the story Ding Ling reveals the prejudices women spies face from their home communities because of their inability to meet chastity norms. This discomfort continued in the divisive and politicised responses to the story published in the communist press during the 1950s, when Zhenzhen and Ding Ling were both accused of sexual deviance as the CCP sought to present itself as hyper-moral. How could the noble CCP ever be described as using sex spies? As the chapters to follow reveal, the post-war rehabilitation of women with compromised virtue is not a smooth process – even if they were 'sacrificing' themselves for the patriotic cause. Our-side stories must be morally clean (or cleansed) and women's virtue (or lack of it) is central to creating that 'reality'. Women who break norms of sexual virtue in wartime service are perfect sites for this ideological work.

Popular culture assists in the process of confirming 'our side' wartime virtue. The romance and danger of the beautiful honey-trap spy makes superb fiction and film fantasy – audiences in both peacetime and wartime have a sustained appetite for stories of sexual virtue given up to the service of victory. But, even more significantly, the sex spy can further society's militarisation by eroticising and glamorising war. Stories of sexy spies and images of seductive agents abound. They make war sexy; they help sell war to populations. The pondering of relatively free sexual liaisons, the moral stain of which is tempered by the 'sacrifice' that is being made for the country, appeals to many people. War looks like more fun if there is some sex, dancing, pearls and cocktails mixed in with the danger. Shortages of basic life necessities, disruptions in transportation and uncertainty in housing and schooling are the mundane realities for even those safe from the front lines, but these grim facts are glossed over in the entertainment replay of war and replaced with smart, savvy, sexy young women who are never short of lipstick. The depictions of women wartime spies and, to a lesser extent, those of the women warriors eroticise war for consumers of popular culture products.

Women's liberation and women's war fighting

For many people women's equal access to participate in warfare is framed within an 'equal opportunity' rubric. Women soldiers are often heralded as feminist forerunners, carving new territory in a male-dominated world. Yet, in the Chinese cultural sphere women warriors have featured as fantastic and bizarre exceptions and for centuries have consolidated, rather than challenged the Confucian patriarchal social order. In the aforementioned satirical piece, Lu Xun alerts readers to the particular Chinese proclivity for regarding women warriors as objects of diversion and entertainment – rather than agents in actual warfare. Commencing with the phrase 'China has long loved its magic tricks' Lu Xun makes the point that in the operas played all over the countryside women soldiers appeared highly decorated with pheasant feathers in their heads and large swords in their hands. 'As soon as they appear on the stage, the audience's elation reaches new heights. They know full well that it is no more than an act but they still watch with great enthusiasm.' The problem, he writes, is that too many soldiers and scholars have waxed lyrical about the stock literary forms that include unlikely figures performing heroic deeds for the greater good – such as 'beggars who rise up and kill the enemy', 'ruthless leaders who suddenly sacrifice themselves for noble causes' or 'remarkable women who save the nation'. When the country faces a real threat and magazines are filled with these romantic stories many people take these make-believe characters for real. He explains: 'I am not saying that young women should all be locked up in their boudoirs. I am just saying that it is rather theatrical when the crack troops retire and the "missies" carry the guns.' Lu Xun alerts us to the fact that while some regarded the military action of Qiu Jin (Chapter 3), Xie Bingying (Chapter 4) and Zhao Yiman (Chapter 6) as forging new ground for women in public space and demonstrating women's physical strength and courage,[18] others understood their actions within a long tradition of make-believe and fantasy.

This fantastic and diverting world of female derring-do was readily contained by a resilient Chinese patriarchy. Just as Goldstein describes the way that myths of Amazon communities of women warriors 'reinforced men's construction of their own patriarchal societies as orderly and natural',[19] China's fictional female knights errant and wondrous all-female armies reinforced not only a patriarchal social order but also men's claim to virtues coded masculine. The lionised women warriors of dynastic China were without exception wives and daughters whose remarkable courage and martial skill were harnessed in the defence of their husbands or fathers. They performed what I have called 'crisis femininity' in which exceptional events provide space for a temporary release from the norms of womanly behaviour (passivity, gentleness and frailty) as they lead armies, wage war and defend cities.[20] Lu Xun's identification of these figures in a list of other *unlikely* types explains why audiences found them amusing – they were fantastic and bizarre diversions from mundane life. As we will see in Chapter 2 on Hua Mulan, her centuries-old story cycle reveals a young woman whose military actions confirm the foundational virtue of filial piety – the spirit of obedience and service to one's parents and seniors that underpins the patriarchal family system. Most women warriors of China's historical and cultural past were presented as reinforcing the loyalty of women to a patriarchal family order – they were far from feminist revolutionaries, even if women in the audiences gained courage from watching their adventures.

However, as China modernised, the fundamental structures of Chinese society, including the gender norms informing women's involvement in war, were being reshaped. Qiu Jin's life and death spanning the late nineteenth and early twentieth centuries (Chapter 3) mark the point where the cultural weight of the old-style woman warrior is sloughed off and the redaction of her martyrdom in newspapers and poetry facilitates the emergence of a new type of woman warrior inspired by women's rights. For example, Xie Bingying (Chapter 4) and Zhao Yiman (Chapter 6) directly subverted the authority of their senior family members when they joined the Nationalist and communist forces, respectively – they effectively declared their loyalty to their parents secondary to their loyalty to the nation. They argued against old ideas about women's roles and contributions to society and fought for the Nationalist Party and CCP that both promised to deliver equal rights in a new society. In the twentieth-century renditions of Hua Mulan's story (Chapter 2) we also see that the 'nation state' replaces the 'father' as the object of her devotion and loyalty.

In the traditional containment of the woman warrior's feminist potential, women routinely dressed as men and passed as men while performing their martial deeds – resuming their feminine status once the task was achieved. This cross-dressing effectively made women temporary, honorary men in order to explain their manifesting of masculine attributes like courage, camaraderie, loyalty and strength. The operas that Lu Xun discussed include copious incidents of female-to-male cross-dressing. Hua Mulan is the exemplar of the way that this device operates to both entertain and tame any radical challenges to existing gender orders. In contrast, the twentieth-century women warriors do not become *men* to go to war, but rather they become *soldiers*.[21] The modern nation state that China was in the process of building created a new social category of person – the woman soldier who wore a new-style military uniform and engaged in mechanised warfare. The coding of this new category of person would eventually lose any association with hyper-masculinity via its adoption as daywear for all PRC citizens in the 'Mao suit'.[22] While some commentators regarded the universal adoption of the Mao suit in the 1960s and 1970s as 'defeminising' women (by not allowing women to decorate themselves in feminine frills) it is also important to acknowledge the suit's role in making the soldier androgynous. And this process had commenced in the 1920s with the inclusion of women in the armed forces of both the Nationalist Party and the CCP – Xie Bingying notes in 1927 that the only difference between her uniform and the male recruits was the addition of the English letter 'W' for 'Woman' embroidered on her left sleeve (Chapter 4). The use of the Roman alphabet instead of a Chinese character further emphasised the modernity of this new social role.

The long tradition of containing the disruptive potential of the woman warrior through devices such as cross-dressing and discourses of filial piety and/or patriotism does not mean that the Chinese woman warrior has no capacity to test the boundaries of male privilege and cannot resist being pulled into reinforcing the status quo of family or nation. In the twentieth century, knowledge of women's rights reorients the way traditional women warriors are understood as well as creates new scope for alternative behaviours among new-style women warriors too. To an audience with even a mere passing awareness of feminist politics, women soldiers and spies declare their freedom from patriarchal notions that position them as men's dependents because they assert their own agency and capacity for killing and self-defence. All the women discussed in this book have been read through the lens provided by the women's movement seeking equal rights and status with men. As a result of the dissemination of feminist political ideas that occurred before and during the twentieth century, the formation, shaping and reshaping, of the woman warrior is more able to resist the long tradition in which any exceptional acts by women were co-opted into the patriarchal status quo. Hua Mulan, dutiful daughter in centuries of Confucian teachings, was mobilised by China's new feminist movement at the start of the twentieth century as a model for woman's independence and strength. New perspectives, such as those provided by the global women's movement, changed the ways that old tropes were regarded. Lu Xun's 1931 comment about young women 'locked up in their boudoirs'[23] juxtaposes participation in the world of war with the discredited ultra-conservative sex-segregation practices common in China only a few decades earlier. But, in harnessing women warriors as feminist icons we risk making feminism a tool of militarisation.

Ironically, the post-Mao years that saw greater political and media freedoms emerge in China have also produced a return to more traditional management of women warriors and wartime spies. Some of the woman warrior's radical challenges to a patriarchal gender or family order are undermined by dramatic remakings of their stories. Between the 1950s and 1980s the young underground fighter, Liu Hulan (Chapter 9), was depicted as deliberately disobeying her backward, hidebound grandmother who seeks to stop her becoming active in the resistance movement. The grandmother was a symbol of 'feudal thinking' about politics and gender roles. But, in the 2000s, where the CCP trumpets harmonious families and a peaceful society Liu Hulan becomes a filial and obedient granddaughter to a grandmother who encourages her to study and improve herself by engaging with the CCP underground. The more dramatic transformations occur in the case of the wartime spies. For example, Zhenzhen (Chapter 8) is depicted in a 2003 film as blowing herself up in a revenge-suicide rather than confidently trekking off to join the communists, as she does in the original story. But the historical setting of the movie in the 'bad-old-days' (i.e. before and after the establishment of the PRC) separates this traditional chaste suicide behaviour from the contemporary viewers' modern moral order. Similarly, in the recent decade's 'back to the wok' rollback of revolutionary women's roles, Zhao Yiman, a ferocious guerrilla fighter, is tamed through the promotion of her status as a pining mother yearning for her absent son.[24] But, even within this moderated version of her life and deeds, contemporary Chinese readers have ample evidence of women's dual roles as mothers and workers without being required to make the dramatic sacrifice of abandoning a child, as did Zhao Yiman. The peace and prosperity of twenty-first-century China makes this choice a historical relic of the 'bad old days'.

Changing soldiers' social status – impact of women

For centuries in China's dynastic past, military skills connected to war fighting were denigrated. Scholar bureaucrats wrote the histories and established a textual tradition in which they garnered social prestige while their military counterparts did not – despite the latter's centrality in the formation, expansion and defence of empires. The phrase 'Good iron is not used to make nails, and good men do not become soldiers' encapsulates the long-standing prejudice against soldiers.[25] Elite men would learn various forms of martial arts for fitness and to cultivate a meditative self-control alongside their calligraphy and poetry but this was not preparation for enlisting in the standing military forces. It was a further marker of their cultivated status. Yet, a change occurred in the late nineteenth and early twentieth centuries as a result of the evident European superiority in military technology in the British attacks on China during the Opium Wars of the mid-1800s. Colin Green has revealed the conscious planning undertaken by numerous Chinese governments in their bid to raise the status of the military and notes the fluctuations in its success.[26] The importance of science and technology in warfare grew more apparent as time went on. Scholars who were otherwise distant from military matters became increasingly involved in new-style military academies and arsenals that aimed to train a new style of soldier and build a modern military hardware for China. Military matters gained new prestige accrued from the modernity of technological warfare. Modern schools that were also appearing at this time included military drills and strategy in their curricula – even the new women's schools, as we will see in Chapter 3 on Qiu Jin. The modern education system connected the literati preoccupation with textual learning directly with military skill.[27]

Robert Culp showed that Chinese governments through the 1910s, 1920s and 1930s promoted military training in physical exercise curricula. He demonstrates that China's leaders regarded the military orientation of schooling as central to the creation of a modern citizenry.[28] Modern military training was integral to the formation of a modern nation and it had explicit support from the highest levels in the country. Edmund Fung summarised this trend in the pithy phrase 'To be militaristic was to be modern.'[29]

Consequently, just as women were entering public schools, schooling placed higher prestige than ever before on war strategy and building military skills among the privileged, educated classes. In the biographies of the women below, there is a close link between their struggle to access schooling and their attainment of military skills. In contrast with the majority of male soldiers of the twentieth century, who were still uneducated, poor and frequently conscripted, the women soldiers were from comfortable families and their path to warfare was forged through entering the new girls' schools. Xie Bingying (Chapter 4) and Zhao Yiman (Chapter 6) are both classic examples of this pattern. Qiu Jin (Chapter 3) was a principal of one of these girls' schools and her students learned shooting and strategy alongside foreign languages. In the military academies established in the 1920s to train CCP and Nationalist Party officers women recruits needed to have attained a high level of education to secure a place. Many women were entering at the upper ends of the military hierarchy and were trained to perform propaganda work, medical work and logistics as well as combat. The considerable importance that Chinese forces placed on propaganda and engaging with the ordinary people from the 1920s in both CCP and Nationalist armies meant that the women performing these parts of the military's operations were highly valued – often, as we read in Xie Bingying's recollections, women soldiers made the first contact with villagers in advance of the full body of troops. Nicola Spakowski argues that the importance of winning the 'hearts and minds' of ordinary people in the Chinese war system during the twentieth century presented specific opportunities for improving women's status that did not require them to engage in direct combat.[30]

The appearance and promotion of women soldiers and officers also performed the function of signifying a changed and improved status for military forces generally in China. Both the Nationalist Party and the CCP were keen to promote the presence of women in their forces as markers of their modernity and revolutionary plans for dramatic change – in particular in their appeal to the mass of Chinese women. In this regard, the twentieth-century Chinese women warrior performs a unique role in militarising the would-be literati class. The presence of educated women challenged the low-class status of soldiering as a profession and had some role in increasing its respectability and modern-ness.

Another function that women warriors in China perform, motivating people to work hard, deserves our attention too since it shows the moral work that women soldiers performed even during peacetime. It is common to read that women soldiers were used to shame men into action – increasing men's participation was the goal for governments that promoted knowledge about women warriors. For example, Laurie Stoff has shown that in Russia during World War One women had a clear 'motivational value' in which they served as 'inspirational symbols to boost morale among war-weary male troops and to simultaneously shame men into resuming their "patriotic duty" as defenders of the nation'.[31] In the PRC, the militarisation of Chinese society has expanded to such breadths that women soldiers would serve as models for women's engagement in productive labour more generally even in the absence of war (see for example the 'Liu Hulan Teams' that formed all around the country in communes and factories during the late 1950s and 1960s, discussed in Chapter 9). Sex workers would be exhorted to 'Learn from Liu Hulan' and take up factory work. Soldiering had been elevated to new heights of social prestige in the PRC and women's presence in their ranks continued to build the idea that 'good iron made a good soldier'.

****

China's journey from the start of the twentieth century has been one of remarkably rapid change – from a feeble hereditary monarchy, through to a troubled democratic republic and on to the present times where a communist party-state, having relinquished its radical revolutionary policies, now drives global economic growth while delivering wealth to millions of its citizens. Over the course of more than a century governments, revolutionary groups and political parties have invoked the crisis of war – real, remembered and imagined – to secure popular support for their myriad policies and actions. Militarisation strategies implemented in China within this overall strategy have necessarily varied as the political goals changed, technology advanced and, from the middle of the twentieth century, wars ended. The chapters below, by analysing the evolving mobilisations of China's key warriors and spies over the course these decades of dramatic twists and turns, show how militarisation is immensely flexible. The militarisation of populations during peacetime heightens the romance of war in commercialised arenas that are both less credible and sometimes impossible to deliver during the progress of war itself. In peacetime, the CCP presented its radical changes to family, factory and farm structures as warlike struggles for survival against hostile foreign enemies, like the USA and UK, who were depicted as plotting China's destruction. Managing the stories of the past, creating new ways of conceptualising traumatic experiences/memories and creating a sense of collective victory against foreign and domestic threats have also been crucial to building popular support for the CCP since the early 1990s. Cultural nationalism, pride in China as a global cultural force, has built steadily among its citizens in part through the propaganda work of the CCP.[32] Legitimacy for the CCP's rule is not premised on open parliamentary elections but rests on its record of delivering staggering economic growth for over four decades and a carefully managed marketing campaign that links national unity and sovereignty to continued CCP control.

By focusing on women warriors and wartime spies, the book demonstrates the centrality of gender to successful militarisation across diverse political systems, in war and peace and during times of dramatic social and technological change. Women make war more appealing – whether that be as heroic poet swordswomen, courageous guerrilla mothers, glamorous intrepid spies, or, as we see in the next chapter on Hua Mulan, self-sacrificing daughters. The militarisation that underpins war needs narratives of manhood and womanhood – gendered discourses of everyday life – to persuade populations of its putative righteousness in communist and capitalist regimes, in wartime and in peacetime.

2   The archetypal woman warrior, Hua Mulan
Militarising filial piety

Hua Mulan has entranced and intrigued generations of Chinese. Since the Northern Wei dynasty (386–534) stories of her remarkable adventures in the military realm, replacing her father in the imperial troops disguised as a man, have been a recurring theme in both elite and popular cultural forms, including poetry, drama, opera and more recently film, television series and video games.[1] Mulan's continued popularity over 1,500 years, in part, can be credited to the flexibility of her story and its redactors' enthusiasm to make adjustments to the plot line and narrative resolution. The various evolving renditions of her story inevitably illuminate the concerns of writers in specific historical and ideological contexts as well as their diverse artistic goals and commercial interests.[2] As Wu Pei-Yi aptly put it, 'She was, and still is, amenable to all forms of fantasizing and manipulation.'[3]

Over the centuries critics have identified a wide range of often-contradictory perspectives on the central significance of the Mulan story – from filial piety and feminism, to maidenly chastity and militarism, onwards through Marxism and patriotism. Distinct consistencies underpin this apparently paradoxical list and these reveal how the many women warriors of China's rich cultural heritage buttressed, rather than challenged, the existing social order. The presumed nascent feminism of China's iconic women warriors is counter-balanced by their stories' role in reinforcing a male-dominated and masculinist gender order. While figures like Hua Mulan did inspire real women to take on new and different social roles – feminists in the early twentieth century explicitly invoked Mulan – the overarching narrative framing China's traditional women warriors consolidated rather than disrupted the status quo patriarchy. Mulan's story embeds militarisation into the core virtue of filial piety – respect for and obedience to one's parents and seniors. And, as we will see in the discussion of the twentieth-century renditions of her story, she is harnessed to promote 'militarised filial piety' as the modern social virtues of patriotism and sacrifice to the nation-state. Hua Mulan is 'grandmother' to all the later women warriors discussed in this book. The retelling of her story across multiple media in the twentieth century set the tone for popular culture and propaganda that used women warriors to promote the militaristic ideologies that support China's war system.

This chapter shows that Mulan's story is not merely an empty vessel into which diverse ideological or commercial interests are poured. At its core it has allowed writers, critics and audiences to wrestle with a key feature of the Chinese moral and social universe – how individuals manage the competing demands from their families and the central state. Her story shows how militaristic logic is embedded into the core values that tie individuals to their family and their state – filial piety and patriotism – through the appeal of the woman warrior image. It shows that regardless of genre (film, play, opera, television series), regardless of period (sixth century through to the start of the twenty-first century) and despite remarkable and extensive elaborations in plot, characterisation and context, these militarisation processes remain central to the narrative tension of a Mulan story.

Mulan's sustained popularity emerges from her disregard for conventional gender norms about soldiering and war by allowing audiences to ponder the putative inevitability and naturalness of these norms. For centuries her daring cross-dressing has titillated audiences as they imagine the pragmatics of her life among male soldiers. Only in the twentieth century did her assumption of a male-gendered military role take on a feminist, anti-patriarchal hue.[4] For the larger tract of history, Mulan's cross-dressing life made the story amusing and entertaining rather than revolutionary or feminist. And, even within the twentieth century, the feminism that Mulan represents is constrained by an overarching preoccupation with the connection between the state and its subjects/ citizens. The weight of traditional ideology she carried with her into these feminist mobilisations of her form meant that her potential as a radical feminist challenge to patriarchy has always been undermined. Chinese versions of her story depict her prime motivation for joining the military as emerging from her desire to defend her country, her father and her family line – not from an enthusiasm to forge new social roles for women.[5] Nor does she challenge the gendered war system by her participation in battle – she becomes temporarily masculine and an honorary man when she performs her martial feats because she dresses as a man throughout and redresses as a woman when she returns to the feminine-coded domestic space. Mulan's cross-dressing serves to amplify the magnitude of her devotion to her father or her country because the transgression of gender norms it represents places her in extreme physical and moral danger. These norms being the desired segregation of men from women that existed for centuries until the 1920s and the long-held notion that divided the masculine space of the battle front from the feminine space of hearth and home.

Today, the story of Mulan is commonly presented as a tale of unproblematic filial sacrifice for 'national' military service – Mulan's heroism emerges from her dedication to her father and her country within a rubric that presents a tidy convergence of family interests with those of the state as both are presented as benefiting from warfare. However, this common-sense analysis elides a notable shift in her story that occurred from the start of the twentieth century – the elimination of the earlier versions' *opposition* to the central state. Resentment of the state's co-option of ordinary people for country-wide projects, such as warfare, that was a marked feature in the pre-twentieth-century versions of Mulan's story diminish in the twentieth century as patriotic military sacrifice for a beleaguered nation-state becomes the dominant discourse. The erasure of the Mulan story cycle's opposition to central government authority, complete with its forced extraction of military service from the family unit, is effected through the subsuming of filial piety into a statist discourse and the militarisation of the virtue of filial piety. From the twentieth century onwards, filial piety is presented as best performed *through* the demonstration of militarised sacrifice to the state. Far from simply being tales of filial piety and/or patriotism, the Mulan narratives tell us about the transformation of filial piety into a statist discourse of war-ready patriotism and of the concomitant decline of discourses of resistance to the central state's imposition of military service on ordinary families.

The materials discussed are drawn from a vast sweep of historical periods and a diverse range of genres. While sacrificing detailed discussion of historical context and text, this pan-historical approach illuminates the transformation in the core themes of the Mulan story cycle. A detailed reading of specific texts from specific periods would elide the subtle changes that have emerged across time and in a wide range of political structures – imperial, democratic, totalitarian, communist and capitalist. I focus on the longer Mulan pieces (plays, novels and films) because these longer pieces often have commercial imperatives to seek wider audiences and thereby more likely to capture the core ideas behind Mulan's popularity.[6]

The chapter moves chronologically commencing with the original Mulan poem of 568, and a four-act play by Xu Wei (1521–1593). Analysis of a novel-length version of her story from the Qing dynasty follows: Chu Renhuo's (c. 1630–c. 1705) *Romance of the Sui and the Tang*. With the advent of film in the twentieth century we see a flurry of cinematic and television versions. These range from film recordings of local operas and plays, through to specifically written film scripts and a multi-episode television series.

These materials show that from the start of the twentieth century Mulan's patriotic credentials had consolidated and her role as a figure of opposition and resistance to the central state's military service has evaporated. Moreover, while gender ambiguity remains central to the story's audience appeal, ambiguity about which *state* Mulan is fighting for dissolves. Where earlier versions presented her acting on behalf of an unstable and fractured country in which competing internal aspirants for power battled, the twentieth-century stories depict her as fighting for a unified 'China' whose borders are threatened by northern land-invading 'foreigners'. Pre-twentieth-century versions describe Mulan as a northerner of indeterminate ethnicity serving 'a Khan' (the Tuoba Wei), or a half-Han, half-Tujue warrior defending 'an Emperor' against northern invaders. In the twentieth century she has been effectively 'nationalised' (and implicitly Hanised) as a loyal patriot defending 'China' against external foreign threats. Mulan's earlier more complex ethnicity dissolves along with her resistance to leaders that would draw her family into their military campaigns.[7] While she undergoes a consolidation of her Han ethnic identity, Mulan's performance of gender migration remains. This latter aspect provides audiences with fertile material for contemplating the gendered nature of a person's service to the family and sacrifice to the state, oftentimes in ribald jokes and diverting mishaps.

The filial Mulan resisting an unreasonable state

The original Mulan text is an anonymous poem that appeared in 568 titled 'The Ballad of Mulan'. The poem is 62 lines and 332 characters, and provides the basis for all later renditions of her 'life'.[8] This poem presents a lively tale of a youthful Mulan who replaces her father in the khan's army. Her brother is too young to fulfil the family's conscription obligations, so the filial Mulan assumes the burden to protect her father. Women could not become soldiers, so she disguises herself as a man – concealing her true sex for over twelve years. The ballad explains that at the end of a period of outstanding military service, the khan offers Mulan a prestigious position as a minister in his cabinet. Mulan declines and instead requests a camel so she can return home to her family. On entering the house she changes into women's clothing. Her military comrades are aghast at their failure to detect a woman living amongst them for so many years.

The ballad is sparing on detail of Mulan's life amidst men. It is precisely this space that the later versions of her story occupy. Audiences for plays, films and television thrill in the risks Mulan takes with her virtue by mingling with men and the danger to her chastity presented by the threat of disclosure of her true (female) sex. While warfare presents men with risk of death, it has sexualised associations for women – rape, sexual torture and sexual slavery were/are among the potential ramifications for women experiencing war. Readers and viewers factor this into their understanding of Mulan's remarkable daring deed – she was risking her sexual virtue.

In contrast, the ballad devotes considerable time to exploring her relationship with her family. Mulan's actions are clearly motivated by her loyalty to them. She risks her personal safety in order to protect her father and, once this duty has been fulfilled, seeks to return to her family. It makes no mention of Mulan's enthusiasm to defend the realm, the khan's empire or the 'Chinese nation' – she is inspired only by a desire to protect her father. Her relationship to the central state is forged by obedience, not devotion. The ballad places ordinary people in a passive position in relation to the khan's conscription demands and Hua Mulan's sacrifice protects her family against the unreasonable state's militarism. The khan's offer of official glory and further imperial service cannot compete with the devotion she feels for her father and her desire to serve him.

The ballad dedicates most of its space to exploring the misery of family separation: Mulan's impending departure, her own homesickness, her parent's anxiety and the joyful family reunion. To emphasise the familial theme, lines 28 and 30 are paired repeated phrases: 'She doesn't hear the sound of Father and Mother calling / She only hears the Yellow River's flowing water cry tsien tsien'; / 'She doesn't hear the sound of Father and Mother calling / She only hears Mount Yen's nomad horses cry tsiu tsiu'.[9] The ballad repeatedly emphasises the physical distance between Mulan and her parents with descriptions of vast and hostile terrain. Descriptions of miserable gusts of cold winds and 'chilly lights' amplify Mulan's suffering and the distance separating her from the warmth and comfort of kith and kin.

In contrast to the extensive elaborations dedicated to family separation and reunion the poem only briefly mentions the connection between the khan and Mulan or her family. The meeting with the khan, where he offers her an official position, is given only six lines in the poem. The ballad's narrative tension, so firmly established as family separation, is resolved by her rejection of imperial honours in favour of family reunion. The conscription letter and the khan's offer of high office are reduced to props that facilitate the poem's central discussion of Mulan's extraordinarily filial actions and signal the tension between the family and the state. The weighting of content in the ballad celebrates ideals of devotion to one's family and sacrifice to one's father and simultaneously presents a muted critique of the central authorities' unreasonable exertion of brute power – the family *had* to provide one warrior regardless of its composition and/or the welfare of its members.

The limited dedication to the central government continues into the Ming dynasty (1368–1644) with Xu Wei's play, 'The Female Mulan replaces her father and joins the military.'[10] Xu Wei follows the basic plot of the original ballad, but includes comic episodes and ends with her crowd-pleasing marriage to a scholar in her hometown. The descriptions of her life as a soldier, her heroic deeds and displays of her swords-skill are extended. He also includes salacious jokes, and on-stage costume changes, as Mulan moves in and out of women's dress. Wilt Idema notes that this on-stage 'dresstease' was 'a novel thrill' for the audience.[11] Xu's play includes her fellow soldiers' salacious commentary about Mulan's effeminate visage and his/her curious modesty in evacuating bodily waste.[12] These devices forged intimacy with the audience as they admire the creative ways Mulan avoids exposure as a woman.[13]

Figure 2.1 Hua Mulan leaves home
Source: Qiu Shouping and Ding Song (1887, 1917) *Gujin baimei tuyong – yi juan* (Odes and Pictures of One Hundred Beauties Past and Present, vol. 1), Shanghai: Zhonghua tushuguan, p. 43.

In keeping with the shift towards the eroticisation of the female foot between the Tang dynasty (618–907) and the Ming, Xu Wei includes extensive references to Mulan's feet. During Xu Wei's lifetime bound feet were a highly eroticised bodily feature and a key marker of the difference between men and women. Accordingly, Xu Wei's play includes descriptions of Mulan painfully unbinding her feet before joining the army. Mulan comments that with practice she was able to walk firmly and stably again. And she tells the audience that she has a magic treatment that will shrink her feet back to their miniature size as required. Siu Leung Li argues that this device 'contains' the feminine subversion with masculine values.[14] This containment ensures the woman warrior does not upset the existing patriarchal gender order. The foot motif is given further play when Mulan's mother comments that she finds her daughter's feet 'big' and 'strange'. The original poem made no reference to footbinding because the practice did not commence until centuries after the appearance of the original ballad, but its anachronistic inclusion in the Ming versions of her story were important to its audience appeal because the foot motif invokes the sexualised and eroticised female body. These discussions of feet highlight the extent of Mulan's remarkable transgression and the extreme measures she undertook to defend her father and family against the militaristic designs of the central state.[15]

Xu Wei's drama, like the original ballad, identifies Mulan's loyalty to her father and family as the motivation for her actions. At the commencement of the play 17-year-old Mulan explicitly likens herself to two famous women from ancient times who risked their lives 'for the sakes of their fathers' – Qin Xiu from the Warring States period (475–221 BCE) and Ti Ying from the Han dynasty (206 BCE–220 CE).[16] Mulan decides that the time had come 'to repay' her father as had these heroic women.[17] Amplifying her virtue, Xu Wei introduces an element to the story that will become commonplace in later versions – a reason for Mulan's father's inability to go to war – his frailty through either age or illness or both. The original ballad provides no such exigencies – she simply wants to meet the family's conscription requirement in lieu of her father. Xu Wei's audiences and readers learn that Mulan's father is too old and sick to fight. Thus, Mulan's filial virtue extends to the provision of care for ageing parents. She is not simply 'replacing' her father in battle; she is protecting him from certain death because his frailty would make survival in battle unlikely.

In keeping with the ballad's emphasis on the misery of family separation, Xu Wei's play describes in depth her tearful departure and her joyous reunion. In anticipation of the inevitable misery of separation, her family entreats Mulan to send regular letters home in order to reduce her elderly parents' anxiety. No mention is made of her desire to defend the country from foreign invaders.

Mulan's sole motivation is to protect her family and repay her filial debt to her father by obeying the central state's conscription demands.[18] Nor is there any expression of family glory garnered as a result of her service to the nation on her departure or return. After their victory, Mulan and her troops are received in the capital and she is granted a ministerial position in recognition of her long years of 'forced service'. Although she is given three months' leave to visit her family prior to this ministerial posting, she demurs and respectfully requests to be able offer her services to the state at another time. The reason Mulan gives for rejecting high office is that she is worried about her family and needs to return home to her parents.

The play also emphasises the dire state of the family confronted with the unreasonable demands made by the khan. On receiving his conscription papers Mulan's father is plunged into despair and the audience learns that he is about to hang himself in response to his intractable situation.[19] He cannot fulfil the khan's demands, but neither can he reject them, so he resolves to commit suicide. Mulan's father would rather die by his own hand, than die in battle serving the dynastic rulers. His preference for death by suicide rather than in service stands as resistance to the unreasonable demands made by the state. Once she hears that her father is planning suicide, Mulan's resolve hardens and her mother's resistance to her cross-dressing plan dissipates. On her departure the family drinks a toast in Mulan's honour, but impatient imperial officials harass the tearful group with shouts of 'Hurry up!' curtailing their final fare-wells. The Hua family's sadness is an inconvenience to the khan's representa-tives. The distance between the khan's interests and an individual family's concerns is amplified.

Although she forgoes imperial honours, when she gets home Mulan receives glories of a familial nature – her years of sacrifice are rewarded with marriage to the esteemed local scholar, Wang, who was impressed by her filial spirit. She accepts this marriage proposal with alacrity and in so doing enables her parents to fulfil *their* final parental duty. Her mother had opined wistfully to the audience, unaware of Mulan's imminent return, that she wished Mulan would come home to marry Wang so that 'we two old folk can die with easy hearts'. The concluding scene's 'wish-fulfilment' is framed in terms of family con-tinuity and the play's resolution confirms the crucial ongoing cycle of duty and responsibility between children and parents.

During the Qing dynasty (1644–1911), Xu Wei's comedic tone is replaced by tragedy in Chu Renhuo's *Romance of the Sui and Tang* (c. 1675; first edition 1695). In keeping with Qing notions of female virtue Mulan commits suicide rather than returning to home.[20] Chaste suicides among women were an official preoccupation in the Qing with state-sponsored celebration of chaste women manifest through the construction of elaborate arches commemorating women of exceptional virtue. The ideology was integral to the Qing moral order so its appearance in a Mulan story should be of no surprise.[21] Robert Hegel describes the *Romance of the Sui and Tang* as 'a virtual anthology of earlier fiction concerning the Sui and the Tang' but its inclusion of Mulan is an innovation – Chu moved the Mulan tale chronologically forward to the end of the Sui dynasty (581–618) so that it could be included in his one-hundred-chapter novel on the Sui and Tang.[22] Chu's 17-year-old Mulan is a half-Han, half-Tujue woman fighting on behalf of a Han-Tujue alliance for control of the country at the fall of the Sui. During her military service Mulan loses a battle to a warrior princess, Dou Xianniang, and is captured. Mulan reveals her true sex to Xianniang – the princess immediately orders her women soldiers to investigate its veracity. Xianniang, impressed by Mulan's secret cross-dressing adventures and moved by her story of filial devotion, invites her to stay as a guest rather than as a prisoner. Their friendship blossoms and Princess Xianniang takes Mulan as a sworn sister – they travel together accompanied by Xianniang's troop of women soldiers. During this period of sisterly togetherness, Mulan returns to her natal home to bring her parents to live with Xianniang. Instead of the much-anticipated happy reunion, she finds her father dead and the Tujue Khan waiting to take her as his concubine. She commits suicide rather than enter his palace.[23]

Through this innovative conclusion the *Romance of the Sui and Tang* emphasises Mulan's fierce resistance to unreasonable imperial authority while promoting her filial piety. Mulan's refusal to submit to becoming an imperial concubine and her dramatic, defiant suicide show the limits of her obedience. She joined the military to protect her father, and once that military service was complete, her family's duty to the state was fulfilled. Mulan anticipated a new life together with her parents and her sworn sister, Xianniang.[24] When this proves impossible, suicide enables Mulan to declare her loyalty to one man alone – her father – and to personally resist the imperial state. Mulan's suicide shows that the state not only made unreasonable demands on men through irrational conscription systems but also sought to 'conscript' women into concubinage.

She commits suicide on her father's grave thereby literally declaring her supreme loyalty to her father over the state. In order to reiterate the significance of this choice, she feigns deference to the khan's power so that his emissaries allow her visit her father's grave. She declares, 'we common people cannot disobey the Chieftain's orders, but please take me first to visit my father's grave to say my farewells. Then, I will accompany you to the palace.'[25] Once at the gravesite Mulan's resistance, rather than deference to imperial power, is revealed in her dramatic death through self-inflicted stab wounds. The only man worth dying for, in Chu's rendition, is one's father. Mulan's grief-stricken mother and stepfather bury her alongside her father.

Chu's book was a political critique of the author's times. Tensions between the Han and their Manchu rulers underlay Qing society – the Han regarded the Manchu as foreign invaders and Chu's novel's harsh judgement of the political order reflects this animosity.[26] Hegel describes Chu's version of the Mulan story as a muted Han critique of Manchu rule saying 'the scene demonstrates graphically that even a half-Chinese woman would prefer death by her own hand to serving a foreign ruler'.[27] But he also makes the broader point noting that the entire book makes a savage critique of China's imperial system as a whole saying that it is 'an exposé of the moral bankruptcy inherent in the imperial institution'.[28]

Chu's *Romance of the Sui and Tang* contrasts the decrepit imperial state with the family's virtue. Mulan's mother suggests her husband participate in the system's corruption by 'buying' an exemption. He rejects her advice and prepares to end his life instead. Mulan overhears of her father's plan and in recalling women warriors of the Warring States period asks 'Did these girls not also have mothers and fathers and were they not also by dint of political circumstances forced into imperial matters, and compelled to join the military?'[29] She resolves to dress as a man and take her father's place in a display of filial piety that contrasts starkly with the state's immorality. But this plan challenges another key family virtue – female chastity.

Chu's tomboyish Mulan had learned martial arts and war strategy as a child and she explains that she wants to protect the family and show up those 'pusball worthless men'. Her mother resists saying that Mulan would compromise her virtue and bring shame to the family gallivanting around the country with men. However, Mulan persuades her parents of her resolve arguing that loyal officials and filial sons are made and not born and insists on her success arguing, 'where there's a will there's a way'.[30] They finally relent and she enrols at the marshalling station without incident. The narrator explains that fortunately Mulan's feet had been relatively loosely bound so she could pass for a man once they were unbound if she stuffed cloth into the toes of her boots. In farewelling her parents she tells them to take care of themselves and to look after her younger sister and brother. Mulan's filial virtue trumps demands for feminine chastity.

Despite her noble motivations, Chu's Mulan is unable to protect her family from the shame her actions produced. Once their neighbours hear of Mulan's deeds they berate her parents for allowing their daughter to risk her virtue in such a foolhardy fashion. Local gossips ponder how she will be picking and choosing sexual partners from among the thousands of men in the troops. Her despairing father worries himself sick and within a year he is dead.[31] Mulan's subsequent suicide on his grave amplifies the cruelty of conscription and the purity of her body. To mid-Qing audiences, her suicide proves her virtue and Mulan emerges a chastity martyr as well as a filial daughter – she defends her maidenly honour against the khan's desire to take her as concubine and simultaneously declares her chastity and her devotion to her father.

The pre-twentieth-century Mulan story cycles place prime value on her loyalty to her parents and her father in particular. Narrative tension and the resolution of this tension revolve around the sacrifice she is making for her family in response to the militarised state, the misery of their separation and either the joy of their reunion, or their continued misery as a result of the futility of her sacrifice. The central imperial authorities make unreasonable demands on ordinary people who are forced to compromise their womenfolk's chastity and whose enthusiasm for military action on behalf of the state is limited or ultimately betrayed. The pre-twentieth-century versions are circumspect about Mulan's loyalty to the country – she chooses her father or death over the khan/ emperor. The central state is depicted as being prone to make unreasonable demands on the family for its wartime ambitions. In contrast, as the following section shows, in the twentieth century with rising nationalism and the consolidation of central state power, China's writers and directors transform the Mulan story into one of noble sacrifice for the Chinese nation and to a government that is worthy of her sacrifice. Filial piety, the overarching virtue of earlier times, finds expression primarily *through* service to the state and most significantly of all is militarised in the process.

The supremacy of state power and the co-option of filial piety

The rapid decline of the Qing court's legitimacy in the first decade of the twentieth century and growing internal pressures for democratic, rather than imperial, rule necessarily transformed the relationship between individuals and the state. David Faure's work shows that at this time the reformist intellectual classes increasingly regarded family-based lineages as a 'source of backwardness'. A modern, strong China required citizens aligned to the state and not to their family lineages. He shows that in earlier times lineages had jealously guarded their autonomy from the centralising forces around the emperor through their invocation of ritual power. With the collapse of the imperial structure, Chinese modernisers proposed the creation of a citizen who was integrated fully into the republican state – disrupting the vigour family-based lineages gained from their long-standing resistance to the emperor. The versions of the Mulan story cycle created in the twentieth century support Faure's point.[32] Filial piety, the cornerstone of lineage loyalty, is gradually absorbed into a state-centric morality where rituals of filial piety dovetail with state military service. This ancient virtue is modernised such that its performance is best realised through service to the state.

Throughout this transition Mulan appears in newspapers, educational materials and magazines as the model for engagement in public affairs and national modernisation.[33] She also emerges as an exemplar of radical politics in biographies of women designed to modernise China's womenfolk. Joan Judge's detailed work on these biographies argues that women warriors, like Mulan, were 'liberated ... from the moralizing overlay that had made their transgressive actions palatable in the past. Ignoring whatever private, familial, or local interests heroic women had historically been made to serve, they turned these submissive agents of patriarchy into daring Han patriots.'[34] But, the process of becoming daring was evolutionary. Judge's work shows Mulan's transition – she was not entirely liberated from family duties even as she became a Han patriot. By the late 1930s the transition was complete and Mulan's family duties have been neatly subsumed into national duties. The former cannot be performed without the latter. To be a good daughter Mulan *must* be a good patriot.

In 1939, in the heat of the war against Japan, Bu Wancang produced an enormously successful film *Mulan Joins the Army*, that illustrates how filial rituals were co-opted into military service for the nation.[35] Poshek Fu describes the film as a lively, engaging and thinly disguised tale of resistance to foreign invasion produced, as it was, in Japanese-occupied Shanghai.[36] Bu's Mulan is a mischievous tomboy who hunts on horseback roaming the countryside despite her parents' objections. Her time in the army provides scope for dramatic battle scenes, carousing, feasting and uncovering of treachery. Sexual tension is produced through the movie's descriptions of Mulan defending her honour from both hetero- and homosexual advances in a series of scenes where she fights off or outwits her would-be molesters. The script written by Ouyang Yuqian includes a group foot-washing session, where the soldiers wash and massage each other's feet. This scene draws the audience's attention to the particular challenge public ablutions present for Mulan in her new life as a man. She solves the problem by rejecting the offer of the footbath saying she preferred to take her pail of water outside – conveniently away from the men's view. The washing of the feet stands as a synecdoche of the broader problems she will face in bathing. Bu and Ouyang also draw audience attention to other eroticised parts of Mulan's sexualised form. At the commencement of the film, a gang of hoodlums surround Mulan (the girl) and with the point of an arrow their leader touches various parts of her body: moving from her lips, face, arm and eventually thwacking her buttocks. Their erotic gaze moves threateningly around her body. Others in the group warn her to behave because he 'still hasn't taken a wife' suggesting that he might like to 'take' Mulan. Mulan outwits this threatening gang and rides off home. The sexualised form of a young Mulan is contained safely within the family.

Bu Wancang's film reveals explicitly how filial piety is subsumed into service to the state by the co-option of ancestral rites. The evening before her departure Mulan pays respects to her ancestors dressed in her father's military uniform; she then toasts her father in their final family dinner thanking him for teaching her the value of defending her nation. She reassures her mother that she will be reunited safely with the family once she has demonstrated her usefulness to the country. Turning to her young brother, who has just expressed his desire to join her in battle, she advises him to obey his parents so that he can grow up to fight for the nation in the future.[37] Once her extensive and glorious military service is completed, and after having been offered high official positions, Mulan begs permission to return to her parents. Once home she changes into women's clothing and is betrothed to her comrade(s)-in-arms General Liu Yuandu. Like Xu Wei's Ming drama Bu's version also includes a happy marriage – but this time to a soldier with whom she had secretly fallen in love, rather than a scholar – reflecting the rising status of soldiers in the twentieth century.[38] Her willing and enthusiastic service to the state complete, Mulan happily returns to her life as a daughter and wife to an esteemed military figure. Bu's film makes 'service to the state' entirely compatible with 'service to the family'.

Her glorious wartime role also delivers national honour to her family and the entire locality. On Mulan's return to her village, she is escorted by a large military procession and well-wishers crowd the streets to welcome their local hero. The Hua family risked losing its daughter in battle, but it gained unparalleled prestige from her ultimate success. Moreover, Mulan's marriage to the esteemed General Liu, impossible to achieve had she not joined the military, underscores the link between national service and familial benefit. The descriptions of her partnership with Liu build the mutuality of state and family interests by the reiteration of a sexed division of moral labour between the twin virtues of filial piety (*xiao*) and loyalty (*zhong*). Bu Wancang's script divides them between his two protagonists. As the film draws to a close, General Liu, Mulan's peer in military hierarchy, declares that he would like to serve Mulan in her new position of high office – a position she then declines in preference to returning to her parents. The emperor immediately declares General Liu to be 'loyal' and Mulan to be 'filial' – affirming their validity as a virtuous couple to the audience who anticipate the heterosexual romance. But it also domesticates Mulan by contrasting her private family virtue with Liu's public ones – ultimately the state has reaffirmed her 'natural' return to the feminine space of the family and reinstated the public martial roles of men. China's wise and generous leader had foreseen the harmony of mutual interests in the institutions of marriage and official service.

Zhou Yibai's 1941 four-act play provides an important contrast to the pattern of 'good patriots and wise national leaders' expressed in Bu's more popular film. Zhou's play is largely humourless and the language and characterisation are dull monochromes compared with those in Bu's lively film of only a few years earlier. Zhou's Mulan is a moralistic figure endlessly preaching the virtues of contributing to the war effort and the movie lacks the playful sexual innuendo in the earlier (more successful) versions. His movie failed to attract wide audience approval.[39] This 1941 play presages the Socialist Realist trend that would come to dominate cultural production in the years after 1949. Mao Zedong outlined the new rules in his now famous 'Talks at the Yan'an Forum on Literature and Art' held in May 1942 and established a set of core principles that would impact China for decades to follow – loosely described as Maoist Socialist Realism.[40] This included formulaic positive characters (steadfast, hard-working patriots) and contrasts them directly with negative characters (lazy, wavering, comfort-seeking, gamblers and drinkers). Zhou's movie adopts a didactic tone but delivers a wavering message to audiences about supporting the war effort. Chang-Tai Hung described the play as being 'marred by the absence of an integrated plot and by an awkward conclusion'.[41]

Zhou Yibai's 1941 version, like Bu's, links the Hua family's ancestral duties to national military service. Zhou's script commences with Mulan's young brother scurrying home to escape from some village playmates who are bullying him. They are insisting that he calls them 'father' and 'ancestor' – a grave insult to his real father and ancestors. Mulan's father, Hua Hu, uses this scenario to explain to his wife and daughter how important war is to the family's interests. 'You may think that nothing good comes from war; but if we *don't* fight then we will suffer.' He explains that the hardship will manifest itself in 'a lifetime of calling other people 'father' and 'ancestor'!'[42] Zhou's script establishes the direct connection between a family's responsibility to pay respect to its ancestors and the state's interests in mobilising men for battle. Hua Hu, despite his age and illness, is an enthusiastic supporter of the war and declares that 'exerting oneself for the nation is in the very nature of a soldier's work'. By 'protecting my country' he reinforces his status as a respectable person – 'If I don't go, how could I still be considered an upstanding man?'[43] The nation's crisis presents the Hua family with a chance to protect its deceased ancestors from humiliation and assert the high morals of its living members – national military service *is* filial piety.

Mulan's motivations reinforce the proximity of filial duty and war service. She declares that she wants to enlist 'for the country, for my father'.[44] Mulan's mother assists in persuading Hua Hu of the virtue of Mulan's scheme saying that she has such a filial heart that he should let her go.[45] Once Mulan has joined the military, her national loyalty becomes the dominant virtue. Acts Two and Three present audiences with ample opportunity for learning about the importance of 'making an effort for the country' and revolve around the problem of identifying traitors. The narrative tension in these two acts focuses on the threat to the collective national project posed by 'spies' and others who would 'sell' their country. The primacy of the family and village as sites of emotional or geographic loyalty common in the pre-twentieth-century versions has receded. By 1941 the 'enemies of the nation' propel narrative tension in the Mulan story.

In establishing both internal (traitors) and external (foreign invaders) enemies, this modern moral order coalesces around the nation, not the family or the natal village.

Once the fighting is over, Mulan is accused of insubordination, despite her central role in the victory, and is brought before the emperor – the movie climaxes around the question of whether she will be punished or praised? In the final battle she and her troops had decided to disobey their superior's orders in order to secure victory. During her interrogation by the emperor, Mulan persuades him of their noble, rather than mutinous, intentions and is duly rewarded by the enlightened and rational state, with an official position in the military bureaucracy. Mulan takes the opportunity to seek permission to return home to look after her parents rather than take up the post. The emperor is puzzled by this 'strange' request. Mulan reveals that she had replaced her father and used his name to enlist. The emperor asks: 'Why did your father want to evade conscription?' Mulan replies that he wanted to enlist but was too sick to be useful in battle. The emperor, again representing the rational and reasonable central state, asks why he didn't simply request a period of sick leave. Mulan responds saying that because the country faced an immediate crisis she resolved to replace her father.[46] The emperor queries the depth of Mulan's loyalty to the nation, demanding to know why she now refuses to continue to serve the country as a minister: 'So, you only acknowledge your parents, and not the country?' He reminds her that her parents could live with her in the capital while she serves her nation as an official. She explains that as country folk they love their farming and would not enjoy city life. Eventually, the emperor concedes that she can return home. But the drama does not end there and Zhou Yibai's unified moral position (that sacrificing yourself for the state is a noble and valued act) unravels.

The emperor discovers that Mulan is a woman because he attempts to reward 'her' military service with marriage to a woman. Faced with this situation Mulan has to reveal her true sex and, in doing so, finds herself sought as the emperor's concubine. Mulan refuses, much to the horror of the gathered officials and the emperor himself. He gives her the choice of becoming his concubine or death – Mulan chooses death. Just at that moment, news arrives that the palace is under attack and Mulan is immediately called upon to rally her troops to fight. She agrees on the grounds that if she survives this battle, she would be permitted to return home. The emperor concedes and the play concludes with Mulan fighting alongside her comrades. Zhou Yibai fails to provide audiences with a satisfactory conclusion – Mulan's survival is not assured, her reunion with her parents uncertain and her relationship with the state spoiled. The leader of the imperial state, to whom Mulan had dedicated herself, turns out to be unworthy of her devotion. While China may be worth dying for, the emperor is a self-seeking leader prone to arbitrary decisions and the imperial state is morally bankrupt.

Ultimately, Mulan's performance of filial piety through national military service is misguided. The last act of the play makes a mockery of the prosaic national service rhetoric that permeates the previous three acts. Audiences and readers in the 1940s faced daily decisions about collaborating with the occupying Japanese or sacrificing themselves for China, and would be unsure at the play's end if they really should identify with Mulan. Perhaps the wavering, war-hating characters they had been coached to disdain throughout the earlier parts of the movie were correct after all? And which of them had not collaborated in some way with the occupying Japanese? Were they also like the sneaky traitors in the play?

After 1949 despite the gradual cessation in actual military battles on Chinese territory, Mulan continued to appeal to producers, writers and directors. In 1956, Liu Guoquan and Zhang Xinshi directed a film of a Henan Opera.[47] The film adheres to the basic ballad plot line and presents an earnest and dedicated Mulan who instructs the audience on service and dedication to the country – comparatively devoid of comedic episodes or salacious jokes this PRC (People's Republic of China) opera creates Mulan as a moral exemplar of a national citizen. In keeping with the PRC's enthusiasm for bringing women into the workforce during the 1950s, Liu and Zhang's opera provides audiences with lessons on the importance of women's contributions to the nation. Amidst the misogyny of the soldiers' in-barrack complaints that men risk their lives while women rest at home, Mulan reminds her comrades that women also shoulder extra burdens during wartime: performing the agricultural work left behind by the absent men, sewing shoes and weaving cloth for the troops as well as providing food for the nation and its soldiers. In this version Mulan is a dedicated patriot and an advocate of sex equality – both men and women have valuable duties, albeit in different spheres, as citizens of the Chinese nation.

In this film-opera, the sexualised danger of her cross-dressing is minimised and her feminist credentials emphasised. This vision of Mulan was not an erotic fantasy – she was a radical revolutionary fighting to strengthen the nation and a warrior battling for women's rights. However, this latter battle was contained within the rubric of the ultimate goal of building the state – women's public engagement would enhance national strength. In Liu and Zhang's opera there is no ambiguity about the value of sacrificing for the central state. The tension between loyalty to the nation and filial piety is resolved in a fresh manner early in the play. Mulan expresses frustration that as a girl she can neither perform her loyalty to the nation nor her filial piety to her parents precisely because she cannot assume her father's martial duties. The equal weighting given to both roles displaces the dominance of filial piety and the suspicion of the central state (or its unreasonable demands) common in earlier centuries. The opera confirms from the outset that Mulan's father would have willingly gone to war in defence of the nation had he not been frail and ill. She engages him in an on-stage practice fight to demonstrate her superior martial skills and his own inability to serve. Once Mulan has persuaded her parents that she can pass for a man, the opera then provides a solution for her un-filial departure from home. Mulan reassures her parents that she will return home to perform her filial duties and care for them in their dotage once peace has returned to the nation and the enemy has been defeated. Her father nods his head approvingly on hearing her declaration. In the moral universe of the PRC filial piety is important but as a quotidian performance it can be legitimately deferred – with no disgrace to the family – when the nation calls upon an individual. Delayed gratification of daily domestic filial duties is expressly advocated and approvingly acknowledged by both child and parent because she is manifesting her filial devotion *through* her military service to the nation-state.

With the militarisation of filial piety established at the start, the remainder of the opera is devoted to reiterating the importance of serving the nation and sacrificing to it in warfare. The enlightened Mulan lectures her comrades in arms when they deviate from these principles. She tells her fellow soldiers, one of whom is a resentful and reluctant participant in the war effort, that the entire nation would be in peril unless they make their sacrifice. After many years of military service, depicted in on-stage battles, Mulan sings that she cannot return home until victory is secured – and affirms explicitly that she does not resent the hardship and sacrifice this resolve entails. National interests, she informs her fellow soldiers and the audience, prevail over those of the individual or the individual's family. National survival becomes the overarching moral code by which all the soldiers unite. Their families are reduced to composite parts of this larger structure and filial service to their parents is expressed through their national military duties to the state.

The wisdom and rationality of the central state emerge paramount in this PRC Mulan story. The Henan Opera depicts a state that understands the limits of its power to impose on family life through the re-dressing of Mulan as a woman. Mulan's performance as a military leader had so impressed her commander-in-chief that he seeks Mulan as a 'son-in-law' for his daughter. Mulan respectfully reports that he/she would need to consult his/her parents before agreeing to the marriage and returns home. The commander visits Mulan's parents, bearing betrothal gifts and expounding at length on the great contribution their 'son' had made for the nation. Eventually the female Mulan emerges from her room and hastily explains that she had only engaged in the cross-dressing ruse to defend the state in crisis. The wise commander does not punish the Hua family but instead lavishes praise upon them for raising such a noble patriot. The representative of the central state bestows honours on a loyal family for their service to the nation. Mulan does not resort to suicide to protect herself against unreasonable demands made upon her female sex nor does she face execution for her deceit.[48]

In 1964, the Shaw Brothers studio in Hong Kong produced a Huangmei Opera (Mandarin language) version with Yue Feng as director.[49] Titled 'Lady General Hua Mulan', it too has a happy ending with Mulan married to her comrade(s)-in-arms General Li. Like the 1956 opera, Yue Feng's Mulan is a tomboy expert in hunting and riding. The insertion of a male relative who colludes with Mulan enables her to maintain her male disguise and protect her feminine virtue while living among rough-drinking, hard-talking men. At the start of the opera-film, her physical superiority above the mass of new recruits is established in training when she defeats one after another in an elimination trial. Complete with acrobatics and drinking games the opera is a lively and engaging version of the story. It is also framed in a comedy that revolves around the stupidity of men and the superiority of women. Mulan invites the viewers to laugh at her male comrades for not realising that she is a woman with repeated references to 'stinking men'. Yue Feng also includes jokes that depend upon heteronormativity to operate. At one point General Li and General Hua Mulan are about to separate and the former is unnerved by the sexual nature of his longing for Mulan. They express their mutual love with Li quickly describing it as 'brotherly love'. Mulan extends this comradely affection to the sexual and romantic realm by replying that if Li could become a woman then Mulan would marry him.

Mulan's playful comment reveals another aspect of the semi-homoerotic themes in the twentieth-century versions of the story cycle.[50] Within these saucy homoerotic references audiences are treated to a reversal of the expected gender order where the male character takes control and directs the desiring gaze. In Yue Feng's 1964 version Mulan clearly desires General Li. The audience often sees *her* looking admiringly at *him*. The power of active desire rests in the female character – at least the character the *audience* knows is female. General Li is disempowered because he does not know that she is a woman. The expected masculine power of the desiring gaze shifts into Mulan's hands since she, like the audience, has 'all the information'.

Yue Feng's opera assumes no disjuncture between the emperor's commands, the nation's needs and family interests. The film makes clear that each family has a duty to protect the nation through military service because ordinary people need defending against the horrors of foreign invasion. The audience is introduced at the very start of the movie to scenes of the misery inflicted on common folk as a result of the war, showing that the central state's conscription request is in the people's best interests. In response to the tales of wartime horror suffered in other villages, Mulan's father, Hua Hu, cries: 'We've got to save these people!' On receipt of his conscription papers Hua Hu is distraught and driven to bed with worry. His misery derives from his knowledge that physical weakness will render his service to the nation futile. The audience learns that Mulan's father is no malingerer – he asserts the Hua family's lengthy and distinguished military service and declares that he must join the forces 'because the country needs us'. The passive or resentful obedience to imperial conscription that typified the Qing stories is replaced by the enthusiastic desire to personal sacrifice in the mid-twentieth century. Mulan's father is re-created as a military veteran whose desire to fight 'for the country and for the family' is stymied only by his age and ill health.

Mulan is clearly her father's daughter as she is unwavering in her desire to serve the nation. To persuade her parents that she can be an effective soldier, she dresses as a man and 'visits' her father pretending to be family friend who has come to learn some sword techniques from the respected warrior, Hua Hu. Mulan assuming the position of an eager student asks Hua Hu: 'When one's country faces invasion, everyone, regardless of sex or age, must take up arms to protect the family and defend the nation, isn't that so?' Hua Hu agrees with alacrity and the two 'men' engage in their duel. Only after Mulan has defeated her father does she reveal her identity. The success of her ruse persuades her father to let her enlist as he declares: 'It doesn't matter what sex she is as long as she kills the enemy.' And in the supreme subsuming of family interests into state projects he resolves, 'As long as she is able to dedicate herself to serving the nation, the Hua family will have produced a good descendent that will bring glory to the family and the nation – and then I can die in peace.' Before she leaves for battle, Hua Hu presents her with the Hua family's famous lance. He solemnly hands this family treasure to Mulan saying, 'This lance has been at my side my whole life. It has killed many enemy soldiers for the nation; it has won untold glory for the family.' He exhorts her to kill the enemy and return home to glorify the whole Hua clan. In this rubric, family honour can only be achieved through national military service.

Even though Mulan's deeds promise to bring honour to the Hua family, an absent child cannot perform the day-to-day acts of filial care and respectful nurturing. Having just won her parents' approval to enlist, Mulan becomes concerned that her absence will cause her elderly parents anxiety and harm their already fragile health. Her mother is already sobbing about the uncertainty of her daughter's fate and wondering about her likely return to hearth and home. Mulan's elder sister steps in to provide the solution to the conundrum by reassuring Mulan that she will care for their parents and help raise their young brother. She exhorts Mulan to put her mind at ease, to go off to battle and to return victorious.

Mulan's beloved country is worthy of her loyalty. Once victory has been achieved Yue Feng's Mulan is awarded imperial honour for her glorious service and offered promotion to high office. Her commander-in-chief, enthralled by her bravery in battle and noble character, seeks her as his son-in-law – as a father without sons, he hopes Mulan will join his family through marriage. Mulan demurs on the promotion requesting permission to leave public life and uses 'his' desire to see 'his' parents to forestall the betrothal. The commander agrees that the Hua family should be consulted and grants Mulan 'his' wish to return home. Once home Mulan returns to her feminine roles. When the commander sends a large procession carrying betrothal gifts to the Hua family, Mulan's female sex is revealed and the final scene shows Mulan's true love, General Li, on his way back to the capital to inform the commander that the marriage is impossible. Instead, Mulan will marry her beloved comrade-in-arms, General Li.

The three decades of comparative peace in China, Taiwan and Hong Kong between the mid-1960s and the late 1990s may account for the relative absence of major Mulan products in these years. The next wildly popular Mulan work to appear came in 1999 in the form of a 44-episode television series produced by Taiwan's Young Pei Pei.[51] The length of the series, compared to the ballad, operas and movies, provides ample scope for elaborations on the plot and the modernisation of its humour and content. Young's diverting television series includes Mulan's romance and marriage to General Li Liang half way through the series with their joint adventures as a married working couple comprising the remainder of the story. Tensions between Mulan and her mother-in-law dominate the middle section as the elder woman struggles to come to terms with a liberated career-minded daughter-in-law.

Mulan's difficulties in avoiding male viewing of her ablutions are repeated features of Young Pei Pei's television series. In one episode Mulan explains to her father, who is visiting the military base, about how she goes to elaborate lengths to avoid being caught bathing – including swimming in icy cold rivers – much to her father's amusement. The audience is treated to comic episodes where she is nearly discovered naked in baths only avoiding detection by a fortuitous twist in plot. Male viewing of females urinating has diminished in erotic appeal during the twentieth century, being replaced with enhanced fantasies about observing female bathing more generally. And her feet are no longer eroticised – the audience's eye moves instead to her breasts. In keeping with the series' comic tenor, she avoids her fellow soldiers touching her chest in multiple scenes of celebratory group hugs. Similarly, when Mulan suffers an injury to her chest in her valiant defence of the emperor during an assassination attempt she nearly dies trying to avoid being examined by a doctor. Denying that she is in need of medical attention she asks for family leave to prevent exposure of her breasts.[52]

In Young's version modern-day nationalism reinstates the central government's legitimacy and subsumes family interests into those of the state. Mulan is inspired to action through the phrase, 'Protect the family and defend the nation,' and repeatedly uses this maxim as justification for her extreme actions – the family cannot exist without the nation. Mulan's father is keen to contribute but knows that his crippled leg will render him useless. Nevertheless, he earnestly dusts off his old uniform and resumes practising his swords-skill only to collapse on the floor with each attempt. His desire to contribute to the nation is undercut only by the inability of his body to perform.

The overarching rubric is that good families want to contribute to the national effort, and in fact *must* contribute in order to survive. This perspective is reiterated through the battle scenes – the emperor's troops explicitly aim to protect the ordinary people from direct foreign attacks. They never engage in unprovoked attacks on the enemy. In 1999 Mulan's military endeavours are not extensions of imperial vanity, rather the emperor has conscripted the troops in order to better protect the ordinary people's livelihoods through an organised, highly trained and rational military system. Individual households would not be able to protect themselves; rather they rely on a central organising authority to coordinate their defence. The distance between the state and the individual family has diminished to the extent that the family depends upon the central state for its very survival.

Following the pattern set in the majority of the twentieth-century versions, Young Pei Pei presents the central state as being rational in determining the limits of its demands on the family sphere – which has emerged as a space for the expression of individual romantic desire – by deploying the trope of inadvertent same-sex marriage. When Mulan saves the emperor's life, the emperor and empress (presented as a conjugal leadership team for the first time in the Mulan story cycle) reward her heroic deeds with the offer of marriage to their daughter. As an offer that cannot be refused, this event prompts the disclosure of Mulan's female sex. Rather than punishing her for breaking military codes and deceiving the royal family, they immediately seek her hand as wife to their eldest son, the crown prince. Unfortunately Mulan has already fallen in love with her comrade(s)-in-arms General Li Liang, and even the prospect of becoming empress cannot stifle her love. After a series of misadventures and near-tragedy, the emperor and empress, aided by the crown prince, recognise the error of their plan and facilitate the love-match between Mulan and Li Liang. This imperial volte-face concurs with Mulan's father's wishes – he had long espoused the importance of a love-match for his daughter. The central state demonstrated its supreme power in determining all three of Mulan's betrothals and then performs its rationality and reveals the harmony of its interests with those of the family and the individual by giving imperial blessing to the love match of Mulan and Li Liang.

Where to next for Hua Mulan: sexless but not loveless?

The penetration of the state's militaristic ideologies into the family was completed over the course of the twentieth century in the dovetailing of family interests with those of the nation. Yet in the twenty-first century the reach of the state extends even further. In 2009 Hong Kong director Jingle Ma directed the full-length feature film *Mulan* with funding from the PRC, starring, Vicki Zhao Wei.[53] This twenty-first-century Mulan becomes a defender of peace and a reluctant warrior since she abhors killing and the needless violence war inflicts upon innocents and soldiers alike. She takes up a warrior role only because it is the duty of families to fight when their country is in danger. She makes a forceful declaration of patriotism with the rallying cry to her troops 'I, Hua Mulan, will never betray my country!' but her dedication to the nation is expressed primarily through her extreme personal sacrifice – not just on behalf of her father but also in her relationship with her beloved.

The narrative tension in the movie emerges from Mulan's struggle to develop a mature, warrior mentality encapsulated by her father's advice that 'There is no place for emotions on the battlefield.' Despite this warning, she falls in love with her fellow General, Wentai, and the remainder of the movie revolves around her personal challenge to overcome the threat emotional attachments pose to her warrior judgement. The apex of Mulan's development into a great general is marked by her ability to put aside her personal feelings so as to make the correct decision for the country as a whole. She stands obdurate and watches her loyal childhood friend die and sacrifices dozens of soldiers in impossible battles, all in the knowledge that service to the nation requires hard-hearted sacrifice. But Mulan's greatest personal sacrifice is the relinquishing of her beloved Wentai. In contrast to other versions of the story destined for commercial markets she and Wentai do not marry at the end. Instead she withdraws to make it possible for him to marry the former enemy Princess Rouran – this marital alliance will secure peace for both nations. Mulan and Wentai relinquish their love to ensure their country can live free from war.

This twenty-first-century, battle-hardened, self-sacrificing Mulan faces none of the salacious jokes of her predecessor Mulans from comrades-in-arms, and only on rare occasions does Jingle Ma use the threat of her true sex's discovery to titillate the audience. The key 'exposure' incident comes when Mulan bathes naked at night in a hot-spring unaware that Wentai is also bathing there – in the darkness Wentai accidently discovers her sex but not her identity. The threat of the exposure is a serious, rather than a comic, matter. After the hot-spring incident Mulan takes the blame for the theft of a wallet in order to avoid a body search and faces execution – she is only saved by a surprise enemy attack and during the chaos Wentai, who has guessed her secret, facilitates her escape from prison. She excels in the battle and receives a reprieve. Jingle Ma's Mulan is a sexless, but not loveless, warrior. Her willingness to sacrifice herself for her country requires the relinquishment of the most personal and private desires of the heart. In the twenty-first century, the state has not only militarised the domestic space of the family, but it has reached to the innermost parts of its citizens' emotional lives.

Conclusion

The many transformations of Mulan's story over the centuries since the ballad's first appearance naturally reflect the cultural contexts of their historical period and her daring cross-dressing life as a soldier remains central to audiences' sustained interest in the story because of the titillation provided by taboos surrounding sex and gender roles. But, as this chapter has shown, the changing details of the many Hua Mulan stories have revealed the ways in which a core virtue – filial piety – was militarised in the twentieth century and put to war service for the modern nation-states that would emerge in that century. The power of the woman warrior to fascinate and exemplify personal sacrifice meant that the insertion of militaristic thinking into the personal and private realm would make it seem natural that families would offer their children up to the state. A male warrior performing identical deeds to Mulan's would fail to excite the same degree of tension – after all, men have long been expected to sacrifice themselves for wars. On entering the twenty-first century, Mulan embraces a perspective on her obligations to family and country that differs little from those expected of men – everyone, regardless of sex, should sacrifice themselves for the nation and their family. Accompanying this dissolving of gender roles has been the disappearance of popular mistrust at the state's right to demand service from individuals and their families – the evolution of a 'modern' Mulan shows the emergence of the 'national family' that has 'children' to sacrifice to war rather than 'sons and daughters'.

3   Qiu Jin

Transitioning from traditional swordswoman to feminist warrior

For centuries, women war fighters like Hua Mulan have featured prominently in China's literary, dramatic and historical texts and the woman warrior icon proved hugely popular with mass audiences. Yet curiously, as we saw in the previous chapter, such stories of fighting women operated in a cultural context where women, to use Qiu Jin's words, 'are prisoners our entire lives, and beasts of burden for half of it'.[1] The patriarchal and oftentimes misogynistic social order of dynastic China produced and sustained the martial female image in a complex discourse that nurtured the contradictions between idealised submissive women and romanticised powerful women. This resilient cultural tradition produced a situation in 1907 in which Qiu Jin (1875–1907) could describe her countrywomen as 'still perishing in the darkest and lowest of the eighteen layers of Buddhist hell without showing any desire to climb even one level'[2] despite viewing dramas and hearing tales featuring strong, sword-wielding, fearless fighting women. Why? Because for centuries, China's women warriors, like Mulan, were exemplars of consolidation and defenders of orthodoxy.[3]

Over the three decades of Qiu Jin's short life the woman warrior would assume new significances as a result of feminist notions of equal rights for men and women that flooded into China from Europe and America in the late nineteenth and early twentieth centuries. The one-time diverting cross-dressing, magical swordswoman who avenged her brother, replaced her father and defended her lord and master in countless opera stages around the country was confronted by Qiu Jin – a knife-wielding, gun-toting *feminist* warrior who explicitly identified the male-dominated gender hierarchy as unjust and sought to overthrow it. As she wrote in one of her impassioned essays, 'The man always assumes the position of power and the woman the position of slave. ... Alas! Dearest Sisters, no one in any other country would willingly bear the sobriquet "slave", so why should we carry it with such docility and without feeling its shame.'[4]

Qiu Jin's incorporation of a feminist political platform into the existing woman warrior narratives was undoubtedly inspirational at the start of the twentieth century. In China, feminism emerges as a militaristic movement at the hands of Qiu Jin. At this point China's elites were seeking to recover their country's international strength after the Qing dynasty's (1644–1911) imperial rulers demonstrated their incompetence time and again in the face of European, American and Japanese economic and military might. Rebels like Qiu Jin wanted to overthrow the monarchy and establish a republic. Strengthening women's capacities was central to this anti-Qing revolution. Some in China's educated elite, newly aware of women's rights, regarded the preponderance of women warriors in China's history as evidence of their nation's advanced status. Qiu Jin's friend, publisher Chen Yiyi (fl. 1909), argued that China's martial heroines like Hua Mulan were superior to western and Japanese women because the former could only indirectly serve their countries and the latter could only support their husband's careers.[5] China's reformers and rebels, like Chen and Qiu, saw a model for feminism and hope for China's future in the beloved stock icon of ancient swordswomen. Qiu Jin presented herself to her late Qing public as a classically virtuous woman warrior in the mode of the female swordswoman of the knight errant tradition, but one bearing the promise of a modern, independent womanhood of a re-strengthened China. The female swordswoman, long-time defender of patriarchy, would be sent out to battle for women's rights and republican nationhood in the form of Qiu Jin.

However, the iconic figure of the woman warrior carried a complex array of social meanings – not all of which could be easily controlled in a battle against patriarchy. The resilience of the ancient women warrior virtues meant that Qiu Jin's feminist aspirations were easily overlooked. The knight errant traditionally roamed the land alone righting wrongs and reminding the people of core virtues of loyalty, justice, courage and personal sacrifice. In drawing on this image Qiu Jin invoked virtues that would mark her as the first and last feminist knight errant. Later female war fighters actively rejected Qiu Jin's knight errantry in favour of professional soldiering. The lone, unconventional swordswoman of great courage and righteousness that Qiu Jin evoked in her life and death would be eliminated as a martial ideal, except as a fantasy figure in popular culture, almost as soon as the Republic of China (ROC) was formed in 1912. This chapter examines Qiu Jin's radical role in a period of violence and destruction as she consciously crafted a persona for herself and presented it to a population bathed in traditional conceptions of warlike female heroes from mass culture, and to her literati peers schooled in Confucian ideals of martyrdom for righteous causes. Her desire to prompt change in attitudes about women's capacities and rights would be restricted by the weight of these traditions and her enthusiasm for using these topoi in propagandising for her cause.

Hu Ying describes her as 'a "transitional figure" *par excellence*: a history of women of traditional China typically ends with her while a study of modern women begins with her. It is as if alongside her the last of [the] "talented women" (*cainü*) was buried and through her the New Woman (*xin nüxing*) was heralded in.'[6] But, as the various women discussed in this book show, her death also marked the end of a particular type of woman warrior for China – later female soldiers would not be witnesses to her values or sentiments. Qiu Jin fought to change women's roles and status, and in so doing rendered redundant many of the very attributes of heroic women that she had invoked to build her fame. She lived during the last years of public glorifying of suicidal, sacrificial, chaste women. Her self-presentation – knowing that early death was inevitable – sought to prompt public sympathy for her and her anti-Qing feminism by mobilising age-old gendered rhetoric about a heroic death for a noble cause. She deliberately waited to be captured rather than fleeing, courting execution in a decision that was embedded in the political culture of her times. Only a decade-and-a-half after her execution-*cum*-suicide, this noble suicide ideal was discredited and the warlike women that succeeded her, like Xie Bingying discussed in the following chapter, specifically argued against Qiu Jin's actions. Bingying eschewed martyrdom and suicide, regarding them as relics of old patriarchal values. Qiu Jin's story and its commemoration marks a turning point not only in the ideology of women's education and women's learning, as identified by Hu Ying, but also in the ideology underpinning gender and war – her life and deeds reflect views and social norms that would quickly be considered futile, defeatist and vainglorious.

Qiu Jin's attitude to militarised violence was at once traditional in her invocation of swordswomen but also very modern in her repeated advocacy of the importance for China to build a strong, disciplined army that garnered respect at home and abroad – and Qiu Jin's desired modern armed forces would include women. She compared Chinese soldiers unfavourably to their Japanese and European counterparts, describing them as dejected 'pitiful creatures who scraped together a few coppers and some grain in wages . . .[and] regarded their barrack commanders as rats would eye cats'.[7] In battle, confronted with a proud and well-trained enemy, these men faced certain defeat. To save China from dismemberment and deliver prosperity to the land her troops needed to be educated and funded. She sought to change the Chinese elite's attitudes not only to women's status but also to the value of soldiering and organised militarisation.[8] Qiu Jin, herself, was part of the rebel Guangfu army that would overthrow the Manchu rulers of the Qing dynasty. The rebel's black and white flag bore the character 'Han' – signifying the ethnic war against the Manchu by their Han subjects.[9] Qiu Jin's poems and essays are replete with militaristic imagery of swords and knives, battles of courage and passionate patriots with iron for bones. Neither women nor soldiers deserved disdain, and reform of both was vital to China's survival.

During Qiu Jin's parents' lifetime, China experienced the British and French attacks of the Opium Wars of the 1840s and 1860s that crippled the Qing government. New military and economic surges threatened to crush the monarchy altogether. In Qiu Jin's view, by mobilising women to the patriotic cause and advancing the status and capacities of women, China might have a chance of survival. China's Manchu-led government was in disarray in the face of foreign gunboats and her society was crumbling before the impact of floods of opium and foreign manufactured products – the time was ripe for foundational social change. For Qiu Jin, foreigners of all forms, including the Manchu, had to be overthrown. She sought to inspire faith among Han Chinese about their capacities writing: 'My fellow Chinese are inherently superior, so why is it so difficult to surpass these white people?'[10] The woman warrior and swordswoman of the popular imagination was called into being to act on the stage of the real-life battle between Manchu and Han, Chinese and foreigners. Her ancestral land, she wrote, had sunk so low under Manchu rule that its very existence was at stake.

> Invaded by foreign aggression,
> And corrupt and rotten within,
> Without a manly hero to take the lead.
> Heaven, you're so blind:
> Can you bear to see these rivers and mountains
> In the possession of foreign barbarians?
> Divided up like beans, cut up like a melon –
> It is all our land of old![11]

On Qiu Jin's reckoning, women of courage like the women warriors of China's ancient past were needed to save their country and their sex. 'Now we must! Must! Must send out the troops! Wipe out the poisonous fog to see the clear sky. Raising a white sword in our hands, seeking out those who would betray the people, sacrificing life and limb to save the people is a sure and sacred act!'[12]

Qiu Jin's life and times

In 1906, Qiu Jin, a 30-year-old mother of two, injured her hand while making bombs with her comrade would-be assassins. Their intended targets were the hated Qing government officials. Calling for blood, death and sacrifice in myriad poems, essays and songs Qiu Jin was martyred the following year – acutely aware that with her execution she had become the first *female* hero (*nü yingxiong*) to do so. While there were other women who engaged in paramilitary plots and formed women's armies, they were few in number and exceptions to the norm. Many of these women were her personal friends and fellow members of Sun Yat-sen's Revolutionary Alliance – a rebel group fighting to overthrow not only the Qing dynasty, but also monarchy as a system of government. The establishment of a democratic republic was their goal – one that would be realised in 1912, three years after Qiu Jin's execution.

There is no doubt that Qiu Jin was exceptional and that the historical context in which she operated was unique. The Qing Court was fractured with political intrigue and failed to quell increasing social unrest. The majority ethnic Han literati began mobilising the population against the Manchu ruling class through an emotionally charged racist rhetoric. Both posed serious challenges to the Manchu hereditary line that had governed China since 1644. After two-and-a-half centuries of rule, the height of which saw peaks in China's international prestige and domestic prosperity, the country was in chaos and faced both internal rebellion and external attack.

The Qing Court was forced to flee Beijing in a humiliating fashion after declaring war on 'foreigners' in support of an anti-Christian rebel groups called the Boxers, so named for their belief in the magical powers of Chinese martial arts. The court's support of the Boxers provoked military reprisals from Austria-Hungary, the United Kingdom, the United States of America, Japan, Germany, Italy, France and Russia. The 'Eight Powers' quickly crushed the Boxers and their Qing army and rampaged through the capital after their 'relief' of the foreign legation diplomatic quarter. The legations had been under siege for fifty-five days between June and August of 1900 before the 'Eight Powers' came to their rescue.[13] Legation residents had reason to fear for their lives since the Boxers had been responsible for the deaths of many missionaries around North China in the preceding months. The Qing government had reached a new nadir with its misguided support of the Boxers and many Han around the country saw this, including Qiu Jin.

She was roused to action – action that would lead her to abandon her safe but dull domestic world for the excitement and uncertainty of military rebellion. She expressed her despair at the events of 1900 in a poem – its lines presaged the cross-dressing warrior woman role that she would soon assume.

> When will the flames of war in the north finally be extinguished?
> It is said that the battle between China and the west will never end.
> The woman from Qishi frets for her country but in vain;
> It is difficult to change women's dress to military attire.[14]

The poem's frustration belies the comparatively privileged life that Qiu Jin lived as a member of the literati elite. Born in the southern province of Fujian she was raised in the family home in Xiamen, where her grandfather had served as Prefect responsible for coastal defence, and in their ancestral home in Shaoxing, Zhejiang Province. She received an excellent education in both literature and the martial arts from a family that valued women's talents. Her feet had been bound, but 'perhaps not very tightly' and ultimately she 'matured into a talented, unconventional, and strong-willed young woman, accustomed to having her own way'.[15]

Her freedom ended with her marriage in 1896 at the relatively late age of 21. Her husband, Wang Tingjun, was a merchant from Hunan Province, and the unhappy marriage produced two children, a son Wang Yuande (1897–1955) and a daughter Wang Canzhi (1901–1967).[16] Qiu Jin performed the roles of daughter-in-law, wife and mother in comparative seclusion from the world, as was customary for women of her class, but wrote frequently of her melancholy. She expressed to her brother her despair and loneliness: 'In the boudoir, no understanding companions; Who can accompany me in my spare hours?... Regrettably, there is no understanding person; realising this, I shed more tears.'[17]

In 1903, she left Hunan and her parents-in-law's household when her husband purchased a position in the imperial bureaucracy and moved the family to Beijing. Once in the capital, Qiu Jin joined progressive political groups. She and her friends read books about life outside of China and spoke regularly about national affairs. But her marriage was still problematic. Her husband was interested in profit and leisure while she sought personal fame, poetry and politics. Tensions increased and her husband sought to take a concubine. Qiu Jin's loathing of her husband is apparent in another letter to her brother dated 19 June 1905: 'That person's behaviour is worse than an animal's... he treats me as less than nothing.'[18]

Qiu Jin's appreciation of the broader political implications of her personal predicament fuelled her enthusiasm for feminism. She formed a 'Natural Foot Society' to oppose footbinding and spoke publicly about the importance of expanding women's educational opportunities.[19] Her famous friendship with calligrapher, poet and reformist intellectual Wu Zhiying (1867–1934) started at this time – Wu would play a significant role in building and sustaining 'the Qiu Jin myth' after her execution. Qiu Jin's patriotism and feminism quickly matured, leaving her dissatisfied with the role of 'arm-chair activist' – she sought to make a direct contribution to ensuring the survival of her country and its rescue from Manchu hands.

In 1904 she embarked on the path that would shorten her life but ensure her a lasting place in the history of China's twentieth-century revolutions. She sold her jewellery, left her children and husband, and bought a boat ticket to Tokyo – a key base for anti-Qing rebels. Her mother and brothers, themselves attuned to progressive politics, supported her decision and provided additional funds and encouragement.[20] Her decision was a feminist act that declared the right of women to determine their own fate rather than obey their husbands. Her most famous poem of this moment directly expresses her feminist motivation. Titled 'Regrets: Lines Written *En Route* to Japan', it runs:

Figure 3.1 Qiu Jin dressed in Japanese style with sword

Sun and moon have no more light; earth is dark.
Our woman's world has sunk so deep; who can help us?
Jewellery sold to pay for this trip across the seas,
Cut off from my family, I leave my native land.
Unbinding my feet, I clean out a thousand years of poison,
Alas this delicate kerchief here
Is half stained with blood, and half with tears.[21]

Her decision to depart was also a patriotic act since it declared her personal war on the Manchu state. And she would soon become a serious threat to the Qing government.

In Tokyo she joined the hundreds of other Chinese students and political activists working to restore China to its former grandeur. Japan was not only geographically close but its rapid rise in military and industrial capacities greatly impressed those Chinese looking for a programme to reinvigorate their own country. Japan's 1895 defeat of China's military confirmed that Japan had something to teach the lumbering giant that was China. Among her friends in Tokyo were women activists such as Tang Qunying, who led the Chinese women's suffrage movement, Chen Xiefen who was one of China's earliest anti-Qing journalists, and He Zhen a leading anarchist.[22] All were firm in their hatred of the Manchu. She became active in the militant secret societies from her home province of Zhejiang and joined the Revolutionary Alliance that would propel Sun Yat-sen to his position as founding president of the ROC in 1912.

Inspired by the increasing radicalism of her fellow students and their expanding skills in explosives and military strategy she decided to return to China in early 1906. Sun Yat-sen circulated his general strategies for the revolution in the winter of that year and specifically contrasted his new-style troops against the old-style rebels of China's past dynastic changes. 'In the past we had revolutions of heroes, but today we have a revolution of the citizenry' and the citizen revolutionaries will have 'the spirit of freedom, equality and fraternity and each will bear responsibility for the revolution'.[23] Qiu Jin envisaged herself as one of these citizens, equal to men and charged with expanding the corps of individuals ready to join the anti-Qing cause. On her return to China she strengthened her ties with the underground movement and like many others combined her revolutionary work with teaching and publishing.

She edited the short-lived *Chinese Women's Journal* – recognised today as one of China's earliest feminist magazines – and secured teaching positions in various new girls' schools including the Datong School in her hometown, Shaoxing. The radical Xu Xilin (1873–1907), with whom she had studied in Japan, established the school and apart from promoting a modern education for women, he intended it to foment anti-Manchu dissent. Qiu Jin became its principal and from this base built her women's army. The curriculum at Datong was modern, physical and warlike. The students trained in foreign languages (including English and Japanese), geography, history and military strategy and undertook a rigorous physical education programme that focused on military drills and weaponry skills.[24] Many of her students had undertaken the painful process of unbinding their feet in order to participate in these training regimes. Children living around the school sat and watched the women during their drills with 'foreign rifles' and crowded around Qiu Jin as she rode horseback about Shaoxing dressed in men's clothes and western leather shoes.[25]

She and her rebel cell promoted anti-Qing sentiment and plotted the assassinations of government officials in Henan and Zhejiang but their plans were cut short by her arrest. When Xu Xilin failed in his bid to assassinate the provincial governor of Anhui, the Qing government had sufficient cause to issue a warrant for Qiu Jin's arrest – since she was the principal of Xu's school. News of Xu's arrest and execution reached Shaoxing ahead of the Qing troops, giving Qiu Jin sufficient time to escape, but she had chosen a martyr's path. Qiu Jin resolved to remain at Datong School and await her executioners – her death, she correctly anticipated, would generate further anti-Qing sentiment. While awaiting their arrival, she wrote a final letter to one of her sworn sisters, Xu Yunhua, expressing her 'determination to die for the revolutionary cause'.[26]

Her colleague from Datong school later cited Qiu Jin: 'I am a pure and spotless woman and haven't committed the slightest crime, so why should I run away and provide people with an excuse to accuse me of fleeing like a coward!' More than 400 Qing troops arrived to arrest Qiu Jin, surrounding the school to prevent her escape. When her students tried to flee 'many were killed by gunfire'.[27] This appears to be the only time the troops she trained faced live fire.

During her short imprisonment and hasty trial she maintained her innocence of any crimes. Instead she argued that her school was well integrated into the Shaoxing community and that the local judicial and government authorities regularly visited for ceremonial functions, had donated funds and even approved the purchase of rifles for military drills. She maintained the position that she was simply running a school that trained women in a modern education curriculum. Her association with Xu Xilin should not be a problem since 'Even though this school may have been founded by Xu Xilin, he is only one of the old teachers, so why should the [current] teachers of the school be implicated in this case?'[28]

Many later reports of her imprisonment say that she was tortured to extract a confession but none was forthcoming so her many published poems were the sole evidence that the authorities could muster to convict her. She was executed at dawn on 15 July 1907 by beheading – the morning after her arrest. Florence Ayscough aptly wrote that Qiu Jin's death was 'fecund'.[29] Despite the failure of the revolution during her life, her death deepened discontent against the Manchus. The controversy over her hasty and poorly managed trial and execution caused serious problems for the Qing officials involved. The press, ranging from the moderate *Shibao* and *Shenbao* to the revolutionary *Shenzhou ribao*, presented Qiu rather romantically as a wronged woman and the extensive media coverage of her life and death was overwhelmingly sympathetic.[30] While some believed she was innocent of all charges, others recognised her crimes but felt that the trial was mismanaged and its verdict excessively harsh.

Many in the government were annoyed that the actions of their Zhejiang colleagues had stirred up more unrest in a country already boiling with anti-Qing discontent. Mary Rankin explains that the careers of the officials responsible for her execution were ended by the controversy and the magistrate who sentenced her to execution committed suicide.[31]

Her fame was not limited to the Chinese language press. The Shanghai-based English-language *North China Herald* reported on both Xu Xilin's execution (his heart was cut out and his head displayed on a spike)[32] and included a lengthy article on Qiu Jin – her life, bungled trial and hasty execution. The *Herald* presents the view that she was not an anti-Manchu revolutionary at all and had no knowledge of the charges that were being brought against her. Describing her as 'heroic' in the face of torture and 'perfectly loyal' in her refusal to name any co-conspirators, the paper disdainfully described the Qing officials as 'miserable' and 'panic-stricken' at the prospect of rebellion in their jurisdiction.[33]

So prominent did she become after her death that she was buried and reburied nine times as national and personal politics invested in or attempted to control the power of commemoration. Sabine Hieronymus aptly describe the journey of her body as 'an odyssey'.[34] Fear of persecution meant that at first, no family claimed her severed head and body so a charitable association buried Qiu Jin in the hills outside the town. In October, several months after her execution her brother retrieved her coffin and reburied her in Shaoxing. Only a few months later again, in January of 1908, her sworn sisters Wu Zhiying and Xu Zhihua (1873–1935) travelled to Shaoxing, retrieved her remains and secretly moved her to a plot they had bought for the purpose at Hangzhou's West Lake. This shift honoured Qiu Jin's wishes to be buried next to the national hero, Yue Fei, who fought to defend the Han-dominated Song dynasty (960–1279) against the invading Mongols who would later form the Yuan dynasty (1271–1368).[35] A ceremony, including the erection of a stele in her honour, marked the occasion. In December 1908, however, the increasingly anxious Qing government instructed her brother to take the body back to Shaoxing, fearing the Hangzhou location near Yue Fei's tomb would provoke unrest. In autumn of 1909 her son Wang Yuande, then only aged 14, obeyed his recently-deceased father's wishes that Qiu Jin be buried in the Wang family plot in Hunan and so her remains were relocated yet again. Following the collapse of the Qing dynasty in 1912 her coffin was moved to the hills of Changsha and then in 1913 returned to lakeside Hangzhou where, after yet another relocation to the hills in 1965, she returned for the last time in 1981. Today tourists still visit her resting place on the lakeside at Hangzhou.

Her public prominence increased after her death, in no small part thanks to Wu Zhiying and Xu Zhihua – both women were Qiu's close personal friends and dedicated considerable time to promoting her causes through writing about

Figure 3.2 Qiu Jin statue in Hangzhou, 2009

her life and deeds. Broader public fascination with the now-dead woman warrior meant there was demand for information about Qiu Jin in the regular press as well. In the first year of the new republic, 1912, and five years after her death, Sabine Hieronymus declares that 'the Qiu Jin cult had reached its zenith'. Freed of earlier fears that the Qing government would persecute attendees, a memorial ceremony was held in Hangzhou and over a thousand guests attended. Schools were established in her name and Sun Yat-sen visited her gravesite penning an elegiac calligraphic scroll with the words 'Female Hero' (*Jinguo yingxiong*). In writing this term, a centuries-old classical phrase used to honour women warriors, Sun, despite his desire for a citizens' revolution and not a heroes' revolution, situated Qiu Jin within the ideology of noble swordswomen of China's past rather than as a revolutionary citizen in which feminists could be part of China's future.

Becoming a swordswoman to become a feminist nationalist

In today's terms, Qiu Jin was a terrorist. She advocated and prepared for the violent overthrow of her government. Yet, as we saw above, reports on her execution reveal her to be extremely sympathetically regarded. This positive appraisal has been sustained for decades through to the present and results in part from her conscious self-crafting as a classic female swordswoman. Hu Ying and Sabine Hieronymus have traced the mechanisms through which she engaged the woman warrior heroine tradition.[36] Hieronymous explains: 'The heroine Qiu Jin had a very good working knowledge of the old myths of her culture, she knew how they worked and instrumentalized them – and thus created a myth of her own. . . and by doing so, deliberately placed herself in the tradition of Chinese heroines.'[37] Similarly, Mary Rankin described her behaviour as being 'closely tied to the image of the hero, which had already crept into her early poetry and now became the model about which she sought to organize her life'.[38] Wu Zhiying dedicated considerable time and energy to present Qiu Jin posthumously as a 'knight errant' in order to commemorate her unusual friend in a recognisable, positive frame.[39] She too positioned Qiu Jin as a lone hero rather than a radical, feminist terrorist.

The 'knight errant' is a stock figure in Chinese literary and historical traditions. They possess advanced martial skill and, according to James Liu, are marked by the following attributes: altruism, a strong sense of justice, valuing individual freedom highly and rejecting conventional morality, personal loyalty, physical and moral courage, truthfulness and a commitment to fulfilling promises, the cherishing of honour and the desire for fame and generosity coupled with a disdain for the trappings of wealth.[40] The historical figures he discusses are male but in his discussion of knights from fiction and drama women also feature. The romance of a swordswoman of superior skill adhering to the highest moral (masculine) codes had huge popular appeal.[41]

Qiu Jin actively sought to present herself as a female knight errant (*nüxia*). She uses the term *xia* frequently in her poems to describe herself and her pen name was 'The Female knight errant from the Mirror Lake' (*Jianhu nüxia*).

Rankin described her youth as being 'engaged in romantic dreams of knight errantry fed by swashbuckling novels, and to have learned to ride horseback, use a sword, and drink considerable quantities of wine'.[42] Her poems also display her interest in China's historical and fictional amazons. In 'Full River Red' she writes 'The memory of Qin Liangyu's fame soaks my gown with tears; At the thought of Shen Yunying's deeds my heart starts to pound.'[43] Wife to a Sichuanese general, Qin Liangyu (1574–1648) took command of his troops after his death in battle. Shen Yunying (1624–1660) was daughter to a heroic Ming general and also assumed command of his troops after his death in the successful defence of Daozhou city in 1643. Significantly both women fought the Manchu, just as Qiu Jin herself aspired to do.

Qiu Jin harnessed the power of these popular women to increase public sympathy. She regularly carried a sword or a knife and made much show of her skills in their use. Many are the reports of her performances of martial arts sword dances. She was not averse to more aggressive uses of knives either. During one of her famous Tokyo speeches of December 1905 aimed at prompting students to return to China to join the anti-Qing revolution, Qiu Jin used a knife as prop – some reports saying she stabbed it into the podium's table and others that she threw it onto the table while threatening death by sword for all those who failed the anti-Qing rebel movement. Qiu Jin's friend, Xu Shuangyu, said that she told the audience 'anyone who sides with the Manchus, sells out friends to pursue glory, or bullies the Han people after their return to the fatherland will take a stabbing from me!'[44]

Although the anti-Qing revolutionaries worked mostly with rifles and explosives the romance of the sword and knife was central to the creation of Qiu Jin as a female knight errant. One of her more famous poems is 'Song of the Precious Sword' in which she invokes the power of the sword as a historical symbol of revolt against poor leadership and as a contemporary symbol calling for the taking up of arms.

> When the allied troops of the eight powers marched north,
> We again handed our mountains and rivers over to others.
> Those white devils coming from the West serve as a bell,
> That woke us Chinese up from our slaves' dream!
> You, my lord, gave me this gold-speckled sword,
> Today as I receive it, my mind is virile and brave.
> These are the days when red-hot iron rules,
> And a million heads are not worth a feather.
> Bathed by the sun and moon, shinier than jewels:
> Risking my life, I am suddenly filled with elation.
> I swear I'll find us a way to lead us from death to life:
> World peace now depends on military armament.[45]

She continues her poem with emotive lyrics on the sword's power.

> A precious sword, heroic bones: who is our equal?
> All my life I've known who are my enemies and friends.
> Don't despise this foot-long iron for not being brave:
> The rare merit of saving the nation is yours to garner!
> Could I but use heaven and earth as my oven, and yin and yang as my coal, and
>   gathering all the iron of the six continents,
> Produce thousands, tens of thousands of precious swords to purify this sacred
>   land,
> And continuing the glorious power and fame of our first ancestor, the Yellow
>   Emperor,
> Cleanse once and for all what, in its thousand-, its hundred-year-long history,
>   has been its vilest shame![46]

This song encapsulates another key feature of Qiu Jin knight errant identity – her capacity for huge personal sacrifice. Qiu Jin, in her self-conscious creation of a heroic identity and her welcoming of capture and execution, saw herself as more powerful in death than in life. She was inspired by the perceived noble status she would achieve on her martyrdom and spoke approvingly of others' heroic deaths. Hu Ying explains that the willingness to die for one's principles is a deep-seated and well-known Confucian principle – the truly great person does not seek to preserve his or her life if it means compromising virtue or righteousness.[47] Hu Ying argues that such martyrdom then demanded a eulogistic response from those positioned as the audience for the martyr's sacrifice. It was precisely this reaction that Qiu Jin sought in her self-presentation as a female knight errant.

In the late Qing, replete as it was with rebels of strong principles, Qiu Jin had many direct role models of martyrdom. In 1898, Tan Sitong (1865–1898) refused to flee from the Qing police after the reform movement he helped spearhead was foiled. Two of his colleagues, Liang Qichao (1873–1929) and Kang Youwei (1858–1927), fled Beijing for Japan but Tan chose martyrdom – advancing their cause among Han literati by displaying his steadfastness to the reform movement and purity of political intention. Similarly, Qiu Jin's friend in Japan, Chen Tianhua (1875–1905), had walked into the sea committing suicide in protest at the Japanese government's increasing restrictions on Chinese students' political activities. Qiu Jin even saw accidental deaths as praiseworthy and ennobling. Wu Yue (1875–1905), died after accidentally blowing himself up during an assassination mission against five Qing officials. Qiu Jin wrote an obituary declaring his death 'pure sacrifice'.[48] The courage to die for one's principles was a key attribute for those joining the anti-Qing movement. The population positioned as audience for these acts of public sacrifice were ideally roused to sympathy for their cause or at least to enormous respect for the individual who had so courageously demonstrated his/her virtue. Tan Sitong had also explicitly invoked the knight errant image for its capacity to arouse the people to action.[49] Qiu Jin would be the last woman warrior to present herself so purely as a classical martyr.

Such was the moral and political context in which Qiu Jin operated. She wrote explicitly of her willingness to die for her cause in a 1905 letter to a friend, Wang Shize, declaring that since the Boxer calamity of 1900 she had already resolved to put her life on the line. She listed the many men who had martyred themselves for the anti-Qing cause, like Tang Caichang (1867–1900) and Wu Yue, but noted that, much to the shame of the 'women's world', there was no female equivalent yet.[50] She offered herself for this role with the pledge 'I vow to give all of you encouragement.'[51]

Her enthusiasm to be a female version of Tang Caichang did not, however, mean she entirely abandoned the audience's expectation that martyred women worthy of emulation reflect long-standing ideals of female chastity. In Qiu Jin's embracing of a violent death she was acutely aware of the importance of appearing morally 'clean' in order to be an effective martyr. She wrote to her brother from Japan saying 'What I care about is that when I am dead and buried my name will be handed down through 10,000 generations.' For this to happen she had to prevent those who 'would damage her future reputation' from gaining any advantage – that is, her husband Wang Zifeng. Qiu Jin declared, 'I will definitely never allow that immoral one, Zifang to pollute my heroic spirit of independence.'[52] Other letters to relatives likewise express her concern at slander and gossip that would sully her 'lofty aspirations'.[53]

Female chastity and virtue were long-standing markers of community virtue and female knights errant, despite their daring, still needed to demonstrate purity. Moreover, during the two preceding centuries China had seen a dramatic increase in the numbers of women 'publicly performing virtue' through suicide or chaste widowhood – events that were documented in reports to government on significant events in each locality and sometimes even commemorated with the construction of huge memorial arches. A chaste and virtuous woman brought respect to the community – suicide was one method of demonstrating these qualities.[54]

Her friend Xu Zhihua supported her desire to be remembered as pure of heart in writing the stele for Qiu's 1908 burial site. Xu explained Qiu's unusual behaviour as follows: 'In closely examining [Qiu Jin's] conduct, [we see that] she was careless of details, tended to give free expression to her emotions, and loved wine and swords – all as if she were not to be reined in by convention. Yet, in her true essence, she was exceptionally upright and prudent. . . Although she loved freedom, in matters concerning propriety, she never transgressed.'[55]

Not everyone was convinced that she 'never, from first to last, overstepped the bounds of morality and virtue'[56] – and rumours about her relationship with Xu Xilin undercut her friends' professions of Qiu's chaste spirit. She wrote several poems about him and his heroism once she arrived in Japan and no other living figure features so frequently in her poetry.[57] Even those on the same side of the battle as Qiu were not entirely convinced of her feminine virtue. Prominent leader of the anti-Qing movement, Zhang Binglin (1868–1936, aka Zhang Taiyan), wrote a preface for her collected poems and criticised her garrulousness – she talked too much and gave too many speeches in public to be a truly virtuous woman. He writes approvingly of her sword skills but less positively of her failure to adhere to a key principle of female virtue – 'prudence in words'. 'I heard that in ancient times, those who were good in swordsmanship held true spirit within and exhibited placid appearance without. Few were garrulous.'[58] One of Qiu Jin's most famous essays is her 1904 'The Advantages of Public Speaking' where she declared that 'an eloquent and honest tongue'[59] could mobilise the masses and, based on Zhang's critique, she clearly practiced what she preached.

The idea that a woman such as Qiu Jin who abandoned her children, rejected her husband and wandered the world independently in apparent disregard for feminine propriety could aspire to anything approximating *virtue* is entirely contradictory – at least on the surface. But, as Hu Ying so deftly explains, this contradiction could be managed within the ideal of the noble warrior knight errant, the *xia*. As a female version of this noble figure, Qiu Jin could be excused her unconventional behaviour. Knights errant were known for rejecting conventional norms in order to achieve higher goals. Qiu Jin, in large part through her friend Wu Zhiying's carefully constructed biographies, emerges as a legitimate knight errant. Her unusual and unfeminine behaviour becomes noble and worthy of commemoration and exaltation through this well-recognised social role. She is unorthodox but understandable within the established cultural system. In this respect the radical nature of her claims for changing the foundation of gender roles is tamed – she is presented as an unusual woman in unusual times and a stock figure throughout China's cultural history.

The knights errant's rejection of conventional morality typically leads others to misunderstand their motives or find them problematic. While in Beijing before embarking on her Japan adventure Qiu Jin wrote of her loneliness at being misunderstood by lesser human beings. But, despite the frequent mournful tone of many of her poems, Qiu Jin equally frequently declares her courage to fight for change in China's miserable circumstances. In the second verse to her 'Full River Red' she wrote:

> My body will not allow me
> To mingle with the men,
> But my heart is far braver
> Than that of a man.
> All my life, has not my liver and gall
> Burned for others?
> But how could they with their vulgar minds understand me?

> In adversity the hero must suffer troubles and woes.
> Where in this world of red dust can I find a true friend?
> My blue gown is soaked with tears.[60]

In self-consciously presenting herself as a female knight errant Qiu Jin was making sense of her own actions within the standard conceptualisations available to her and these were also connections that others viewing her actions would readily grasp. However, like the women knights errant of yesteryear, she also had to become a man temporarily to achieve her goals.

Becoming a man to become a soldier

Qiu Jin was famous for her propensity to dress in men's clothing. She left photographs and poetic commentary on her dress choice as part of her presentation as a noble swordswoman. Cross-dressing as men was a key trait of the traditional women warriors and was central to their allure. To be effective, heroic soldiers they had to first pass as men. War fighting and the social role of soldier were ascribed to men at the exclusion of women. The other key public role, that of the scholar, was also denied to females and deemed the exclusive preserve of men and masculinity. Women were prohibited from sitting the imperial examinations that selected the bureaucrat literati who would rule the country and hold moral authority as their nation's political leaders. Nor could they join the military examinations that selected the officer elite let alone be conscripted or volunteer for battle as regular soldiers. That is, the roles of scholar and soldier were denied to women unless they assumed the persona of men – and the key method for achieving this was through dressing as a man. Women, like Hua Mulan, passed as men to fulfil masculine military social roles. Others, like the protagonists in the popular and well-loved stories of Huang Chonggu and Zhu Yingtai, dressed as men to become scholars.[61] By dressing as men, such women did not upset the gender hierarchy in which masculinity and maleness were integral to legitimate scholars or soldiers. Such women usually returned to their feminine social roles – their adventures being a sojourn that confirmed the matrix where the social roles of scholar and soldier could only be mapped onto the male form.

Soon after her arrival in Beijing she became known for her public appearances dressed as a man – variously in Chinese or western clothing. From the autumn of 1903, after a particularly nasty episode with her husband, she resolved to dress as a man and wear no cosmetics. Her rejection of traditional female attire marked her rebirth as a political and military being. On an inscription to one of the many photos she had taken of herself dressed as a man, she wrote that the clothing reflected the arrival of this new person and the eradication of her former self. The poem shows how she believed her female

Figure 3.3 Qiu Jin dressed in Chinese men's clothing

body had to be disavowed as fake before she could take on the task of saving her nation's future. Using Buddhist notions of reincarnation she implies that in a previous life she had been a man – who unfortunately found himself reborn as a woman – but at least a woman who can recognise her masculine alternative core.

> 'Inscription on My Photo – in men's clothing'
> Who is this person, staring at me so sternly?
> The martial bones from a former existence regret their female embodiment.
> The flesh of this world is from the start a deception,
> The land of the future, surely, is real.
> You and I should have been together long ago, to share our feelings;
> Looking out and lamenting these difficult times, our spirits garner strength.
> When you see my friends from the old days,
> Tell them I've scrubbed off all that old mud.[62]

Mary Rankin explains that, in dressing as a man, Qiu Jin was imitating heroes like Hua Mulan but also 'demanding the right as a woman to play male roles and, relishing the impropriety of her behaviour and dress, dramatising her protest against restrictions'.[63] There was no doubt that her cross-dressing increased her fame and her husband's frustration while also signalling her decision to challenge the distinction between the social roles ascribed to men and women. Lingzhen Wang, like Rankin, argues that this was more than a mere imitation of Hua Mulan because unlike Mulan's donning of men's clothing Qiu's 'anticipated no return to any existing female role or conventional female embodiment'.[64] Qiu Jin was making a personal decision to model the capacity for the female body to have manly or masculine social attributes.

But, in contrast to later women soldiers she was still trapped in the traditional mindset where she *had* to dress as a man to assume what she perceived to be 'manly roles'. Only two decades later, women would not have to 'pass as men' to become soldiers – they would feel quite comfortable as women soldiers dressed in specialist military uniforms – i.e. they were dressed as 'soldiers' rather than as 'men-who-are-soldiers'. In the next chapter, we see that by the 1920s women like Xie Bingying no longer needed to deny their femaleness as a prerequisite for soldiering. Women soldiers dressed in military uniform still perceived themselves and were perceived by others as *women* – strange and exotic women, but women, nonetheless. They were not masquerading as men, as was Qiu Jin in her performance of the noble female knight errant role.

Qiu Jin did more than simply don men's clothing – she also altered her physical body to become more effectively martial. Undertaking strenuous physical exercise after arriving in Tokyo she described her exertions to her brother as follows: 'Everyday I practice calisthenics that have made my body strong.'[65] In Shaoxing, her school's curriculum included extensive physical training for male and females alike. Reformist intellectuals tried to spur on their fellow Han by describing China as 'The Sick Man of Asia'.[66] Only through improving their physical body and intellectual state would China survive – and in the eyes of those mobilising this epithet women were far sicker than men because of the crippling impact of footbinding. But, it was not only in the physical realm that women were deficient. In the Chinese context masculinity connoted a set of noble moral and spiritual qualities that women were generally regarded as lacking – heroism, ambition, high-minded patriotism and courage of conviction. She revealed her frustration at the mismatch between her female physical form and her manly mental frame in a poem to a Japanese friend whom she met while in Beijing. Titled 'Walking through the Sedge-Grass' it proceeds:

> My ambition is manly,
> My life is too narrow,
> To no avail is my mind filled with heroic daring!
> Let me question High Heaven about my bad fate:
> Although a mere woman, I suffer like the poet Qu Yuan!'[67]

The story of Qu Yuan (343–278 BCE) is central to Chinese cultural history. He represents the archetypal, manly patriotic poet because he drowned himself in despair at the state of his country. Even today, annual festivals are held to celebrate his life – known as Double Fifth or Dragon Boat Festival.[68] To Qiu Jin, Qu Yuan's circumstances mirrored China's current dire situation.

Qiu Jin's enthusiasm for masculine gender roles fuelled her feminist sentiment but her thinking was locked into existing conceptions about male and female social roles and moral capacity. Women, trapped by their bodies, had to become men in order to take on masculine roles. Only a decade after her death women who sought to create new roles for themselves in the public sphere as workers, professionals, or soldiers were able to invoke the increasingly powerful icon of the 'Modern Woman' or the 'New Woman'. They no longer needed the female knight errant persona to justify their claims to this public world of national affairs. While the Modern Woman idea had been circulating around the world during the last years of Qiu Jin's life it would only take concrete form in China from about 1915 onwards. When they did emerge these new-style women did not pretend to be men in order to enter the public spaces of political power, military impact and economic influence, they presented themselves as Modern Women and proudly claimed their rights as women. So significant was the Modern Woman as a social force that she became a site of contestation from the political class that sought to ensure she was a politically oriented patriotic woman, not one that simply pretended to be modern while using newly won access to public space for shopping and flirting.[69]

From nationalist swordswoman to feminist warrior

The female knight errant model that Qiu Jin and her friends invoked were extraordinary women who appeared during extraordinary times to take up arms with and for their brothers, husbands and fathers. But, none of these women, historical or imagined, fought for women's rights – they were firmly creatures of a patriarchal order that required women to extend themselves in times of crisis.[70] Qiu Jin invoked their fame and the positive emotive connections of these ancient women warriors as saviours of the country – but extended their significance by including a woman's rights agenda. She achieved this shift firm in the belief, like the 1898 reformers who influenced her generation so powerfully, that women's dependency and weakness was central to China's failure to withstand the impact of foreign powers.

In her many writings on women's rights and the importance of mobilising women, Qiu Jin targeted women's dependency on men and passivity in relation to their own oppression. While she clearly identifies men as the opposition in phrases like 'With their theories and tricks men deceive us,' she also challenges women to rouse themselves from their passivity. 'My sisters, my compatriots! Those who cannot be independent should be determined to be independent. Those who can be independent should nourish the desire to save all their sisters in the world from the sea of suffering, they can put it off no longer!'[71]

Qiu Jin's campaign against footbinding drew on the idea that the forced crippling of women was central to their weakness as a sex and by extension their country's vulnerability. The pain of undertaking physical activity on newly unbound feet was likely excruciating for many of her students. 'Alas! These girls – Why did they have to suffer this mutilation at such a tender age? A bloody mess of broken bones – they could hardly walk!' A life of immobility, dependency and sickness accompanies this crippling, leaving Chinese women more prone to illness and death in childbirth than Japanese or European women, according to Qiu Jin. 'Why are our women willing to risk their lives and endure all that suffering for a pair of feet, to put up with every kind of pain, even to the point of having their bones broken? ... It is their own fault for considering themselves as totally worthless. They do not try to acquire a craft or knowledge of use to their own lives, they know only how to rely on men and devote their entire lives to serving them.'[72]

Her efforts at providing women with education, independence and physical strength stemmed from her belief that women had too long been passive in the face of their misery and, when active, had sought only to inflict misery on other women. Mothers break their daughters' feet and ignore their pain as they bind them. Mothers-in-law oppress their daughters-in-law and treat them like prisoners. Parents use matchmakers to choose slave-like wives for their sons. To Qiu Jin, these travesties occur because women do not rise and fight. 'We women suffer a myriad kinds of oppression that are truly unbearable!' Only by overcoming 'layer after layer of nets and snares' that 'lock women up deep inside the inner quarters' can women be independent and participate equally in a new republic.[73]

In addition to rousing women's awareness of the depths of horror to which they have sunk, she also uses an age-old rhetorical strategy – drawing negative comparisons with men to inspire action. In 'Full River Red' she writes:

> In this ugly and dirty world
> How many men, I ask you, are heroic and wise?
> Only from the ranks of those with painted eyebrows
> From time to time do stalwarts emerge!

She then continues by beseeching her fellow women to take up arms.

> I urge those of you present here
> To exert yourself to the utmost.
> Be fired by the desire to ensure the future of your race,
> Prosperity does not depend on showing off your jewels.
> These bow-like shoes, three inches long, condemn us to inaction:
> This must change!'[74]

The failure of men, on her logic, demanded that women arise and transform themselves. Another poem uses the same negative appraisal of men to remind women of their capacities. In her commentary on a Qing story, 'Records of the Sesame Niche', Qiu challenges its Manchu triumphalism and asserts the importance of mobilising women for success in battle. Stanza 5 reads: 'Banished into this dusty world, what a shame to be a man / Shouldering dagger-axes, young beauties became generals / Now the names of the loyal and the filial belong to women.' Stanza 8 sustains her theme that women from China's past have recorded martial skills oftentimes superior to men. 'Officials who eat meat are all useless; / Beautiful women defended the nation. / Two extraordinary women commented on military affairs, / They rivalled Hua Mulan.'[75] The two women she refers to are the anti-Manchu Ming dynasty (1368–1644) loyalists, Qin Liangyu and Shen Yunying.

Just as we saw in the section above discussing Qiu Jin's cross-dressing, her elevation of women and denigration of men is far from a radical, new trope in Chinese cultural traditions. Advancing the idea that the women of a particular time or place are better than the men is a centuries-old stock moral framework. China's most famous novel, *The Dream of the Red Chamber*, first circulating in the 1760s revolves around the proclaimed superiority of the young female characters, who serve as foils for the decrepit men presiding over the once-great family's decline.[76] Excellence among womenfolk signified the declining state of the menfolk – as manifest in the maxim 'When *yin* dominates, *yang* declines.' In this cultural context, having strong women is nothing to celebrate.

Rather, it stands as a warning to men that they need to improve. Readers of Qiu Jin's poetry would have filtered her claims of female supremacy through the lens in which it signalled broader societal calamity and crisis. At such times, it was expected that a female knight errant would appear – and equally expected that such a woman would die a sacrificial martyr. Although Qiu Jin sought to create a new world rather than rebuild the old patriarchal order, many viewing her actions, listening to her speeches and reading her poems would have understood her as another old-style loyal, exemplary woman.

Feminism was a key motivation for Qiu Jin's radical action – but it is marked by the times in which she lived. Not only was it mediated by long traditions of exemplary cross-dressing women who appeared in times of crisis and male incompetence, it was also read within a strong tradition of eulogising women's suicides as markers their virtue. Qiu Jin's willingness to await capture and her enthusiastic martyrdom were problematic for later Modern Women and other critics of chastity suicides. The radical advocates of modernisation who emerged during the New Culture Movement years (1915–1925) explicitly targeted female suicide and chastity as backward and harmful to women's progress. During Qiu Jin's era, however, the prospect and eventuality of her martyr's death was an unproblematic noble and heroic act well within the realms expected of the woman knight errant.

Problematic women knights errant in modern and communist China

Awe of Qiu Jin's romanticised and mythic martyr's suicide dwindled in the Republican era when warfare and military systems modernised as quickly as social attitudes. Not everyone remained convinced of the effectiveness of her martyrdom and many saw her active seeking of personal fame as outdated. Writer Lu Xun (1881–1936) witnessed Qiu Jin's knife-waving 1905 speech when he was a student in Japan, but he ignored her exhortation that Chinese students quit Tokyo and return to China. He developed a sceptical attitude about spectacles as political action, noting that Qiu Jin sought the limelight, performed sensationalism, provoked her audiences and was ultimately 'clapped to death'[77] – a victim of her own publicity machine. In a 1919 short story based on Qiu Jin's execution, 'Medicine', Lu Xun explored the futility of these spectacular sacrifices – ordinary people simply came to watch the execution 'show' and did not understand the politics behind the sacrifice. They merely moved on to become passive audiences for the next spectacle.[78] However, Qiu Jin was primarily addressing her fellow literati who carried the same class-based cultural codes of sacrifice and public performance. The idea that the 'masses' were an appropriate audience only emerged in the 1920s as

China's elite adopted more democratic attitudes and rejected Confucian ideals of leadership by enlightened literati.[79]

A similar questioning of Qiu Jin's decision to become a martyr appeared in Xia Yan's 1937 play about her life titled *The Spirit of Freedom*[80] performed at the start of the eight-year war against the invading Japanese – in which women fought alongside men in formal and auxiliary military roles. In the play the significance of a self-sacrificing death is discussed explicitly between Qiu Jin and her colleagues as they debate her plan to await the Qing troops. Qiu declares that 'The decision to "die for a just cause" is inherent to the revolutionary party' and 'A lot of our comrades' blood has been shed for this failure. They bravely died for this just cause, so if I feel danger now how can the revolutionary party talk about having a righteous faith in the future?' To which her friends replied in the most modern of terms: 'I didn't know you were so stupidly stubborn. You have been ruined by those books of old on virtue and righteousness,' and, 'Commander, my final words: Suicide means that you have given up your fight against the Qing government! It means that you admit your personal failure.'[81] Xia Yan depicts her fellow rebels as encouraging her to escape and arguing against traditional knight errant ideals of self-sacrifice to a righteous purpose.[82] In the 1920s, 1930s and 1940s, a Qiu Jin-style 'female knight errant' martyrdom seemed like an anachronistic vestige of older and debunked morality. While Qiu Jin was a model of sorts for many other female warriors in the struggle against Japan from 1937 to 1945, her welcoming the martyr's death was problematic. Soldiers, female or male, had to really fight to the death rather than sit writing poetry performing patient, suicidal martyrdom.

The shift away from glorifying suicidal martyrs partly grew from the influence of western, socialist ideology on the military forces that emerged in the 1920s – the Communist International movement provided core organisational and financial support to both the Nationalist Party and the Chinese Communist Party (CCP). Their party-armies were designed to be disciplined fighting forces – enlistment and survival, body counts and the burden of the injured were central to the strategic operation of military troops facing conventional battles. For Qiu Jin and her rebels, this level of military professionalism did not exist. There was no concept of sustaining a war, rather it was one of destabilising the Qing through assassination, small-scale uprisings and civil unrest in the hope of building larger resistance and inspire Qing troops to turn against the Manchu.[83] Martyrs to a rebel cause were effective in this disruptive role. Women martyrs held particular popular appeal because they combined the romance of the woman knight errant mythology and the virtuous female suicides of the Qing – thousands of whom had asserted their chastity or honour through suicide.[84]

The following chapter on Xie Bingying shows how the Qiu Jin model of glorious martyrdom fell from favour in the 1920s and surviving to fight another day became the prized attribute. Qiu Jin would be one of the last women warriors to present *herself* as a female soldier martyr. Helen Foster Snow noted this in her 1967 chapter on Qiu Jin: 'She [Qiu Jin] also believed in personal heroism, which the present-day Communists in China hold in little esteem.'[85] That is not to say that martyrdom would not be mobilised in the communist militarisation processes after 1949 – but, individuals were not praised for their self-conscious orchestration of their own martyrdom. The CCP produced large numbers of communist martyrs after 1949 but unlike Qiu Jin's 'vainglorious' self-determined death – passive suicide was not eulogised whereas struggling-to-a-certain-death in battle clearly was (see chapters on Liu Hulan and Zhao Yiman below). In the many contradictory twists of People's Republic of China's (PRC) literary and political campaigns, Xia Yan faced vehement criticism for his depiction of Qiu Jin's as 'suicide' rather than a 'sacrosanct act of revolutionary martyrdom'.[86]

Apart from its utility in providing evidence to attack Xia Yan and his drama, Qiu Jin's story was not given particular prominence in the PRC until after Mao Zedong's death with the winding back of radical, revolutionary politics from 1978 under Deng Xiaoping. Traditional virtues and ideals began to make their reappearance. Commencing with a series of events in 1979 surrounding the centenary of Qiu Jin's birth and the renovation of her 'old home' for tourists, the CCP's embrace of Qiu Jin would continue into the twenty-first century. She is now a stock patriotic figure in school texts and popular reports on the 1911 revolution.

Two full-length feature films were produced that reveal the return of the romanticised self-sacrificing woman knight errant. In 1983 renowned film-maker Xie Jin made a film of her life.[87] In 2011 a Hong Kong–China co-production directed by Herman Yau released *The Woman Knight of Mirror Lake*, explicitly invoking her 'female knight errant' appellation in the Chinese movie title *Jingxiong nüxia*.[88] In both films her feminism is muted and her patriotism amplified. The gendered and militarised narratives underpinning both movies show the increasing reluctance of the post-Mao PRC government to promote antagonistic social movements and their concomitant desire to buttress family cohesion. In 2011 Qiu Jin is presented as being frustrated by her incompetent husband but she does not loathe and despise him – as is documented in her letters and replicated in the 1983 Xie Jin version. The desire for China's revolutionary heroine to have a happy nuclear family dominates Yau's 2011 film. Its final scene shows her husband on his deathbed requesting to be buried with Qiu Jin followed by a lyrical image of Qiu Jin running along a grassy bank flying kites joyously with her children. She was, after all, a good mother as all good women should be – national heroic martyrs or not. The feminist who rebelled against patriarchy and abandoned her children is banished. Xie Jin's 1983 film romanticises Qiu Jin's misery at being separated from her children but makes no attempt to repair her relationship with her husband. Instead, 1983 audiences see Qiu Jin forming close revolutionary bonds with other like-minded people, such as Xu Xilin. Audiences of Xie Jin's 1983 film witness the intense training – ideological and physical – that went into crafting Qiu Jin as a soldier. These old communist values of striving hard to continuously improve one's skills are central to her success as a martyr in 1983. In Yau's 2011 film, audiences are told that she was a child prodigy – skilled in martial arts from an early age, naturally rebellious and filled with patriotic fervour. Her talents magically emerge just as her capacity to bounce off walls and leap from buildings are superhuman too.[89] By the twenty-first century Qiu Jin has been re-incorporated into the ancient woman knight errant myths of magical, incredible exceptional woman – harmless to the status quo, be that patriarchy or one-party-state, simply because she is so unbelievable.

Conclusion

Qiu Jin imagined herself as a romantic and heroic figure so it is not surprising that later retellings of her story make use of this trope in their commercial or propaganda roles. She was without doubt a brave, loyal, self-sacrificing, noble and pure-spirited individual with martial intent. But, the traits absent from this list reveal a considerable amount about the various social and political ideals that emerged after the end of the Qing dynasty. Her anti-Manchu views are muted in later stories of her life. Once China became the multiethnic states of the ROC from 1912 and the PRC from 1949, hatred for Manchus by a lauded patriotic martyr was problematic for social cohesion. Similarly, her antagonism towards men's unequal access to power as a structural and societal problem is diminished and even twisted to deny its primacy in her political agenda. Equally, contemporary stories of her life minimise her advocacy of political violence as a tool to produce regime change. Instead she becomes a poet and propagandist or a fantastical super-human kung fu fighter abstracted from the world of real military struggle. The utility of the female knight errant in real-world battles was always questionable but she is resoundingly exposed as a myth in the pragmatic world that emerged in the ROC. As we see in the following chapter, real military engagement required the invention of an entirely new set of ideological tools to enable women's participation in warfare – the romantic knight errant would return to her fantasy-land box. The New Culture New Woman who claimed public space in employment, travel, school and the army would emerge to really join the battle.

4 Xie Bingying opening public spaces to women
Fighting patriarchy and fighting militarists

Born a year before Qiu Jin's execution, Xie Bingying (1906–2000) lived in a fashion that Qiu Jin had struggled to make possible for other Chinese women. During her long life, only six years short of a century, Xie Bingying secured for herself a school-based education, trained and fought in the military, wrote and published creative works, polemical articles and autobiographies and maintained her commitment to fighting for China's independence from foreign control and freedom from internal chaos. Bingying demonstrated that women could achieve both literary (*wen*) and martial attributes (*wu*) – qualities, when found together, were traditionally the twin preserves of men in their performance of ideal masculinity.[1] The matchmaker who negotiated her first marriage declared in a 'premature triumph' to her new mother-in-law: 'Not only is she perfect in both literary and martial skills, she can handle every household chore.'[2] Xie Bingying escaped this arranged marriage and secured a divorce to make a love match and an independent life. Her publicly recognised exercise of both literary and martial talents was sustained over decades as she worked at the front lines of battle in three major military events – the 1926–1928 Northern Expedition in which Nationalist and Communist troops joined forces to crush the disparate warlords and unify the nation under one rule, the 1932 Shanghai Incident to repel Japanese attacks on that city and the full-scale Japanese invasion of China in 1937.

Xie Bingying is one of modern China's most remarkable women – a fighter for women's freedom from patriarchy and for China's freedom from chaos and foreign occupation. Her story shows us that the singular position Qiu Jin had created, as a feminist anti-Qing warrior, had by the 1920s become a more common phenomenon. In Xie Bingying's generation, women's participation in the military was an organised, group activity, not a lone act of a knight errant. Their patriotism was directed at unifying their republic, rather than overthrowing a monarchy, and this republic was one in which men and women would be equal partners. Bingying and her comrades-in-arms aimed to overthrow men's dominance of women through their participation in expelling militaristic aggression from China's territory. She described the prejudice that women soldiers overcame in her report on their gathering at Changsha train station prior to leaving for the front in 1937 as follows.

"Look, we are going off to the front battle lines!" Chinese women were always looked down upon as a result of oppressive feudal domination. People did not believe that women could be as courageous as men and head into the front lines, and neither did they believe that women were capable of shouldering the burdens required to save the nation. If you told them about the women soldiers who took part in the Northern Expedition ten years ago, they would open their eyes wide and exclaim "Nonsense! Nonsense!"[3]

This chapter shows the impact of Qiu Jin's legacy on women of the immediate subsequent generation – women and girls, like Xie Bingying, born into the new republic and who sought to participate in the building of the nation as equals alongside men. Bingying sought inspiration from the memory of Qiu Jin in order to survive the three weeks she spent in a Japanese prison in 1935 facing torture and interrogation.[4] Women's rights to equal opportunity and equal responsibility for national affairs were relatively new ideals, but as Xie Bingying's experience reveals, many young women soon saw them as axiomatic principles upon which they would base their whole lives. From her autobiographical writing it is clear that at this time, the entrance of women into schools and their enlistment in the military were equally strange and radical acts – the military aspects of her life were not merely a further, higher level of rebellion – rather, the two were connected acts since schools were the major recruiting grounds for both men and women officers during the 1910s and 1920s. The Nationalist Party sought to build its Party–Army leadership from among the educated and politically aware population in order to raise the status of soldiering. Schools and military academies were intimately linked through this model. Xie Bingying joined the military *through* her school and had to sit a written examination to gain entry to the force's Wuchang Academy. Women students became soldiers.

The young women of Bingying's cohort, although only two decades younger than Qiu Jin, regarded their brothers' naturalised privilege with a now-naturalised indignation – so widespread had ideas of sex equality become among young people. Many of their brothers were instrumental in supporting their radical life choices against their parents' wishes. Xie Bingying often said that she owed much of her freedom to her elder brothers.[5] They supported her decisions to secure school-based education, arranged her travel and provided books to feed her mind, assisted her with her first publications and were demonstrably proud of her rebellion against centuries of traditional gender norms. The seeds planted by Qiu Jin came to fruition in Xie Bingying's generation.

Xie's work in promoting the role of women in public civic and military life is substantial. Her writings about her radical life and struggle to overcome the

Figure 4.1 Xie Bingying in military uniform at Hangkou, 1937

many blocks placed in her path were immensely popular in China and even had international reach. Her most famous books have been republished multiple times: *War Diary* has nineteen editions; *A Woman Soldier's Own Story* was republished over twenty-five times in Chinese and translated into four different English versions with the first appearing as early as 1940.[6] She wrote

Figure 4.2 Xie Bingying writing her *New War Diary*, 1937

frequently about her struggle for access to schooling, her defiance of her parentally arrange marriage, her battle to overcome prejudice against women in public life and her commitment to ensuring that women had equal access to all social, political and economic spheres. Facing personal danger and public ridicule, imprisoned by her parents and the Japanese, Bingying's life was lived to the full and informed by principles we now regard as feminist ideals of 'equal opportunity'.

This chapter demonstrates that women at this pivotal moment in China's history saw warfare and participation in the military as an extension of the wars they were fighting on the family-front against the denigration and suppression of women – feminism was a militarised political position. Through Bingying's diaries, essays and autobiographies it is evident that fighting on one front gave her the courage to fight on the other – and both required equivalent ingenuity and fortitude.

One of China's foremost bilingual writers and commentators, Lin Yutang, described their first meeting and provides a compelling insight into the character of this, China's most well-published woman warrior.

The translator [Lin Yutang] had an occasion of being introduced to her, after her return from the expedition – Miss Hsieh [Xie] comes from a revolutionary family, having two brothers all serving in the Revolutionary Army. She is barely over twenty, with a small face and bright eyes, light, joyous, enthusiastic, and with still something of a tomboy in her. She talked in a winning manner in a husky, staccato voice, on account of the bad throat contracted from a night's exposure on the homeward voyage, but it did not prevent her from telling us stories until it seemed the heavens were going to fall down upon our heads. In a cap and sandals she appeared, in true war attire. Once, as the conversation turned upon the question of knapsacks and the average weight they carried, the translator ventured the question about whether the amazons as a rule carried mirrors and powder puffs in them, and was immediately answered with an annihilating look. 'You have even combed your hair?' she asked playfully, after subjecting my head to along scrutiny. There was no use explaining I had not come back from the front as she did, and for a moment I wished my hair had been more shaggy and in the revolutionary order.[7]

Biography of a woman rebel

Xie Bingying clearly loved being involved in war. She wrote enthusiastically about the energy she garnered from the crises she encountered at the front. The comradeship she felt among the troops, both male and female, is palpable. The thrill of her excitement of war comes through in gushing tones. 'How can I describe the happiness I feel?' Xie Bingying asks her readers[8] as she and her woman comrades don their military uniforms in preparation for battle. This life course was not one that would have been predicted for her in her early years.

Born in rural Hunan to a scholar father and imperious and domineering mother, Bingying was an unusual child from the outset. Her love of running around made footbinding more problematic for her to bear than for other girls – but, Bingying's mother, like most of this era, resolved to perform the bindings to secure her daughter's marriage prospects. Betrothed to the son of a family friend at age 3, Bingying's life was mapped as millions of women in her region had been for centuries before – she would bind her feet, build her trousseau through spinning and embroidery, marry a youth selected by her parents and leave home to become a dutiful daughter-in-law in her husband's family. But, Bingying was not such a dutiful and obedient individual and around her the world was changing, rapidly opening more opportunities for women than ever before.

Instead of the traditional path of physical crippling and oppressive marital and domestic servitude, Bingying left her village home at age 12 to attend Datong Girls School in Changsha city. She moved around Hunan Province attending different schools (sometimes because she was expelled for her political activism) and at age 20 joined the Nationalist Party's newly established Central Military and Political Academy in Wuchang – the training ground for leading Nationalists and Communists, including the communist martyr Zhao Yiman (see Chapter 6), who entered the academy in the same year, 1926. Her scholar father praised her courageous decision, calling her a 'Second Mulan' and encouraged her to write of her military experiences.[9]

From this point Bingying's life entered an entirely new phase in which her physical strength and courage would be tested in the battlefield and field hospitals and her political consciousness would reach new heights as she moved among war-ravaged villages, determined to alleviate the suffering of ordinary people. Inspired by the Nationalist Party's then-commitment to socialist principles she was active in propaganda units and worked particularly among the women of the villages they traversed. But, with the Nationalist Party's purging of the Communists in mid-1927 radical women like Xie Bingying, marked by their bobbed hair, risked being executed as leftists regardless of their political affiliations – so their unit was disbanded and the women fled penniless back to their hometowns.

For Bingying, this homecoming proved to be a crucial juncture in her resolve to fight against patriarchal family norms and parental authority. Her mother insisted on proceeding with the arranged marriage despite Bingying's fervent resistance. She attempted to flee her family home three times – each time finding herself foiled by her mother. She was locked up until she crossed the threshold of her husband's home; Bingying's new husband respected her wishes not to consummate their marriage and to consider annulment. Biding her time in her new home, she performed her domestic chores expertly and gained in-laws' trust when she rescued her footbound mother-in-law from a bandit raid – supporting the crippled woman and her sister-in-law to safety in the forests. Her opportunity for freedom came when she was offered a teaching position at her old school, Datong Girls School. Wrongly assuming it to be a temporary teaching post and trusting that Bingying had reconciled herself to life as a wife, her parents-in-law permitted her departure.

Instead of joining the school she moved to Hengyang and Shanghai in 1928 variously teaching, writing and studying. Her first major book *War Diary* was to be published and an advance on the royalties barely enabled her to survive months of cold and hunger. Segments of the book, written as letters in diary format, had been published in the Nationalist Party's newspaper *Central Daily News* in 1927 as she sent copy from the front lines. She completed the remainder of the manuscript after her demobilisation in 1928 – making it a reflection of the past and a rallying cry to her woman comrades not to lose their passion despite the dismantling of their brigade.

She honed her writing skills as a student in the Shanghai Academy of Art but in 1929 the French Concession government forced the academy's closure so she joined her elder brother in Beijing with the goal of enrolling at the Women's Normal University. Successful in the entrance exam, she commenced her degree, and soon formed a common-law marriage with an ex-army comrade, Fu Hao. In 1930 they had a daughter, but the relationship foundered, Fu Hao was imprisoned for his left-wing political views and Bingying struggled to pay for her schooling, her baby and her imprisoned husband. The Beijing government soon directed their attention to her and she was advised to flee to avoid arrest. She went first to Fu's mother's home and then visited her own natal home – mending her difficult relationships with her mother – who still smarted from her daughter's rejection of the arranged marriage. Unable to support her child and continue her work, she left her daughter with Fu's mother and decided to go to Japan to study. There she found the Japanese celebrating their occupation of North East China.[10]

The tense political situation in Japan sees her return to Shanghai by 1931 – writing, publishing and editing. Her role as editor of a weekly newspaper called *Women's Light* served as the base from which she would mobilise Shanghai's writers to support the troops fighting Japanese attacks in the 1932 Shanghai Incident – a three-month battle for the city. Her essays on this period reveal the invigoration she felt with her return to war – the emergency pulled people together and concentrated their energies as they moved back and forward from the front lines bringing supplies and caring for the injured. It is clear that Bingying loved the adventure of war as much as she hated the Japanese militarists and was disappointed not to be able to extend their fighting to liberate the North East from Japanese occupation. She recalls that not all the writers in her organisation, the Shanghai Writers Association of National Salvation to Resist Japan, were equally courageous as many fled the front lines for the safety of their desks.[11]

In the next few years she travelled around Fujian Province and her home province of Hunan, writing, teaching and publishing. She made another attempt to pursue her studies in Japan only to find herself imprisoned for three weeks, beaten and tortured for refusing to acknowledge the Japanese controlled state of Manchukuo in North East China[12] (see Chapter 5 below on a woman commander of this new nation, Aisin Gioro Xianyu). She later wrote of her rage at reading the Tokyo newspaper headlines describing the visit of the Manchukuo emperor, Puyi, the deposed emperor of China's last dynasty, as a great glory to Japan.[13] Her participation in anti-Manchukuo events organised by resident Chinese students led to her arrest. The photographs of Bingying dressed in a soldier's uniform that the police found during their search of her lodgings did not help her case. 'Are you a woman soldier, they asked?'[14] Her writer and scholar credentials came into doubt. Consular intervention enabled her to return to China where, in 1936, she finished another of her major books – *A Woman Soldier's Own Story*. Within a year Japan's full-scale invasion of China had commenced and Bingying once more pulled on her soldier's uniform and organised women from her home province into the Hunan Women's War

Zone Service Corps. They left for the front and provided first aid for the injured. Overwhelmed by the Japanese, she retreated with the Chinese troops along the Yangzi River, from Suzhou through Nanjing and Wuhan on to Chongqing and then Xi'an. In Xi'an she married Jia Yizhen and between 1940 and 1943 had a son and a daughter while editing the literary monthly *Huanghe*. Throughout this period behind the lines, Bingying continued to write and propagandise for women's rights and China's independence – her months in the front lines of battle provided ample material for her subsequent books – including *New War Diary* which was published in 1938. In 1940 she published a book titled *Inside a Japanese Prison*, recounting her experiences of five years earlier.

During all her adventures and despite starvation, privation, cold and illness she never stopped writing. She wrote and published dozens of pieces of fiction, diaries and essays in major newspapers and with larger and smaller presses. Lin Yutang, a major literary figure of these years, described her as 'a rising star in the revolutionary literary world' on the appearance of her first essays about her experience as a woman soldier in the *Central Daily News* in 1927.[15]

Of all the women in this book, Xie Bingying left the largest corpus of materials about her war experiences. Yet, she is the least well known and certainly least celebrated in the People's Republic of China (PRC). The split in the United Front between the Nationalist Party and the Chinese Communist Party (CCP) that occurred in 1927 would see her placed on the side of Nationalists despite her disdain for party politics and refusal to belong to any specific party.[16] Once the Japanese were defeated in 1945 and China descended into civil war, Bingying's patriotism, like many others of her generation, was insufficient to bridge the vast gulf that would form between the two parties. The men and women she trained with at the Wuchang Military and Political Academy comprised an entire generation of military and political leaders in both major political parties. These comrade students were variously partners in battles against disparate warlords (1923–1927), then mortal enemies (1927–1936), allies against the invading Japanese (1936–1945) and mortal enemies again in the civil war (1946–1949).

In 1948, months ahead of the CCP's victory over the Nationalists, she left China for Taiwan to teach at Taiwan Normal University, never returning to China mainland and instead living her life in Taiwan and the USA – dying in San Francisco, the city she had made her family home from 1974. Xie Bingying's presence on Taiwan, the Republic of China (ROC), meant that little was said about her either as a writer, soldier or a feminist in the PRC until the liberalisation of the 1980s that brought about a thaw in ROC–PRC hostilities.

Before she left the mainland in 1948 her refusal to 'choose a side' in an increasingly bipolar world split between the Nationalists and Communists meant that the Nationalists regularly accused her of being pro-Communist, or at least anti-Nationalist. Her *War Diary*'s descriptions of the Wuchang

Academy training makes the socialist origins of both political parties evident as she sang the socialist 'Internationale' and chanted 'Down with International Imperialism!', 'Complete the World Revolution!' and 'We have no home, the party is our home!'[17] The 1927 split within the United Front that had torn left and right asunder placed radical women, like herself, in perilous positions. The Wuchang Academy had been a locus for socialist training, so its members were all suspected of left-wing sympathies. Her forced demobilisation during the anti-Communist purges of 1927 would be echoed in 1933 when she had to make a hasty escape from a teaching position to avoid imprisonment after being accused of being the woman's organiser in an anti-(Nationalist) government resistance movement.[18] She, herself, remained as a patriotic feminist fighter with unique experiences of wartime action, regardless of the suspicion her actions and public profile aroused.

The life of a woman soldier

Xie Bingying gives us rich detail about the ways that women soldiers managed their training and battlefield lives. The women soldiers were acutely aware of their unique position and wanted to succeed in their training and performance not only out of patriotic passion but also because they sought to radically reform their culture's treatment of and attitude to women. Their instructors at the academy exhorted repeatedly: 'You are the first ever women soldiers in Chinese history and you have to be excellent models. Any future decisions from the Academy about whether to accept women students or not will depend entirely on how you perform.'[19] Their enthusiasm to commence this historic journey is evident in Bingying's description of the enrolment period when the women gathered in Wuchang to prepare for the entrance examination. 'We didn't care about anything, we just hoped to enter the Academy as soon as possible, to put on our military uniforms, to make our bodies as hard as iron as quickly as possible, with spirits of steel we would speedily learn our military tactics and risk our lives against the enemy.'[20]

To achieve their desired levels of discipline, skill and precision, they rose at 5.00 am and only got to bed at 9.00 pm. Bingying explains the hopes she and her friends had at the start of their training: 'We want to experience the Academy's more rigorous training, we want to do the same amount of work as the men students, we want to withstand suffering and hardship, we want to eradicate the divisions between men and women's spheres.'[21] They worked six days each week and often did not leave the school on Sundays because they were required for cleaning duties. Xie Bingying wanted to record her military life so she also spent time each night writing and editing. Each morning the women soldiers had four hours of military drills and in the afternoon they had classes on politics, speeches from prominent figures, group discussions on topics like Sun Yat-sen's political philosophy and international affairs. When they felt homesick the women cheered each other along with reminders that 'Revolutionaries only shed blood, they don't shed tears!'[22] Bingying described her pride when during a military parade and troop inspection she heard the audience saying 'The women soldiers are really incredible!'[23]

But, military training was not to every young woman's liking. In her *Reminiscences* she writes that when one trainee fled the academy it caused the others considerable grief since it reflected poorly on all the women soldiers. 'It's really a loss of face! She's run away. She couldn't handle the rigours of the training,'[24] wrote Bingying after one of their comrades fled Wuchang. The discussion among the remaining women revolved around the deserter's reluctance to forgo fine clothing and cosmetics. They suspected her of enlisting out of vanity and then escaping when she realised it was too much hard work. 'Lucky it is only one person, otherwise we would really lose too much face!'[25]

Many of the women were terrified of breaching academy rules and being punished. As you entered the grounds, the gates were pasted with ominous paired banners that read 'A martyr's blood is the flower of ideology' and 'The Party's rules are iron clad and military orders are as solid as rock.' Bingying explains their anxiety: 'The Academy's rules really were too strict. If you dressed untidily, if your hooks and eyes were not fastened correctly, if your leg bindings were not tied well, if your cap was not perfectly straight, if your salute was awry, if your legs were not positioned correctly when at Attention, if any of this was the slightest bit off, everyone would be severely criticised and receive a severe reprimand.' If the morning inspection went poorly, the soldier knew she would face a hard day ahead.[26]

The men and women students were separated in the academy for their military drills but came together for events such as when prominent speakers arrived or for formal parades. She explained that there was a wall between the two training grounds and at one point the men dug a hole about the size of a teacup through it so they could watch the women train. The hole was discovered when one infatuated young man inserted a love letter into the cavity ready to be picked up by his paramour – he was expelled. The women's modesty was tested most severely when, according to Bingying, they came together with the men for parades. The reason for their concern was that their names were written on their uniform pockets for all to see 'Central Military Academy Women's Students Brigade, Company X, Platoon X, Student XXX'.[27] The public knowledge of their names made it possible for the men to single individual women out for flirtation. Sometimes when the men were jogging they would turn to look at the women, lose their rhythm and trip over.

Bingying notes that while some women were 'too trapped by feudalism' to think about choosing their own love match, others saw the academy as a place for exercising their modern-style romantic choices. One of Bingying's friends was punished for going to the cinema with a young man and returning late. She was put in solitary confinement for three days and on her release said 'I would rather never have a boyfriend my whole life, than go back into solitary.'[28] Although Bingying opposed arranged marriages and sought to make a love match of her own choosing, she was also extremely firm about the appropriate timing of such choices. While at the academy and during her war service Bingying regarded romantic love as a hindrance to revolutionary work. She wrote to those 'comrades-currently-in-love' at the academy, 'Ultimately, I hope that we can work diligently on our revolutionary work, and smash the dream of romantic love!'[29]

Once deployed for battle the women found themselves primarily occupied as field medics and propaganda teams – roles that Bingying found equally invigorating and meaningful for different reasons. Each soldier she saved represented another dead enemy; each person she persuaded to support their cause raised their chances of victory further. The women soldiers were particularly effective in propaganda roles because, as the section to follow outlines, they were able to talk to the women villagers where male soldiers found themselves objects of fear and suspicion. In the medical sphere, Bingying describes how they worked non-stop for hours during battles where some 700 soldiers lay wounded awaiting attention. In her diary entry from 23 September 1937, aptly titled 'Warriors' blood dyes our hands red', she explains that her comrades became immune to the vast quantities of blood as they moved from one injured soldier to another without rest.[30]

The women worked in physically demanding conditions. Her *War Diary* reminds her comrades of the arduous work they undertook as soldiers.

You have carried on your backs tens of kilos of military equipment – food bowls, water jugs, dry footwear, bundles, blankets, cases of vegetables – everyday under the blazing sun you climbed mountains, traversed peaks, walked rugged, uneven mountain paths. Beads of sweat drenched every single strand of your hair, and fell like precious pearls. Your faces burnt purplish red, white skin long gone, although your legs were aching as you ran, not one person fell behind and not one person complained. When you drank, you squatted by ponds in the fields using your hands as cups to scoop the water. When you were hungry you paid a few coppers for a wheat-cake to block the hunger. Your bed was the floor or the ground. On rainy days you went barefoot or wore straw sandals. Ah! Ah! In those days your spirit was the type that won people's praise and respect![31]

The propaganda roles that women soldiers played in the war effort were as important for Xie Bingying as saving soldiers' lives in front-line medical units. In her 1928 *War Diary* she describes how she enjoyed the propaganda work since it enabled her to work with village people, and in keeping with the socialist origins of the training she received at the Wuchang Military Academy, she wrote in gushing tones: 'I'm really happy to be going, really going to the chicken-squawking, dog-barking countryside so that the revolutionary army becomes the army of farmers and workers, and so that we can let the soldiers understand the farmers! Those poor folk have been so terrified by Bandit S – that when they first see us, they run and hide.'[32] Although the conditions are filthy, the women soldiers' spirits are high and in their conversations with the farmers they soon forget their own difficulties when confronted with those of the villagers. 'All six of us woman soldiers wanted to talk to them, but because they [the villagers] only understood Hubei and Hunan languages, four comrades from the north couldn't be understood so they eventually went to bed in a huff.'[33]

In her descriptions of the War of Resistance against Japan, women soldiers are vital to the propaganda efforts as they move easily among the people. 'Ordinary village people hid from male soldiers but not from us women, so we were able to give considerable help to the military without having planned it. For example, each time the army arrived at a new destination, tasks such as hiring coolies, hiring boats, finding lodgings, and borrowing necessary items were ones that we women easily accomplished after we had explained things to the local people.'[34] The propaganda work among ordinary rural dwellers was vital to building a spirit of resistance. Bingying noted that ordinary people often had no idea who was fighting whom. She narrates that some villagers asked 'What country are you from?' – the dialects and languages of the Nationalist troops being as foreign as the Japanese language to many rural folk. She surmised that they had received no information about the war from any source at all and that 'our own people were being turned into traitors by our enemies' so 'we must hurry up and get them organised or the future would be unthinkable.'[35] Her medical unit soldiers spent their spare time working with villagers explaining the nature of the war and the importance of resisting the Japanese. The task was made easier as new comrades arrived equipped with knowledge of local languages. Their status as women soldiers with education was central to their success in propagandising for the war effort.

Bingying regarded changing the hearts and minds of people as integral to the military effort. In some cases she regarded working with the ordinary folk, educating them about war and representing new roles for women, as the real marker of victory. Even though she was part of two major military retreats – one in 1928 and the other in 1937 – she wrote 'we had established the foundation for revolution by planting in the mind of every common citizen a belief that could never be shaken. This was our biggest victory: we had taken from the warlords the allegiance of thousands of common people who had met us and who now believed and trusted us. We had scattered everywhere the seeds of revolution. Having won this victory, we returned from the front.'[36]

The bonds that were formed in the hardship of the experience at the academy and the loyalty that the women felt for each other are evident in the passion with which Bingying writes of its closure after the left was purged from the Nationalist Party in 1927.

The Central Military and Political Academy is disbanded. Such a spectacular, world-leading vanguard; the women students' brigade has disappeared without a trace! But, their spirit has not been extinguished, and every student that experienced the baptism of revolution will become more and more vigorous and intense. And not only are they themselves like this, but so are their friends, and all the ordinary people they contacted. They will not forget the past and they will definitely not stop loathing the present situation and hoping that something akin to the past [unity] will re-emerge. The women's student brigade is disbanded only in name, and has disappeared only in form. But, the real revolutionaries and the majority of loyal and brave comrades, they are ceaselessly coming together for support and working hard to struggle together, uniting to create a new future![37]

This optimistic perspective is tempered by her realisation that not all the demobilised women soldiers would remain advocates for the new future. She writes in emotional and lyrical terms of their potential future paths as follows:

The pitiful ones who have come from their struggles against the thoroughly evil feudal families to take the Party as their lives and the Academy as their family, how will they continue on living? Ah. . .! The brave ones who sacrificed with their blood flowing; the pitiful ones who became ghosts at the warlords bayonets; the weak ones who surrendered to the feudal capitalist class; the reactionary ones who will become tools for the enemy. And there are even those that made narrow escapes and are now working ceaselessly and tirelessly for the creation of a new life![38]

Popular responses to women soldiers

As Xie Bingying and her comrade 'women soldiers' travelled through the country on duty in 1927 they caused a stir wherever they went. The reactions of ordinary people to these strange creatures are documented vividly in her diaries as part of the narration of her political work – Bingying knew that she was representing a new style of life for women that was independent, and free of domineering mothers-in-law and husbands – these women soldiers were not just representing the Nationalist Party's military agenda.

In her first celebrated book, *War Diary*, she wrote of the arrival of the women soldiers in Fengkou as follows: 'Oh, the number of people, both old and young, male and female, who gathered at Fengkou to see us! I believe woman soldiers will occupy an important position in China's history, more particularly in China's revolutionary history.'[39] This scenario was not unique. Almost everywhere they went the women soldiers caused a stir among the locals. The enemy bandits did not include women soldiers – so the appearance of women in the Northern Expedition troops would have been a remarkable and unique identifying feature. Their education and commitment to the ordinary people's future marked their troops as special.

On 27 May 1927 she entered Jiayu, riding alone into town on horseback, to secure accommodation for the arriving troops. She was greeted by growing crowds of people as word circulated about the 'Woman Teacher', 'Woman Commander' and 'Woman Officer'.[40] She wrote that the shouts of 'A woman soldier is here! A woman solider is here!' drew women who would normally stay indoors onto the streets. 'Even the young maidens normally shut in their towers came scrambling out to see.'[41] 'I had become an exotic curio reflected in an illusionist's mirror, no, I was a weird figure from the new era.'[42] In the typically refreshing style of her diaries she explains that her major concern at that moment was to *not* fall off the horse – as a novice rider – and humiliate herself in front of the gathered crowds.

The villagers' responses ranged from humour to concern. One woman laughed until she cried as she said 'I've lived to over eighty years of age and never seen a woman with such large feet, no hair and wearing a soldier's uniform!'[43] Another worried about what her parents would do if they lost such a lively young daughter on the battlefield. Bingying replied to the woman that if she died for the revolution then she would be happy since some people had to sacrifice themselves in order that the majority achieve happiness and prosperity. The old people gathered around muttered, 'Poor child' as they pondered her misguided thinking.[44]

A decade later, in 1937, she wrote about how the novelty of women soldiers continued to provoke public interest in the war and the importance of resisting the Japanese invasion. She described how, as she paraded with her troops prior to departing for the front lines, 'The entire city of Changsha was stirred with emotion by us women soldiers. When we arrived at the train station a huge crowd hemmed us in on all sides. ... News reporters arrived in a rush, took photos, did interviews, kept us all very busy.'[45] Before they departed an old man with a shock of white hair passed his daughter to Bingying saying in a modern version of the Hua Mulan story, 'I am giving my daughter to you to take to the frontlines and I am very happy. I am old and cannot serve on the battlefield so I can only send my child. You must urge her to always work hard. And, if she is injured, or killed, I will not be sad. In fact I will feel proud!'[46]

Bringing attention to the impact of war on women

In her first publication about the war, Xie Bingying introduced readers to the horrors of sexual violence as troops intermingle with the civilians whose territory they occupy. Sexual assaults causing death or prompting suicide and forced or coerced prostitution are regular features of her reports from the field.

In June 1927, after a little girl was instructed by her father not to be afraid and to escort Bingying to the toilet, Bingying wrote in a letter to her editor friend: 'Ha ha! Mr. Fuyuan, why do they not fear "women soldiers" and only fear "men soldiers"?'[47] The episodes of sexual violence reported in her diaries provide a clear answer to her mocking, rhetorical question. In 1938, when writing of the War of Resistance against Japan she reports a similar reaction from local people when she was trying to arrange accommodation for her squad. A 70-year-old woman initially refused her request for lodgings but once she finds out there are no male soldiers, she declares, 'Oh! So you are all women, no worries, no worries, you can all stay anywhere here.'[48]

Xie's *War Diary* that record her first battlefield experiences of May and June 1927 include numerous incidents of sexualised violence against women perpetrated by the soldiers of 'evil warlords'.[49] In the village of Tuditang she was told that: 'One of the bandit soldiers under S – attempted to violate this brother's wife, but the woman defended herself by holding her child tight to her breast, so the heartless beast just bodily wrenched the child into two pieces. How cruel and inhuman!'[50]

In Fengkou on 12 June 1927 she wrote:

Raping, looting, killing, extorting money and forcing labour – these are the specialties of the militarist [warlord's] troops. In a little village about ten *li* [Chinese miles] away from here, they raped to death three young girls aged between thirteen and fifteen. In the city, there was a widow who having lost her husband when she was eighteen had remained chaste until she was thirty-two. But, as a result of the humiliation she suffered she committed suicide by swallowing opium![51]

Her intent in writing of these episodes is clear in the context of the rest of her diaries. Not only is she depicting the brutality of the enemy troops, in contrast to 'our brave and ideologically inspired soldiers'[52] of the Northern Expedition forces, but, as is evident in the section above, she also wrote of the oppressive patriarchal feudal system that the women labour under. These are particular and specific harms perpetrated against women and girls.

Writing her autobiography of this time some ten years later, Bingying also reflects on the fear she held for her own personal safety when she and another female cadet were accidentally left behind at a train station overnight on their way to join the Military and Political Academy. Still young school girls without military training, they feared they would be kidnapped and sold when they found themselves being trailed by two men – luckily a woman allowed them to stay overnight in her house and they were safe from their feared attack.[53]

The wars and disruption also produced high demand for sex work. She describes with disgust the prevalence of prostitution in Xindi during the Northern Expedition after having been mistaken for a young man – she was wearing a 'very charming foreign suit' borrowed from a male colleague and was approached by sex workers as she walked along the street. Her reaction reads:

Oh, how sorry, how angered I felt to think that a blossoming young girl should be allowed to go rot. But is this their fault? Haven't they been driven here by poverty, and was it not the lure of the filthy lucre that sent them on to their present position? My dear comrades of the revolution, we cannot afford to scorn their impudence and dishonour, we can only blame our present economic system. If we wish to save them, and cleanse them of their shame and iniquity, we must overthrow the present unfair and wicked economic arrangements. If we want to redeem them, to make them come back and live the life of normal human beings, then we must go forward in the spirit of firm determination and dauntless courage and fight against the old society! Let us fight with all our power and fight to the end![54]

The moralising tone of her passion is typical of activists at this time who sought not only to liberate women from prostitution but also from concubinage. The impact of Marxism on the politically active people during these years is also clear – the economic system determines all and the militarists must be overcome before the economic system can be reformed.

Ironically, her concern about the moral peril of sex workers was matched by many older women's concerns about the moral peril facing women soldiers. She describes the commentary of the women in the crowds that gathered to see these strange woman soldiers. 'Good iron is not used to make nails, and good men do not become soldiers. What then do we make of maidens who strut around showing themselves in public to join the military!'[55] Bingying explains to her readers that the older women were misguided because they did not realise that the National Revolution soldiers were unlike earlier soldiers – the former protected the people and were sacrificing themselves for the overall good of the country, fighting for freedom and peace.[56] The women soldiers' special status was consolidated in their special clothing. Their uniforms were identical to the men's except for the addition of the letter 'W' sewn in red cloth on their left arm. The 'W' marked them as 'Women' and many resented this distinction. Bingying describes how their male comrades would tease them and say that the 'W' stood for 'Wife' – infuriating the women soldiers. She led a delegation of all the women soldiers in her unit asking that the officers change the 'W' to three horizontal stripes that would represent 'truth, goodness and beauty' – but the officers refused.[57]

In recalling the scenes only weeks after the Japanese retreat in 1945, Bingying describes the 'Comfort Stations' all around Wuchang that housed Japanese and Korean women who 'serviced' the Japanese soldiers. One major building had been divided up into small rooms which were identifiable by a large map that described the separate sections in romantic terms – 'Pacific Lodge', 'Bright Happiness Chamber', 'Pine and Bamboo' – 'Why did nobody remove this map?' she asked.[58] Xie describes how they chatted to several young Korean women amidst the empty rooms of the 'Comfort Stations' abandoned as the Japanese Imperial Army vacated the now desolate and ransacked city.[59] Locating a few Japanese military documents they left the city optimistic that it would regain its former glory.

During the anti-Japanese war Bingying recalls meeting women experiencing a variety of new problems as the war dragged on and they were left in their family homes alone. The men had joined the military and the women were left to feed themselves and their hungry parents and children as best they could. She tells of a particularly resilient woman who gave birth to a son in an air raid shelter amidst an attack. Despite her weakened state and the offer to rest a few days at the military camp she insisted on trying to go back to her mother-in-law lest the older woman fear she had been killed in the raid. She collapses on the road so Bingying's troops secure permission to carry her home on a stretcher, assuring each other that this child would surely be a major figure in his life since he dared to be born as the bombs dropped.[60]

Her concern about the social structure that underpinned sex inequality runs through all her writings. And, the wars she joined were fought not only to quell domestic militarists and expel foreign forces; they were also battles to change the traditional Chinese social system. In writing about the military war, Bingying also writes about the war she is waging against 'feudal values'.

War for women's rights

For Xie Bingying and the other women soldiers, their participation in the war effort was integral to their personal struggle for independence as women who would form part of a new and just China. In the Wuchang Academy she recalls that the trainees were particularly inspired by the lessons on Sun Yat-sen's Three Principles of the People – a philosophy to underpin China's reconstruction that aimed to provide prosperity and democracy to all. For Xie and her women comrades, this new China would be

an incredibly beautiful society, where everyone had freedom and each person was equal to the other, where women and men alike enjoyed the pleasures of life, and were no longer subject to oppressive feudal ideology, it would be so happy! Such pitiful women, in the past they lived as non-people, slaves to men, chattels of men. They had no freedom and no capacity for economic independence, so we really should thank our founding father [Sun Yat-sen], he forged a bright path for us women, from here we can be independent, free thinking and the same as men in using our knowledge and capacities to contribute to the nation for the benefit of society.[61]

To the women soldiers, this was more than a war against militarists; it was a war to liberate women from centuries of feudal oppression. Bingying's writings on her war experiences are filled with commentary about the importance for women to fight for their own independence.

After only three weeks at the Wuchang Academy, Bingying wrote a letter to her women comrades that outlined the historic nature of their particular participation in the war. She exhorted her peers to work hard to be models for all Chinese women and to lead their participation in the National Revolution. They should strive to eradicate vanity and she warned them against being preoccupied with glamour titles such as 'fashionable women soldiers', 'leaders of the women's revolution' or potential 'women politicians' and 'women officials'. Such self-centred thinking would, according to Xie, harm the revolution. She also encouraged them to eradicate any feminine conditioning such as dependency or doubts about their capacities relative to men. 'We don't want the school to give preferential treatment to us, because "preferential treatment" means they pity us and think that women are weaker than men, aren't as capable as men, aren't able to suffer hardships the same as men, so it's best if we don't seek sympathy.'[62]

She wrote to her third brother prior to setting out for the front the first time that they had three objectives for their mission. The first was a straightforward goal of providing care for the injured and raising morale among the troops. Her second and third objectives were directly about increasing women's awareness of the possibilities of changing their social status and to ensure that women's roles in forging social change were broadly recognised and welcomed.

We must awaken women and enable them to see for themselves the origins of the suffering and oppression they experience – the oppression of feudal society and its economic system – enable them to realise their own strength, and to know themselves as individuals, as people that ought to have their own lives. Consequently, they must rise up to liberate themselves, and save themselves, so they must join in the revolution.[63]

The National Revolution to create a new and equitable society could not succeed without women's liberation and the women's brigade saw itself as integral to that purpose.

Little wonder, then, that after their brigade was disbanded in 1927, she grew despondent and struggled to complete her *War Diary*. The feminist agenda she felt so passionately about appeared to have been crushed in the purging of the left wing of the party. She was persuaded to continue writing when her editor, Sun Fuyuan, told her that her book would be the only account of the women's brigade within the Wuchang Military Academy and that for the historical record she was obliged to complete her work.[64] This book would become part of the annals of Chinese women's struggle for independence. The feminist fervour with which she continued her writing is evident from the moment she recommits to the project. And she seeks to inspire other demobilised women soldiers to regain their commitment as well. 'You are the vanguards of a worldwide women's revolution, you are the creators of a new era! You have forgotten that you were animals that had emerged from thousands of years of feudal society, you simply didn't recognise yourselves as women–physically weak and incompetent women.'[65] With these words she hoped to remind them of the importance of their participation as *women* in the revolution.

The military action itself was explicitly feminist action and not only motivated by patriotism and party political loyalties. For example, in *War Diary* Bingying commented repeatedly on the status of women in the villages and towns they passed through in Hubei Province in 1927 during the Northern Expedition. The most horrifying aspect to Bingying was the large numbers of footbound women – some still involved in farm labour despite their crippling. Her passionate and impatient reaction against footbinding was no doubt prompted by her own rebellion against her own experience of footbinding in 1918, nearly a decade earlier. She describes her rebellions against her mother's attempts to bind her feet as 'The first signs of my war against feudal society'.[66] Her mother would bind her feet in the morning and Bingying would loosen the bindings herself at night. In this way she prevented her feet from being crippled. 'Although my feet had been bound, somehow I was able to still walk long distances and I could walk fast.'[67]

Some of her friends in the women's military units had also been footbound by their mothers and found it difficult to make the long treks between operations – but like her friend Guanghui, they had unbound their feet and persevered to fight against the cruelty of the custom despite the physical hardship it caused.[68] The slow pace of change in rural China created incredulity among her urban friends and impatience in Bingying. One of her friends refused to believe that she actually saw a pair of feet that were 'a little over one inch long, while feet of two inches long were quite common'.[69] Her diary letter of 17 June 1927 describes footbound women working the pedals on the water wheels that shift water from one field to another. She wrote:

I cannot help thinking of the misery caused by their small feet, especially while engaged in such arduous labour. Mr. Fuyuan, I believe footbinding is really the greatest misfortune of the female sex. In this era where individuals seek liberation for themselves, these women are still willing to be eighteenth-century slaves. This is the greatest disgrace of our women's world, a disgrace that cannot be washed clean for thousands of years.[70]

While she was billeted at Jiayu, Bingying and some woman soldiers became the subject of jokes among village women laughing at their natural feet.

Mr. Fuyuan, the footbinding here is really too intolerable! Their smallest feet are only two inches long and the longest doesn't extend beyond four inches. One day I was sitting on a grassy hillock writing a letter and several "family women" rushed over, and I put down my pen to propagandise to them about liberating their feet. One of the older Three Inch Golden Lilies[71] said: "Your feet are so huge, won't you and your 'boss' (husband) put on the wrong shoes?" Ha Ha Ha Ha. . .they giggled and laughed. . .so that eventually the Political Instructor and some other soldiers standing near me burst out laughing as well. They laughed so much that even though I am a courageous kid I blushed from top to toe.[72]

Bingying's impatience at the women's inability to comprehend the possibility of change to their conditions continues in the next paragraph.

One time a Company Commander wanted them [the villagers] to cut their hair [into a revolutionary bob] and he said: "Once you have cut your hair you can avoid being pulled by your hair when your old men beat you." They replied "Right! If we liberate our feet we can hit them but [even so] they'd still win." They were very aware of the pain of footbinding but said that big feet used up too much cloth [in shoes]. We said but aren't the untold lengths of bindings used to wrap your feet also using cloth? [They regarded] the binding of their feet as a way to save cloth![73]

Xie Bingying's military academy included a 40-year-old woman, Comrade Deng, whose feet had been bound since she was a child. She struggled to keep up with the other women during training drills as her body had to twist and turn to maintain balance as she moved – she was always the slowest to complete the drills. Her daughter was also in the academy so Bingying asked her why she had enlisted. Deng replied. 'My daughter is my daughter and I am myself, I am not going to replace my daughter to eat, just as my daughter is not going to replace me in joining the revolution.' She explained that feudal thinking had caused her such deep suffering during her life that she wanted to join the revolution, and that it was not just the footbinding to which she was referring. Her married life had been one of enslavement to her husband who treated her and their daughter like animals. In contrast, her son received superior treatment and privilege. She described her escape to the academy as 'the arrival of the bright days'.[74] But prejudice against such 'backward' women was evident even in the academy as Deng tells Bingying that her daughter pleaded with her to quit because it was embarrassing to have such a country-bumpkin mother present among all the bobbed hair, natural footed young 20-year-olds.[75]

To many of the progressive women of this period, the battle was not against men per se, since their brothers and fathers were sometimes supporters and their mothers and grandmothers their most ardent opponents. The Deng case was more the exception than the norm. Older women were the more formidable direct opponents of new roles for women since they had control over the young women as either mothers or mothers-in-law. The older women had the most to lose in any changed family power structure. Bingying's relationship with her mother is a case in point. She argued constantly with her mother but could not outwit her or escape. She won permission to enter school through her father and elder brothers and these same brothers assisted her entrance to the military academy. In contrast, her mother bound her feet, battled relentlessly to ensure she married in accordance with the betrothal arrangements made when she was 3 years old and became a forceful jailor when Bingying tried to escape. Yet, the close of Bingying's *War Diary* includes a heart-wrenching letter to her mother explaining why she cannot come home, despite her mother's pleadings that she return for Spring Festival. She had left her marriage and natal province for over a year and had no intention of returning anytime soon. She writes, 'But, Mother, I cannot return as you so fervently desire .... Mother, this is definitely not cruelty on my part... Oh, Mother, it is the thoroughly evil feudal power that blocks me.'[76] The war for women's rights was a serious war against the authority of older women over their juniors. 'Mother, remember, that thoroughly evil feudal society is disappearing before your very eyes.'[77]

The rigidity of views about the morality of women taking roles in public and long-standing prohibitions on women intermingling with men were equally as frustrating for Xie Bingying. She finds this 'feudal' thinking in both the countryside and the cities and even among the educated classes that she had expected would reflect a more open-minded position. She was asked to resign from one of the schools that she taught in because she was seen talking too often with a male teacher; her friendships with male colleagues and students were frequently misread as evidence of her loose morals; and even her common-law marriage to Fu Hao, father of her first daughter, foundered upon his mistrust of her friendship with another former soldier. She refused to adhere to traditional moral codes that restricted contact between men and 'good' women.

In the countryside she often found herself in situations where she tried not to bring the National Revolution troops into disrepute. She explains that when it came to bathing the women soldiers did not insist on going into Xindi's male-only public baths partly because 'The simple-minded country-folks are already scandalised and puzzled to see us going about in the company of men, our male comrades, and spread all sorts of rumours about "communism" and "common wives"; how then could they stand anything else [such as seeing us use men's bathhouses]?'[78] The assumption among some of the Xindi residents appears to have been that the women soldiers were the camp-wives of the soldiers – so Xie and her comrade soldiers were at pains to demonstrate their independence and difference from other women the villagers may have seen in the company of soldiers.

On the journey from Fengkou to Xindi in June of 1927, Xie writes of her frustration at constantly being asked in every locality (immediately after being asked their ages) 'Where are your old men (husbands)?' or 'Where's your mister? Are you married yet?'[79] To the women of inland China the idea that unmarried women would move about in public without a male 'owner' was inconceivable. Moreover their failure to secure a husband at their advanced ages (in their early 20s) was regarded scornfully as evidence of personal failure. Bingying grew tired of being asked the same questions. 'Sometimes when we'd lost patience with questions about "marrying off" and "old men", I would bluntly tell them: "Nowadays we are only concerned with the revolution. We don't want any 'old men'".[80] Some women responded with the knowing comment: 'They're afraid that marriage will cause them trouble and stop them coming out to fight, so they are all maidens.' Bingying writes her thoughts: 'We are indeed still maidens at this [advanced] age, but we pity you lot that have become slaves at seven or eight.'[81] The prejudices against unmarried women and the suspicions at their 'immoral' gadding about with non-family men were integral to the high levels of public interest in National Revolution forces at this time.

For Bingying, the frustration of being confronted with backwardness was balanced by the hope provided by the many women with progressive aspirations who were involved in women's committees in their towns and villages and often had bobbed hair. For women in the 1920s and 1930s having short hair was a marker of their rejection of traditional attitudes to women in their roles as daughters, mothers and wives. The short, cropped hair marked a woman's progressive views about her own independence. In *War Diary* she writes that this trend had spread to Xianning as well. 'Among the women members of the Woman's League at Xianning, three quarters have cut their hair short, although, unfortunately, due to inadequate propaganda, they are unwilling to take part in public rallies, and are especially unwilling to march through the streets and shout slogans.'[82] People would laugh at them if they did so, explained the women's league representative. Bingying learned later from a Xianning comrade that when the warlords recaptured the town, women with bobbed hair were rounded up as radicals and executed.[83] The executions of women with short hair was widespread in China during 1927 and 1928 – warlords hated them as supporters of the Nationalist Party's Revolutionary Army and the Nationalists suspected them of being Communists.

Bingying's braids were cut when she entered school – but not without some resistance on her part. Later, she described her advocacy of long hair in Confucian terms invoking the maxim that one should not damage the body given by your parents, and that braids marked the distinction between men and women. Her school friends called her 'backward' and a 'criminal running against the times'. Her second brother explained that short hair was more hygienic, easier to wash and comb – leaving more time in the day for more productive activities like reading and writing. But in her stubbornness, she resisted cutting her hair – until eventually her friends forced her to cut it. Xie Bingying describes this episode as one where her stubbornness and refusal to admit error led her along a foolish path.[84] Once she had enlisted, of course, her hair was cut extremely short. As they were escaping police round-ups of radical women after their demobilisation, she and her friends tried desperately to hide their short hair beneath hats bought especially for the purpose. 'All of us had hair that was very short, especially Shurong. Her head was shaved almost like a potato.' As they left Wuchang ahead of the purges they reluctantly cast aside their uniforms and donned simple dance dresses. 'Because our heads were not fit for public view, we also went to a department store and each of us bought a foreign hat of woven straw.'[85]

Reading Xie Bingying's works it is evident that the idea of fighting for one's beliefs and being prepared to die for them was integral to her life journey. War metaphors abound in the description of her fight against feudalism. She saw no alternative for women but to persistently struggle for their own liberation – using violence and disobedience if necessary. 'Better to let society curse me as a rebel and as a disobedient daughter than to yield to a feudal code of ethics,'[86] she declared in response to the gossip circulating in her hometown. The contact with ordinary village women who willingly subjected themselves to oppressive practices – despite the new times of 'self-liberation' – clearly frustrated Bingying. Overthrowing feudalism required a warrior-like attitude, according to Bingying, and resisting her mother and the pressure from her family was harder, required more courage and persistence, than fighting a military battle. During the period of her imprisonment at home, repeated escape attempts and forced marriage, she explains to her elder brother that 'I want to formally declare war on feudal society – I will stand firm to the end.' He replied 'Good luck in your struggle as a lone soldier.' He warned her that even though she was braver than the others in her family 'even you can only fight the war outside – you cannot make a revolution at home.'[87]

In her darkest moments of despair during her imprisonment at home, Bingying contemplated suicide. Her description of the mental anguish this caused is also dotted with military metaphors. Ultimately, she opted to survive since suicide would be a victory for feudalism – a criticism levelled against Qiu Jin's suicide-esque martyrdom (see Chapter 3). Bingying's rationale for staying alive was framed in a new rhetoric of struggle and persistence rather than a dramatic death that women just one generation earlier had romanticised.

Think: you have been baptised by revolution. You have the mission to change society. You have been to the frontline and worked under fire to kill enemies and save comrades, and you once swore to struggle for the liberation of millions of workers of the world who have been repressed. You are not a weak and old-fashioned female who lacks abilities. Rather you are a modern woman, resolute, courageous, strong willed. You are a warrior who opposes all feudal rules. . .now, have you really forgotten your duties? Death would show your failure and tradition's victory.[88]

During her time in Shanghai as editor of the *Women's Light* she worked among the women workers of Shanghai's many factories to promote women's rights. International Women's Day was a key point for the organisation of rallies and public events, but in 1932 during the three-month Shanghai Incident, Japanese bombing of the city disrupted their plans.[89] The war ceased only on the 3rd of March – less than a week before International Woman's Day – but the *Women's Light* collective resolved to hold their events regardless. Bingying notes that the women workers were the most direct and dedicated of their group and less prone to gossip and politicking than the educated women. Sadly, only a day prior to their planned events the police from the French Concession arrested the women organisers. Bingying explains that while many people thought of Shanghai as being a 'free city' the police of the foreign concessions frequently clamped down on political activities they deemed problematic – International Woman's Day being one such example.[90] At no point in her life did she cease fighting for women's rights and advocating for equal opportunities for women.

Despite her enthusiasm for women's equality with men and the special roles that women could play in war, she expressed doubts about women's physical capacities. In her *New War Diary* from 1938 she includes a fascinating entry about the differences between men and women and concludes that 'Women really aren't as good as men.' The conclusion comes after she found herself plagued by illness in October 1937. She visits the home of leading left-wing woman leader, He Xiangning (1879–1972).[91] At that time He Xiangning led the National Salvation Association to mobilise civilians against the Japanese. Bingying learns that despite a serious illness, the 42-year-old He Xiangning remained constantly preoccupied with the organisation of the war effort. At this point Bingying ponders the lot of some of her other woman soldiers and their ongoing illnesses and concludes that 'Women really aren't as good as men' for no other reason than that their bodies are inferior. She determines that in terms of courage women are men's equals and sometimes even surpass them, but in physical stamina women are weaker. 'It's really too annoying!' she declares emphatically.[92] Her next diary entry is aptly titled 'Really sick!'[93]

Conclusion

Xie Bingying's life as a writer and a soldier tells us a great deal about the motivations for women's participation in the military in the 1920s and 1930s – patriotism and feminism together drove their actions as well as a healthy dose of adventurism. The instability of the national borders and the internal chaos prompted by warlords and bandits provided fertile ground for women to step into alternative public roles and advance their campaigns for greater equality with men in every sphere. Participation in war would demonstrate their capacity to achieve as much as men and contribute as much as men. But in patriarchal systems, there is a danger that women's military work is contained within the rubric of 'crisis femininity' – where women are welcomed temporarily out of the confines of regular feminine expectations to meet the needs of a particular national or community crisis. Bingying's narratives show that attempts to return women to traditional modes after they have performed their duty in 'crisis femininity' mode are not always successful. She was emboldened and strengthened through war to fight her family and to survive the financial and physical hardships that would plague her life as a writer, teacher and mother in an unstable world. Her enthusiasm for war and the excitement of military life are matched only by her joy at being involved in effecting social change. Her life and deeds show how deeply feminism had become militarised in China by the 1920s and 1930s.

5   Aisin Gioro Xianyu

'Joan of Arc of the Orient' or 'Mata Hari of the East'?

In early March 1948 the Chinese press reported that the Manchu Princess Aisin Gioro Xianyu (1906–1948? 1978?) had been executed as a traitor to China. She was well known to ordinary Chinese through a media profile that crafted her as a dangerous, cross-dressing monster and femme fatale. One of dozens of trials investigating traitors held in the aftermath of the War of Resistance against Japan, Xianyu's generated huge popular attention and mobs forced their way into the Beiping (now Beijing) courtroom just to catch a glimpse of this evil, royal beauty. The mysterious woman they saw in the docks was dressed as a man illustrating her fame for skillful disguise. The legal case and media reports confirmed her treachery by studiously using her Chinese or Japanese names, Jin Bihui and Kawashima Yoshiko, rather than her Manchu name. The court ruled that Xianyu was guilty of spying for Japan, but she regarded herself as fighting to establish a Manchu state independent of China – a Manchu nationalist rather than a traitor to China. Xianyu's very public life and death encapsulate the dangers for individuals of mobile identity and ethnicity when wars change 'national' borders and complicate post-war memorialising.

From her earliest childhood in the palaces of the declining Qing court, Xianyu was trained to assume a leadership role within the Aisin Gioro imperial line that had ruled China since 1644. With the collapse of the Qing dynasty in 1912 Xianyu was sent to Japan, a child of barely 7 years, as a member of an exiled imperial line seeking territory to rule. Her task was to become equipped with the linguistic, military, political and cultural skills to bring a new Manchu nation into being – and in March 1932 with the formation of the Japanese-controlled state of Manchukuo in the traditional homelands of her people, this goal seemed realisable. When Xianyu returned to China in 1927, aged in her early twenties, it was to live a dramatic life filled with cross-dressing, espionage, soldiering and myriad sexual liaisons with a domestic media profile to match. Outside of China also her fame grew and she became known variously as 'the Joan of Arc of the Orient' or 'the Mata Hari of the East' – the latter in reference to the Dutch 'exotic dancer' executed by the French as a German spy in 1917.

Figure 5.1 Signed photograph of Aisin Gioro Xianyu in military uniform

This chapter examines the debates about her life that occurred in China while she was alive and those that have continued decades after her death. Her adventurous life has appeared in novels, films, documentaries as well as academic studies and media reports.[1] The twists and turns and contradictory appraisals of Xianyu reveal how wartime celebrities, even those of notoriety, participate in perpetuating the seeming logic of violent conflict and post-war nationalistic reconstruction. During the war China's political leaders and media interests presented Xianyu as an evil, dangerous freak – her sexual and ethnic ambiguity amplifying traits deemed typical of traitors and distinguished her from loyal people. But, from the 1980s she has been reclaimed as yet another sorry Chinese woman degraded and duped by the Japanese military. In peacetime memorialising of war, even infamous in-between women like Xianyu prove useful to building multiethnic national unity if they are presented as *victims* rather than as agents of aggression and violence.

Manchu imaginings of an independent ethno-nation are overshadowed by her celebrity/notoriety and tales of a vulnerable, puppet princess. Contemporary Chinese narratives emphasise her susceptibility to larger forces of war, politics and predatory Japanese men – reminding readers of the division between the Japanese and Chinese races, rather than between Manchu and Han. Xianyu's Manchu relatives and friends are amongst the most vocal promoters of the view that she was a victim rather than a treacherous aggressor.[2] Most sensationally, there is a widespread belief that she was not killed in 1948 but escaped death through a body double and lived out her quiet life as Granny Fang in North East China, dying a natural death aged 72.[3] Audiences indulge in salacious voyeurism as they dissect her unorthodox sex life, her connections to the rich and famous and her courting of notoriety while sympathising with her fate. As is common to the memorialising of complex women living in dangerous times, historical fact becomes intermingled with sensationalised and eroticised fiction.

During the wartime peak of her fame, the Chinese media presented her as a figure to fear and revile – a dangerous spy capable of remarkable disguises and fluent in multiple languages, she was irresistible to men, devoid of any moral sense and completely unscrupulous. The contrast between that view and the post-1980s' rewriting of her remarkable life reveals a key feature of the gendered nature of war culture – that being, 'our' women are most comfortably incorporated into the peacetime national story as victims rather than aggressors. Once Xianyu became 'Granny Fang' she was one of 'us' in the multiethnic PRC (People's Republic of China) nation. Her production as a pitiful victim rather than a dangerous vamp is central to completing this transition. Victimhood prevents the traitorous woman from languishing in the historical record as an evil, despicable slut.

Women as war victims

Purveyors of war create a symbolic order in which individuals confronted with its brutality are assisted to make sense of its operations and 'logic'. As we saw in the introduction, gender is integral to this symbolic order. Women are presented variously as beacons of 'hearth and home', objects requiring protection, icons of nurturing motherhood and symbols of collective yearnings for peace. Within this rubric belligerents often recognised women and children as non-combatants deserving evacuation from danger. The flip side of this protection sees women and girls subject to sexual assaults as troops ravage each other's symbolic 'home and property'. War propagandists highlight enemy attacks on 'our innocent women and children' to elicit disgust among their target audiences. In performing this symbolic work, women emerge as passive victims, pure in their lack of aggression in war and innocent of responsibility for any actions undertaken during its occurrence.

In contrast, masculinity is frequently depicted as exemplified by war service and imbued with an intrinsic propensity to violence. Manhood is often constructed through narratives of warfare – military forces and militias promise to 'make men out of boys' through their training. Carol Cohn explains it as a gender order 'where being "a good soldier" is synonymous with having the characteristics of being a "real man"; and where "male bonding" is seen as crucial to a fighting unit's effectiveness'.[4] In this dynamic, masculine figures engage in warfare and their feminine counterparts are passive in its face.

Women who participate actively in war, despite being marked as 'naturally feminine' by their sex, confound this tidy symbolic schema. Xianyu, with her rejection of orthodox Chinese positions on national, ethnic and sexual boundaries and her refusal to embrace the role of passive innocent, on first glance, should be assigned to permanent ignominy. But, as this chapter shows, in postwar recreations of war histories problematic women can be reintegrated into a unifying story of multiethnic national harmony if their redactors emphasise their victimhood and amplify their inherently feminine lack of choice. Men who played similar wartime roles – enemy soldiers, spies or collaborators – are not able to deploy the 'helpless victim' narrative because gendered ideas about warfare posit men as intrinsically capable of agency. A victim-man is not 'a real man'. For women, even those as troubling to the boundaries between 'us and them' and 'men and women' as Xianyu, narratives of victimhood enable their paladins to restore them to the (Chinese) national story.

Aisin Gioro Xianyu's life and nation/s

Xianyu's life is complicated since it involves 'repeated crossing of national and cultural boundaries', to use Dan Shao's words.[5] Japan, China and even

Manchukuo – if the latter had continued as a nation-state – could each claim her within their respective national histories. Her execution in 1948 was an affirmation of Chiang Kai-shek's Nationalist government's desire to assert the territorial integrity of his republic. There was no possibility that she could be regarded as a Manchu fighting to advance the interests of Manchukuo against China since this would give implicit recognition to the validity of that state. Chiang's government was asserting its 'symbolic regime of authenticity'[6] through the execution of Xianyu. On this same logic, her story can reaffirm the PRC government's right to rule north China and consolidate its ideal of the nation-state's fifty-six nationalities, including the Manchu, living peacefully together within these borders. Scholars from the PRC call the government that she was fighting for 'pseudo Manchu' and steadfastly adopt the term 'the North East' to refer to the territory that was once Manchukuo. The compass references in the provincial title imply that territory's connection to *China's* 'South East' and 'North West'.[7]

Despite the PRC view that regards Manchuria as an inalienable part of China, Prasenjit Duara discusses how the territory's position in the PRC nation-state is 'largely as a consequence of the demographic and cultural integration that took place in the first half of the twentieth century and not because of some primordial or age-old claim to it'.[8] Xianyu's participation in a project to establish Manchukuo as an independent state was not at all a bizarre concept during her lifetime. The Qing dynasty's Manchu leaders had tried to keep the territory as a preserved homeland free from foreign and Han immigration. The ban on Han migration to the area was lifted in 1902, as a result of population pressures in north China and Qing reaction to expansionist designs from Japan and Russia. Rich in forest, mineral and agricultural resources, the territory presented a tremendous opportunity particularly to land-limited Japan.[9] Over eight million people immigrated to Manchuria between 1890 and 1942[10] – one of the largest human migrations anywhere in the world. With China in chaos during the 1920s and 1930s, the warlord Zhang Zuolin (1875–1928) and his son Zhang Xueliang (1901–2001) ran the territory largely autonomously of the rest of China but in constant dialogue with various governments and power holders, including the Japanese.[11]

Japan's influence over the region increased rapidly in 1905 when it took control of Russian-occupied territory after winning the Russo-Japanese War. Japan's South Manchurian Railway claimed Russian assets and resumed land along the rail network as it expanded. After Japan's colonisation of Korea in 1910, Japan exerted even more economic influence over Manchuria supported by a military force called the Kwantung Army – a special unit dedicated to Japan's Manchurian operations. Japan's desire to harness the region's natural resources faced competition from like-minded Chinese and unrest between the two groups developed. Japan sought a pretext to extend its military control of the territory. On 18 September 1931 the Japanese Kwantung Army bombed the rail tracks of the Japanese-owned South Manchurian Railroad Company and declared it to be the work of Chinese forces. This 'act of aggression' became the pretext for occupying all of Manchuria in a series of battles collectively known as the 'Manchurian Incident'.[12]

To most Chinese the date of the railway bombing, abbreviated to 'Nine One Eight', immediately invokes Japan's aggression against all of *China* and builds into China's primordial claim to Manchuria and its inherent rejection of any post-Qing dynasty Manchu nation-state. In popular consciousness this date instantly prompts memories of 'national humiliation' thanks to songs, schooling, film and direct propaganda by Chinese governments and activist groups. 'Nine One Eight' is a rallying point for nationalistic and anti-Japanese sentiment and has been since the 1930s.[13]

The Manchurian railway 'incident' presaged Japan's 1932 proclamation of the Republic of Manchukuo and the installation of the last Qing emperor, Aisin Gioro Puyi, as its head of state with the reign title 'The Kangde Emperor'. Manchukuo was established with all the trappings of a fully formed nation-state – a national flag, a new capital city (literally called 'Xinjing' or 'New Capital') and a national anthem. Louise Young says that the Japanese 'laboured mightily to convince themselves and others of the truth of Manchurian independence'.[14] The Japanese government justified the expenditure in money and soldiers to its domestic population by propagandising the natural link between Japan and its new 'independent colony'.

Despite Japan's best efforts the League of Nations did not recognise the new nation and called for the removal of all Japanese troops from the territory. Disunity in China, with the Chinese Communist Party (CCP) and Nationalists vying for power and regional military commanders wreaking havoc as well, resulted in an unconvincing Chinese sovereignty claim. Significantly, while the league recognised Chinese sovereignty over the territory it also recognised Manchuria's historical autonomy *from* China.[15] The ruling compounded the uneasy position of both China and Japan in the League of Nations – Japan quit the league in 1933 and continued as puppet master for the 'independent' Manchukuo nation. This nation was only disbanded with Japan's defeat in August 1945 as Soviet troops invaded from the north. They captured Manchukuo's Emperor Puyi as he tried to flee by plane to Japan. Handed over to the Chinese, Puyi was imprisoned and underwent a decade of re-education, after which he declared his support for the CCP and the PRC. His reintegration into the PRC national history would emerge through the documenting of his lengthy reform – rather than an amplification of his victimhood as would occur with Xianyu. His autobiography was published in 1960 in Beijing as testimony to his conscious, pedagogically driven conversion to loyalty to the PRC and renunciation of Manchu secessionist sentiment.[16]

Aisin Gioro Xianyu becomes Kawashima Yoshiko and dies as Granny Fang

Determining truth from hearsay is extremely difficult in the case of Xianyu simply because she was the subject of so much public commentary and fictionalisation during her life. This confusion facilitates the later amplification of her victim status. Some of the speculation was spurred by popular desire for exotic tales of women soldiers and sex spies during the war but it was also fuelled by her own enthusiasm for fame. Nonetheless, through this 'created history' of the Manchu princess-soldier-spy there are some common threads that provide the core for later embellishments and fantasising.

She was the fourteenth daughter of Prince Su, an ardent advocate for restoring the Qing dynasty and creating an independent Manchu state with Japanese support. Prince Su, in a time-honoured tradition of trading women as hostages for diplomatic goals, gave Xianyu in adoption to Kawashima Naniwa, a one-time advisor to the Qing security forces.[17] Kawashima had helped protect the Qing palace, the Forbidden City, during the Boxer Rebellion of 1900 and spied for the Manchu elite during the 1911 revolution that would crush the Qing dynasty – the project for which Qiu Jin, discussed in Chapter 3, had martyred herself. Prince Su and Kawashima became close friends and allies in their joint political agenda – hence the gifting of Su's daughter to Kawashima.

Xianyu moved to Japan with her stepfather in the spring of 1913 and began her life in Nagano training for an as-yet-unspecified role in a restored Manchu imperial order – inextricably entwined, as it was, with Japan's dreams of great empire. Xianyu was educated as a Japanese but also studied martial arts, English and equestrianism. She attended elite schools in Japan, where the teachers and her schoolmates regarded her royal presence as bringing great prestige to their school and she was afforded the special treatment deemed worthy of her status as a princess. She apparently grew into an 'arrogant girl prone to acting arbitrarily'.[18] Her love of horses meant that she often rode to school rather than taking a carriage as would be expected of an elite Japanese girl. Her stepfather's house was regularly full of leading figures in the Manchu independence movement and members of the secretive Black Dragon Society. Witnessing these men's conversations from early childhood was integral to her political training as a future leader of the nation-in-waiting. Her unique personal qualities and unusual behaviour for a young woman, let alone a princess, would become crucial in the choices she would make and actions she would take as an adult once back in China. These 'choices and actions' would be minimised in the later recreation of her history as 'victim' of Japanese aggression.

Her childhood comes to an abrupt end when, it is generally accepted, around the age of 20 she is the victim of sexual assault by her stepfather. For later historians, writers and filmmakers, as we will see below, the trauma of this experience becomes the dominant explanatory incident in the recreation of Xianyu as a victim of circumstances generated in the war that engulfed her, rather than as an agent in determining her own fate, or a warrior for Manchu independence.

In 1927, she returned to China as the bride of a Mongolian, Ganjuurjab, the son of a military leader also committed to the Japanese-sponsored idea of a Mongolian-Manchurian alliance independent of Han China. The marriage was a strategic, political relationship devoid of affection and only lasted two years, enough to have secured her independence from her stepfather in Japan. She began her espionage work for the Japanese military, supposedly providing vital information that enabled the Kwantung Army to blow up military strongman Zhang Zuolin's train in 1928, resulting in his death. Zhang, one-time supporter of Qing restoration and close collaborator with the Japanese, became involved in a number of complex political and military endeavours that eventually rendered him problematic to the expanding Japanese interests in Manchuria. His enthusiasm to remain the supreme ruler of Manchuria did not endear him to the Manchu independence movement either. Xianyu's role in providing the intelligence that ensured Zhang's assassination is one of her most famous early roles on behalf of the Japanese.

After the end of her marriage she left for Shanghai where she circulated among the Japanese residents in the foreign concession and formed links to the Shanghai gangster, Chang Yuqing – another collaborator with the Japanese in the rollicking world of Shanghai's espionage. Her precarious financial situation and expensive, glamorous lifestyle meant that her pecuniary needs underpinned most of her liaisons and romances. She formed a relationship with Tanaka Ryukichi (1896–1972), military attaché and spy for the Japanese government – they lived together in Shanghai. When Tanaka was recalled to Japan she became an intelligence agent for Major-General Doihara Kenji (1883–1948), a man known through the anglophone world as 'Lawrence of Manchuria'. News reports from the 1930s and 1940s show that he was held in some awe for his exploits in north China. One Australian paper described him as 'an outstanding political genius in the Japanese army's intrigues in Manchuria'[19] and a year later he was described as a 'Romantic Figure in China'.[20] Xianyu also became mistress to Major-General Tada Hayao (1882–1948) – Emperor Puyi's military advisor. Tada would go on to become vice chair of the Imperial Japanese Army General Staff and maintained a firm view that Manchukuo should separate from China. In only few years Xianyu maintained multiple, ever-changing personal and sexual relationships with the top echelon of the Japanese military in China.

Xianyu was primarily a networker forging communication between the remnants of the Manchu imperial family and the Japanese military. She played a role in persuading Emperor Puyi to move from Tianjin to Manchuria to accept the Japanese invitation to head the new state of Manchukuo in November 1931. The Japanese had garnered influence in the Qing imperial family throughout the preceding decades – Puyi stayed in the Japanese embassy in Beijing for eighteen months after leaving the Imperial Palace in 1924 and moved to live in the Japanese Concession of Tianjin from then until 1931.[21] International news reports from 1934 described the 'Daring Exploits of "Manchukuo's Joan of Arc"' when reporting on Xianyu's dramatic evacuation of Puyi's Empress, Wanrong, from Tianjin to a Japanese ship off the coast. Had the empress remained outside of Manchukuo it would have been 'extremely inconvenient' for the new country. The report explains Xianyu's 'boldest and most ingenious endeavours' (using her Japanese name, Yoshiko), as follows:

During the tumult in Tientsin [Tianjin], when machine-guns were barking everywhere from behind street barricades, Yoshiko disguised as a taxi-driver, calmly drew up before the house of the Empress and ordered her in the cab. Several times on the way to the harbour they were stopped by Chinese troops, but the resource and coolness of the girl spy brought the fugitive Empress to the safety of a Japanese destroyer.[22]

Xianyu's work on behalf of Manchukuo was not limited to espionage and diplomacy – it also included direct military action. In 1932 she formed a 'counter insurgency cavalry' comprising 3,000–5,000 men to crush anti-Japanese, anti-Manchukuo elements. This military unit, called the 'Pacifying the Country Army', operated until the late 1930s. It participated in the Japanese military actions at Rehe (Jehol) in the spring of 1933 when Japanese forces attacked those of Zhang Xueliang, son of the assassinated Zhang Zuolin, and wrested control of a section of Mongolia – annexing it to Manchukuo. This military action is the high point of her active military career since although pictures of her dressed in military uniform circulate well after this time, her work increasingly focused on intelligence and networking. Phyllis Birmbaum's study of the Japanese military records shows that they saw her army command as a propaganda role, rather than an actual military force.[23]

In Japan her sensational activities attracted considerable media attention during the 1930s. Xianyu's story reinforced the validity of the Japanese actions in Manchuria – her cross-dressing created a fad among young women and her frequent appearance in men's military uniforms connected well with Japan's growing militarist urges. The title of Muramatsu Shofu's 1933 book, *A Beauty Dressed in Male Attire: A Biography of Kawashima Yoshiko*, directly appealed to this fashion trend. She featured in numerous news reports and appeared on Japanese radio where she gained the moniker the 'Manchurian Joan of Arc'. Xianyu achieved such a degree of public fame that it rendered her useless as a spy – she made radio shows, released recordings of her songs, and her espio-nage and military exploits were widely discussed in the popular press.

Figure 5.2 Aisin Gioro Xianyu wearing western men's clothing in recording studio

Nonetheless, her propaganda value for Japan as an enthusiastic advocate of Manchukuo's independence from China far outweighed any losses from her withdrawal from espionage or military action.[24]

Stories of her exploits circulated throughout the world as Xianyu's enthusiasm for fame and the promotion of the Manchukuo nation expanded. The English-speaking world was treated to a biography care of an American graduate student, Willa Lou Woods. Woods travelled around Asia in the 1930s and was captivated by the stories circulating about a warrior princess. She published a thirty-page book called *Princess Jin: The Joan of Arc of the Orient* in 1937 – the year of Japan's full-scale invasion of coastal China.[25] Unlike the Chinese reports of her activities of this time, Woods was entirely sympathetic to Xianyu, an orphaned, tomboy who fled to Japan after narrowly escaping assassination by 'revolutionaries' in 1911. Woods creates a character for her Anglophone audience that links the princess into well-loved narratives of royal lineages fleeing certain death as a result of political revolutions (e.g. the French and Russian revolutions) and of a cross-dressing woman 'making it' in a man's world. Woods describes Xianyu's lifestyle in Tianjin as one of bicycling, dancing, horse riding and meeting Manchu activists. Xianyu's military and espionage work is a tomboy adventure of a charismatic princess leading a loyal band of followers. Woods asserts the reliability of her biography despite it only drawing on a five-day residency in Xianyu's Tianjin home. The book is fraught with errors but the romance of the tomboy princess is not compromised.

Woods describes Xianyu's political views as being independent of both Japan and China and her dedication to Manchukuo stemming from her status as an 'heir to the throne'.[26] Woods writes that Xianyu explained her collaboration with Japan as instrumental to securing an independent homeland. Her mistrust of China resulted from its treatment of her parents and the deaths of her brothers, the appalling conditions of the Manchus after the collapse of the Qing and continued Chinese mismanagement of their nation. Xianyu's household was apparently modest by royal standards and meals were limited to three dishes in order to 'save money for our soldiers'.[27] In writing a tale of a young princess in a man's world 'envied and much publicised because she goes where she pleases and dresses as she pleases',[28] Willa Lou Woods became part of the Xianyu's Manchu publicity machine.

But from 1937 as the war intensified between China and Japan, Xianyu became increasingly disenchanted with the Japanese exploitation of Manchukuo and she largely slipped from public view. That is, until her sensational arrest in Beiping by the Nationalist government in 1945. Tried as a 'traitor to the Han people' even though she herself was not Han, she was presumed executed in 1948. The trial caused a media frenzy – so prominent was her celebrity status. The trials against traitors mostly involved non-descript men so the arrival of a beautiful woman famed for cross-dressing, spying and soldiering was bound to generate mass interest.

Not long after her 'execution' Beijing newspapers wrote that a body double was used and there was widespread suspicion that her high-level contacts in the Nationalist Party arranged for her escape. The *Life* magazine reporter who witnessed the execution, by rifle shot to the back of the head, included a photo of a corpse with a 'mutilated face' covered by matting in his article.[29] The speculation died down for a few decades but once revived in the twenty-first century, proceeded apace and the Granny Fang story gained wide public attention. Historians Wang Qingxiang,[30] Li Gang and He Jingfang[31] conducted extensive investigations and declared that they are '100% sure that Granny Fang is Kawashima Yoshiko [Xianyu]'.[32] For their books and a television series, they interviewed two women from a village in the North East from the Duan family. Their father and grandfather, Duan Lianxiang, claimed on his deathbed that their neighbour, Granny Fang, was Xianyu. Granny Fang was able to speak Japanese, was highly educated and remained singularly close to the Duans. The Duan family had kept gifts by Granny Fang and after much tortuous investigation these confirmed Duan's claim.

Wang, Li and He argue that Duan was instrumental in securing her escape from Beijing – he had previously worked with Xianyu in Manchukuo and Tianjin. Their families had ties reaching back to the Forbidden City where Duan's relatives had worked for Xianyu's father, Prince Su. The researchers also interviewed Xianyu's relative, Aisin Gioro Decheng, who remembers, as a child, a secretive visit to his home in the winter of 1955 of a woman who spoke with his father in Japanese and Manchu. Thus, the circumstances surrounding Xianyu's 'death' were as mysterious and romantic as those of her life. The rediscovery of the cultured, genial and harmless Granny Fang would underpin the Xianyu-as-victim narrative to facilitate her reincorporation into PRC history. However, the stories of her circulating during the war paint a less benign picture.

Wartime Chinese commentary – an evil, dangerous and immoral woman

Chinese wartime media reports on Xianyu built her celebrity through sensational stories of her sexual immorality and ethnic ambiguity. Images of her dressed as a man, either in western suits or in military uniforms accompanied descriptions of her moving across linguistic, social and political borders. These all created the general view that she was a loose woman politically and morally. No attention was given to her struggle for an independent Manchu nation-state. In the process of becoming a media celebrity Xianyu was depoliticised and hyper-sexualised. Any goals she had for using fame to advance her political cause were destined to failure as an eager public gobbled up stories of sex, spying, glamour, gossip and treason.

The popular Shanghai entertainment magazine *Linglong* presented its readers with a story on Japan's 'most famous woman spy', creating a vision of a mystery and danger. The author, Li Jun, reports that Xianyu had been spotted entering China three weeks earlier on 1 March. Emperor Puyi, ruler of Manchukuo, had apparently sent Xianyu on missions to Beiping and Tianjin. 'Without doubt some serious matters are afoot.'[33] The threat posed by this woman emerges from Xianyu's superior Japanese education, her talent in Russian, English, and French as well as many Chinese regional languages. Nicknamed the 'Mata Hari of the East' *Linglong*'s readers learn that she is expert in disguise variously dressing as a taxi dancer and as a man to circulate among the military while gathering intelligence.[34] The article creates a sense of imminent crisis built upon the mystery of a woman who, while famous, is so capable of disguising herself that she moves with ease across sexual, moral and national borders.

Once the full-scale invasion of China started in the autumn of 1937, the attitude towards Xianyu hardened and she emerges as a monstrous freak. That year, a leading women's rights magazine, *Women's Life*, launched a racialised attack describing Xianyu as yet another Manchu woman traitor to China. The author, Bi Quan, places her within a genealogy of other treacherous and devious Manchu women aristocrats who have meddled in foreign affairs. Xianyu is presented as 'The Third Shrew' in the list. The first shrew is Empress Dowager Xiaozhuangwen (1613–1688) who was instrumental in the foundation of the Qing dynasty that overthrew the Han-dominated Ming dynasty – she used her beauty and sexuality to gain influence and lead Han Chinese to betray the Ming. The second Manchu shrew was Empress Dowager Cixi (1835–1908), loathed for usurping the throne and using a series of child emperors to sustain her power. Cixi's mismanagement and lust for power are still popularly regarded as making China vulnerable to foreign subjugation. As the third shrew in this list, Xianyu is presented as a treacherous and devious Manchu in a genealogy of corrupt, sexual predators.[35]

Bi Quan explains that Xianyu's Japanese stepfather raised her as a 'slave girl' intending her to become a femme fatale specialising in espionage. After a year in a girl's school her stepfather transferred her to a boy's school where she wore men's clothing: 'from that moment on through to today she became the monster, a so called "beauty in men's clothing"'. The article distinguishes 'good' cross-dressing women, such as Hua Mulan discussed in Chapter 2, from Xianyu, the monstrous freak. Xianyu's cross-dressing is 'not for those noble purposes of loyalty and filial piety that marked Mulan's decision to replace her father in battle'. Rather, just like the last emperor Puyi, Xianyu betrayed her country. 'She did not hesitate to degrade her own body, and become a most shameless traitor, [someone] who would stop at nothing – a spy who turned from a woman into a man.'[36]

The article continues by outlining her activities disguised as a taxi dancer during the Japanese attacks on Shanghai on 28 January 1932, the so-called 128 incident, gathering intelligence behind the Chinese lines. This was the same battle that Xie Bingying wrote about in ecstatic terms (Chapter 4, this volume).[37] The article continues with a discussion of Xianyu's military actions as commander of her own army in the Rehe campaign. The list of Xianyu's travesties continues: she was known as the owner of a bar in Beiping where Japanese troops and their friends relaxed; she was the Elder Sister to 'hundreds of hoodlums and gangsters' organising rackets in both Beiping and Shanghai. Xianyu's love of media attention also gained a mention in Bi Quan's article furthering the narrative that while she was a beautiful woman, she was a shameless freak.

Lest her feminist readers admire Xianyu's capacity to operate in a man's world, Bi tells readers that Xianyu was not motivated by aspirations for forging broad sex equality in society. In a Japanese *Women's Club Magazine* Xianyu was reported as telling her Japanese readers that she felt uncomfortable with young women imitating her cross-dressing style: 'I had no other choice but to adopt men's clothing in order [to secure] my life (work). Why should young Japanese girls upset the natural order of *yin* and *yang*? Cutting their hair, wearing men's clothing and spouting equal rights for men and women, there is no reason for this behaviour.'[38] Xianyu continued saying that women's most noble path was to serve their husbands as good housewives and to bear and raise children. To Bi Quan this position was hypocritical. While Xianyu was out in the world doing as she pleased and engaged in every sort of scandalous behaviour, she was advocating that other women stay at home and be 'chaste wives and good mothers'.[39] Xianyu's lack of political dedication to women's rights further confirmed the freakish, immoral and untrustworthy nature of her actions.

Other publications used Xianyu to promote espionage as a legitimate 'profession' with the potential for liberating women. A *Linglong* article by Yun Qiu discussed women's spying in its international context as part of the inevitable movement of women into all professions. It explained that women in Europe and America received special training for espionage – a profession that was regarded as patriotic rather than illicit and immoral. This was legitimate work and required education – 'there are few [female spies] without education'.[40] With the increase in hostilities, the call for women to imitate Xianyu was explicit. *Linglong*'s readers were reminded that the key people in military and political circles during the 918 Incident were charmed by her seductive feminine beauty – 'Who knows what secrets they let slip?'[41] Despite her cover being blown during the 128 Incident she managed to smuggle some crucial maps into Japanese hands. Her success as an agent confirmed, the article reveals that Xianyu is back from Manchukuo and in Shanghai again, living secretly in a hotel in the Japanese-dominated Hongkou area of the city where she goes out to dance halls in disguise. 'We don't know what her mission is.'[42] But, readers are left in no doubt that women can be effective espionage agents and China needed its own Xianyu-like spies. 'This is the best opportunity for action for China's young, patriotic women. For our ancestral land, for the race-nation, rouse your courage and stride forward, ... drape yourselves in your most beautiful, delicate silks, apply your sexiest cosmetics, step out the doors of your barracks, transcend death's limits, and mask any worries with a smile.'[43]

Linglong had established the idea amongst its readers, largely women who would consider themselves cosmopolitan and modern, that women's work in espionage was patriotic and glamorous, albeit frightening and dangerous. Xianyu was the model for a raft of potential Shanghai women spies.[44] An earlier article detailed the professional training spies undergo internationally: foreign languages, the history and status of intelligence work, investigation techniques, psychology and photography, military strategy and planning and (in case that list was not enticing enough) explosives.[45]

Communist magazines discussed women's participation in espionage through Xianyu's work as a sex spy as well. In 1940 the Yan'an women's journal *China's Women* revealed how stories of Xianyu's activities were used to inspire female students to form spy brigades whose joke-motto was 'Our station is in the bedcovers of the enemy.' The author, Wu Qun, opposed relegating women to spying and aimed to secure for them front-line battle positions but the start of her article explains at great length how in 1938 a speaker at a women's meeting described Xianyu in the most glowing terms and presented her as a model for women's war work. The unnamed speaker was quoted as saying:

Of all the women in the world, I only admire one – and that person is Kawashima Yoshiko [Xianyu]. Her greatness arises from her unstinting readiness to make whatever sacrifice is required for the future of her country. She is not like the regular female heroes, who once they start political work only want to stand at the very front lines, but are unwilling to put their heads down and get to work. And unlike her, are not prepared to bravely use their special womanly attributes to undertake the most difficult and arduous work, espionage – which has the least scope for garnering the limelight. Look at Kawashima Yoshiko [Xianyu]. From the outset she occupied that most difficult and arduous station, nowhere else, a place where nobody wanted to go, into the beds of the enemy. But, her contribution, her contribution to the whole Japanese nation, is even greater than in military terms. I hope you will learn from Kawashima Yoshiko [Xianyu], learn from her noble personal attributes, and I hope that you resolve to take up espionage, make the most of women's talents, you know that espionage really isn't that vulgar![46]

Wu Qun continued saying that after hearing this speech dozens of students formed a spy group and they practiced dancing, wearing high-heel shoes and applying cosmetics. The sex-specific nature of the work is evident in the fact that there was no male students' spy brigade. News that Xianyu had turned up a dancehall in Hankou with a team of over twenty Japanese dance girls prompted even more vigorous activity from the student spy brigade.[47]

An article in the Nationalist Party's women's journal from 1938, the very year that saw the flurry of student spy brigades, included a piece by Wang Pingling titled 'The Special Duties of Women during War: We Ought to Acquire the Knowledge and Techniques of Women Spies'. She uses the story of Xianyu to explain the particular uses of women in espionage. She explains:

The Japanese military have a deep understanding of human foibles when it comes to sex and money. Accordingly they have sent young women all around the world tasked with gathering military intelligence. Currently the most advanced of these, like Kawashima

Yoshiko [Xianyu], are the most useful tool for the Japanese military in their invasion of China and their harassment of Russia.[48]

Wang asserts that Xianyu's most powerful tools were her beauty, spoilt child naiveté, fluency in many foreign languages and the timbre of her voice, which was as coquettish as an oriole's. Moreover, she moves freely from one man's embrace into next because, as men become enraptured by her charms, she milks them for information and carries it straight to the Japanese military or her intelligence contact. She has not only harmed China but she is actively spying against Russia as well.

From all this information, Wang concludes that 'espionage and especially the work of women spies is of the utmost importance to military developments; so why are the young women of China not working hard and learning this type of work on behalf of their ancestral land?'[49] The skills women need to learn are extensive. Other than foreign languages, dancing and singing applying cosmetics and adopting various costumes, they need to learn military strategy, how to swim, ride horses, fly planes and drive cars. Wang comes to the conclusion that 'Chinese women should learn these skills in order to make a glorious sacrifice to the nation.'[50]

Xianyu, always referred to by her Japanese name, Kawashima Yoshiko, was both a *Japanese* model for drastic wartime action by Chinese women and a demonic, freak devoid of morality. Interest in Xianyu's activities and personae covered both popular commercial and political publications. The former had a prurient and voyeuristic interest compared to the latter's enthusiasm for using her as a model or anti-hero. Both glamourised the world of espionage and romanticised women's potential war contributions in the process. Her sexualised celebrity ensured that once she was captured and put on trial public attention to her treachery would be enormous – none were interested in her Manchu political agenda.

The celebrity trial: a freakish spy paraded

With the defeat of Japan the Nationalist government embarked upon a series of trials against key collaborators – Xianyu was among those arrested and tried as 'traitors to the Chinese people'. The huge public interest her trial attracted was a natural result of the extensive and emotive media commentary and publicity over many years, some of which she herself had generated and welcomed. Her celebrity status had some disturbing impacts on the quality of the justice dispensed and the accompanying media frenzy intended to further profit from her celebrity. Moreover, the Nationalist party-state operating the courts in Beiping had a vested interest in ensuring that any Manchu independence ideals were discredited through her trial. Her work for the Japanese had effectively ceased well before her trial because she was disillusioned by their failure to deliver real independence to Manchukuo. The Nationalist prosecutors disregarded her quest to build a distinct Manchu nation and instead created the impression that she was plotting for the Manchus to retake China.

On 11 October 1945, two months after Manchukuo's Emperor Puyi had been captured by the Soviets, the Nationalist government's police arrested Xianyu. Official charges would only be pressed in 1946 and the trial would last until 1948. Her crimes were: 'Serving as an official at the Manchukuo Court and as chairman [*sic*] of the Manchukuo Overseas Students' Association in Japan, recruiting bandits and organising the Dingguo Army for Manchukuo, participation in the Rehe campaign against China, passing confidential information to Japan and trying to "revive the Manchus" and move Puyi back to Beijing'.[51] The prosecutors asserted that based on international law traitors and spies faced the death penalty.[52]

Xianyu's defence revolved around two aspects – her age and her nationality. She claimed that she was only 15–16 years old at the time of the 1932 'Shanghai Incident' so she was too young to have been involved the type of military action described. Her lawyers also argued that she was a Japanese national because she had been adopted and raised in Japan from early childhood – as a Japanese she should be tried as an enemy combatant not as a traitor. Later, her defence referred to her as a Manchu, asserting it was natural that she should fight to restore her people to leadership in their own nation. On this premise, her activities were a domestic *Chinese* dispute between Han and Manchu and should not be dealt with in a treason court. If recognised as either Japanese or Manchu she could secure a reprieve or a lighter sentence. The court rejected these ethnicity claims on the basis that she was a Chinese citizen because her birth father had Chinese nationality.[53] Even at the final hearing her lawyers declared: 'The defendant should not be considered a Chinese person.'[54]

The Nationalist authorities ignored her Manchu identity – the trial used only her Chinese and Japanese names – neatly obscuring any claims to independent Manchu nationhood. But Dan Shao also notes that increasingly her Japanese name was dropped in favour of her Chinese name – confirming her status as a *Chinese* who should be tried for treason.[55] The use of her Chinese name, Jin Bihui, also accelerated in the Chinese-language news reports. Pre-empting any verdict, they increasingly called her 'The traitor Jin Bihui' even though the trial was in progress.[56]

Dan Shao's analysis of her trial documents shows that Xianyu was appalled at the quality of the Nationalist government's legal system since 'the officials involved used only some letters, a Japanese novel, and a movie as evidence'.[57] Muramatsu's 1933 novel, although based on her life, was not written as a factual account warranting legal standing – yet its wide influence enabled the prosecution to use it as 'fact'. Kenji Mizoguchi's 1932 movie *Dawn of the*

Manchurian-Mongolian Nation was a propagandistic romance rather than a historical documentary of her life, but it too was used as formal evidence of her crimes.[58]

In garnering fame to legitimate her new nation, she had encouraged the production of novels, stories and films – in Japan, China and elsewhere – now these romanticised and likely exaggerated stories would be used against her as *evidence* of her treachery. The theatrical nature of the trials was revealed in a report published in the major daily newspaper, *Dagong bao*, that described the closing session of the trial as 'having the quality of a drama' because the lighting in the courtroom cast shadows that created a solemn atmosphere.[59] All charges against her were upheld but explicit mention of her role in trying to revive the Manchus was removed from the summary verdict of October 1947. The Hebei Supreme Court sentenced her to death on 3 March 1948 and she was supposedly executed on 25 March in Beiping. *Dagong bao* reports that a Japanese monk claimed her body and buried it in the city's Japanese cemetery.[60]

English news reports about her imminent execution maintained the sensational media frenzy associated with her trial. 'Ching [Xianyu] – popularly known as Radiant Jade and referred to in the Chinese Press as "Mata Hari of the East", "Queen of Spies" or "The Human Devil" – was the first woman in China ever to be given the death sentence for treason'.[61] This Australian report narrates her 'financially successful' life in Beiping as she organised rackets and blackmailed a succession of prominent lovers.

The enthusiasm to demonise and romanticise this mysterious woman abounded in the popular entertainment press in China. A 1946 article told readers that Xianyu was called 'Commander Jin' for her military prowess. While fighting on behalf of the Japanese in north China she was wounded and from then on took regular injections and increasingly large doses of morphine to dull the pain. The author, Hai Yi, likens her to Empress Wu Zetian of the Tang dynasty (618–907), known for her supposedly unnatural lascivious ways, declaring 'She lived a dissolute life in pursuit of sex, such that Wu Zetian would have candidly admitted defeat.'[62] A sex-crazed drug-addicted spy with propensity to violence abnormal in a woman, Xianyu received no sympathy from this Shanghai journalist. Another reporter, Ping Er, explained in an article provocatively titled 'A Masculinised Japanese Female spy' that as a 'beauty in manly garb' Xianyu was a monster.[63]

Little wonder that crowds gathered when she appeared in court. So enthusiastic was their presence that foreign media reports from October 1947 describe how 'five thousand unruly Chinese caused the postponement of the trial'.[64] Crowds inside the courtroom apparently 'smashed windows and a chair' during the hearing as she confessed to being connected with top-level

Japanese military officers such as Prince Konoye Tojo and Doihara but simultaneously denied committing treason.[65]

The Chinese reports suggest that the mobs that gathered were not prompted to violence by anything she had said because the first day of the hearings was postponed before it even commenced. Rather the unruly behaviour appears to be a result of poor crowd control and mass enthusiasm to witness the trial of such a mysterious, celebrated figure. The *New People's News* described the trial of 8 October 1947 as uncontrolled and bordering on a riot.

An hour before the court opened there were several thousand people waiting to see the hearing. The crowds still surged like a tide at the single main door. The southern entrance was closed tight to those outside, who pounded on the doors and windows . . . they smashed glass in the windows, injuring the left hand of the bailiff, and wrecked the threshold to the door.[66]

It continues describing damage to the inside of the courtroom and the authority's concern that the building would be damaged irreparably. Accordingly the judge ruled that the hearing would be postponed. Xianyu was returned to prison but still the crowds refused to disperse. The reporter noted that the damage to the courthouse and the delay in the trial were costly.[67]

The second convening of the case, 15 October 1947, was marginally better. The authorities constructed a temporary court in the gardens of the courthouse complete with the press gallery in a pavilion. Barricades were built to contain the crowds and when the court opened over 5,000 people were there to witness the event, pushing against the barricades to get a better view. Xianyu arrived dressed in a steel grey jumper, coffee-coloured western trousers and, when combined with her short hair, she looked all the part a middle-aged man.[68]

The complexity of the emotional response Xianyu generated is clear in the *Dagong bao* report on her execution. Her progress to the execution ground is described as being extremely sad and Xianyu is presented relatively sympathetically. She thanked the prison staff for looking after her during the previous two years and when the shots rang out indicating her death, fellow prisoners in the women's section wept in sorrow at the passing of their 'foolish elder brother'. She had sent a letter to her stepfather asking him to 'advise Japanese youth to love China' and encouraging him to come to serve China.[69] Most revealing of all is the reporter's comment that 'She was probably evil, but she was definitely intelligent and beautiful right up to just before her death.' The journalist's equivocation about her moral state was prompted by her confession in which she poetically claimed: 'The person I am today is like a snowflake before a blazing hot stove.'[70] No mourners came to cry over her coffin – her brother's and sister-in-law's absence was explicitly noted. The Japanese priest performed his Buddhist rites without their presence.[71]

The lust for sensation generated by commercialised media that promote celebrity systems sullied the quality of the justice she received. And, her celebrity status as an immoral female freak made her legal sentencing as a Chinese traitor inevitable. The huge public attention she drew meant that the Nationalist government could use her trial and execution to mark its leadership over the North East and all China's multiple ethnic groups – wartime sexual deviance by a Manchu princess helped make the message more interesting.

Reclaiming 'our' woman, Xianyu, as victim

In 2004 twenty people gathered at a conference in the offices of the Changchun government in North East China determined to reveal the truth about Xianyu's life. Some had personally known her, including historians, relatives and provincial leaders. The gathering produced a book by Li Gang and He Jingfang in 2009 that claimed to present new evidence on her story. It moved chronologically through her life with the goal of revealing its tragedy – she was abandoned by her parents, abused by her stepfather, and duped and used by the Japanese into believing that by supporting them she would be able to build a Manchurian-Mongolian kingdom. Xianyu emerges as a victim of trickery by powerful manipulators, rather than an evil, depraved traitor.

In the twenty-first century Xianyu's status as a victim of sexual violence at the hands of her stepfather becomes the overarching determining factor explaining her inability to make correct moral and political judgements. Sexual deviance had dominated media reports on Xianyu throughout the war and pushed her political agenda aside. Sexual violence would dominate discussions on her among those that sought to bring her back into the Chinese historical fold. During her lifetime, few Chinese sources discuss her as a victim of sexual assault – she is presented as a sexual predator. Wang Pingling's 1938 article was one of the few to discuss her sexual assault. Wang says Xianyu was so ashamed that she tried to commit suicide but with that option thwarted she instead lived a dissolute life.[72] Rape explains her path to depravity rather than national identity confusion. In the PRC from the 1980s onwards as commercial opportunities build on an increasing official acceptance of depictions of sex in media, fiction and film, Xianyu's sexual assault becomes more commonly discussed – spurred by the translation of previously unavailable Japanese books on her life.

Three Japanese-language biographies were translated into Chinese and published in the early 1980s. All mention the sexual assault and while they are less explicit than later Chinese texts, the topic of sexual assault is introduced. The 1972 biography by Watanabe Ryusaku, the so-called Yoshiko Kawashima [Xianyu] Researcher, was published in Chinese translation in 1982. Watanabe explains Xianyu's aberrant behaviour as resulting from being treated like a 'toy doll' by her father and stepfather – discarded, sent to a foreign country and left to an extremely lonely and isolated life. 'Most likely her wanton personality and crazed behaviour gradually emerged from within her attempts to break out of this loneliness.'[73] He then proceeds to discuss the accusations of sexual assault against her stepfather made by Xianyu's brother, Aisin Gioro Xianli. Xianli had reported that after Xianyu's parents' death, her stepfather had stolen much of their family's money and that in his 'thick skinned and importunate fashion entangled himself with Yoshiko Kawashima [Xianyu]'.[74] Watanabe explains that some people believe that Xianyu's preference for male clothing was a ploy to repel the unwanted attentions of her stepfather. He cites Xianyu's brother as evidence. Watanabe is unconvinced: 'I don't think that her stepfather would change his lascivious nature simply because … [Xianyu] changed into men's clothing. Nor do I think that the reason she changed her clothes was only a result of this. But, it can be material in an analysis of the distinctive temperament and eccentric behaviour of this type of female psychology.'[75]

Following quickly from Watanabe's book was the 1984 release of Umemoto Sutezo's 1980 Japanese-language biography. This book also mentions that there was some suspicion about Xianyu's stepfather's behaviour arising from Xianli's comments. Xianli described a conversation in which Kawashima waxes lyrical about the potential strengths of a child born of a combination of his great samurai lineage and the Manchu imperial line. The suggestion being that he secretly lusted after his stepdaughter.[76] But, apart from this brief mention, the book goes no further and does not make the sexual assault a central part of Xianyu's subsequent dramatic behaviours.

The Chinese translation fest of Japanese materials on Xianyu continued with the publication in 1985 of Kamisaka Fuyuko's 1984 novel. The book explicitly mentions its debt to the Muramatsu novel that had been used as evidence in Xianyu's trial. Kamasaka also describes the sexual assault as precipitating Xianyu's transformation into a boy in hairstyle and dress choices.[77] But she also points out that some historians, like Harada Tomohiko (1917–1983), suspect that the rape was merely gossip circulated by Xianyu's brother in response to resentment he felt about the handling of his parents' estate.[78] The translation of these Japanese texts opened the door for a new wave of Chinese research on Xianyu and to the discussion of the impact of sexual assault as an explanatory rationale for her behaviour.

In PRC accounts drawing on the multiple translations of Japanese material emphasise the trauma Xianyu experiences during her sexual assault and subsequent abuse by powerful Japanese aggressors rather than her wilful deviance. By the 2000s Chinese redactions of her life are dramatic and credit her irregular behaviour directly to her sexual assault. Li and He go into detail in their book about her experience of rape as a young girl by her stepfather.[79] This event is positioned as a pivotal moment in her personality development and explains her subsequent erratic actions. According to their version of the assault, Xianyu's stepfather became jealous as she was becoming romantically involved with boys her own age and so took it upon himself to 'have her first'. He explained to Xianyu that she could not form normal marital and romantic bonds during her life because of her political mission and that it was his responsibility to instruct her in every aspect. She was hospitalised after the rape and attempted suicide by shooting herself in her arm. Li and He explain that while recovering from the suicide attempt Xianyu realised that her best course of action was to continue to live and to realise her Manchu birth father's dreams of an independent Manchuria. The researchers explain that her personality altered dramatically from this moment and she soon manifested an 'abnormal psychology'. She increasingly spent time with men, dressing as a man and was more and more ruthless in her interactions with people generally.[80]

Li Yiming's 2010 study extends the narrative of her as a victim of a traumatic sexual assault. He describes her stepfather as 'regarding her like the prostitutes he visited so frequently' and Xianyu as 'having no strength to resist' his attacks.[81] Li fleshes out the story with fictional detail. Xianyu cried into her pillow at night and eventually developed a fever and lost consciousness. Her stepfather took her to a local hospital where one of his friends was the doctor. The bruise patterns on her body indicated the events of only a few days earlier. The doctor, unaware that the stepfather was the perpetrator, advised him that Xianyu had likely been attacked and raped. Both men resolve to protect Xianyu's reputation by keeping the information quiet. In keeping with the style of many 'popular history' books, Li includes dialogue and internal monologue to give the text urgency. Xianyu is described thinking: 'He can go fuck his mother, the rapist.'[82] There is no possible way that Li Yiming or any of the authors of these texts could possible know this level of detail – yet the Chinese-language 'biographies' regularly include rich details of this sort.

'The results of Kawashima Naniwa's [her stepfather's] brutal assault were that Yoshiko's [Xianyu's] temperament started to change and become erratic, she became a woman of easy virtue who liked to join in whatever fun was going and she became shameless. From this point she turned her brain toward the crotch, and used her intelligence and beauty in a crazed vengeance against men'.[83]

Xianyu turned her body into a weapon in the bedroom. This kind of exaggeration not only serves to draw readers into the book, but also helps explain that she is a victim of Japanese aggression and her aberrant behaviour subsequent to this has a legitimate explanation. She becomes a completely understandable figure if her life choices are reduced to the trauma of sexual assault. Deeper consideration of her political and military motives is neatly elided within this salacious pondering of the young rape victim turned sexual predator.

Hong Kong's Eddie Fong also makes this transformation in her personality the climax of the first part of his 1990 movie.[84] Based on Lillian Lee's popular novel on Xianyu, the motives for this choice are likely to be commercial – sexual assault makes exciting viewing.[85] Eddie Fong depicts the young, naïve Xianyu, played by darling of the cinema world Anita Mui (1963–2003), returning home with her boyfriend, a young lieutenant. Their childish flirting and modest kisses are interspersed with playful teasing and the sharing of treats Xianyu had made – they parted with promises of further dates. The scene of innocent, youthful romance amplifies Xianyu's personality change in the scenes to follow. After the rape, Xianyu is no longer a playful, giggling and teasing youngster – she is hard, ruthless and strategic in all interpersonal relations. The trauma she experiences as a result of the rape is manifest in a scene where she cuts of her relationship with her boyfriend in a dramatic moment where he hands her a gun and she shoots herself in the arm. Director Fong depicts a further suicide attempt from her hospital bed as she begs the doctors to sterilise her so that she can never be a parent. From that moment, according to Fong's version of her life, she seeks to become a man; she insists that the hospital staff cut her hair short and wears only men's clothing. Her rejection of feminine grace and charm throughout the remainder of the movie are explained as reactions to this early betrayal and rape trauma.

In addition to feeding his audience's prurient interest in watching a rape in progress, Fong's movie includes lesbian sex. When Xianyu returns to Tianjin to arrange for the Empress Wanrong's escape from the city, Fong includes a scene in which Xianyu seduces the empress who becomes compliant to Xianyu's plans while in the throws of her opium-induced lesbian lust. Xianyu callously manipulates the empress's loneliness and sexual frustration in order to achieve her Manchukuo political goals. Xianyu had been told that Emperor Puyi and Wanrong had not shared a bed for a very long time. Fong's empress also declared offhand that Puyi did not like women – adding another layer of homosexual interest to the story. Xianyu pretended to be facilitating their escape as new lesbian lovers but in fact she was tricking Wanrong into leaving Tianjin for Manchukuo to assume her public role as empress in the new state.

The key theme throughout Fong's movie is Xianyu's struggle with her *Chinese* identity. It commences and closes with her trial where Anita Mui's Xianyu is asserting, that she is 'a Japanese' and therefore cannot be tried for treason since hers were acts of war. In keeping with the confusion that Dan Shao noted in her court documents, she is operating outside of the framework of nationality and citizenship of her Nationalist government prosecutors. She saw no confusion with being a Japanese citizen of Chinese race. Within Fong's movie Xianyu's fluid attitude to race and nationality is central to the sympathy that his 1990s' viewers felt towards her life and death. Her Japanese school-mates are depicted as asking her 'Are you Chinese?' To which she gives no reply. Other characters in the movie also explicitly discuss her muddled loyalties. The male lead, heart-throb Andy Lau, who plays a patriotic Chinese opera actor, emphatically rejects her declaration that she is a Manchu and therefore justified in her actions against China and collaboration with Japan. At the end, just prior to her 'execution' (the movie leaves it unclear whether she was shot with blanks or real bullets) she declares to Andy Lau's character 'Maybe China would be better off with me being executed' among another number of comments that position her as seeking to advance China's welfare – regardless of the incompetence of its governments.

Central to this confusion is the film's depiction of her betrayal by nation-marked authority figures in her families. Her birth father identified with the Manchu revival within her home city of Beiping, China, and yet he abandoned her. Her adoptive father claimed to be pursuing the interests of Manchukuo but was driving Japan's interests and following his own lustful desires. On hearing that her stepfather will not lie about her age in order to prove that she was too young in 1932 to be involved in military and espionage work, Xianyu says: 'A man who has lied all his life, why does he suddenly decide to tell the truth when he is so close to death.' Within Fong's version of her life, the rupture in her personality caused by the rape and her early isolation from her parents and her Chinese homeland explains her inability to accept a straightforward Chinese identity.

Anita Miu's Xianyu is clearly unhinged – a damaged mind driving her towards a tragic end. But the viewers are invited into a different world, led by Andy Lau – one where an innocent young woman has been turned into a sociopathic, sexual predator through the machinations of the men whose political ambitions were to render Manchuria beholden to Japan and to weaken China. She becomes nothing less than a pawn in their grand plot misleading her into thinking that her actions are in her own interests. Yet, the long-lasting sympathy and affection that she elicits from key male protagonists, their emotional attachment depicted as being at odds with their common sense and official duties, reveals a core sincerity and goodness that is hidden by her 'rough diamond' beauty. Her first teenage love returns to the film as a Kwantung army officer and helps her escape assassination, directly defying the orders of his superior. Andy Lau's character tells her that the bullets will be blanks and she must just pretend to die. The casting of Anita Mui as Xianyu would also have prompted a sympathetic response from audiences – revered as she was as a pop star and movie goddess throughout Hong Kong and much of the Chinese diaspora.

Eddie Fong's Xianyu is more complex than the figure recreated by academic researchers in the PRC. In their assertion that they are narrating the 'true facts' of her life the researchers are forced within the PRC's comparatively rigid containment of correct and incorrect history, to present a clear vision of her as a Chinese woman who was led astray by sexual abuse. In contrast, the movie leaves open the possibility for her to be reincorporated into several 'national' histories as a victim of the machinations and abuse by Japanese, Manchu and Han men playing global politics and promoting competing national interests and personal ambitions. Fong's Xianyu, for example, remains wary of assassination attempts from Chinese patriots and the Japanese military throughout the movie – staying one step ahead until the trials of the traitors by the ROC's Nationalist Party-led court system – where her *Chinese* identity is confirmed.

Conclusion

The contemporary PRC narratives present sexual assault as the explanatory point for her later 'deviant' behaviour. Alone in the world she was left to make her way as best she could. Xianyu emerges less as a sexual predator and more as a confused victim of a brutal sexual assault that crushed her capacity to determine friend from foe. Her troubled national and ethnic loyalties were a product of sexual assault at the hands of a Japanese militarist. As 'more victim and less vamp', she has a new place in China's national, multiethnic history.

Aisin Gioro Xianyu was born in the Qing dynasty when Manchus ruled China but was raised in Japan. She regarded herself as a Japanese-educated Manchu (sometimes 'Chinese' and sometimes not) at a time when it was possible to conceive of an independent nation for Manchuria, carved from the northern reaches of the Qing Empire led by the deposed monarchy of that dynasty. Japanese interests in establishing a client state in North East China matched Manchu and Mongol desires for a distinct homeland from Han-dominated China. Yet, over many decades of commentary, PRC scholars have found a way to draw her back into Chinese national history by creating the narrative of her victimhood – first at the hands of the Manchu aristocracy, then by Japanese imperialists and finally as a confused victim of sexual assault. In this form of sexualised victimhood available only to females and given the nationalist sentiment generated around wartime rape of 'our women', Xianyu can be effectively cleansed and incorporated into a history of multiethnic China struggling to maintain its dignity and territorial integrity. Just as the Japanese political and propaganda art world used her in the 1930s to promote its vision of an 'independent' Manchukuo, the Chinese masses thrilled reading stories of this mysterious wartime sexy spying princess and international commentators enjoyed the thrill of the cross-dressing Mata Hari of the East, PRC historians turn Xianyu to their own purposes. It takes considerable ideological work to rehabilitate women like Aisin Gioro Xianyu into simple historical narratives based on a unified nation-state. In contrast, the loyal CCP woman guerrilla, Zhao Yiman, who fought against Aisin Gioro in the North East is foundational to PRC commemoration of war and the formation of their nation, as we see in the chapter to follow.

    Guerrilla resistance leader, Zhao Yiman
Warrior teacher and self-sacrificing CCP mother

In 1948, in anticipation of their victory in the civil war, the communist authorities controlling Harbin City opened a memorial hall called 'The North East Martyrs' Museum' to mark those who had died in the struggle against the Japanese and the Nationalists. The woman guerrilla fighter, Zhao Yiman (1905–1936), occupied a significant part of the exhibition space – lodged, as it was, in the very same premises in which she had been tortured during interrogation by the occupying Japanese twelve years earlier. The major thoroughfare leading to the museum is called 'Yiman Road' in her honour. In 1960 a museum also dedicated to her opened in her hometown, Yibin, in the western province of Sichuan and in 1996 a further commemorative building dedicated to her memory was opened in Shangzhi City – the location of key events in her heroic life and early death. The Chinese Communist Party (CCP) has built and sustained stories of Zhao for decades, consolidating her status as *the* premier communist woman warrior martyr right to the present.

During her lifetime, few people knew her name. Unlike the infamous Aisin Gioro Xianyu discussed in the preceding chapter, against whose Manchukuo state Zhao's forces waged their guerrilla battles, Zhao Yiman only became known years after her death when the People's Republic of China (PRC) commenced its memorialisation of wartime heroes. The PRC propaganda system adopts a 'total propaganda' approach – all ages, classes and localities are targeted with carefully constructed, subtly evolving messages using diverse media and formats. As well as the museums and memorial halls, she is the subject of two full-length feature films, multiple serialised comics, poems, paintings, textbooks, websites and biographies.[1] The great wall of narrative surrounding figures like Zhao Yiman recreates war 'memories' as emotionally charged pedagogical experiences of political and moral self-improvement.

Her status as a guerrilla mother is central to her efficacy in the total propaganda system because it enables the CCP to prompt people's emotional responses around their fears of the integrity of their family units. The CCP positions itself within the propaganda narrative as a supra-parent caring for the national family. At the start of her propaganda life, as early as 1951 Zhao gained the esteemed moniker of 'the immortal daughter of the Chinese people'.[2] On the discovery of her son's existence, her status as a daughter in the national family would be complemented by her role as self-sacrificing national mother.

Within this rhetoric of the national family, the CCP is chief mourner maintaining family obligations to the nation's war-dead, as a virtuous Chinese would in the ancient rituals of ancestor worship. As members of the national family dead heroes warrant regular commemoration from other family members. At her hometown museum opening, senior Marshall, Zhu De (1886–1976), penned a calligraphic epithet declaring that 'The revolutionary hero, martyr Zhao Yiman, is immortal.' Death as a wartime hero secures eternal life; but, such state-sanctioned immortality demands participation by ordinary people to be realised. Everyone must contribute to 'never-forgetting' their deceased national family members.

The total propaganda system of the PRC requires the cultivation of knowledge about appropriate immortalising processes among audiences – they form an ongoing pedagogical relationship with the immortal one. In the consumption of Zhao Yiman tales, audiences are drawn into an educational paradigm in which they read/view narratives about Zhao, persuading others of the veracity of the CCP's plans and, in the process, are being themselves simultaneously transformed. In the propaganda system's dramatisation (and fictionalisation) of war history, readers/viewers experience Zhao Yiman's passion. Emotive descriptions of her dangerous underground guerrilla life, the daring of her battles, the pain of her forced separation from her son and the repeated and often-graphic narrations of her torture and interrogation, all bring excitement and tension to the lesson being taught. Otherwise dry political lessons about patriotism become emotional journeys that show the reader/viewer how to transform themselves under CCP guidance and how to re-transform when the message changes.

Since 1949, Zhao Yiman's story has taught two contradictory messages. In the early years of her propaganda life, immediately after the PRC state was formed, Zhao was heralded as a patriotic forerunner for women's equal participation in society and labour – a symbol of Mao's famous epithet that 'women hold up half the sky'. Her leadership in that most manly of work, war fighting, was presented as reflecting the CCP's broader campaign to transform the country's gender relations. In these early years, she often explicitly advocates for women's rights. In the twenty-first century, the CCP-state has promoted 'traditional' family values and social harmony over revolutionary change. The lessons audiences learn from engaging in the immortalisation of Zhao Yiman have altered accordingly. Marriage and motherhood have become central to the quantification of the glory of the female guerrilla warrior. Zhao's sacrifice to the nation is now amplified by the 'double burden' of a soldier mother that makes her martyrdom immeasurably weightier than that of her male counterparts.[3] This chapter shows how the PRC's total propaganda system, with its desire to reach every single citizen, actively teaches its messages of patriotism and loyalty to the CCP's leadership through presentation of images of extreme sacrifice by women. In this case a woman who abandons her infant son to join the guerrilla forces in a region where they are hopelessly outnumbered by the enemy. Depictions of maternal sacrifice by a guerrilla fighter and CCP member brings the day-to-day hardship of warfare directly into the family unit and in the wake of the emotions produced audiences learn how to appreciate the CCP's dedication to China.

From radicalised youth to guerrilla martyr

Zhao Yiman was born in 1905 in Baiyangzui Village, Sichuan, to the family of a local doctor. One of eight children, she would change her name several times during her life with each shift marking a transformation in her ideological growth. Originally named Li Shuduan, she adopted the name, Li Kuntai, on entering school. When she joined the Socialist Youth League she called herself Li Yizhao or Li Shuning and once she began her military work in the North East she used the alias, Zhao Yiman.[4]

Zhao was drawn into politics through left-wing journals and newspapers brought into the family home by her elder sister and brother-in-law. In 1923, with their support, she joined local communist youth groups where she began her revolutionary activism. By 1924 she had published an emotive denunciation of her eldest brother for his refusal to fund her education. In the article, the 19-year-old Zhao called all 'sisters of the world' to be indignant at her brother's backwardness.[5] Her passion was evident in a text dotted with exclamation marks. The article was published in the radical left-wing women's newspaper *Women's Weekly*. Zhao's entrance into public politics was completed when she formally joined the CCP in 1926 and was sent to the Central Military and Political Academy in Wuchang.[6] As we saw in Chapter 4 on Xie Bingying, this academy emerged from the brief alliance between Chiang Kai-shek's Nationalist Party and the CCP known as the First United Front (1924–1927), which aimed to build a strong military and political force to unite a fragmented China. The terms of the United Front, as engineered by the international socialist organisation, the Comintern, to which both the Nationalist Party and the CCP were tied, meant that the CCP joined the Nationalists en bloc and in effect became a party within a party. This collaboration lasted until April 1927 when the Nationalists brutally purged the communists from their ranks in a nation-wide campaign. CCP members fled into hiding but many lost their lives. Leading left-wing activist and editor of the newspaper that had published

Zhao's article in defence of women's education, Xiang Jingyu (1895–1928), was captured and executed as part of this purge.[7]

Zhao Yiman escaped China in September of 1927 and made her way to Moscow to study at the Comintern's Sun Yat-sen University where Chinese socialists, including many Nationalist Party members like Chiang Kai-shek's son, were being educated in internationalist and socialist political leadership. Zhao's unique educational opportunity was curtailed when she became pregnant to fellow student and CCP member, Chen Dabang (1900–1966).[8] Radical ideas about free love circulated among the Chinese students in Moscow and the relative shortage of women meant that few went without partners – unwanted pregnancies were frequent.[9] Sheng Yueh writes that 'All of them [the pregnant women] came under heavy fire from the Party branch . . .. [which] had taken the position that Communist women must not bear children.'[10] Since abortion was legal in the USSR many chose this solution but a nursery for 'little revolutionaries' also operated for those that kept their babies.[11] Zhao Yiman did not follow either course and instead returned to China in the winter of 1928–1929 to have the baby. There is considerable confusion about the timing of her marriage, her departure from Moscow and the birth of her baby. None of the official histories of Zhao Yiman discuss whether her 'illegal' pregnancy was the sole reason for the termination of her studies. Her poor health and the extreme cold of the Moscow winter are mentioned. The status of her relationship with Chen Dabang is also unclear. Did they formally marry before she left Moscow or was theirs another of the very common de facto bonds that formed between radical youth in these years?

On returning to China she worked in the CCP underground in Jiangxi and Shanghai building networks that faced annihilation from Chiang's ongoing campaign to exterminate 'leftists and radicals' – a process that included the execution of many women who were deemed to be radicals just for the bobbed cut of their hair. It was still an extremely dangerous time for all progressive women when she returned and as we saw Chapter 4 on Xie Bingying, even non-communist women from the Military and Political Academy feared for their lives. Constantly on the move to avoid capture, Zhao gave birth to her baby and cared for him in dire circumstances – short of food and oftentimes unable to secure shelter, the baby's early months were extremely difficult. Ultimately, in 1930 Zhao sent her infant son to live with his paternal uncle – she was unable to care for him and continue her political work. Mother and son would never see each other again.

With the Japanese military's increasing aggression in China's North East, Zhao Yiman was sent to Shenyang and Harbin to work as a labour organiser, where she participated in the famous Harbin Tram Workers' strike. Her involvement in the resistance against the Japanese and their Manchukuo government extended into the rural areas in 1934 when the CCP sent her to politicise

Figure 6.1 Zhao Yiman and son: their last and only photo together, 1930

peasant women in Zhu He County outside Harbin.[12] After leading the 'women's work' section she became party secretary of Zhu He north. In 1935 she formed anti-Japanese self-defence units among the peasants in the county and launched guerrilla attacks against the Japanese military. From here she was promoted to political commissar in the North East Democratic United Army for Resistance against the Japanese – Third Army, Second Unit. The United Resistance comprised volunteer troops of local people and communist activists from elsewhere in China – Chiang Kai-shek's Nationalist Party government had downplayed Japan's occupation of North East China in a bid to concentrate its energies on eradicating the communists and in anticipation of building his military capacity.[13] In contrast, the CCP presented itself to the public as the patriotic defenders of China's border integrity even though United Resistance forces were hopelessly outnumbered throughout Manchukuo. Zhao's Second Unit was no exception and in October of 1936 they were surrounded, and Zhao was injured in battle and captured. Tortured and interrogated by the Japanese, she was executed on 5 July 1937 aged 32 years.[14]

Teaching and learning and the warrior woman

The CCP state developed Zhao Yiman initially as a model of the 'soldier educator' and later as a 'mother-soldier educator'. Undertaking ideological work among civilians is a duty required of every soldier and deemed central to military success. Communist military personnel are trained not only in combat techniques and discipline, but also in persuading ordinary people to support their cause. Soldiers, ideally, integrate themselves with the people and become naturally interconnected with them. A 'fish and water' metaphor is used to explain this relationship. Fish (the communist troops) cannot live without water (the people). The ideological objective of this proximity is to educate the people so that they understand the rationality and benefits likely to accrue from supporting the CCP. It is not sufficient to win the military battle – a communist warrior must win the hearts and minds of the masses. Zhao Yiman's prestige as a female communist guerrilla is constructed around her exemplification of both military skill and pedagogical talent.

The screening of the *Zhao Yiman* movie on 1 July 1950 served as the first major opportunity for guerrilla Zhao to become a teaching and learning device – the date marked the twenty-ninth anniversary of the founding of the CCP.[15] *Zhao Yiman* was given pride of place with this anniversary screening amongst all the films produced in the first months of 'new China's' existence as a nation-state. The film encapsulated the CCP's ideology that linked the battles that gave birth to the nation with the promise of future prosperity through 'the inevitable mass support' the CCP's righteous policies would elicit. And it was no accident that film was the medium in which this connection of past and present was celebrated. In the first months of the PRC's existence the central government dedicated considerable resources to developing the state-run film sector. Party leaders saw film as the most important tool for large-scale propaganda. Using studios in Shanghai, Beijing and Shenyang they produced over twenty-six films in the first eighteen months of the formation of their new state. Commentators on the film industry routinely cited Lenin, Stalin, Mao Zedong and Liu Shaoqi, showing that communist leaders around the world recognised that 'Of all cultural forms, movies are the most important.' They reflect the spirit of the masses and their lives and struggles – they are 'the most powerful tools for educating the masses in order to raise their political, ideological and cultural levels'.[16] As Paul Clark noted, the party's messages could be delivered consistently at each screening – this contrasted with its earlier use of drama troupes that sometimes altered the script or show in response to audience demands.[17]

Zhao Yiman, directed by Sha Meng (1907–1964) from the North East film studio, stands prominent among these early PRC propaganda film efforts.[18] The official news media kept readers up to date with progress on the film reporting in June 1949 even before the official declaration of the PRC in October 1949 that the script for the movie was complete and filming was under way.[19] Throughout the movie, audiences are left in no doubt that the 'army and the people are one family'. The socialist realist characterisation techniques, in which characters have clear national, class and political loyalties advanced in Mao Zedong's 1942 'Yan'an Talks on Literature and Art' are evident throughout the film. The Japanese, collaborators and traitors are physically deformed, animalistic, stupid or callous brutes. In contrast, the communist and their peasant supporters are cheerful, kind, unified and loyal. In preparation for the film's release, a Zhao Hongben comic book tie-in was published titled *Woman Hero of the North East, Zhao Yiman*.[20] The pedagogical function of the film and its comic book are evident through their scripts but also in the media accompanying the film's screening.[21]

Both these foundational documents in the Zhao narrative discuss her skill in teaching diverse types of people – workers, peasants and even collaborators and Japanese soldiers. Zhao's propaganda is depicted as being effective on men and women, young and old and under her guidance their positive attributes are nurtured. The movie includes a scene where an elderly farmer shares all his tobacco with the communist troops billeted in the village. His wife comments that until he received Zhao's training he would never have shared such a large quantity of his precious tobacco. Similarly, Zhao is depicted as eliciting the best labour from the peasants by modelling her own hard work. The young peasant women sewing soldiers' uniforms and shoes spend all day in the hot sun because they are hiding from the Japanese amongst the corn fields and unable to work in the shade of the village. Despite their hardship they compete with each other with protestations of 'I'm not tired!', 'Neither am I!' These newly propagandised peasants all recognise that Zhao Yiman works harder and longer than all of them and that she has grown thinner as a result of her dedication.

Her persuasive talents are not even diminished by the impact of torture on her body. After her initial interrogation, the Japanese decide to revive her with the goal of trying to 'crack' her at a later date. She is hospitalised and while rehabilitating Zhao propagandises the righteousness of the CCP cause to the nurse responsible for her care, Han Yongyi, and the sentry guard charged with her security, Dong Xianxun. Both these young collaborators are persuaded by her ardent lessons in patriotism, and her strength of resolve, particularly after she survived a second round of brutal torture and interrogation. Together, Han and Dong facilitate her escape and decide to join the communists themselves. Their escape is hampered by a terrible storm and all three are recaptured. During their time in prison, Zhao propagandises further and her comrade prisoners mourn as she leaves the jail shouting her loyalty to the CCP ('Long Live the CCP!') and cursing her captors ('Down with Japanese Imperialism!'). Zhao is led out to her execution a heroic and resolute communist whose educational efforts include propagandising for the CCP right to the very last minutes of her life.

The accompanying comic book even includes a frame where, prior to her imprisonment, Zhao educates a group of captured Japanese soldiers about the criminality of their invasion of China. One picture depicts Zhao pointing her index finger directly at the captured Japanese as villagers stand by and watch the lesson. The soldiers were deliberately taken alive in order to be the object of communist teachings and their re-education is conducted in front of the gathered peasants.[22] Later readers of the comic book have a participatory panoptical view as they observe the educational experience from all sides and are educated themselves in turn. The book's final frame depicts the North East Martyrs' Museum in Harbin with crowds of ordinary citizens (just like the readers themselves) moving into and around the building. Readers are told that the street leading to the museum was called Yiman Road[23] – a navigation service that further facilitates their appreciation of themselves as potential visitors participating in immortalising the glorious daughter of the PRC.

The CCP's national newspaper, the *People's Daily*, dedicated much space to teaching its readers about the correct way to respond to Zhao Yiman's story. Film reviews were useful vehicles. Qiu He's lengthy review told readers that the movie shows that ordinary people from all walks of life and in all parts of the countryside were resolute in their resistance to the Japanese after the 'bandit Chiang Kai-shek had betrayed the nation and given Manchuria to them'. These ordinary people did not fear starvation, bitterness, beatings, or extremes of cold or even death in their struggle against the Japanese. In this lengthy and dramatic report, readers are told of the central role of the CCP in training Zhao's courage and political consciousness, and then directly connects her story to the readers' own experiences of learning how to develop similar qualities. The paper reprints her final report to her CCP command on the night before her execution – dedicated to the last minute she expresses 'the fearlessness and nobility of CCP members'.

The enemy is about to execute me. I am already prepared for this. In the end, I have examined myself, and my conscience is clear and at peace, my thoughts are directed to my beloved party, to the great struggle of the people against the Japanese, and to my fellow warriors. Today, I offer my life, and use my last act to report to the party. I proudly hold my head high, and offer my life to my troubled nation.[24]

In this expression of resolve and certainty in the validity of her sacrifice, Zhao Yiman, according to Qiu He, 'manifests the Bolshevik spirit'. The origins of this spirit are explicitly outlined for readers: 'This spirit was nurtured through her experience of being educated by the Party and through undergoing a long period of training and exercise.'[25] Zhao is described as a 'model' worthy of ordinary people's emulation but in addition to this direct deployment of her in the form of a USSR Stakhanovite propaganda model she is also presented as demonstrating the CCP as virtuous leaders – in contrast to other political contenders, such as Chiang Kai-shek's Nationalist Party.

Celebrity was another useful vehicle for instructing citizens on how they could correctly transform themselves by participating in commemorating Zhao Yiman. Shi Lianxing (1914–1984) gained huge fame playing Zhao in the movie and won Best Actress prize at the fifth International Film Festival held in the Czech Republic city of Karlovy Vary in 1951. On her return to China Shi Lianxing published an article in the *People's Daily* explaining the importance of the party in her career success. 'This award belongs to the Party, to Chairman Mao and to the Chinese people,' Shi declared. The article explains how the 'guidance and nurturing' of the party and Mao were central to her achievements. She began acting in Ruijin's Worker-Peasant Theatre Troop and then entered the Gorky Theatre School and performed with various troops within the communist base areas in the 1930s and 1940s. Although she only joined the CCP in 1948 she was active in the left-wing art scene from the beginning of her career.[26] By 1951, she expresses her complete and utter dedication to the CCP. 'The Party educated me and helped me to overcome petty bourgeois thinking, and to serve the workers, the peasants and the soldiers . . . the Party is always guiding us, wanting us to listen to the criticism of the masses . . . and so, we progress everyday under our Party's guidance.'[27]

Shi explains that in 1947 she participated in land reform in the liberated areas and came to appreciate Zhao Yiman's spirit of forming close bonds with the people and correctly carrying out the party's missions. She reveals that her own experiences with the army formed the basis of her portrayal of Zhao's armed struggle but that it was more difficult to understand how to best perform the scenes in the jail and interrogation. For these Shi turned to those who had experienced such events and sought their advice – former prisoners of war. Shi Lianxing expressed joy at the new nation's formation and recognised that she needed further training and declared that she would continue to practice, practice and practice again. Her closing lines to the article reiterate Zhao's pedagogical role. 'My deepest respect goes to the good daughter of the Party, the heroine of the Chinese people, CCP member Zhao Yiman! My heartfelt thanks to you because by acting as you I learned from you!'[28]

The *People's Daily* continues its lesson on Zhao Yiman and builds a direct emotional connection through the publication of a letter to the editor by a middle school student, Zhao Qi. The student explains that s/he was deeply moved on reading Shi Lianxing's 'Heartfelt Thanks' article. Zhao Qi says that Shi's portrayal of Zhao Yiman calling the masses to battle with her gun held high 'left a deep impression on my heart'. Through reading Shi's article about learning to act as Zhao Yiman, the middle-school student, Zhao Qi learned the 'correct creative method and spirit'. Shi Lianxing was praised for observing and learning from real life and for undertaking a process of self-correction.[29] At the heart of all the embedded layers of teaching and learning rests the CCP. Zhao Yiman learned from the CCP; Shi Lianxing learned from the CCP and Zhao Yiman; and Zhao Qi learned from them all.

Other comics and storybooks of the 1950s and 1960s followed very similar patterns. For example, Wang Xuanqiu's 1961 comic book version of her life emphasises her power to mobilise the people to military action against the Japanese and teach them why they should support the CCP. In keeping with her role as teacher, the book concludes with a frame in which children are gathered around her portrait while an older youth holding a long pointer directs their attention to Zhao's face and declares: 'The martyr's spirit, forever inspires people advancing along the road of socialist reconstruction!'[30] Socialist reconstruction involved reform of all aspects of family and social organisation.

Changing ideals of womanhood – from worker to mother

For the CCP's propaganda system Zhao Yiman exemplifies the role that soldiers play as advocates for the communist cause and its desire to achieve concrete social benefits for the population – among them improving the status and rights of women. For most of the first four decades after 1949, the CCP promoted women's involvement in the paid workforce, challenging age-old customs about the division of male and female spheres as 'outside' and 'inside' of the home, respectively. Radical social experiments with agricultural and industrial production and the formation of communes through the 1950s and 1960s made dramatic changes to the connections between the home, labour and production. Communal kitchens and childcare were supposed to obviate the

Figure 6.2 Zhao Yiman, guerrilla fighter

need for women's domestic work within the family home and release them for farm and factory labour. In Zhao Hongben's 1950 comic book, Zhao Yiman advises women villagers: 'We women must organise ourselves, unite together to join the movement to save the nation. Only in this way can we give full reign to women's strength and fight for women's social status!'[31] By the start of the Great Leap Forward in 1958, Zhao Yiman's capacity to hold up half the sky with any male comrade was used to bring more women into 'productive labour'. The overall educational project was 'To liberate women's labour power in achieving "greater, faster, better and more economical results" in the service of building socialism'.[32] Zhao Yiman was the model for encouraging women to participate in agricultural labour because she manifested the spirit of dedication, sacrifice and willingness to step beyond the domestic realm.[33]

When Deng Xiaoping took control of the nation his new government instituted a series of economic and political reforms from the 1980s that moved away from the radical social experiments of the previous decades. Deng's policies saw the closure of thousands of unprofitable factories and the lay-off of millions of workers, leading the government to celebrate women's unpaid domestic work and special skills in homemaking – eulogised as 'flower vases and housewives' once more.[34] Zhao's status as a mother-teacher became more important in her story as China's leaders promoted domestic options for women. In the twenty-first century, this trend has continued apace with rising numbers of women aspiring to housewife status within the nationally promoted dream of achieving 'moderately prosperous households'. The CCP now presents itself as the producer and defender of family stability and prosperity rather than radical reformer of domestic relationships.

The discovery of Zhao's son enabled the government to instruct its population in the ever-changing 'correct' connections between individuals, families and the party-state. As a working *mother* revolutionary guerrilla Zhao became useful to the CCP in new ways. She has enabled the CCP to position and reposition itself in relation to motherhood, childhood and the importance of family units in a constant evolution of family policy. Many of the texts on Zhao Yiman now feature a picture of her seated on a cane chair holding her infant son. The boy, Chen Yexian (1928–1982), rightly assumed his mother to be dead. Both Yexian and his father, Chen Dabang, saw the movie *Zhao Yiman* but had no idea that the woman depicted was their mother and wife. The discovery came to light in 1952 when Zhao's elder sister, a CCP cadre in Sichuan, located her sister's history through the North East CCP military offices. She sent a letter to them explaining that her sister had studied in Moscow in 1927 and 1928 but had not contacted her family after returning to China.[35] She enclosed a photograph of the sister she knew as Li Kuntai with as many details about her status and position within the party and the army as she knew. The picture matched those of Zhao held in CCP's file. In an instant, the heroic martyr had a pre-war family history.[36]

Between 1952 and the 1980s the discovery of a husband and son for the revolutionary martyr Zhao Yiman only slightly altered the official use of her story. Until the 1980s the party wanted to have its model soldiers and citizens primarily linked emotionally to the CCP and the nation. The minimising of family sentiment in the Zhao Yiman propaganda prior to the 1980s was in keeping with the CCP's desire to replace the family bonds with political and institutional bonds. Emotional connections between comrades, citizens and the CCP were emphasised. But from the 1980s onwards the CCP uses Zhao Yiman to position itself as a conduit for legitimising emotional links between mothers and children. While the propaganda from the pre-1980s and post-1980s both depict the nobility of individuals who sacrifice their families to the CCP and the nation, the texture of the sacrifice differs between the two periods. Prior to the 1980s Zhao Yiman's relinquishing of her son to the care of the baby's paternal uncle is presented as a pragmatic decision. The choice was not particularly difficult given the exigencies of the crisis facing the country and the dedication she felt to serving the CCP. The CCP's official mouthpiece, the *People's Daily*, makes no mention of her status as a mother or her son's existence until 1993 – even though it was a known fact from 1952. Those depictions of her life that do discuss her identity as mother of Chen Yexian tread a delicate path of recognising her sacrifice as a mother but minimising the maternal emotions relative to those she feels for the party and for China. On balance, the pre-1980s propaganda presents the story that *naturally* her love of the CCP came above any love she felt for her son. However, from the 1980s onwards, the CCP's liberalising 'opening and reform' policies centring around the ideal of happy and contented families benefitting from a 'moderately prosperous society' required them to be advocates for familial bonds. The more maternal aspects of Zhao Yiman are highlighted. In this new context the CCP becomes a sympathetic supporter of families. It recognises the primary bond between mother and child and is a grateful recipient of the mother-soldier's sacrifice. The son, Chen Yexian, becomes the emotional voice of the party's gratitude to Zhao for her sacrifice.

When her status as a mother is mentioned in the first significant biographies and school readers produced in the later 1950s they show greater weighting of the bonds between mother and party rather than mother and son as demanded of good communists at this time. Zhang Lin and Shu Yang's 1957 book, simply called *Zhao Yiman*, reprinted many times and used as the basis for Wang Xuanqiu's 1961 comic, provides a core template for the management of mother-soldiers and married comrades. Good comrades do not willingly let their personal lives interfere with their professional, political and military lives. Zhang and Shu explain that Zhao Yiman found herself subject to a series of misfortunes after one crucial decision to form a relationship with Chen Dabang – but her later action to abandon the child corrected the error of this initial mistake. In this version Zhao and Chen met on the boat journey to Moscow and within half a year announced that they would marry.

Her close comrades advised her against marriage because one could only have one love in one's life and now was not the time to think about one's personal life. Zhao laughed it off indifferently. Precisely because she didn't want her personal life to consume any more of her energy she made this hasty decision. But, things turned out contrary to her wishes and one blow followed another. She got pregnant, fell sick, and terminated her studies.[37]

Luckily, Chen was very obliging and considerate. Zhao was extremely annoyed by the situation and found married life dull and unchallenging.

She was extremely competitive by nature and rejected the idea that she could be conquered by anyone. She wanted to break free of the state of inertia. So without consulting her husband, she resolved to return to China. She was the kind of person that made rapid decisions, even if they sometimes appeared rash, but once they were made she never regretted and never looked back because hesitation was worse than haste.[38]

The story of her work after returning to China focuses on her activities in a port town with the CCP underground, helping comrades move around the country. They explain how she suffered prejudice and discrimination as a young, pregnant woman – but her work was important to the survival of the communists who faced the Nationalists purges, so she continued relentless in her dedication. Just as she went into labour the landlord locked her out of her rooms in fear for her own reputation. After much pressure, she allowed Zhao Yiman back into the house to give birth. One line of the text explains that the baby was born and the next sentence moves to the troubles that the party was experiencing and Zhao's own escape with her newborn.[39] From here the narrative provides readers with the story of Zhao overcoming the hardship of living an itinerant life with a baby and without money. The baby becomes increasingly ill and cries continually. She struggled to maintain her links with the fragmenting party organisation as the mother of a sick child so she resolved to send the baby away. Her maternity is a hardship that allows the manifestation of her true deep dedication to the party. In this version her final words as she faces execution are for the party – no mention of her son.

In 1959 Wen Ye and Zang Xiu's *Anti-Japanese Hero Zhao Yiman* is also matter-of-fact about her parenting decisions. A short twenty-seven-page reader, *Anti-Japanese Hero* explains her decision to relinquish her son in a few brief sentences. The scene is set in which her work became dangerous and put her son at risk so: 'Not long afterwards she sent the child to Hunan to her husband's family to be raised by Chen Dabang's elder brother. Although she was loath to part with her child, she had to do it for her work and for the revolutionary enterprise. From this point they would never see each other again.'[40] Chen Yexian's identity was well established and formally recognised by the publication of this book but readers are not drawn into the emotional and personal lives of the martyred hero – instead they are taught of her love for the party.

The post-1980s' narratives make motherhood and family harmony central to her women warrior's identity. As readers of the *People's Daily* in 1995 learn, 'Women are the mothers of humankind and hold up half the sky. Women soldiers are the most progressive and organised of mothers.' Their advanced standing comes through their work in liberating all women through their profession and in 'giving free reign to the infinite wisdom and breadth of maternal love'.[41] Zhao Yiman, guerrilla mother, is drawn into the government's new-found attention to the virtues of motherhood. Motherhood, previously minimised, regains full emotional power in the new era propaganda through the recalibrating of mother-soldiers, their roles in society and their connection to children.

In 1993 the *People's Daily* published an article that described the emotions of a visitor to a museum where her portrait and other North East martyrs were displayed. The author, Pan Yan, writes about how moving the stories of the revolutionary martyrs were but most heartbreaking of all was 'when we stood in front of the portrait of Martyr Zhao Yiman and heard the tour guide, her eyes brimming with tears, recite the letter Zhao wrote to her son just before her execution'. The recently discovered letter ran:

Ning'er [Chen's baby name], your mother has sacrificed her life today in order to resolutely fight against Manchukuo and the Japanese! Mother has no chance to say goodbye to you .... I hope that you, Ning'er, can grow up quickly and comfort your buried mother and after you have grown up I hope that you will not forget that your mother sacrificed herself for the nation.[42]

Lest the readers miss the lesson to be learned from this invocation of a mother's grief, Pan Yan reminds us: 'In this letter are the last words of Martyr Zhao Yiman to her son. Does it not also stand as a hopeful reminder to us, from all those countless revolutionary martyrs?'[43] The female warrior martyr, Zhao Yiman, is mobilised to forge an emotional bond between the masses, the party and the nation *through* her motherhood.

On its 'discovery' the letter to her son would play a major role in the amplification of her maternity from this point. It apparently came to light from Japanese and Manchukuo papers relating to her interrogation and execution. She was being sent to Zhu He for execution and on the train journey asked the transit guard if she could have pen and paper. After she had written it, the guard submitted it to his superiors as evidence of her crimes and it was included in their military court files – this is how we came to have these 'precious letters from which to educate her descendent'.[44] It is not specified precisely when the letter was discovered. Some sources say 1956[45] and others say 1981.[46] Significantly, the letter is not discussed in any of the propaganda until 1993 but few biographies of her published after this year fail to mention her last heart-wrenching missive. A number of variations on the letter have been reproduced. In 1996 a CCP publishing house in Guangxi Province included a new version of Zhao's letter in a compilation of martyrs' farewell letters to their families and friends. This 1996 version includes the additional line, 'Mother doesn't need to teach you with thousands of words, but instead teaches you by actions.'[47] This line reinforces her triple burden as a warrior, teacher and virtuous mother. Wen Ye's 2005 book has Zhao Yiman exhorting her son to be a good student. 'Study hard my child, that is your mother's last thread of hope.' This twenty-first-century letter suits the current parenting model recommended in the 'moderately prosperous society' ideology where mothers become like the ancient Confucian icon of Mencius' mother – attentive teachers for their children.[48] As the CCP's presentation of itself to the Chinese people changes so do the 'artefacts' of their martyrs.

Propaganda around Zhao Yiman boomed in 2005 – the centenary of her birth. The *People's Daily* included an article with a picture of one of Zhao Yiman's granddaughters that declared in the most emotional of terms the value of family ties and the tragedy that often befalls the families of martyrs. The authors, Zhu Yu and Bai Ruixue, describe the moment when her son, Chen Yexian, read the letter from his mother as follows:

Twenty years have passed. And it has been twenty years since the martyr gave her life in the service of the nation. A mother finally calls to her son, and her adult son finally knows that the mother he hasn't seen since he was small sacrificed herself! With that final letter from his mother, Chen Yexian could not control himself! A mother's love cannot be forgotten! A nation's hatred and family revenge cannot be forgotten! Chen Yexian took some ink and using a needle he repeatedly carved the characters "Zhao Yiman" onto his left arm.[49]

Zhu and Bai remind readers of their own happy family situations in contrast to the children of martyrs who gave their lives in the creation of the current happiness that China's citizens enjoy in the 2000s.

A new movie was released to mark her centenary celebration too. In *My Mother, Zhao Yiman*, director Sun Tie achieves new heights in his romanticising the sacrificing mother-soldier.[50] The adult son narrates the movie and speaks directly to his mother in emotive, lilting tones. The son-narrator provides the common voice threading through the movie and is positioned as watching his mother's suffering *as she is experiencing it* with mournful exclamations such as 'Mother, so much suffering!' The audience of the film is simultaneously hearing a son agonising over his mother's suffering and seeing her suffering. The layering of familial emotion over the story of the woman guerrilla fighter touches new audience needs in early twenty-first-century China. Appeals to abstract ideological and revolutionary ideals are no longer adequate for bonding the party to the people. Instead, family bonds are used as proxies for patriotic feelings – the party situates itself in the role of a clan elder presiding over the emotional world of the family of heroes.

The same year, a new book on her life was published – Wen Ye's 2005 sole authored *The Spirit of the Hero That Shed Blood in a Just Cause: A Biography of Zhao Yiman*.[51] It dedicates an entire chapter to Zhao's separation from her son – albeit with the reminder of her continued duty. Unlike previous books this one describes the separation in the chapter title: 'Chapter 16: After mother and child separate she continues to work in Shanghai'. This twenty-first-century version depicts her marriage to Chen but makes no mention of the CCP's resistance to romance. Instead, it explains that in order to prevent their romance disturbing their studies, Zhao and Chen resolved to marry to regain some stability. Wen says they married in April 1928. The story of the happy communist family deepens under Wen's pen. The marriage apparently did have the desired stabilising effect and they formed a loving couple that cherished each other and formed a happy household. Husband and wife helped each other progress in their studies. Zhao Yiman was a good housewife and organised their outings and their expenditure; she was frugal and clean. Despite all their happiness, Wen Ye explains that she suffered from a lung infection and fell pregnant leaving her body weak, so during the summer the school sent her to a hospital to recover, and although she improved, once she returned to Moscow and resumed her studies her health took a further bad turn.[52]

Within Wen's story the CCP's twenty-first-century modern 'moderately comfortable' family appears in full glory with the CCP as its guardian. The party organisation knew that she was unable to study and that the Moscow winter was detrimental to her health so it allowed her to return to China early. There was a pressing need for cadres to mobilise women so she would not be idle. Wen's text explains that the party was concerned for her health and her career, and rather than *ordering* her return to China for an illegitimate pregnancy, *allowed* her to come back early. It was a rational decision taken in the best interests of the mother, a party professional.

Once they heard the news, they were really sad. How could this newly married husband part from her? He also worried about how she would work with such a weak body on her return home. So they discussed the matter together and considered waiting until the child was born in order to return to China together. The critical state of her health meant that requesting permissions from the Party organization to delay her return would be reasonable – it would not be regarded as disobeying an order. But, Yiman's Party spirit was very strong and she had never before bargained with the [party] organization so she said to her husband: "Love must be subordinated to the revolutionary enterprise. Even if I suffer, I want to follow the party's needs. The child can be born back in China."[53]

This imagined scenario establishes the party as capable of being rational and caring of the couple's relationship, her health and their baby. It also posits the husband and wife as a team working together to advance China's prospects. They love each other, share each other's joys and hardships, learn together and sacrifice together. This collaborative and consultative couple completely replaces the 1957 depiction of Zhao Yiman as unilaterally making the decision to return regardless of her husband's wishes. The reality of CCP women's harsh experiences in Moscow is elided completely.[54]

The process of her labour and delivery alone with the unfriendly landlord is also discussed but this time with more specific detail – the baby was born on 21 January 1929 (most other sources place Chen Yexian's birthday as

December 1928). She called him Li Shining since he was born on the 5th anniversary of Lenin's death.[55] The amplification of maternal love manifest in the 2005 movie also occurs in Wen Ye's book. After the birth, Zhao has no milk and the baby cries incessantly in hunger. Zhao was losing her mind and decided to throw the baby into a nearby river to end their misery. She stands at the riverside but:

The baby's cries tugged at her heart and seemed to be calling "Mama". She then thought about her husband far away in a foreign land and thought if she threw the baby into the river, how could she ever face him again. Her deep feelings of motherly love and longing for her husband, ultimately prevailed and she calmed down and she carried the crying sleepy baby home.[56]

Wen Ye's book includes an essay from a communist active in Shanghai with Zhao Yiman at this time and it narrates how she continued to work with the baby in tow and how comrades in Shanghai tried to help her. But, feeding the baby was a problem since they couldn't find a wet nurse. The story of Zhao balancing political work and a perpetually hungry baby continues for several pages until we reach the chapter dedicated to her decision to give up the baby. Wen Ye explains that she was heartbroken by the decision – taking the famous photo of mother and child to send to father Chan Dabang. These dramatic descriptions of her motherhood from the 1990s contrast markedly with the rather perfunctory treatment of this theme in earlier years.

The emotional life of the son is also given play in Wen Ye's narrative. He explains, although not in great detail, that Chen Yexian was 12 years old before he knew of his tragic early years. Wen Ye notes that Chen was completely shaken by the news and it affected him badly his whole life. He would suffer repeated psychological problems through high school and university.[57] Wen Ye was not exaggerating Chen Yexian's suffering, as his colleagues would attest only two years later.

Chen graduated from high school and moved to Beijing to attend the People's University – at this point he assumed his mother was another of the many CCP members lost in the wars that had ravaged China. In 1955, three years after the discovery of Zhao Yiman's original identity, her son Chen Yexian, then in his mid-20s, was awarded compensation for his mother's sacrifice – a privilege he refused to accept. A year later he graduated and was assigned to work at the Beijing Industry Institute as a lecturer in politics. His colleague at the university, Yuan Baoshan, reminisced in a series of articles published in 2007 that as a young lecturer Chen fell in love with a student in one of his classes, Zhang Youlian, and immediately upon her graduation they married. Zhang gave birth to their daughter in 1959 but the marriage started to unravel. They divorced and the pressure was too much for Zhang, who suffered a psychiatric illness and was unable to work. Chen's situation was not much better. He mismanaged his salary, slumped into depression and was hospitalised. He remarried the still-unstable Zhang and they had a second daughter even as Zhang moved in and out of hospital. The tumultuous Cultural Revolution descended upon this already fraught situation. In 1966 rebellious student factions within the university accused the CCP leaders of 'oppressing the son of a revolutionary martyr' – Chen. In retribution for their crimes against Zhao Yiman's son these Red Guards physically beat the university's party secretary and deputy party secretary. However, typically for those times it was not long before Chen himself was accused of being 'anti-party' and placed under house arrest in his staff quarters. By 1969 the university was closed down and all staff were sent to work in factories. Chen was still working in this assigned task, becoming increasingly morose, unkempt, malnourished and isolated when he committed suicide in 1982.[58]

As if his own troubles were not enough, Chen Yexian's birth father also suffered during these years. Father and son had not formed close ties after years of separation and only came back into contact after Yexian's graduation. Chen Dabang, long-serving communist, was locked up as a counterrevolutionary during the Cultural Revolution as well.[59] Chen Dabang's extensive experience in the USSR and France during the 1930s and 1940s led to accusations that he was a Soviet spy – China and the USSR had become enemies in 1960, making all those with close ties to the one-time ally subject to suspicion. Chen Dabang died in prison – one of many of his generation with similar political credentials to suffer maltreatment and beatings during this period of party purges. Wen Ye's 2005 biography explains that Zhao Yiman's spirit can be comforted by the fact that her two granddaughters have happy families with beautiful lives.[60] No mention is made of the young women's revolutionary credentials – rather, readers are reassured of the return to domestic family happiness for Zhao's descendants.

Conclusion

The propaganda life of Zhao Yiman over the course of seventy years shows us that while the woman warrior remains a teacher of the masses during the entire period, the lessons she transmits are far from uniform. From warrior guerrilla icon to inspiring those around her to join the CCP movement she ends the twentieth century as a model mother, concerned about her son's grades and worrying about how her sacrifice will impact his life. Her capacity to suffer hardship, physical torture, hunger and pain is matched only by her ability to inspire others through her sacrificing of a happy family life. Only in the more liberal twenty-first century do we become aware of the extent of the actual impact of her choice on her son – rendering her maternal sacrifice even more poignant and her warrior's courage more impressive. But consistent throughout her propaganda life is that her active participation in violent acts of warfare is significantly less important than her pedagogical achievements in promoting the virtues of the CCP and its military. War fighting emerges in this narrative as a short-term necessity and in its multiple media recreations one that provides terrain for educating and encouraging more people to come into the light of the CCP's worldview.

7 Negotiating sexual virtue
The glamorous, honey-trap spy, Zheng Pingru

Women's involvement in wartime activities puts them in complex moral positions. Any belligerent activity for either side renders them unconvincing as victims of enemy aggression – the premier feminine role in the myriad reinventions of war. Those who take up arms, women soldiers, are contained within the moral order of gendered warfare as noble, courageous but *unusual* women. Those who trade in secrets are more problematic to manage in the post-war narratives and oftentimes provoke uncomfortable debates about morality, loyalty and sexual virtue. The woman warrior prepared to take a bullet on the front line is a far less ambiguous moral figure than the woman spy who moves information between opposing forces.

Zheng Pingru (1918–1940) is one such contested Nationalist honey-trap spy from the murky world of Shanghai during Japan's occupation of the city. Pingru's mission was to facilitate the assassination of Ding Mocun (1901–1947), a fearsome security chief-*cum*-gangster who was collaborating with the Japanese. Japan attacked Shanghai in mid-1937, extending its ambitions to dominate China and its resources. The Japanese took control of the Chinese sections of the Shanghai in 1937 and at the end of 1941 their control reached Shanghai's foreign settlements – the British controlled International Settlement and the French Concession. Japan remained in charge of the city and its population until the end of World War Two in 1945. In this complex context multiple groups competed to negotiate better terms with the Japanese, resulting in a pro-Japan government being formed in 1940 under the one-time Nationalist Party leader, Wang Jingwei (1883–1944). This 'national' government's members are today still derided as 'collaborators' and 'traitors'. Throughout these years Shanghai was dominated by a brutal group of men, including Ding Mocun, comprising a security apparatus of secret police, assassins and gangsters. Shanghai was a city of drugs, murder, duplicity and terror.

Shanghai's pro-Japan Security Police executed 23-year-old Zheng Pingru in 1940 after a failed assassination attempt on Ding. In 1946, at the end of the War of Resistance against Japan, her execution came to public attention during the trials of 'traitors against the Han people'. In the trial against Ding, her mother, Zheng Huajun, asserted Pingru's integrity as a courageous 'patriotic daughter'[1] and demanded that Ding be held to account for her illegal killing. Ding painted a less glowing picture of the young beauty and the popular press revelled in the stories of sex, spying and glamour manifest by this dead, Shanghai beauty.

Questions about her morality reemerged in the twenty-first century after her story was used as the basis for Ang Lee's influential film, *Lust, Caution* in 2007. Lee's film script was based on Eileen Chang's novella of the same name that fictionalised Zheng's descent into the murky world of intelligence. Eileen drew on her own personal and romantic connections with the collaborationist regime. She wrote and rewrote the piece between the early 1950s and 1979 but it would only achieve international recognition with the 2007 film. Ang Lee's version depicts Pingru's conflicted emotional and sexual relationships with the cruel collaborationist spymaster rather than resolute patriotism, dedication and sacrifice.[2] Outraged, residents of Zheng's hometown, Qingpu, denounced the movie for smearing the integrity of a heroic woman. They constructed a memorial park complete with a statue of her execution to commemorate her 'properly'. The Zheng Pingru debates reveal that unlike the woman warrior, the sexual morals of the female espionage agent are subjected to close public scrutiny – she is a touchstone for boundaries of acceptable feminine morality in ways that the masculinised woman warrior is not.

Sex and spying

The reason that women spies invite this very-public defence of their virtue is because of the perceived close link between spying and prostitution. Prostitution and spying are wryly described as the world's oldest and second oldest professions. The continued currency and geographic spread of this 'joke' reflects the sustained anxiety women of indeterminate or unstable loyalties generate. While men can also work as spies and prostitutes, the term 'profession' usually invokes a *woman* prostitute and a *woman* spy. The joke elevates two derided forms of work, selling sex and selling information, to the ranks of the 'professions' in order to mark their place as roles of the lowest esteem. In this rubric all spies are suspected to be prostitutes and all prostitutes are suspected to be spies.

Feminist scholars have long noted the dangers inherent in the manner in which governments use female spies and the subsequent presentation of women spies in popular media and official propaganda. Tammy Proctor's study on women spies in Europe during World War One argues that the persistent linking of women's espionage roles to illicit sex discredits the professionalism of women as intelligence officers and diminishes their con-tributions to intelligence gathering.[3] Her book presents ample evidence that the majority of women working in intelligence were not involved in any form of sexual entrapment of men. Neither was the 'honey-trap' female agent the sum experience of women in China's spy scene either. Allison Rottman's work on espionage in Shanghai during Zheng Pingru's lifetime reveals a rich variety of espionage and underground work – including carrying messages, materials, money and people in and out of the city.[4]

However, there was clearly a significant assumption that women would be called upon to use their sexuality for espionage work in China during the War of Resistance against Japan. As we saw in the chapter on Aisin Gioro Xianyu, some argued that it was a patriotic duty for women to use their 'natural talents' to help the war effort while others protested the relegation of young women to spying since it robbed them of front-line combat opportunities. It was also debated as a workplace equality issue. In 1940 CCP (Chinese Communist Party) member, Wu Qun, wrote about the callous treatment of young women working in sex spying as part of a broader report on the impact of war work on the reproductive and physical health of women and children. She noted that only unmarried women were eligible for espionage duties. This stipulation led at least one woman to abort a pregnancy (she had just entered her second month) in order to disguise her marriage and ensure herself a place in the espionage team. Wu argues that these regulations limited women's careers unfairly since women should not be discriminated against on the basis of their marital status.[5] The report does not explain why married women were deemed unsuitable for espionage work, but one can surmise that the link between sex and female espionage work would jeopardise the honour of any husband whose wife was involved in such war work.

Women spies threaten to break a gendered moral code that positions the female sex as beacons of sexual virtue and an extension of men's honour, and this produces a generalised anxiety about women's engagement with intelligence work. Proctor describes women espionage agents as risking being trapped in the roles of 'perpetual concubines' and 'sexual servants for the state'.[6] She argues that the link between sex and spying is a powerful and debilitating exaggeration of the actual work of women as wartime spies. In its very pervasiveness and sustained currency, 'sexspionage' requires our atten-tion if we are to unpack the connections between gender and war.

Espionage in Shanghai: Zheng Pingru's world

Loyalty, virtue and treachery are difficult to determine at the best of times but in China during the 1930s and 1940s these qualities became even more problematic. Security and intelligence agents variously infiltrated each other's organisations, crossed over to their former enemy and cooperated with each other in complex schemes of temporary mutual benefit. Nationalists spied on the Communists, the Japanese and the pro-Japanese government of Wang Jingwei – stocked, as it was, by former Nationalist Party agents – and each of these groups spied back on each of the others. So complicated were the intelligence webs of these years that Frederic Wakeman describes the situation as follows:

As a consequence of this fractured clandestine politics, most of which was totally impenetrable to the public, their [secret agents'] ultimate loyalty remained very much in question throughout the war; and despite the extreme polarisation between "warriors" and "traitors" there was not quite the same clarity of choice as one could imagine in the case of the French resistance to the Nazis.[7]

During Zheng Pingru's short life, the espionage world of Japanese-occupied Shanghai included a wide variety of political groups and numerous deadly, nefarious characters. The four key groups operating in the city are as follows. First, the Chiang Kai-shek party-government had its Nationalist Party intelligence agency, the Central Investigation and Statistics Bureau (CSB) and a military wing called the Military Affairs Commission Bureau of Investigation and Statistics.[8] The Nationalist Party agents in Shanghai operated via a series of underground networks through two men, Chen Baohua and Ji Xizong. Employment in the Southeast Bank provided cover for Ji's espionage work. Chen Baohua was embedded in a major faction of Chiang Kai-shek's central leadership group – the 'CC Clique' – through his familial relationships with the clique's key figures, his fraternal cousins, Chen Guofu and Chen Lifu.[9] Chen Lifu was the founder of the CSB.[10]

Second, tenuously allied with the CSB, the CCP also ran its own spy networks in Shanghai. CCP agents mobilised Shanghai's citizens in various relief activities ostensibly in aid of the refugees that flooded into the city but these activities also gathered materials and money for the CCP's New Fourth Army.[11] Work for both the CSB's and the CCP's agents became more difficult when the Japanese extended their control over the 'foreign concessions' on 8 December 1941 – nearly two years after Zheng Pingru's execution. Overlapping with Zheng's time in Shanghai was CCP spy Guan Lu (1907–1982). A reasonably well-known author, Guan was recruited in 1939 by soon-to-be PRC (People's Republic of China) premier Zhou Enlai to infiltrate the pro-Japan security apparatus. She worked closely with the Japanese occupation authorities through a magazine called *Women's Voice* and became close friends with the wives of key figures in the security offices. So successful was she at hiding her secret agent status that at the end of the war she was identified as one of the 'educated traitors' or 'cultural traitors'. Guan escaped jail in the post-1945 round-up when her CCP handler, Zhou

Enlai, evacuated her to communist-held areas. But after the formation of the PRC in 1949 she was repeatedly criticised for her activities in Shanghai and was jailed for ten years – her name was only cleared in 1982 and was followed quickly by her suicide.[12]

The agency that Guan infiltrated was the third, and extremely dangerous, Chinese force operating in Shanghai – the ex-Nationalist Party agents who moved to collaborate with the Japanese during their occupation of the city. On the formation of the Wang Jingwei-headed Reorganised National Government of China in March 1940 the unit was called the Special Work Section. This organisation emerged from the Nationalist Party's own CSB and comprised key agents who moved to support Wang Jingwei.[13] They ran a ruthless operation suppressing dissent and assassinating activists with impunity. These Wang Jingwei agents cooperated with the Japanese military police and operated out of a mansion located at No. 76 Jessfield Road in western Shanghai in an area known as 'the Badlands'. Brothels, nightclubs, gambling halls, drug dens and gangsters ensured that this area of 'illicit pleasures' maintained its not inconsiderable notoriety.[14] The offices at Jessfield Road became simply known as 'No. 76' and it was a much-feared address among ordinary Shanghai residents. Former CCP and Nationalist Party member Li Shiqun headed this unit along with Zheng's target, former Nationalist Party member, Ding Mocun.[15] CCP agent Guan Lu became close friends with Li Shiqun's wife and was a regular figure in the No. 76 social gatherings.

The Japanese Military Police also ran operatives throughout the city in a complex web of different units. The sections that are discussed the most in relation to Zheng Pingru are the Plum Blossom Agency and the Plum Organ, the Special Services group for the Japanese army in East China and the Special Services Corps of the Japanese Military Police.[16] The Japanese agents were coordinated from Hongkou at the northeast edge of the International Settlement – a favoured base for Aisin Gioro Xianyu in the early 1930s, as we saw in Chapter 5. Like their Chinese collaborators, the Japanese spy networks were heavily involved in drug running, protection rackets and general gangsterism – partly to raise revenue and partly to destabilise the foreign concessions so as to justify an expansion of their occupation. The USA and various European governments ran their own espionage agents from Shanghai at this time as well – but they appear to have little connection with Zheng Pingru.

Zheng's death in February 1940 came just before the formal establishment of the Wang Jingwei puppet government in March that same year and well before the formal occupation of the Foreign Concessions by the Japanese military in December of 1941. The political and military landscape was hotly contested and unstable. The world of the spy in Shanghai during the late 1930s and 1940s was sordid and treacherous full of assassinations, betrayals and torture. The threat of assassination and counter-assassination occupied the minds of all the players regardless of their political affiliation. Wakeman summarises the situation as: 'political assassinations soon became a way of life and death in Shanghai, where killing was in the air'.[17]

One such victim of assassination, in the very winter that Zheng Pingru was arrested, was the underground communist woman, Mao Liying. Mao was chair of the Chinese Women's Vocational Joint Friendship Society – a philanthropic front organisation that raised funds and gathered intelligence for the CCP. On 12 December 1939, just as she was leaving the society's offices, she was set upon and shot.[18] Wakeman says that her assassins were so brazen that once they had fought off the police they drove straight back to No. 76 to report to their handlers.[19] Mao was one of the many women underground agents operating in Shanghai outside of the 'honey-trap' mode. She is hailed as a heroic martyr and is buried in the Shanghai Martyrs' Cemetery. Zheng Pingru would have to wait until after the 2007 movie *Lust, Caution* to receive a monumental burial – and this was conducted not in the name of party or nation but in the process of defending *local* honour through asserting the virtue of a 'local woman'.

Zheng Pingru's life and death: the 'facts'

Just a month before the Japanese attacked central Shanghai, Zheng Pingru appeared on the cover of the fashionable Shanghai pictorial magazine, *Young Companion*.[20] This dimple-faced beauty with crimped, bobbed hair and rosy cheeks had come to the publisher's attention through her performances in local university drama performances. Although a student of the Shanghai Political and Legal College, she performed with the Datong University troop in such plays as Tian Han's (1898–1968) 'Father Returns'. Her talents in the performing arts extended to playing the piano and singing Peking Opera and she seemed destined to make a name for herself in Shanghai's glamorous entertainment sector.[21] The advent of war would change her life irrevocably and her acting skills were turned to espionage purposes.

Zheng Pingru also had a particularly valuable set of linguistic skills that, when combined with her acting talents, youth and beauty, made her a particularly attractive espionage 'asset'. The second daughter of Zheng Yue and his Japanese wife Zheng Huajun (Hanako Kimura), Pingru has spent some years in Japan with her mother's family and spoke fluent Japanese. Through her mother, she also had close ties with the elite of the Japanese community in pre-war Shanghai. Her lawyer father was active in politics as a member of the

Figure 7.1 Zheng Pingru featured on the cover of *Young Companion* 130 (1937)

Nationalist Party and had been a member of its forerunner party, Sun Yat-sen's Revolutionary Alliance. During the occupation of Shanghai her father was a prosecutor in the Second High Court of Jiangsu. The family's pro-Chinese position was consolidated after Japan's attacks on China when Pingru's elder brother, Zheng Haizheng, died serving as a pilot in the Nationalist Government's air force.

Zheng's combination of beauty, cultural talents and high-level Shanghai family connections drew her to the attention of the Nationalist Party's CSB.

In 1937, Chen Baohua approached Pingru to join them.[22] Her task was to become close to people like Ding Mocun and key figures in the Japanese Military Police with ties to No. 76. The CSB was keen to secure Ding's assassination through Zheng's information – this was not a simple task because Ding was well protected and always alert to attempts on his life.

Her opportunity to insinuate herself into Ding Mocun's world arrived in March 1939, when the Japanese captured a Nationalist Party's military leader, Xiong Jiandong (?–1946). Xiong's wife, Tang Yijun, approached the CSB to seek clemency for her husband so Chen Baohua introduced Zheng Pingru to Ding Mocun in the role as intermediary for Tang – a young woman pleading clemency on behalf of the older woman. Ding's predilection for young beauties was well known – Pingru was to perform the classic 'honey-trap' role. She presented herself at No. 76 full of charm and elegance and flattered Ding by reminding him that she had been his student while he was the principal at Minguang Middle School. This establishment of a previous connection as a student beholden to her mentor proved to be an effective entrée into his world. Zheng Pingru soon became Ding Mocun's 'girlfriend'.[23]

On 10 December 1939, Zheng informed the CSB that she and Ding Mocun were going on a date that could provide the awaited assassination opportunity. Zheng was to lure Ding to her house and assassinate him there. However, once they arrived at her house, despite Zheng's increasingly amorous advances, Ding did not alight from the car. The plan was foiled and Ding continued safely on his way. A few weeks later, on 21 December, Ding arranged that Zheng accompany him to the home of banker, Pan Sansheng. She immediately arranged with the CSB to make another attempt on Ding's life. The plan was to have Zheng persuade Ding to buy her a fur coat – pretending that it was an impromptu desire resulting from their chance passing of the Siberian Fur Shop on Jing'ansi Road. Two armed assassins waited outside the fur shop on the chance that Zheng would be successful in her persuasion. The plan looked to be proceeding smoothly as Ding indulged his mistress, agreed to the unscheduled shop and exited his bulletproof car. As they entered the shop, Ding noticed two suspicious figures lingering on the street outside and immediately turned on his heels, ran out of the shop and back into his car. Ding leapt into the car with bullets flying and his driver speeding him away to safety. Zheng was left in the store alone.

To keep her cover intact, she rang Ding to show her concern and apologise that her desire to buy a coat had placed him in danger. Ding maintained the fiction that all was normal between them as patron and mistress despite his suspicion of her loyalty. He agreed, on her request, to send her a new tranche of money to cover her ongoing daily expenses. Unbeknown to them both, Ding's superior in No. 76, Li Shiqun, was

informed of the contents of their phone call and Ding's brush with death –
an eventuality that Ding was keen to avoid in the dog-eat-dog world of
No. 76's internal power struggles. On 26 December Zheng Pingru returned
to No. 76, to consolidate her cover as a devoted girlfriend concerned for her
patron's health and happiness. She went accompanied by a Japanese friend,
a member of the Military Police, on the assumption that even No. 76's
agents were scared of the Japanese Military Police. She misjudged and as
soon as she stepped inside the compound, one of Li Shiqun's men arrested
her. Ding was initially unaware of her arrest and, once apprised of her
detention, pretended to be unconcerned about Zheng's fate. Relinquishing
her to his superior, Li Shiqun, Ding tried to salvage any dignity he could
from his lapse in judgment about the reliability of this young beauty.[24]

Held in detention for several weeks, Zheng was interrogated regularly
but seemingly informally. First she faced two women – Shen Gengmei, a
translator, and Yu Aizhen, the wife of gangster Wu Sibao. Zheng Pingrui
confessed that she had initiated the attack but presented it as emerging from
sexual jealousy – she was angry that Ding took other lovers and wanted to
punish him. Soon all the wives of the Wang Jingwei security apparatus
came to visit her – Wang Jingwei's wife, Chen Bijun, Li Shiqun's wife
Ye Jiqing, and Ding Mocun's wife, Zhao Huimin.[25] Apparently, Ding also
came to interrogate her himself.[26] Pingru's brother told the court investigating Ding's treachery in 1946 that she telephoned him to say that she
was being held at No. 76 but not to worry. She asked that he bring her an
outer coat and told him to keep the 'Chop' (signature seal) for the bank
account safe.[27] At the beginning of February Li Shiqun decided that she
should be executed. Indicating that her 'imprisonment' and 'interrogation'
must have been relatively benign, she was told that a group was going on a
picnic – fruit and snacks were purchased and Pingru dressed up for the
occasion. Once the car headed to a small forest outside Shanghai – a killing
ground commonly used by No. 76 – she realised her error and, instead of
begging for her life, asked that her executioners not shoot her face. Li
Shiqun's bodyguard, Wang Jin, shot her in the chest in consideration of her
wishes.[28]

This dramatic narrative remains largely intact across multiple versions of her
life – although some of the dates vary a week or so. However, the narratives
diverge considerably when debating her sexual morality and commitment to
the patriotic cause.

Good girl making a sacrifice

The first attempts to assert her virtue came in 1946 during the post-war trials of
traitors and specifically in the case against Ding Mocun. Zheng's mother and

brother made depositions to the court placing responsibility for her death firmly at the hands of Ding Mocun.[29] Her brother declared on 11 December 1946: 'My sister was killed by Ding Mocun.'[30] In their version of events, Pingru was a young girl trapped in a set of social relationships that left her little room to move. Her vulnerability to the 'system' is amplified alongside the entire family's patriotic credentials. On 16 November 1946 Zheng Pingru's mother presented a formal document to the court about the murder of her daughter. Written in comparatively formal legal language, Zheng Huajun's testimony establishes a familial patriotic lineage commencing with her husband's early anti-Qing activities and his despair at the recent Japanese attacks and ultimate occupation of Shanghai. Her son followed this patriotic dedication to the war effort through his sacrifice in the Nationalist air force. And her daughter, she declared poetically, had 'a patriotic will that exceeded those of bearded men'.[31] The Nationalist Party's underground intelligence unit contacted Pingru in 1937 to join their ranks on the basis of her known dedication to the patriotic cause.

A month later, on 11 December 1946, her brother continued the exegesis on his sister's virtue. Zheng Nanyang explained to the court that Ding and Pingru became connected in March of 1939 when Pingru sought clemency for Xiong Jiandong using her 'old school ties' connection with her former principal. Ding saw her approach as an opportunity to coerce Pingru's father, prosecutor in the Jiangsu High Court, to work for the 'peace movement' – that is, the Wang Jingwei collaborationist government. According to her brother's testimony Ding told Pingru that her father would be killed if he failed to cooperate. Later that year, on 23 November, a colleague of her father's, a judge in the Jiangsu Criminal Court, Yu Hua (1884–1939), was assassinated for his refusal to cooperate with Wang Jingwei's regime. Zheng Nanyang explained to the court that Ding told his sister that this deed was 'Killing a chicken to show the monkeys'.[32] The Nationalist Party's underground agents Ji and Chen then worked with Pingru to assassinate Ding. Within this narrative, Pingru was effectively trapped in Ding Mocun's snare as a result of her loyalty to her father and to China.

In the middle of the trials against Ding, a respected woman educator, scientist and daughter of a military family, Zhang Zhenhua, wrote a letter to the editor of the *Datong bao* that aimed to 'represent the extraordinary injustice Miss Zheng faced and to confirm Ding Mocun's guilt'. Although written as a 'letter to the editor', the document was presented as evidence to the court and is included in subsequent official records of the trial. The letter provided considerable detail about the indignities of Pingru's imprisonment and interrogation. Another of No. 76's agents, Lin Zhijiang, lusted after Zheng – 'Lin Zhijiang was inherently lascivious and thought about raping Miss Zheng, although he never realised this goal' and 'wanted to turn Zheng to the anti-Nationalist Party cause.'[33] It is unclear precisely how Zhang Zhenhua came to learn of this level of detail but the public narration of Lin as the unsuccessful sex-crazed predator, and the absence of any discussion about Zheng Pingru as a 'honey-trap' sex spy, confirms Pingru's image as a noble, patriotic Nationalist Party supporter.[34]

The advocates on Pingru's behalf extended even to the government of the Republic of China after its relocation to Taiwan. This 1964 record confirmed her 'familial' status by discussing her father and brother's contribution and reminding readers of Pingru's potential as a wife. The Republican Government Investigation Bureau in Taiwan produced a formal version of the life and death of 'The Martyr Zheng Pingru', which revealed that she had a fiancé, another martyr, Wang Hanxun – an airman in the Nationalist Party air force killed in fighting around Guilin. The document narrates that in the spring of 1939 Wang had written to Zheng twice asking that they meet in Hong Kong to marry. They decided to postpone the marriage until the war was over. This version neutralises any sexual relationship with Ding by providing a vision of 'true love' and the noble sacrifice of that love through revelation of a legitimate, albeit tragic, marital connection with another patriotic Nationalist Party fighter. The treatise embeds her sacrifice into a family narrative by reporting that her father was also detained for questioning during the winter of 1939 but was later released when he denied knowledge of his daughter's activities.[35] These stories of a young patriot prepared to sacrifice her virtue to the patriotic cause were competing with more colourful versions of her activities and more complex political allegiances.[36]

A woman of dubious morals

Ding Mocun's testimony at the trial paints a less flattering picture of Zheng Pingru. Through his narrative Ding reminded the Nationalist Party court that Pingru had close ties to the Japanese and was likely to have close ties with the CCP as well – attempting to diminish the tragedy of her death because of her uncertain political allegiances. With the civil war between the CCP and the Nationalist Party in full force by the time of Ding's trial, hints to a Nationalist Party court that Pingru had communist sympathies was a strategically astute move. As well as projecting the view that Zheng was a woman of wavering political loyalty he also suggested that she was a woman of loose sexual morals. All the while, Ding distanced himself from any close personal knowledge of her. Trying to save his own life, Ding saw no reason to save Zheng's reputation.

On 19 November 1946 he explained to the court that he hardly knew Zheng Pingru but vaguely remembers lending his car to a young woman who claimed to be his ex-student so she could go shopping. He later heard about the shooting and her arrest, but was not clear about the details. Instead, he suggested that it was possible that Pingru, being half-Japanese and having lots of Japanese friends as well as an excellent command of Japanese language, found herself on the wrong side of the Japanese secret service. Many of her Japanese friends were arrested around the same time for their communist activities. According to Ding, Zheng Pingru was killed by the Japanese military for her ties to Japanese and Chinese communists. Further diminishing her rising status as a heroic underground agent for the Nationalist Party he declared that he had 'no idea whether or not she was a member of the CSB underground' – but expressed his considerable respect for that type of patriotism.[37]

In his 12 December testimony he recommenced with his programmatic assault on the foundations of her fame – her patriotic loyalty to the Nationalist Party. He simply noted that her mother was Japanese and she had 'lots of Japanese friends after 1937' [the year Japan invaded and occupied Shanghai] and lots of connections with Japanese communists. He asked the court to investigate whether it was the Japanese or the Chinese who had killed her.[38] Ding expressed his bewilderment at being blamed for the murder of a young woman who clearly had ample enemies in Shanghai in the winter of 1940. By the time of his 3 February 1947 statement, Ding outlined a rich and internecine world for Zheng Pingru. He explained that the Japanese regarded her as 'one of their own' and she had been working as a secret agent for the Japanese from as early as 1935 and 1936, spending large amounts of time in Hangkou – the Japanese area of Shanghai. This comfortable position in Japanese-occupied Shanghai came to an end in the winter of 1939 when some of her many Japanese friends were exposed as communists. They were arrested and she was detained as well. Only then, did the Japanese determine that she was spying for the CCP and the CSB. Ding declared that the Japanese gaoled both Pingru and her mother during this interrogation and that he was helpless to act since it was a case in which the Japanese military police had arrested Japanese people – it was none of his business.[39]

Ding did not stop with raising doubts about her political loyalty. He also raised doubts about her sexual morality. In the November hearing he simply hinted at her dubious behaviour with the phrase 'On the matter of Miss Zheng's personal morality, I had better not speak.'[40] In Ding's testimony Pingru was a young woman who liked to have access to powerful men's cars to transport her around shopping venues – a service Ding was happy to provide. In his 1 February 1947 testimony he developed the idea further and stated: 'I am not willing to say whether Zheng Pingru's personal morals were really bad.'[41] The prosecutor directly challenged this assertion on the pretext of trying to determine whether or not Ding was in the car at the time of the fur shop shootings. 'A young girl sacrificed her chastity while conducting espionage work on behalf of her country, it is a fact that you accompanied her to buy the coat, correct?'[42] To which Ding replied with the direct statement that he did not accompany her in the car.

Ding's attitude during the trial did not endear him to the court. In summarising the trial on 8 February 1947, the judge wrote that Ding did kill the 'patriotic high minded person and underground member, Zheng Pingru'.[43] When the final verdict came down, on 1 May 1947, the judge declared that Ding showed no remorse for his actions and should be put to death.

Ding was not alone in his assessment of Zheng Pingru's personal morals. Two other operatives in No. 76 described her in less than flattering terms in their testimonials written during re-education in the 1960s. Ma Xiaotian and Wang Manyun were in a CCP reform camp and wrote about their involvement with Wang Jingwei's No. 76 office – the two men possibly presumed they would improve their own situation by providing negative appraisals of the CCP's archenemy, the Nationalist Party. Their original report of Zheng's introduction to the Nationalist Party underground espionage world was ripe with sexual overtones.[44] Her contact in the CSB, Chen Baohua, was described as a playboy and Zheng Pingru herself as 'dissolute by nature'. The two of them 'got along very well'. The sexual origins of her induction into espionage are clearly asserted in Ma's and Wang's testimonials. Patriotism was not mentioned as a motive. They continue by declaring that the Nationalist Party's CSB knew that she was 'a coquettish seductress' so they thought she would be perfect to entrap the sex maniac, Ding Mocun.[45] Ma and Wang explain that once arrested, the wives of No. 76's dissolute men decided to punish the seductress assassin – they visited her room to see the 'beauty who brought disaster'. Their jealousy and desire for revenge would not be sated until she was executed.

According to Ma and Wang, Zheng continued to use her charms even while imprisoned. Li Shijun's trusted deputy, Lin Zhijiang, was given the task of executing Zheng – but his resolve was tested as she entranced him with her beauty and protestations of undying love for him. He genuinely waivered in his resolution to kill her – hence the ruse about the picnic trip that turned instead into an execution. To the last minute, Zheng declared her love for Lin and her happiness that she would die at the hands of the man she loved. To avoid marring her beauty in death, it was Lin who gave the orders for his henchmen to shoot her in the chest.[46]

The narratives about Zheng Pingru presented in both the context of the law courts and the re-education process complicate the simple narrative of a young woman who sacrificed her chastity to serve her country. Self-interest contributes to the negative appraisals by Ding, Ma and Wang. Ding's negative depiction of her political and sexual morals aimed to reduce any blame apportioned to him in relation to her death or even absolve him from any connection with it. Ma and Wang would have been unlikely to say anything positive about a

Nationalist Party woman spy during their re-education at the hands of the CCP. Nonetheless, their suppositions also gain credibility from commonplace prejudices about women spies and their dubious moral and political principles.

Flawed individual: a woman out of her depth

Many of the popular stories circulated about her death during the trials describe her as being simultaneously sexually immoral *and* patriotic and courageous. This ambiguous figure draws on a long tradition of noble and heroic prostitutes in Chinese literary and historical texts – women of compromised sexual virtue who nonetheless adhere to other non-sexual codes of virtue, such as loyalty.[47] Zheng Pingru's life is frequently presented within this rubric – a sexually immoral figure that turns to serve higher purposes. In Zheng's case the counterbalancing moral virtue is patriotism.

The leading historical model for patriotic prostitutes is Sai Jinhua (1874– 1936). While working in a Suzhou brothel, 13-year-old Sai met a scholar-bureaucrat, Hong Jun (1840–1893) and a year later became his concubine. Leaving employment as a courtesan she joined Hong Jun in Beijing and then accompanied him around Europe in 1887 when he represented China on a diplomatic mission to Russia, Germany, Austria and Holland. Returning to China after three years abroad, Sai was equipped with high-level contacts among European royalty and familiarity with foreign social norms. On Hong Jun's death, Sai returned to work as madam in a high-class brothel but her international experience enabled her to play a diplomatic role during the siege of Beijing's foreign legations in the 1900 Boxer Rebellion that had so enraged Qiu Jin (see Chapter 3). She used her fluency in German to positively influence the commander-in-chief of the invading Joint Forces, Count von Waldersee, helping end the European pillaging of the city. She gained recognition for her role as negotiator between the Court and the capital's foreign occupiers. But, her close ties to the Germans were assumed to derive from her sexual relationship with Waldersee – a patriotic prostitute. Shengqing Wu described Sai's diplomacy as averting 'a national crisis by employing her sexual charms'.[48] So famous was Sai that fiction and drama versions of her life circulated during her lifetime and after her death. Xia Yan wrote a play about her that was performed in Shanghai in 1936 – a year prior to his drama on Qiu Jin's life (see Chapter 3). Popular understandings of Zheng Pingru's life and death would have been refracted through these prisms of noble, albeit sexually compromised, figures like Sai Jinhua.

Zheng Zhenfeng, a writer who would later become vice-minister of culture in the PRC, is typical of those who romanticised her moral ambiguity. In 1945 he wrote a short piece of reportage about woman spies that tracks his discovery of 'a real woman spy and genuinely tragic story'.[49] In setting the scene for his discussion of Pingru (who he surnames 'Chen' rather than 'Zheng'), he eloquently juxtaposed the female spies' 'beauty and charm, soft and gentle manners' with their 'spirits forged of steel'. These attributes enabled women spies to have lives full of dancing, dining and glamour while always remaining alert to the possibility that they would have to call upon their organisational skills to make rapid escapes from imminent danger.[50] Confirming the link between a sexually compromised woman and espionage, Zheng Zhenfeng commences his piece with a reference to the executed Dutch 'exotic dancer', Mata Hari. In so doing, he immediately draws audience attention to the connection between sex and spying and execution. Zheng mentions Mata Hari to set the stage for his piece on Pingru. Mata Hari, whose lovers included German officers and French officials, was executed on the basis of flimsy evidence about her supposed espionage work. Subsequent research on her life shows that no actual evidence existed to prove she presented a risk to military security. But, Mata Hari did present an affront to the sexual/moral order of peacetime recovery because of her multiple partners and sexually explicit dancing.[51] Stories of Mata Hari circulated globally and many women working in prostitution or espionage around the world became known as 'The Mata Hari of such-and-such a location' (see Chapter 5 on Aisin Gioro Xianyu).

Zheng Zhenfeng draws readers into a world full of allure and sexuality but he also presents the possibility that Pingru was 'a good girl who was playing a bad girl'. His narrative device is a time-honoured form – 'a friend of mine told me (the author) and I am now sharing his story with you'. Zhenfeng's friend was rumoured to be spending time with a very 'romantic' young woman – a woman who frequented dance halls and music venues in the company of traitors and collaborators. Zhenfeng pressed his friend to tell more about this woman and eventually the three had a chance meeting in a café on Xiafei Road. Zhenfeng describes the young woman as not the glamorous 'romantic' figure he expected at all. 'Her clothes were not at all eye catching, but were instead were plain albeit expensive; her hair was not curled with a perm but instead was combed up into a bun at the back, neat and tidy. She really had the look of a proper young lady about her, and certainly didn't look like a "romantic" girl.'[52] From this description, readers are invited into the world where authenticity and pretence are hard to distinguish.

Zhenfeng reports that about a month later his friend told him the woman had been killed and that she was actually a spy who used her fluency in Japanese to get information on the activities of traitors and the Japanese. Her attempt to facilitate Ding Mocun's assassination was her undoing and led to her martyrdom. The two men sadly contemplated their close encounter with a 'patriotic female spy'. Zheng Zhenfeng closes his article with the rousing and emotive lament:

For her ancestral land, she repeatedly braved untold dangers; For her ancestral land, she went heroically to her death! More heroic even than dying on the battlefield! ... A women spy's life is not a rose, but is full of thorns and is one of extreme suffering. But, for her ancestral land, she walked the path towards her death without looking back.[53]

Zheng Zhenfeng's romanticisation of Pingru's life and death asserts the high morals of the real person behind the spy. Other commentators suggest that the spy persona dominates and eradicates anything of the *real* person that may once have existed. Jin Xiongbai (1904–1985), a journalist whose close ties to the Wang Jingwei regime earned him two years imprisonment for treachery, wrote about Zheng Pingru in a section of his *Memoirs of the Rise and Fall of the Wang Regime,* from his post-1949 home in Hong Kong. He commenced with sex from the outset of his article:

There was too much indulgence in wine and women in the Wang Jingwei regime and Ding Mocun of No. 76 was a particular satyr. Despite the fact that his body was weakened with Stage 3 Tuberculosis he kept himself in his debauched lifestyle through tonics that boosted his masculine essence. His sexual intimacy with the actress Tong Zhiling were already a public secret that year, and news of the spy case of Zheng Pingru spread far and wide with huge clamour.[54]

Jin claims to have seen Pingru cycling to her family home in Fangyi Lane in the French Concessions – a beauty with a smooth white face, limpid eyes and delicate brows – as fresh as the spring. 'How did she come to work in espionage for the CSB? Nor do we know how she came to have such a "warm and tasty" relationship with Ding Mocun.'[55]

The story of her interrogation and imprisonment presented in Jin's memoirs puts Ding Mocun at the centre. It was he, and not his rival Li Shijun, who imprisoned Pingru and conducted the first round of interrogation. She apparently confessed to working for the CSB. In the hope of garnering detailed intelligence from her, Ding handed Pingru over to former-CSB member, Lin Zhijiang. Lin locked her up in his Huxi house. Jin wrote that Lin personally told him of this period of Pingru's imprisonment – Lin had also relocated to Hong Kong where he died. Lin described how Pingru used her feminine charms right through her imprisonment and tried to seduce Lin with promises of a life of pleasure if they both escaped. Lin told Jin that she was so pathetic and sad that it was 'really heart-wrenching' and he nearly succumbed to her charms a few times.[56] Even Ding apparently still had some feeling for her and was wavering about whether to execute her or not. It was only when the wives of the Wang regime got involved that her fate was sealed.

Jin writes that one night at a dinner with Zhou Fohai, soon to become the president of the Executive Yuan in Wang Jingwei's government, the conversation turned to Pingru and her imprisonment in Lin's house. The wives decided to visit the treacherous seductress and once their curiosity was satisfied the wives lobbied for her execution lest she lure their husbands into danger.[57] During the trial against Ding Mocun, each of these women denied knowledge of Pingru's imprisonment and denied ever having seen her – including Ye Jiqing, who, in the court's version, had conducted the first interrogations and been told by Pingru that she had acted recklessly and only out of jealousy prompted by Ding's infidelity.[58] These 'collaborating wives' would soon face their own trials[59] so 'no knowledge' was their best defence. Jin describes Pingru's entreaties to Lin Zhijiang on realising she is to be killed:

On such a beautiful day! In such a beautiful place! Under clear blue skies, a beautiful woman suffers a cruel fate, and off I go returning to the west [i.e. to her death]. Zhijiang! In the end, our feelings for each other have only been for a few days but we can still escape together now, there is still time. But if you are really merciless, then shoot me! But, I beg you, please don't damage the face that I cherish so much![60]

Lin wavered – so charming were her looks and so pitiful her words. But ultimately, he turned his back and ordered the guards to shoot her. Jin explained that the only way to avoid her charms was not to look upon her beautiful face.

Jin's editorialising on her death further romanticises the noble-if-sullied patriot. He emphasises her youth and vulnerability in times of war.

In this way, this flower-like, jade-like beauty sacrificed herself for her country [lit. sacrificed her *body* for her country]. But who remembers her anymore? It seems that after victory was won, no lists of the noble dead have any mention of Zheng Pingru! In times of chaos, human life is as cheap as a dog's. I don't know how many promising young lives we have crushed in the past![61]

A contemporary version of sullied-but-noble prostitutes sacrificing themselves for the nation emerged in the 2010 Yan Geling novel, *Thirteen Beauties of Jinling* turned into a movie with the English title *Flowers of War* directed by Zhang Yimou in 2011.[62] Set during the brutal Japanese occupation of Nanjing in the winter of 1937, the climax of the plot involves a group of sex workers sacrificing themselves to the sexual abuses of Japanese officers in order to protect some young female students. The innocents are protected and the sullied-but-noble prostitutes face the inevitability of a degrading death. Despite starring Hollywood's Christian Bale as the male lead and the fame of its director, the movie drew little interest outside of China.

Local woman's virtue reclaimed!

Representation and reality have a dynamic existence in China – with fiction and history intermingling in ways that ensure the past resonates with the daily lives

Figure 7.2 Zheng Pingru memorial at Qingpu in 2009

of ordinary folk. Two years after Ang Lee's film *Lust, Caution* was screened townspeople from Qingpu near Shanghai, unveiled a statue in Zheng Pingru's honour and held ceremonies to commemorate the 95th anniversary of her birth in order to 'restore her reputation'. The character in Ang Lee's film that was assumed to be Zheng Pingru, Wang Jiazhi, used her sexual charms to win the trust of a leading figure in the collaborationist government, Mr. Yi (i.e. Ding Mocun), with the ultimate goal of securing his assassination. But, as Mr. Yi's trust in Wang Jiazhi builds she develops a confused affection for him. At the vital moment, when Mr. Yi is about to purchase a rare and extremely expensive diamond for Wang, her love for him leads her to jeopardise the assassination plans. She signals to him that he is in danger and he flees the jewellery shop leaping into his car as bullets fly. Wang and her co-conspirators are rounded up and executed. Yi showed no mercy to his one-time lover despite her warning to him. The film is replete with graphic sex scenes as Wang Jiazhi works under-(the bed)-cover as a classic wartime sex spy. The graphic sex scenes contributed to the emotional reaction by Qingpu residents.

They felt that the film's depiction of her sexual conduct and the protagonist's ultimate treachery deviated from historical reality and brought Zheng's name, and therefore their locality, into disrepute. The 'Zheng craze' that followed *Lust, Caution* has focused on 'rectifying the name of a hero'. Zheng's paladins declared that in contrast to the racy character depicted by lead actor, Tang Wei, she was neither a craven sex spy nor a traitor to China. In fact, her townspeople argued, the assassination attempt had only failed because her gun jammed; not because she had wavered in her resolve. Qingpu locals felt compelled to cleanse her sexual reputation and declared her to be a patriotic agent – not a sex spy – and erected the monument to consolidate their position. Zheng's now-elderly sister made a public statement of support. She declared that Pingru was a 'good girl' who had only had one boyfriend in her life (a local lad) and was not involved in trading sex for secrets with the collaborationist spy master at all. According to this sister, now living in the USA, Pingru was a good person who was known for her beauty and came from a family of patriots.[63]

The PRC government also became involved in the rescuing of Zheng Pingru's reputation – a sign of the warming relations with Pingru's Nationalist Party and Taiwan in general. In 2008, the State Administration of Radio Film and Television in Beijing banned media material featuring the actor who had played Wang Jiazhi, Tang Wei. Authorities in the PRC deemed Tang's depiction of a Nationalist Party secret agent in Japanese-occupied Shanghai to be 'a glorification of traitors and insulting to patriots'.[64] The political and moral deviancy of the fictional character Wang Jiazhi made her anathema to PRC censors – but the real actor, Tang Wei, faced concrete consequences on Wang's behalf.

As a result of Ang Lee's film the fictional Wang Jiazhi, the 'real live' Tang Wei and the 'real dead' Zheng Pingru faced extended public scrutiny of their sexual virtue and their capacity for loyalty.[65] The three 'women' generated a frenzy of public debate and criticism of Ang Lee reached fever pitch with critics seemingly oblivious to the fact that Wang is a fictional character, Tang is an actor *playing* a fictional character and Zheng Pingru's life was merely *one* prompt for Eileen Chang's original novella. Eileen herself had been attacked as a collaborator in the post-war press since she had married prominent collaborator, Hu Lancheng.[66] A similar slippage between authors and characters had occurred in the 1950s in the furore over a fictional spy/comfort woman, Zhenzhen, as we will see in Chapter 8 to follow. The popular and official reaction to these three figures marks the complex emotions women espionage agents evince even years after their war is over and their enemies defeated. These incidents reveal the importance of women's 'sexual reputation' in the moral order of the CCP state and the importance of 'appearances' of morality as well as its 'reality'.

Conclusion

The reality of the life of this complex woman is difficult to determine since as a 'honey-trap' spy her cultural impact, like that of Mata Hari, lies in the repeated circulation of an eroticised boundary-crossing persona. Large sections of the population *want* to imagine these women as highly sexualised, beautiful, glamorous, dangerous and duplicitous. At the same time, the memorialising of the women must also include a considerable component of rectifying their soiled sexual reputations. Declaring them to be innocent victims of bigger games is the only caveat available in the face of overwhelming evidence that they were in fact 'sleeping with the enemy'.

Why is this the case? The answer lies in part within the roles that women play in establishing cultural, national and moral borders within society. The particular heightened attention that boundaries have in times of war, the way ordinary people experience war and the way that it is memorialised place very particular duties on women. Women carry the burden of being sentinels that mark the idealised clear borders between 'us and them'. Those women who publicly cross those borders become immediately interesting phenomenon to an endlessly distractible public. They are interesting because such women challenge the fundamental organising principles of society that revolve around feminine virtue. During war they challenge the fundamental organising principles of warfare, which require clear enemies and clear friends in order to present war as a rational action.

We know of the important role that women play in reinforcing borders *after* the war is over in the post-war reconstruction from the horrific European experiences of humiliating women in public if they were deemed to have collaborated with the enemy. Timothy Brook has shown that while all people living in occupied regions are forced into a daily engagement with the enemy in order to achieve some semblance of order in their lives, once the enemy is defeated, this uncomfortable reality is rapidly erased from public memory and official history. In its place stand cleansed narratives of local resistance and collective suffering.[67] Margherita Zanasi describes the post-war enthusiasm for clear boundaries as being driven by 'a resistentialist narrative' that glides over the complexities of life in an occupied territory.[68]

In the aftermath of war, women are frequently judged for their sexual activity during the conflict while men escape this form of scrutiny. And, as Claire Duchen has revealed of France after World War Two, punishing women's wartime collaborationist misdemeanours and sexualising their 'crimes' partly helped atone for the humiliation experienced by French men during German occupation. Women who had worked in domestic environs with the enemy became scapegoats and faced brutalisation in the form of public head shaving in a ritualised public punishment of 'deviant female sexuality [that] safeguarded the integrity of the new post-war Republic'.[69] In China, Xia Yun has shown, the round-up of female 'traitors to the Han people' focused on celebrities and prominent wives and girlfriends rather than ordinary women in both official trials and popular media.[70] At the cessation of hostilities, in the restoration of 'normalcy', debates about a woman's wartime sexual virtue or promiscuity become sites through which new versions of community honour and political legitimacy are asserted. Female spies are at the front lines of this reconfiguration of collective contradictory emotions of guilt and shame; pride and glory in the remembering of war. They become lightning rods for the popular anxiety about collaborationist or treasonous acts almost all people are forced to undertake during occupation or invasion. For decades after 1949, the CCP prohibited their undercover agent, Guan Lu, from marrying her love, a diplomat – Guan remained single until her suicide. The CCP repeatedly subjected her to criticism campaigns and imprisoned her for a decade, despite Premier Zhou Enlai having directed her undercover role. She was clearly deemed too unreliable for marriage to an internationally mobile government figure.[71] Glamorous, female undercover agents like Guan Lu and Zheng Pingru require sexual chastity to cleanse their reputations. But, by remaining alive during the Maoist era Guan was of little use as a propaganda icon. Had she died, like Zhao Yiman, Zheng Pingru or Liu Hulan (Chapter 9), her story too may well have been recreated and reinvented.

8 Ding Ling and Zhenzhen

Female chastity and good communist governance

All military operations require spies to gather and deliver information about enemy activities. Espionage and counter-espionage are central to the war effort and women are regularly involved in all aspects of intelligence work. As we saw in the preceding chapter both the Nationalist Party and the Chinese Communist Party (CCP) maintained extensive underground networks of agents and informers throughout the wars against Japan and each other. Frederic Wakeman noted that the Nationalist Party's Central Statistics Bureau (CSB) included women both as agents and as sex workers for his male agents.[1] And, as we saw in Chapters 5 and 7 above the sexualisation of women's espionage was explicitly discussed in the popular and political press. During war 'our' use of women as sex spies is comparatively unproblematic and the existence of women sex spies is a topic that is debated publicly and in a matter-of-fact fashion as a necessary feature of war strategy. But, once the fighting ceases, the woman sex spy's utility ends and discussion about her work for 'us' becomes problematic. The post-war rewriting of history routinely depicts 'our side' as clean fighters and 'their side' as the source of 'dirty tricks' – with activities like sex spying and opportunistic or punitive rape associated with the latter. This reappraisal of sexuality and women sex spies occurs because once peace is restored national, social and moral borders need to be reaffirmed. 'Our' soldiers were heroic and 'our' women chaste, while 'theirs' were dastardly and cheap. Memories of the humiliation of enemy invasion of national borders, the forced fragmentation of families and the degradation of the national citizens' bodies are all reframed within the rubric of noble, sustained resistance and ultimate, victorious repulsion. Evidence of the woman sex spy's solicitation of this very same degrading penetration and her duplicity in tricking men – even if they are enemy men – blurs the moral borders that are being actively rebuilt. The incorporation of women sex spies into a history of a glorious and upright national struggle is difficult given the high moral value placed on women's sexual loyalty in most societies, including Chinese society.

This chapter explores the myriad ways that the re-absorption of 'our' female spies into post-conflict solidarity narratives is managed. For national governments the difficulty lies in asserting the moral legitimacy of their rule in the face of evidence about their deployment of women as sex spies. For national populations the difficulty lies in the desire to construct reassuring victory stories within which the peacetime normalcy can be restored. While this book primarily focuses on real women warriors and spies in this chapter I examine seventy years of exegesis around Ding Ling's 1941 short story about a woman spy. The story is titled 'When I Was in Xia Village' and the extended discussion around its protagonist, Zhenzhen, and author, Ding Ling – one of China's most important modern authors – show that decades after the hostilities cease 'our' women sex spies still require 'explaining'. The evolution of this process of 'explaining' reveals the importance of sexual morality to governance in China despite the many challenges made to 'feudal' values during Xie Bingying's heyday (see Chapter 4) and radical Maoist years between 1949 and 1976. Through the analysis of the critiques of 'Xia Village' I show that female chastity and the high sexual morality of 'our side' during the war has been and continues to be an important commodity in establishing and sustaining popular perceptions of the moral virtue of the People's Republic of China (PRC) as a nation, and the CCP as its legitimate government.

Restoring normality and establishing a new sexual morality

As we saw in the previous chapter discussing Zheng Pingru, in the immediate aftermath of war, women are frequently judged for their sexual activity during the conflict. In Europe this took the form of public head shaving, humiliating parades and other forms of group revenge. As far as we know, there is no documentation on mass physical humiliations of Chinese women charged with 'sexual treason' after the war against Japan or the civil war. But there is clear evidence that women of 'dubious' morals, including sex spies, were useful for the post-war PRC government's assertion of its moral and political legitimacy – for example, through the well-publicised campaigns to eradicate prostitution through re-education of sex workers. From these campaigns, ordinary people learned of their new government's upright views on matters of sexual propriety. The official media's silence on living women undercover agents like Guan Lu until the mid-1980s, discussed in the previous chapter, shows the leadership's reluctance to link its military success to sex spying practices. The CCP's desire to confirm the sexed nature of its moral legitimacy is not new for moments of political transition in China. There is a long-standing tradition wherein China's imperial rulers asserted their good governance skills through the promotion of a secure sexual order.[2]

Unlike its imperial predecessors the PRC government sought to achieve a fundamental and ongoing shift in the way its new citizenry perceived the society around them. It aimed to teach all citizens about the 'correct' way to view history and appraise their current world through an interactive process of teaching and learning that revolved around the privileging of 'reality' through Socialist Realist aesthetics. Chapter 6 on Zhao Yiman revealed some of the mechanisms by which this pedagogical process operated, and Chapter 7 explored the intermingling of reality and artifice within the film representations of Zheng Pingru. This current chapter delves deeper into the link between education, commemoration and artistic production and critique. Literary works and critiques of these works, such as that circulating around 'Xia Village', are elevated to new heights of importance as texts through which the 'correct reality' is created. In the new regime, producers of historical texts or creative works were charged with recreating a 'truth' in which facts and ideal meet in a form of aesthetic synthesis. All consumers of these texts were charged with responsibility for 'actively viewing' them in a process in which viewers or readers become participants in the ongoing recreation of 'reality'. This task places responsibility for correctly appraising given texts onto each individual citizen.

In this new environment the CCP became the teacher of 'reality'; intellectuals, artists and writers (as the producers of texts) disseminated correct knowledge about 'reality'; and ordinary people became active students in a three-way process of perpetual interaction. The reconfiguration of wartime memories, along with myriad other social and political phenomenon, can be managed within this evolving didactic process of critiquing representations (e.g. film, literature, art) as if they were reality. The 'teaching and learning' that circulated around 'Xia Village' shows the complex ways in which wartime female chastity operates in the PRC governance system. Ding Ling clearly wanted to call readers' attention to matters of sexual virtue and its connection to broader military or governance roles because her sex spy protagonist's name, Zhenzhen, literally means 'Chastity'.[3] Ding Ling probably did not anticipate that it would become a text upon which national yearnings for community virtue and the CCP leadership group's aspirations for legitimacy would be manifest for seventy years.

'Xia Village': the original story

'Xia Village' is China's most famous story of a female spy of the anti-Japanese war and one of the most famous from the entire twentieth century.[4] Published in June 1941 in a journal titled *Chinese Culture* that was produced in the communist base area of Yan'an, the story tells of 17-year-old Zhenzhen, who is abducted from Xia Village by the invading Japanese. She returns home a year later to reveal that she has been raped, forced into sexual servitude, 'married' to a Japanese officer and become riddled with venereal disease. The people in Xia Village variously regard her with horror, disdain, awe and sympathy. Some say she is a disgrace for returning home in her despoiled state; others pity her fate and respect her resilience and courage. Zhenzhen herself seeks neither their sympathy nor appears to care about their disdain. She is managing her illness and fragile psychological state with plans for the future and faith in the imminent cure for her diseased body. The horror of her experience in Japanese hands is mitigated by her participation in the CCP's espionage work. She describes how her fear of the Japanese soldiers diminished once she 'made contact with our people (the communist forces)'.[5] During her year away from Xia Village she learns to speak Japanese and engages in three important missions for the Communists. She describes her work in the heart of enemy territory with a clear sense of personal agency. These were actions she chose to undertake in her desire for vengeance on her Japanese attackers and the consequences of her actions were hers alone to commiserate and celebrate. She tells the story's narrator (a CCP cadre) that the party is arranging her medical treatment and that she plans to go to Yan'an to start a new life free of illiteracy and the gossip of the village. The party had used Zhenzhen's sexuality and it would now help in rehabilitating her physically, psychologically and intellectually.

Yi-tsi Feuerwerker described the story as showing the 'resiliency of her [Zhenzhen's] spirit'.[6] Ding Ling would no doubt concur with this view because at the time of its writing she was enthusiastic about revealing the 'dark sides' of life in Yan'an – while also showing that there was hope for improvement. For Ding Ling, resilience was a key quality in reaching that improved China. Her description of Zhenzhen's determination to achieve a new life partly absolves the CCP for their use of her body – only through personal sacrifices is a new life won. The villagers' prejudices about unchaste women meant that there was no scope for her successful reintegration in Xia Village life. Only the party gives her hope for restored health and a fresh life.

Ding Ling's description of Zhenzhen's return trip into Japanese territory, despite the advanced state of her illness and the accompanying crippling pain, shows the extent of her dedication. The communist guerrilla leadership told Zhenzhen that despite the diagnosis that 'her insides were rotting away' she had to undertake the mission back into Japanese territory because nobody else knew the locality. She walked alone in the dark for ten miles and 'every single step was painful'.[7] With these descriptions of extreme sacrifice Ding Ling emphasises the depth of Zhenzhen's dedication to the party's anti-Japanese cause, but she also reveals the limits of the party's compassion for its agent's physical health and safety. Moreover, Zhenzhen appears alone and unsupported in her descriptions of the missions and alone again in her return home to face the

Figure 8.1 Ding Ling in military coat and cap

vicious gossip of her neighbours. The party provides a very distant form of support for a woman who has performed these gruelling tasks on its behalf. In creating the sense of Zhenzhen's isolation, Ding Ling hints at the repugnance women sex spies invoke among the people they serve but also the grudging admiration they garner for the extent of their sacrifice. The story provides a grimly realistic vision of the emotional and physical costs for spies performing sexual service for the CCP in 1940s' China. It resonated positively with her peers in the CCP literary elite for more than a decade and a half after it was published, as the following section reveals.

Zhenzhen: the noble resistance fighter

In her foreword to the English translation of 'Xia Village', Tani Barlow wrote that the story 'upset literary policy enforcers because it reverted back to Ding Ling's earlier preoccupation with sex and justice'.[8] The precise timing of the negative appraisal of 'Xia Village' is crucial to our understandings of the ways in which chastity fluctuates in political, military and social values. From its publication in 1941 and throughout the years prior to the 1957 anti-Rightist campaign, the story was not a target of criticism. In Yan'an, Ding Ling had indeed come under attack – but not for 'Xia Village'. In December of 1941 she was upbraided for her story 'In the Hospital' (published in November 1941) which criticised incompetence and callousness in a party-run medical facility.[9] And, she faced criticism again only months later in March 1942 for her essay 'Thoughts on March Eighth' that challenged the party on its poor treatment of women in Yan'an.[10] As editor of the literary pages of *Liberation Daily* she was also criticised between March and July 1942 for encouraging creative works that exposed the dark side of Yan'an's communist society. These bouts of criticism were central to the party's larger Rectification Campaign designed to tighten control of writers, artists and cadres and ensure that they adopt the new Maoist prescriptions for creative works.[11] The tasks for all those working in film, art and literature were to depict only the positive aspects of the new communist society and its workers, peasants and soldiers and only the negative sides of the old society and individuals with bad political credentials – ambiguity was anathema. Readers and viewers were to learn the 'correct' way of understanding their world through engaging with Maoist creative works. During 1942 and 1943 Ding Ling's work was scrutinised for possible deviations from these principles and contrary to a common assumption that 'Xia Village' was also problematic from the moment it was published, the *Liberation Daily* shows that it escaped direct criticism.

'Xia Village' was not only free from negative critical attention prior to 1957, but it received positive appraisal from prominent literary cadres like Feng Xuefeng, Zhou Yang and Hu Feng. It was included in multiple editions of collected works organised by these leading CCP intellectuals. In 1944 Hu Feng edited a collection of Ding Ling's short stories and published them under the collective title of *When I Was in Xia Village* showing that the story was a flagship for her work in general.[12] In Luo Binji's review of the book published in *War Literature and Art* the same year it is evident that the collection was received as an epic of survival, resistance and hope for a new social structure.[13] The sustained popularity and official party support for the short story continued in 1947 when it appeared as the lead article in Zhou Yang's volume, *Collected Short Fiction from the Liberated Areas*.[14] In 1948 Feng Xuefeng praised the story for demonstrating human resilience and heralded Zhenzhen's character as showing how people can create new lives in the face of insurmountable odds. 'Under the extreme circumstances produced during the rollout of the revolution and despite experiencing extremes of misfortune, the fulsome radiance of greatness shines in the spirit of this young girl from an impoverished remote village.'[15]

Even for a few years after the establishment of the PRC, the story remained in circulation and was endorsed at the highest levels. The Hu Feng 1944 edition was republished in 1950 and 1951 in Beijing by left-leaning Sanlian Bookshop. In 1954 'Xia Village' was republished along with the author's postscript by the party's own People's Literature Publishing House. In the postscript, penned in 1950, Ding Ling expresses her gratitude to Comrade Hu Feng for his encouragement around the story's republication.[16] Again in 1954, it appeared in a volume of her short stories titled *The Yan'an Collection* also published by People's Literature Publishing House. This edition included some extra sentences to explain the value of Zhenzhen's espionage work to the guerrillas and the uniqueness of her local knowledge in undertaking the mission. It also includes Zhenzhen's desire to start a new life, free from prejudice, in Yan'an.[17] Neither of the problematic works – 'In the Hospital' and 'Thoughts on March Eighth' – appeared in the 1944, 1950, 1951, or 1954 volumes, indicating that these stories were in a different 'political' category to 'Xia Village'.[18]

The positive appraisal of 'Xia Village' and Zhenzhen in the first decade and a half after the story appeared would come to a dramatic halt in 1957 and 1958 with the 'anti-Rightist Movement'. Mao Zedong launched this campaign to consolidate his power within the party by criticising, purging and jailing individuals who had either spoken critically of party policies or had 'bad political backgrounds' – those with links to the Nationalist Party or relatives living overseas. Writers, artists and intellectuals, regardless of party membership, were favoured targets for mass campaigns and public criticism.[19] Everyone would learn of the CCP's power through the public humiliation and punishment of leading cultural and political figures. Ding Ling's adversaries already had considerable evidence of her 'bourgeois' tendency to criticise the CCP in 'Thoughts on March Eighth' and 'In the Hospital' but 'Xia Village' provided additional ammunition against Ding Ling by querying her sexual morals. This debate provided space for the CCP to reaffirm the moral basis of its rule. Attacks on 'Xia Village' enabled the new Socialist Realist critics and readers to construct a vision of the CCP as a champion of a secure sexual order and to posit Ding Ling as a threat to that order. Female chastity became a synecdoche for good governance – social stability had a sexed nature. With Socialist Realist reading/viewing practices the CCP emerged as the defender of a sexually secure social and political system. In keeping with the merging of reality and fiction promoted by Socialist Realism's didactic impulses, Zhenzhen also became a target for commentators' criticism as if she were a real person.

Creating the barrack whore

The story's sudden negative appraisal in the Anti-Rightist Campaign turned Zhenzhen from a noble wartime patriot into a sordid barrack whore – she moves from a symbol of 'fulsome radiance of greatness' to become a slatternly traitor to the Chinese people and nation. In these new appraisals of Zhenzhen we witness critics explicitly defending the new party-government through indignant declarations that the leadership would never countenance the use of women as sex spies. On this view, Ding Ling's depiction of the CCP engaging in such immoral tactics was further evidence of her anti-party thinking since she had 'obviously' tampered with 'reality'. The re-inscribing of the political and moral significance of 'Xia Village' requires considerable creativity on the part of critics and readers alike as they participate in the reaffirmation of the CCP's role as defender of social, sexual and political stability. The recreation of 'reality' requires a wilful contradiction of a story's written content – texts become unreliable witnesses of their 'real' selves. Fiction authors become purveyors of lies and deception as they are presented as deliberately hiding their 'true' thoughts behind the surface of their texts. Readers are directly invited to seek the truth behind the false witnesses provided by texts and their authors and are led in this process by high-profile figures from the establishment who publish their courtroom-like judgments in prominent official newspapers and journals.

As we will see below, during 1957 and 1958 critics deny or ignore Zhenzhen's intelligence work for the party; they diminish her expressed hatred of the Japanese troops, and pass blithely over her personal resilience in the face of remarkable hardship. No mention is made of her pride in the impact of her intelligence work in securing the communist guerrilla's victory over 'the Japanese devils'. To the literary critics unpacking an unreliable text, Zhenzhen is nothing more than a collaborating whore who dared to sully the

CCP's name by claiming she was working in intelligence. The CCP emerges as a defender of female chastity and purity of patriotic intent. In the Anti-Rightist campaign, 'Xia Village' became an anti-party text and it remained so until the political thaw of 1979 – only from the 1980s onwards did 'Xia Village' reappear in collections of Ding Ling's work.

Ding Ling and Zhenzhen lost support from the highest levels during the campaign. Zhou Yang made a spectacular volte-face – he was reportedly moved to tears on first reading the story in 1941,[20] but in 1958 described it as the beautification of a camp-following military prostitute.[21] Leading PRC cultural and political figure, Guo Moruo, claimed that he had disliked the story when he first read it in the 1940s because it was sympathetic to a young girl who despite having lost her chastity to the enemy had the vanity to treat ordinary villagers as if *they* had no sympathy.[22] But, in keeping with the usual practice for PRC criticism campaigns, the first volleys were fired from less famous individuals but given top-level support through their appearance in prominent official journals.

In 1957, the key literary quarterly *Literary Research* published Wang Liaoying's lengthy critique of Ding Ling's wartime stories, including 'Xia Village' and showed explicitly the extent of 'active viewing' required to consolidate the CCP's position as the upholder of sexual-social order.[23] Wang's article, unlike some later ones, does address Zhenzhen's claim to have worked in intelligence for the Communists but argues that it is a completely unrealistic aspect of the story and was fundamentally flawed in conception. Within Wang's Socialist Realist frame, Ding Ling was accused of fabricating lies about the real CCP in her story. Wang presents readers with two tasks: first, readers are asked to respond to a series of direct questions that demand their indignant expression of faith in the uprightness of the CCP; second, readers are actively encouraged to pass judgment on Ding Ling themselves by being invited into the scenario of 'hearing' Ding Ling's defence. There is no place for a detached reader in this critique as all participants in the contextualised Socialist Realist literary process engage with a sexualised didactic impulse. Wang writes:

Would our revolutionary intelligence teams really 'deploy' their own women comrades one after another to the enemy to be degraded? Would such a thing really happen? Had revolutionary intelligence work already slumped to such a stage that they had to do this? If this really was the case, then where were our army scouts and where were the mass-based intelligence networks that were widespread behind enemy lines – every village with its peasant intelligence workers, every centre's intelligence station, and the Party's extensive underground organisation, where had they all gone? And... wouldn't the enemy wonder about a barrack prostitute that 'runs away' and then 'runs back? Wouldn't the enemy's counter intelligence organs have a part to play in this? Would a girl who had once wanted to become a nun in a Catholic Church be capable of recognising this type of 'important work'?[24] Here was a girl that had served as a barrack prostitute and regarded it as 'nothing much' and 'so-so', would the Organisation's leadership really entrust her with this intelligence work? ... We don't need to investigate why the author [Ding Ling] wanted to defile our intelligence work, because it is clear that this fraudulence would prevent her from ever presenting a plausible defence.[25]

Readers of the critique are schooled in correct attitudes about the CCP's position on sexual virtue and their congruence with these attitudes is sought through the 'self-evident' nature of the answers they are supposed to deliver to Wang. They learn that sexual chastity is a prerequisite for service to the party and unchaste women are anathema to the social and political order of new China. Moreover, this principle is projected backwards to include the CCP's military forces that fought to create this new state before 1949.

As further evidence of the party's position as the defender of a stable (sexualised) social order, Wang invites the readers to consider the likelihood that Zhenzhen was an unwilling participant in sexual liaisons with the Japanese soldiers. He reassures readers that the CCP was able to protect the sexual integrity of respectable Chinese women. Wang describes Zhenzhen as one of a very few Chinese women forced into military sex work to 'comfort' the Japanese. He notes that the Japanese tricked 'good girls' from Korea and Japan and other colonies (an oblique reference to Taiwan) into this work, and also that Chinese prostitutes (flower girls) were often used for 'temporary "comfort"'. But he reassures readers 'I still haven't heard of any Chinese women becoming "camp following barrack prostitutes."'[26] His first-person declaration emphatically denies that there were any Chinese women who had sex with the enemy that should elicit readers' sympathy. Those engaged in sex service with the enemy were either foreigners or Taiwanese or the unchaste prostitute who had already reneged on her right to sympathy through her immoral acts. In this version of 'reality' Zhenzhen must have willingly participated in sex work because the CCP was able to protect 'our' good women from such humiliations.

Wang's querying of the likely presence of a good Chinese woman working unwillingly in the 'comfort stations' builds upon an invitation to readers to actively ponder the 'evidence' of the case. Zhenzhen and Ding Ling are on trial and Wang encourages readers to consider the 'facts' and make a moral judgment about their sexual virtue. He writes: 'There is still uncertainty about the extent to which Ding Ling's Zhenzhen hated these beasts. At the start she was indeed forcibly kidnapped and humiliated, but there is no reason to say that after this [initial instance] that she was [again] forcibly kidnapped and humiliated.'[27] Wang leads his readers to conclude that Ding Ling and Zhenzhen were insufficiently thorough in their resistance to Japanese

humiliation, and he surmises, living as a barrack whore was not that hard –
Zhenzhen was probably enjoying herself.

Later in 1957, China's new Socialist Realist literary critics extended their
active participation in text re-creation by developing entire new scenarios
surrounding the story. Critics positioned Ding Ling's text as merely one document amidst a far richer corpus of 'facts' that could be actively marshalled to
enable readers to learn the truth – in this case the truth about the party's
unimpeachable sexual politics. For example, Lu Yaodong's 1957 critique
published in the key party literary journal of the time *Literary News* draws no
evidence from the story itself for its argument that Zhenzhen is a 'barrack
whore'. Instead the essay provides readers with new background material to
assist them in making their judgment on the virtue of this character and her
creator. Lu tells readers that Zhenzhen went willingly with the Japanese, she
put up no resistance to them and she let the Japanese fascists humiliate her and
had relations with lots of Japanese men until she got venereal disease. Ding
Ling, in this reading, was lying to readers about Zhenzhen's life and trying to
dupe them into having sympathy with this immoral girl. In this single article,
Lu demolishes the story's integrity as a published literary work complete in and
of itself. He invites readers to make their own conjectures about its veracity and
provides guidance about the preferred ideological position in relation to this
deceitful text. Sexual virtue is central to the political lesson. The story is not a
reliable witness to itself and it must be 'actively read' to unpack its 'real'
meaning; the meaning that it is attempting to hide from the readers.

Lu summarised his perspective on Zhenzhen with the declaration that she
had 'lost her feminine moral integrity' (*sangshi jiecao*). He distinguished
between the 'feudal' interpretation of *jiecao* that focused entirely on sexual
chastity, and the 'new' type of *jiecao*. The new form included patriotic moral
duty, had political ramifications and signified a problem of ideological
'standpoint'.[28] In this 1957 view, sexual chastity was inextricably linked to
loyalty to the nation. Zhenzhen was devoid of both her feminine chastity
(*zhenjie*) and a decent person's patriotic moral integrity (*qijie*) that demanded
responsibility to her Chinese race/nation (*minzu*) when faced with enemy
attack.[29]

Readers are reminded that Ding Ling aimed to deceive readers about
Zhenzhen's sexual virtue and her loyalty to China and the Chinese people.
Without Lu's tutoring, reading 'Xia Village' becomes a dangerous act for
ordinary folk since it may lead them to unwittingly sympathise with a traitor.
He warned that Ding Ling had romanticised a prostitute who was serving in
enemy barracks. In creating such a character, Ding Ling exposed her own
innate immorality and treachery – the author was writing from her own
personal experience. She was accused of attempting to transform Zhenzhen,
a woman who was 'devoid of feminine chastity' into a hero and in so doing was

wilfully tricking readers into following this immoral path.[30] The story's first-person narrator, 'I' was not safe from Lu's attacks, either. Lu described 'I' as remaining distant from the villagers and only having interest in this immoral woman. He argues that the three individuals: the real Ding Ling, and her two fictional characters, 'I' and 'Zhenzhen', stand as evidence of each other's guilt. Through the character 'I', Ding Ling reveals her own thinking; 'I' and 'Zhenzhen' are completely in the same faction. Ding Ling tries to eulogise both characters in order to explain her own guilt.

The attacks on Ding Ling continued into 1958 with an article by the editor of *Literary News*, Zhang Guangnian writing under his pen name, Hua Fu. Titled 'Critiquing Ding Ling's "avenging goddess"', he argues that Zhenzhen, whom Ding Ling has described as appearing raging like 'an avenging goddess' is actually seeking revenge against the villagers rather than against the Japanese.[31] To Hua, Zhenzhen has no hatred for the Japanese but, rather, maintains a clear distance between herself and the party and herself and the villagers. Readers learn the importance of personal pronouns when referring to the CCP and the now-infallible rural masses. In Hua's reading, Zhenzhen's repeated reference to the party as 'them' reflects her (and Ding Ling's own) separateness from, rather than proximity to, the party.[32] Zhenzhen has betrayed her country, the party and the ordinary villagers of China.

The CCP, through its literary critics, was consolidating the legitimacy of its rule and its moral standing as guardians of the people. It emerges as the upholder of an ordered, well-defined sexually moral society. The disciplining of Ding Ling and Zhenzhen provided a succinct lesson to readers of literary journals on sexual virtue, loyalty and the importance of keeping political boundaries clear in the new China. Zhenzhen was duly transformed into a traitorous enemy prostitute and Ding Ling into a bourgeois reactionary of dubious virtue.

Rehabilitation through national victimhood

Reclaiming one's sexual virtue after such a thorough and well-orchestrated smear campaign is not a simple task – even for a pliable fictional character like Zhenzhen. Ding Ling, herself, was rehabilitated in 1978 and many of her previously problematic works began to reappear in print. But, in the socialist realist practice of 'active viewing' the rehabilitation must be a process of being 'engaged' in this transformational exegesis. It is not enough to simply declare 'rehabilitation' – readers and viewers must also participate in it. While the more liberal political atmosphere that prevailed from 1978 onwards permitted a greater diversity of views to appear in print, there is a continued enthusiasm to engage audiences and readers as agents of transformation and actors in the creation of a rehabilitation process. Socialist Realist rhetoric has diversified but the didactic impulse remains. The nature of the rehabilitation in the case of both Zhenzhen and Ding Ling reveals the continued utility of female chastity in the creation of national morality and the CCP's virtue. The participatory rehabilitation process since 1978 evolved to recreate Zhenzhen as a victim of foreign abuse and readers, viewers and critics are drawn into active identification with her victimhood. Zhenzhen, the one-time barrack whore, emerges in the late twentieth and early twenty-first centuries as a troubled patriot and as China's first fictional comfort woman who defended her honour with her life. The agency and strategising inherent in the woman spy is diminished and along with it recognition of the party's deployment of women's sexuality for espionage. Not only is the party's position as defender of the correct social-sexual order reasserted, but also China's population is coached to identify themselves as morally pure victims of foreign sexual abuse.

The process of Zhenzhen's transformation reflects shifting political concerns but throughout we see the didactic impulse played out in its sexualised form. The first signs of her rehabilitation came in a 1981 article by Liu Jie. The article moved point by point through the 1957–1958 critiques of Zhenzhen's morality, political position and motivations and discredited each in turn. To Liu, Zhenzhen's story shows how Chinese women rose up and overcame the wartime foe and repressive feudal attitudes to chastity. Readers are directed to understand the earlier critics' erroneous appraisals as evidence of the extreme leftists' influence and their complete lack of objectivity.[33] Liu then asks readers, 'Why do these critics hate Zhenzhen so much?' and answers that they 'either consciously or unconsciously' revealed their feudal literati standpoint by using traditional feudal thinking about female chastity to criticise a story from the 1940s.[34] Readers learn that times have changed and attitudes to female sexuality are key markers of that change. Liu continues by directly reassuring readers about this dramatic shift by saying, 'At first glance this may seem a bit bizarre, but it actually really is the case' and continues with the comment that many other literary works faced the same problem from critics writing in the 1950s – but 'Xia Village' was one of the most extreme instances.[35] Readers and critics are reminded of their 'serious responsibility to thoroughly eradicate the poisonous influences of feudal thinking and feudal morality'. Liu frames his/her article around this individual personal responsibility for the mission and amplifies the urgency of the campaign by reminding readers of the untold misery and suffering of women in the old society as they laboured under the weight of the 'Three Huge Mountains' (feudalism, bureaucratic-capitalism, imperialism).[36]

A year later, Yang Guixin provided readers with yet another way of understanding the controversy around the story and its evolution to a new didactic purpose while making comprehensible the attacks of the late 1950s. Yang reminds readers that from the point of view of the villagers, Zhenzhen's morality was problematic. They, quite understandingly, doubted her story: 'Would the Party really send a prostitute camp follower of the Japanese invaders to perform such a sacred and noble task [espionage]? This despicable Zhenzhen, is so audacious, she dares to profane our glorious, great and correct Party!'[37] But Yang goes on to explain, invoking Mao Zedong, that art should reflect life and should help readers understand how to push history forward through the depiction of all kinds of people. And, during the war, Zhenzhen's tragic experience of been trampled by Japanese troops was not unique. The lesson readers of Yang's article learn is one of collective suffering, and collective suffering with a sex-specific significance. 'This was a humiliation for our race-nation (*minzu*) and, even more was a humiliation for the men of China. Even today when we think about it, it is an extremely sad and shameful matter.'[38]

The rehabilitation via the race-nation shame narrative also extends to Ding Ling as author for not depicting Zhenzhen as a chastity martyr (*lienü*). Yang praises her for instead for creating a 'non-chastity martyr' (*bu lienü*) – a woman with a new consciousness. Ding Ling therein 'manifested the lofty sense of revolutionary responsibility of a Communist Party member and writer with their extraordinary courage and insight'.[39] Yang concludes with a lengthy quote from Lu Xun's 1918 essay 'On Chastity' that queried the traditional morality of forcing women victims of sexual assaults to their deaths. By crafting a vision of backward rural dwellers steeped in traditional ways of thinking about female chastity, Yang is also implying that the critics of the 1950s that called for Zhenzhen's further humiliation were equally as 'backward'. Readers learn instead about the courage and insight of party's members and their close understanding of the vicissitudes of wartime life that ordinary people endured.

By 1993, the 'comfort woman' histories gaining recognition around Asia had reached into literary circles and this feature, in conjunction with the concomitant unleashing of race-nationalism, would irrevocably change the way Zhenzhen was appraised. Zhenzhen's militarised sexual abuse stood as a powerful trope for the abuse of every Chinese person. Initially, the discussion of Zhenzhen as a 'comfort woman' continued to be a vehicle for training the readers in their collective victimhood – and the helplessness of women in the face of this systematic abuse by the Japanese military. The desperate situation of China's womenfolk signified the weak state of the nation in the 1990s just as it had in the first decades of the twentieth century.[40] And, the didactic impulses of Socialist Realism continue into the liberalised decades of the end of this same century.

Zhang Mu's 1993 article in *Literary and Art Debates* is among the earliest Chinese language critiques to explicitly engage with the narrative of Zhenzhen as a victimised 'comfort woman'.[41] Zhang explains that despite her terrible circumstances, Zhenzhen maintained a rebellious spirit and bravely sought to repel the devastating impacts of foreign imperialism and feudal morality on her future. Her sexual acts with the Japanese enemy are framed within the notion of a helpless woman trapped by circumstance and there is no mention of her conscious participation in information gathering for the CCP.[42] The readers' attention is drawn to the suffering, the 'blood and tears' and the sex – while the spying and strategy is occluded. Sexual abuse becomes a shroud to cover a core aspect of Zhenzhen's agency as described in Ding Ling's story; the willingness to serve as a sex spy for the communist forces and their willingness to use her for this purpose. Instead, readers learn of Zhenzhen's personal courage as a woman who overcomes the devastating humiliation of wartime rape.

The creation of a modern day chastity martyr (*Lienü*)

By the start of the twenty-first century, literary criticism has become less important as a social engineering tool. Intellectuals are perceived to be less of a threat to the political status quo and literature is less important as a platform for idea dissemination. The story, its author and its protagonist along with the literary critics that write about them, are relieved of the burden to adhere explicitly to the current political concerns. Critics can distance themselves from the story's characters and authors can focus instead on conversations with their peers rather than with political players.[43] The PRC literary scene has been increasingly liberalising and integrated with international critical norms, but significantly literary criticism is no longer a prime vehicle for exercising the party's didactic impulse. Film and television have prime position.

In 2003 the first mass media version of the story appeared in China and has provided the most dramatic transformation of Zhenzhen's story to date.[44] Simply titled *Zhenzhen*, director Qiao Liang opens his film with a credit line declaring that it is based on Ding Ling's 'Xia Village'. But, the movie bears little resemblance to the original story and Zhenzhen has been 'modernised' back to the Qing dynasty with a celebration of female suicide as a signal marker of a woman's determination to prove her chastity. The movie amplifies national victimhood and humiliation through the trope of the raped Chinese woman and promotes the romance of suicide as a personal absolution of shame and noble vengeance. *Zhenzhen* denies Ding Ling's protagonist any agency whatsoever and becomes a celebration of female suicide. At the start of the movie Zhenzhen watches a fellow-escapee from the Japanese 'comfort stations' drown herself in a well rather than return home to bring shame to her son (who would never find a wife if it was known that his mother had been a 'whore' for the Japanese); and at the close of the movie Zhenzhen blows herself up in these same barracks when she realises that there is no hope for her future as a disgraced, unchaste woman. No mention is made of her espionage work, her survival, her determination and her service on behalf of the party. Rather she progresses through the film as a lost soul vulnerable to social prejudices about 'dirty' women. Ultimately she becomes a classical chastity martyr defending her sexual honour in a dramatic suicide.

The changes to the plot are significant but equally important are the ways that the audience is drawn into an active participatory role in her experiences. Viewers experience Zhenzhen's multiple rapes through repeated flashbacks in which the camera position is that of Zhenzhen's eyes. The audience sees the rapes just as Zhenzhen did when they were occurring with the camera angled up from the ground as men, one after another, walk through the door and lean over to block the lens as the rape commences. Traumatic and uncontrollable memories invade Zhenzhen's dreams and waking hours and again the camera positions itself from Zhenzhen's vision point. Whirling and spinning rapidly in blurred images of violence and terror, the audience participates in Zhenzhen's horror. The sounds of her multiple rapes invade her consciousness and provide the soundtrack so the viewers experience her memories as well. We participate in her fear, madness and terror rather than Ding Ling's character's resilience, strategic determination and optimistic plans for the future.

The first-person narrator party cadre, 'I', from Ding Ling's original story has disappeared in Qiao Liang's movie and with it the party's supervisory eye. Zhenzhen is horribly alone throughout the movie. Her contact with the CCP comes only at the very end when she returns to Xia village on an intelligence-gathering mission for the bandits with whom she has sought refuge. Zhenzhen's spying is now undertaken for the bandits who want to her find out if they would be welcome to join the Communists. On arriving at the village she is greeted by the sister-in-law who had previously spurned her and welcomed with open arms by women cadres who have heard of her story and longed to meet her. Under the cadres' guidance the village is a friendly and orderly place. The CCP's teacher-ly role is explicitly presented to the viewers. It has established a women's school and a community choir where women learn communist ideology on their path to liberation from feudal values. Whereas in Ding Ling's original tale reunification with the party was a distant goal and Zhenzhen had to travel far to find their promised medical and educational attention, in this 2003 version, the CCP's school has penetrated the village and the teachers have arrived on the doorstep.

Qiao Liang's dynamic, bright and orderly CCP women's school with its beautiful young cadres teaching the importance of unity against the Japanese invaders inspires Zhenzhen and she heads enthusiastically back to the bandit hideout to relay the good news. But, Zhenzhen's tragic life continues as she discovers her bandit friends and her common-law husband, the bandit leader, slaughtered. Rather than return to the safety of Xia village and promise of new life with the CCP, Zhenzhen resolves to exact a gruesome and suicidal revenge on the Japanese. She returns to her previous 'comfort station' and kills herself along with some Japanese soldiers in a massive explosion. By the 2003 screening of Qiao Liang's movie Zhenzhen reassures viewers through her suicide that the PRC's social, sexual, moral, racial and political order is secure more than half a century into its existence.

Conclusion

Since the New Culture Movement, Chinese radicals and reformers have pointed to 'female chastity' and the 'double-standards of chastity' as key problems for China's modernisation. The phenomenon Matthew Sommer alerted us to in his analysis of the role women's sexual virtue played in community honour and the legitimacy of imperial governance in the Qing faced serious challenges during the first decades of the twentieth century.[45] New Culture era advocates of political reform undermined this long-standing connection between female sexual virtue and political virtue by promoting sex equality in all aspects of family life, law and politics.[46] By advocating equal access for women in politics, wages, inheritance and employment, China's modernisers sought to delink female chastity from its broader ideological roles in public narratives of social stability and government legitimacy.

Despite their efforts, as we can see from the myriad PRC reworkings of Ding Ling's 'When I Was in Xia Village' over the course of seventy years, female chastity has been integral to the reaffirmation of a sexual/political order that legitimises CCP rule. The repeated enthusiasm of critics, readers, film makers and politicians alike to engage with a story of sex, spying, chastity and national integrity in the face of foreign invasions underlines the point that female chastity continued to have currency as a marker of good governance and national dignity in the PRC just as it had in earlier times. This continued utility of discourses about female chastity in political, academic and commercial cultural products alerts us to the resilience of a patriarchal gender order in China's social and political systems. It also reveals the mechanisms through which the retelling of war stories, replete with the vicissitudes of wartime sex spies or 'comfort women' place gender at the core of the militarisation processes that keep the war system operating. The official 'rehabilitation' of Ding Ling's political and moral reputation only came in 1978 with Deng Xiaoping's more liberal political policies. Ding Ling herself would become the messenger to notify wartime spy and fellow writer, Guan Lu, of her own rehabilitation in March 1982.[47] Guan Lu committed suicide in December that same year – her own political and moral honour restored.

9   Mobilising and militarising rural China
     through the girl martyr, Liu Hulan

In the winter of 1947 a teenaged girl from a small Shanxi village was beheaded with a hay-cutter-turned guillotine – Liu Hulan was another victim of the bloody Chinese Civil War of 1946–1949 in which the Chinese Communist Party (CCP) and the Nationalist Party vied for control over the country. Her membership of the CCP and active involvement in its armed struggle within the local People's Militia drew her into danger as the village came into Nationalist hands. Within weeks of her execution, the CCP mobilised the story of Liu Hulan to rally support for its campaign. Mao Zedong himself declared that hers was 'A great life and a glorious death' and personally penned the calligraphy of this epithet that now graces the various memorials and materials constructed and produced in her honour. A peasant girl of enormous courage and bravery, defiant in the face of death and resistant to her captors' demands that she recant her communist beliefs and betray her comrades, Hulan has been hailed as a heroic communist martyr for well over half a century.

This chapter explores the use of the story of the girl warrior, Liu Hulan, to understand the CCP's militarisation of ordinary citizens – particularly rural dwellers. From the establishment of the PRC (People's Republic of China), the CCP and its military, the People's Liberation Army (PLA), have maintained an extensive network of People's Militias – building off those that had operated in rural China during the wars against Japan and the Nationalist Party. The chapter shows that women warriors can be particularly effective in propagandising the ideal of 'citizen soldiers' because they are able to simultaneously invoke martial valour *and* virtues of the 'hearth and home' while also revealing the permeability of the boundaries between home and battlefield. In the case of the girl martyr/woman martyr warrior, we also see how proponents of militarisation promote the ideal of youthful passion and use the tragedy of early death as emotional hooks to draw the audience into sympathy with their ideology.

The People's Militia (*minbing*) is 'a civilian mass organisation of politically reliable and physically fit men and women under the dual leadership of the Chinese Communist Party and the PLA'.[1] Integral to the CCP's military and political success in the years leading up to 1949 the organisation became regularised and actively promoted after 1949. In peacetime the militias engage in production projects (e.g. large-scale irrigation or mass harvesting), lead the implementation of political campaigns at the local level (e.g. land reform and the establishment of the People's Communes), maintain local law and order and be in readiness to support the PLA in event of internal or external threats. Members are trained in weapons use and basic strategic and military skills. Publicity around the militias reached fever pitch in 1958 during the 'Everyone a Soldier' campaign in which 'Two hundred and twenty million men and women of predominantly agricultural population were to be transformed into an "ocean of soldiers", equipped and prepared to defend their homeland against the invader'.[2]

For propagandists desiring the large-scale militarisation of civilians through the People's Militia system, the military activities of an ordinary village girl, like Liu Hulan, were perfect material. Even among people unlikely to join the militias the propagandising of Liu Hulan's story had the effect of drawing them into a culture of war in which their active and willing participation was invited. The literature on militarisation often focuses on understanding the preconditions leading to international wars.[3] But, long-term and widespread militarisation, such as through the People's Militia system, can be a significant mechanism for exerting control in the domestic sphere too. The sense of imminent danger produced in militarising processes buttresses an existing power holder's control since it calls for 'unity' and positions dissent or diversity of opinion as 'treachery'. The state uses external threats to maintain an authoritarian hand on its own population – a common ploy around the world. However, in the PRC domestically oriented militarisation has always had a deeper significance.

Maoist military doctrines formulated in the 1930s emphasised the role of the people, rather than weapons, as 'the decisive factor in war'.[4] Known as 'People's War' this philosophy of national defence demanded the militarisation of broad swathes of China's population. Ordinary people had to be trained to be able to support the formal military forces within a strategy that would 'draw the enemy deep into China's hinterland, mobilise the population for total war, and wage guerrilla and mobile warfare to erode the enemy's strength in a protracted war'.[5] The People's Militias were deemed central to the success of any war on China's soil. Accordingly, the PRC state's propaganda bureaus actively sought stories of individuals and events that would draw the population into this state of war-readiness.

The militarisation of societies, such as that required in a 'People's War', seeks to effect change in the entire targeted population (i.e. people of all ages) and it is inherently a gendered process. It mobilises existing discourses of femininity and masculinity as central tools in its normalisation of a militarised culture in everyday life. But significantly, it often pays particular attention to

Figure 9.1 'Joining the ranks' (*Rudui*), by Xu Jiping, Shanghai renmin meishu chubanshe, 53 × 77cm, 1965
Used with permission of Chineseposters.net, Call number: BG E15/210 (Landsberger collection). Children becoming Young Pioneers beneath the statue of Liu Hulan.

militarising women and children, since war and war cultures are often posited as a masculine preserve into which women and children need to be drawn for the total militarisation of society. Women must be schooled to 'give up' their sons and husbands to the war machine. Children enjoy the pseudo-military nature of scouts and air force cadets as militarisation reaches into their leisure time around the world. Orna Naftali has deftly chronicled the ways in which PRC children have been encouraged to adopt positive views of the military through play, toys, story and film in campaigns consciously directed by the PLA.[6] She builds from work by Mary Farquhar and Stephanie Donald that explored how PRC children's literature, film and posters have constructed childhood as an active military space.[7] Naftali also explains how children in Cold War era socialist discourses 'often embraced a vision of children as revolutionary warriors' who should 'not be insulated from war but should play an active part in the fight for social justice.'[8] In this logic, Liu Hulan was a major agent of the militarisation of women and children, especially girls, during the years immediately after the formation of the PRC and continues to be so in the twenty-first century. The particular potency of a 'martyred girl' to the task of militarising society rests in the myriad ways that her story is presented for mass consumption.

Liu Hulan proved to be an effective vehicle for propelling militarisation deep into civilian life in the early PRC years because the image of the martyred girl warrior achieved a crucial propaganda function – the generation of an emotional response. Militarisation needs to generate emotional resonance among target populations to be most effective.[9] Liu Hulan's story provided that vital emotional hook to appeal variously to men, women and children, and both soldiers and civilians. Repeated discussion of her young age at death, constant calls to 'seek revenge for Liu Hulan' and invocations of the voices of her family members all combine to create this emotional response among ordinary Chinese.

Liu Hulan's young age at death generated more horror and more sympathy among audiences than the death of an adult. The murder of a young person makes the enemy appear more cruel, oppressive and unreasonable. However, her girlhood is a mobile 'fact' in the story cycles and reports on her life. Some sources claim she was 18 at death and others 14. Yet, in 1930s' and 1940s' China, ascertaining an individual's age was not a simple matter and there are extensive debates about her 'real' age at death. Local Wenshui practices interact with the comparatively recently adopted European system and as a result it is commonplace for an individual's age to vary up to three years. But human error and political needs also play a role. Early reports of Hulan's age at death note that she was 17 years old, yet later determinations show that she was born on 8 October 1932 – making her 14 years and 3 months at the time of her execution. Tiao Yang's detailed investigation into the various confusions about her age based on materials in the Shanxi Provincial Archives explains that by Shanxi's Wenshui County reckoning she was 16 *sui* or 15 years old. He refutes any reports that she was 17 when she died.[10] Most CCP materials describe her as being 14 when she joined the party and 15 when she was martyred. She is frequently hailed as 'the youngest' communist martyr.[11] Regardless of her actual numerical age, the stories of Hulan that have circulated so powerfully for decades were dominated by her *narrative* age as being 'childhood' and 'girlhood'. The contestation about her age reflects more than a dedication with securing the 'facts' – it shows the PRC state's shifting parameters of political maturity in relation to biological age. In the first three decades after the formation of the PRC, political maturity was only loosely linked to an individual's age. Children with the correct attitude were regarded as mature political and martial actors. In these years, Liu Hulan was included in this category. It is only with the post-1978 retreat from radical revolutionary Maoism, complete with its promotion of family sanctity, that we see the celebration of 'childhood' as a period of innocence in which individuals ought to be protected from politics, war and harm. Liu Hulan's teenaged martyrdom became a problem to be solved, rather than celebrated in that new context. As we saw in Chapter 6, these same years saw the glorification of Zhao Yiman's maternalism alongside her guerrilla heroism – mothers and children carry new valence in the twenty-first century.

Only recently has the positive value attributed to Liu Hulan's early politicisation and martyrdom been challenged. For example, in 2005 primary school teachers expressed concern about teaching her biography to Year 3 students given the gruesome nature of her execution and her young age at death. Teachers no longer feel that it is appropriate to encourage children to undertake sacrifices that 'should be the responsibilities of adult men'.[12] The militarisation of society through the emotional hook of a child martyr faces resistance in the new century and new versions of life minimise her military actions in favour of her service roles.

This chapter outlines the evolution of her figure as national hero, exploring the myriad mechanisms through which the party-state has promoted knowledge of her life and death for over sixty years to audiences of adults and children and across periods of radical communism, war and the comparatively liberal twenty-first century. It commences with an overview of the various versions of her propaganda life that PRC citizens consume and then moves to explore how discussion about her life and death are deployed to build confidence in the righteousness and legitimacy of the PRC justice system through the jubilant capture of her killers. I then explore how Liu Hulan plays a crucial role in mediating the boundaries between the home front and the battlefront. Her redactors used Liu Hulan to create new models of managing tensions between family values and the needs of the party and nation – her noble sacrifice was made only after reconciling these competing obligations in favour of the latter. The role of Liu Hulan's stepmother in mobilising families to encourage their sons to enlist for the Korean War through emotive pleas to honour the martyred girl is the subject of the final section of the chapter. Together the sections present a vision of the successful total militarisation of family, childhood, farm and labour.

Creating a national heroine: from historical fact to mythologised 'faction'

Liu Hulan was born Liu Fulan on 8 October 1932 in Yunzhouxi village, Wenshui County, Shanxi Province. After her mother's premature death, her father remarried a young woman named Hu Wenxiu. Liu Fulan's new mother replaced the character 'Fu' in her stepchild's name with her own surname – producing a new composite name, Liu Hulan. Liu Hulan's childhood straddled that unhappy period of the Sino–Japanese War and the slide into civil war from 1946. Extraordinary circumstances often produce extraordinary individuals and the young Liu Hulan proved to be one of these. CCP histories relate that Liu Hulan participated in political activities from a remarkably early age. In 1945, at only 13, she joined the CCP's Wenshui 'Women Cadres Training Class' and after a month of literacy training and political study returned to her village to join the Women's National Salvation Association – a group mobilising to resist the Japanese who still occupied large parts of China.[13]

In May 1946, with Japan's defeat imminent, she shifted her focus to Women's Work for the CCP within five districts neighbouring Wenshui. In June of the same year she officially joined the CCP and returned home to participate in land reform programs and was elected secretary of the Women's Committee in August. Political work turned to military activity when, in the autumn of 1946, the Nationalist forces arrived in Wenshui – after a fierce battle they occupied the town and almost all the CCP cadres retreated to the hills. Liu Hulan resolved to stay in Wenshui from where she participated in resistance and espionage activities.

She organised women to sew shoes for the communist troops and prepare supplies for the front lines; she secretly housed injured soldiers and nursed them back to health.[14] Her concern for CCP soldiers reportedly extended to making moon cakes and preparing melon seeds for them at Mid-Autumn Festival.[15] After just over a year of operational activity, on 12 January 1947, her political allegiance to the CCP was leaked to the enemy and she was arrested.[16] CCP histories tell us that she gave her stepmother a few of her most precious belongings – all items given her by CCP comrades – and left home to face execution with half a dozen other CCP activists.

In total twenty-four villagers from Wenshui and a neighbouring village were killed. The province's left-wing newspaper, *Shanxi-Suiyuan Daily*, reported their deaths in its 5 February 1947 issue.[17] The following day the newspaper published a longer front-page item specifically promoting Liu Hulan's sacrifice. Titled '17 Year-Old Girl CCP Member, Liu Hulan, Vehement and Firm in Her Martyrdom', the article tells the story of her capture and her steadfast devotion to the CCP. The report relays how, on her capture, she was asked: 'Are you a CCP member?' 'Yes!' came Hulan's reply. 'Why do you want to be a CCP member?' her interrogators asked. 'Because the CCP are for the ordinary people!' 'Will you continue to work for the CCP in the future?' 'As long as I am alive, of course, I will work for them!' The narrative continues with Hulan's defiant replies to their attempts to frighten her into betraying the CCP as she stands on the execution mound: 'What's so scary about death?!' As her head went beneath the hay-cutter she shouted: 'Come on! If you want to kill me, do as you like! If I came back for another 17 years, I'd do the same again!'[18] The news report closes saying that all the villagers who witnessed the execution scene would remember the heroism of this 'daughter' forever.[19]

These newspaper articles appeared less than a month after her execution and together present a clear and effective mobilisation of her story for the CCP's campaign to promote unity among its members and engender popular support for the war. Both pieces appeared on the front page of the *Shanxi-Suiyuan Daily* with the first article outlining the 'facts' of the execution. The second, longer piece, complete with dialogue and ample 'eye-witness' detail, provides strong emotional hooks for readers. Together they assert the veracity of the story and outline a model of CCP heroism and sacrifice. They establish a pattern for commemoration of youthful, female heroism and sacrifice and present it as emerging spontaneously from the anger of the masses, confronted with the raw brutality of child-killing enemies.

On 6 February 1947 the newspaper's presentation of Liu Hulan as a 'CCP model' for emulation was reiterated in another article. Titled 'Respects to Comrade Liu Hulan', its first-person response to the horror of her execution entreated fellow CCP members to honour her memory. The article concludes with two direct calls for action from readers: 'Learn from Liu Hulan!' and 'Seek revenge for Liu Hulan!'[20] A week later, on 13 February 1947, the paper provided readers with a 'brief history' of the martyr's life that outlined her activism as a party member and her support for the troops.[21] With these four newspaper articles, the promotional machinery of the girl warrior Liu Hulan had commenced its operations.

On 25 March 1947, Mao Zedong read of her sacrifice from his base in Yan'an and penned his famous tribute, 'A Great Life and a Glorious Death'.[22] Although the original text was reportedly lost within the chaos of war a new version of his calligraphy was penned on 1 November 1957 and sent to her home village.[23] This 1957 document is housed in the Shanxi provincial archives.[24] Other Liu Hulan propaganda relics did survive the war including a 1947 cadre training manual titled *Learn from Comrade Liu Hulan*.[25] Over the course of 1948 and 1949 the CCP's Northwest Combat Dramatic Society collectively wrote an opera called *The Woman Hero Liu Hulan* for performance in liberated areas.[26] This early material on Hulan targeted CCP cadres and soldiers and the ordinary people within CCP-occupied areas to promote the desired level of devotion and commitment to the party, its troops and the war effort generally. But it also addressed specific programs; for example, the opera promoted the 'speaking bitterness and seek revenge' campaign designed to promote militant and oftentimes violent action against local elites among village audiences undergoing land reform.[27] After the establishment of the PRC in the autumn of 1949, the Liu Hulan campaign moved to address a broad, national audience and was wildly popular even in urban China. During the 1950s Liu Hulan featured in more dramas,[28] comic books[29] and biographies.[30] In 1954 a new operatic version based on the 1948-49 original was produced with lyrics by Dong Xiaowu and musical score by the respected Luo Zongxian.

This opera produced the most famous aria of her life to date – 'Heavy snow in the depth of winter'. It is still performed today and there are multiple new and old versions available on YouTube and Youku. A movie about her life was among the first dramas produced in the PRC, along with that of fellow woman warrior, Zhao Yiman, discussed in Chapter 6. Directed by Feng Bailu, this 1950 film featured Hu Zongwen as the teenaged Hulan and was hailed as a model of the new socialist cinema.[31] She appeared in materials designed specifically for children's education within the 'Stories of Revolutionary Fighters and Model Heroic Figures'.[32] One of the PRC's most famous poets, Guo Moruo, penned a poem in praise of Hulan. The poem is an excellent example of the use of clichéd four-character expressions in poetry on CCP heroes and the repetition of known phrases associated with particular individuals. 'You really did have "a great life and a glorious death"! / Great Liu Hulan, you are immortal'. Guo concludes his poem with 'You are a good daughter nurtured by the party, / Your revolutionary convictions surpass life and death'.[33]

The visual arts were also active in promoting her story. In 1950 Wang Chaowen forged a statue of her form, shoulders back, clenched fists, cropped hair and purposeful gaze, it has become the model for most subsequent reproductions.[34] A 1957 oil painting by Feng Fasi depicted Hulan's defiance and courage on the execution ground with the villagers and her family members gathered in horror at the fate that awaits her.[35] Her long-term place in PRC history was assured when in 1956 the central government funded the construction of the 'Liu Hulan Memorial Hall' in her home village. Officially opened on the tenth anniversary of her execution, 12 January 1957, the museum houses memorabilia from her life and comments on her contribution to the nation by a host of prominent political and cultural figures. It incorporates the location of her execution site and burial mound. The museum now covers an area of 6,300 square meters.[36]

From the mid-1960s, as the radicalisation of China gained speed, Hulan was mobilised with renewed vigour. Another play was written in 1965 and performed around the nation.[37] Jin Qing's short reader on her story was released for children's recreational reading in 1972.[38] Yang Lanchun and Niu Guanli reworked the 1956 opera in 1979.[39] Renowned artist, Meng Qingjiang, drew dramatic colourful pictures to illustrate a Li Xueao rhymed-verse comic of her story in 1977.[40] More posters of her image were released for mass purchase and display and variously featured young people sitting under her statue amidst their political instruction or visions of her fearlessness in the face of the enemy.[41] Her now widely recognised statue in the Memorial Hall grounds appeared on one of the three postage stamps released to commemorate the thirtieth year of her martyrdom in 1977. A year later, famous and respected author, Ma Feng, released his version of her story illustrated by Mao's calligraphy.[42] During these years children sang a skipping rhyme that extended her memory to the kinaesthetic realm. 'Liu Hulan, 18 years old / Joined the revolutionary guerrilla brigade. / She sacrificed her life for the people / Chairman Mao says she did the right thing!'[43]

Memorialising Liu Hulan continued apace during the post-1978 years of 'reform and opening up' and particularly after the commencement of the Patriotic Education Campaign in 1991. Children still read of her bravery and sacrifice in their Year 3 Readers rote learning the phrase 'The big red flower grows redder and redder, the heart of Big Sister Liu Hulan is the reddest'.[44] In 1994 the Central Chinese TV and Shanxi Theatre School cooperated to produce a television show titled *Liu Hulan* and in 1996 Shanxi Cinema produced a movie by the same title.[45] Her natal village continues to be known as 'Liu Hulan Village. There was talk that twenty-first-century movie star Zhao Wei was being cast in a new version timed for release at the Sixtieth Anniversary of the founding of the PRC in 2009. This appears to have been nothing more than a rumour – but it attests to the ongoing power of Liu Hulan that she is linked to celebrities like Zhao Wei. Her sustained popularity is due in no small part to the inclusion of her memorial museum in the authorised list of 'Patriotic Education Key Bases' in the mid-1990s.[46] This status makes it a regular destination for school tours as well as people following the Red Tourism wave that has swept China since the start of the twenty-first century.

The makings and re-makings of Liu Hulan's life are vast and have continued unabated since her death. These renditions cover almost all genres and art forms and are promoted endlessly through formal and informal systems with audiences of all ages and sexes targeted. Along with the later 1962 soldier martyr, Lei Feng, Liu Hulan stands as a central figure in official narratives of the war and national development.[47] Over the course of more than half a century of commemoration, Liu Hulan's story has evolved and adjusted to fit the needs of the particular times. It is the detail of this re-freshing process that enables us to see the mechanisms behind the broader militarisation of Chinese culture and the shifting perceptions of appropriate gender roles in times of war and crisis.

Veracity and authenticity: tools for eliciting active popular engagement

While the technologies promoting Liu Hulan's story have evolved throughout these decades, the propaganda machinery consistently seeks to confirm the authenticity of the story and the accuracy of its narration. This self-conscious and repeated process of 'verifying the facts' is coupled with calls for 'revenge' and with declarations of the government's effectiveness in realising this vengeance. In the Liu Hulan narratives the CCP party-army state is presented as satisfying the people's desire for justice. Her betrayers are hunted down, captured and executed. Readers are encouraged to 'Seek Revenge for Liu Hulan!'[48] creating a sense of proximity between the young girl martyr/woman martyr and the ordinary person as well as a sense of responsibility for action and engagement within the overall campaign for justice, revenge and the establishment of a righteous social order. The unsullied virtue of the girl martyr/woman martyr is matched only by her unflinching dedication to the party. Her betrayal at the hands of bad elements is amplified to generate emotion among audiences and their active desire for revenge.

Central to the assertion of veracity of the official Liu Hulan narrative was the well-publicised campaign about the capture, trial and execution of her murderers. This process of seeking justice and revenge for Hulan took over a decade with the trials of those involved occupying national media attention in 1951 and 1959. With their execution 'The fresh blood of the martyr had not been spilled in vain'[49] since the capture and punishment of those involved enabled the new state to rid itself of bad elements. Having promoted the story of Hulan's execution to the population in order to inspire their patriotism, the capture of those responsible for her death neatly ties the loose ends of the story and affirms the new state's strength and the power of its courts. Despite the murderers' evil deeds prior the formation of the PRC they 'ultimately could not escape the net of the people's justice'.[50] Many of the fictionalised versions of her life have dramatic scenes where the party brings her enemies to justice – even before it had actually happened.[51]

In 1951 *People's Daily* ran a series of articles about the men responsible for her capture and execution. Complete with details of their home villages and military service records, the reports confirm that these were thoroughly nefarious individuals – bandits and/or soldiers for the leading warlord of the region, Yan Xishan. The capture of Hou Yuyin, Xu Fengying and Zhang Quanbao was presented to readers as evidence of the party's ongoing victory over the opposition and its continued military superiority over remnants of the pre-1949 power holders.[52] A photograph of their public trial reveals the new orientation of justice in new China – the masses are being avenged and are being directly addressed. A photograph reproduced in Xu Jinsheng's 2004 article tracing the trials shows Hou and Zhang kneeling chained on a stage facing the masses, surrounded by their captors. A speaker in mid oration stands behind a microphone directing his comments to the masses rather than the judicial officials seated behind tables along the back of the stage.[53] This layout for a staged public trial reverses earlier and later formats – in which defendants, witnesses and prosecutors have their backs to the audience and direct their comments to the officials and judges. These trials, like many of those held in the first years of the PRC, were performances of justice being executed for the masses – rather than for the state.[54]

The youthful Liu Hulan's centrality to CCP activities in Wenshui is also confirmed in the confession provided by Zhang Quanbao, one of her executioners. The six other CCP activists executed alongside Hulan fade into the background as the story of the emits its brilliant glow. The *People's Daily* reported that Zhang confessed that he was ordered by his superior, Battalion Commander Hou, to dispose of 'Liu Hulan and the others' since the investigation into their activities was complete.[55] In the 1951 report of the official investigation into her death, Liu Hulan was *the* prime figure among the 20-odd members of her village captured and executed. It is *her* murder that the current round-up and investigation is avenging and *her* contribution as a that is being glorified in the process. The primacy of Liu Hulan in the investigation and trial narratives, as publicised in the press, confirms the authenticity of ordinary people's feelings of indignation and grief at her untimely death. These descriptions confirm the reality of her importance and hide the constructed nature of her elevation as a martyr among all the other deaths of the wars of the 1930s and 1940s.

The second major round of publicised 'real' justice seeking occurred in 1959 with the capture of the last remaining 'extremely vicious enemies' – the people who had betrayed Hulan to the enemy.[56] Two men from her home village were brought to justice between 1959 and 1963 – former CCP member, Shi Xiyu, and middle peasant, Zhang Sheng'er. Both men were captured by the invading bandit forces and, in order to save their own lives, betrayed Hulan and her fellow activists. Shi received the death penalty – executed by gunshot – because of the gravity of his 'betrayal of the party and his defection to the enemy'. Zhang was jailed for ten years for his role. With these two batches of public trials, the 'murder case of January 12' was resolved and all those involved were captured and punished according to law – 'the legal system of the people's democratic dictatorship delivered implacable justice' ensuring that 'the revolutionary spirit of Liu Hulan is immortal'.[57]

In the early years of the PRC, consumers of the various Liu Hulan narratives are also reminded of their responsibility to seek out traitors, backsliders and those who would betray the young revolutionary China – as embodied by Liu Hulan. Liu Hulan's story reminded people to be ever vigilant in their behaviour and actively participate in protecting the country against external and internal threats. Their vigilance was required to battle remnants of the Nationalist Party. An article on Liu Hulan's story in the *People's Daily* closed with the lines: 'Friends! Let's work even more enthusiastically! Comrades! Let's struggle even more bravely! Seek revenge for Liu Hulan! Resolutely, thoroughly, directly completely exterminate the remnants of the strength of the reactionary Nationalist Party'.[58]

The 1965–1975 Cultural Revolution 'Learn from Liu Hulan' campaigns reached fever pitch each anniversary of her execution and reminded readers of the leadership's willingness to rule through evoking ruthlessness, hatred, death and violence and of the ordinary person's duty to participate in this governance model. In 1966 a group of young revolutionaries visited Liu Hulan's memorial and the *People's Daily* subheading reporting on their visit carried the banner: 'Determined to be like the martyrs, infinite loyalty to carry out revolutionary work, maintain a deep-seated hatred of the enemy'. Its headline ran 'Learn from Liu Hulan's Revolutionary Spirit and Her Unyielding Proletarian Spirit'.[59] A year later the paper reported that over 60,000 Red Guards and young revolutionaries had visited the Liu Hulan Memorial Hall during the high tide of the Cultural Revolution. The tens of thousands gathered for the twentieth anniversary of her execution were determined to 'carry forward the unyielding rebellious spirit of the martyr Liu Hulan and thoroughly smash the new counterattack of the bourgeois reactionary line, and thoroughly rout the small group of authority holders who are taking the capitalist road'.[60] In 1974 Liu Hulan's mother exhorted visiting delegations of airforce and navy personnel to be like Hulan for her 'fearlessness in the face of hardship and death and success in learning to kill enemies to protect the ancestral land'.[61] As the party purges against Mao's one-time comrade Liu Shaoqi took hold in 1970, Liu Hulan was invoked to educate readers that they should now oppose the former leader – the masses that gathered at her Memorial Hall were described as 'ruthlessly criticising the "renegade philosophy" and "personal survival at all cost philosophy" of the turncoat, traitor and scab, Liu Shaoqi'.[62] Furthermore, they should 'prepare for war and prepare for natural disasters' on behalf of the people.[63] The state, through Liu Hulan, demonstrated that it was determined to promote the virtue of uncompromising and, if necessary, violent punishment of those who were deemed to oppose its authority. Liu Hulan showed that there was righteousness to the state's violence against its citizens. The proven reality of the violent crime that was committed against her as a child stands to justify the state's violent revenge on those who would be likely to commit similar acts again.

The *reality* of her story is important for its capacity to draw the values Hulan's martyrdom represents closer to the 'masses'. Even fictionalised versions of her story appealed to veracity. In the 1978 Ma Feng short novel on her life and death, the author was at pains to stress the authenticity of his version by declaring in the postscript that the first draft was written in 1964 and circulated to cadres from Yunzhouxi village and Hulan's family for suggestions. On receiving their 'precious comments', Ma Feng reworked the manuscript to produce his final publication.[64]

In recent years these assertions to factual recounting continue with descendants of those involved trumpeting their association to the Liu Hulan history. For example, Wen Jianming published an article titled 'My Father Captured Liu Hulan's Murderers'.[65] Individuals' brushes with fame are published to personalise the hero such as Du Jie's reminiscence titled 'I Worked with Liu Hulan for Half a Year'.[66] Articles like Hong Ni's 'I'll Tell You about the Real Liu Hulan' include pictures of her younger sister Liu Fanglan and younger brother Liu Jilie, as well as her neighbour Chen Delin.[67] The article's emotive tone is set from the outset in its replication of the conversation she has with her executioners just before her death. Hong Ni continues with her own commentary on Hulan's courage in the face of her imminent death:

She was not deaf, she was not stupid, nor was she devoid of feelings like a wooden person. She was a young fifteen-year-old girl made of flesh and blood, she had her happiness and hardships, her loves and her hates. Fifteen years old, the fifteen year-old girl Liu Hulan had experienced the gamut of human emotions and had her beautiful dreams.... she yearned for a set of clothes made from machine woven cloth, and probably also imagined much, much more, even love.[68]

Hong Ni's article humanises the rather tough CCP heroine in its depiction of Hulan's dreams and desires and, for an audience in twenty-first century China, makes her seem more real – she's just an ordinary girl yearning for the latest fashion and love. But, before she comes closer to being a 'regular' twenty-first-century teenager, Hulan was militarised through party action.

Moving between martyred girl cadre to martyred girl warrior

The narratives of Liu Hulan's life repeatedly invoke the sentimentality of 'hearth and home' *and* a warrior's violence. Each aspect is invoked according to the propaganda needs of the party-state at any given time and each matches the goals underpinning the People's Militia – a villager's life of agricultural productivity morphs into battle preparedness at a moment's notice. In the reworking of Liu Hulan's form we see the shifting boundaries for women's appropriate engagement with war over the twists and turns of the CCP's social, economic and political policies. Women 'warriors', unlike male warriors, can embody both the sanctity of the patriarchal village family and the ferocity of the soldier willing to die for the bigger cause. Through the recreation of Liu Hulan's form we can track how the low-level militarisation of women-in-the-home alternates with a more direct and aggressive action of women-in-the-world as antagonists in war. The 'hearth and home' Liu Hulan is spatially bounded by her village and its neighbouring counties and her duties are primarily described as providing food and clothing 'for the troops' – she is not part of the troops within these narratives but takes violent action only in response to attacks from others and in self-defence. The earliest reports on her activities from the *Shanxi-Suiyuan Daily* were quite clear in outlining her role as 'support for the troops' and the heroism and glory of her martyrdom emerges from within these 'more womanly' wartime roles conducted from the heart of 'home and hearth' – her natal village. However, in keeping with the ideals of the People's Militia, every loyal villager should also have the capacity to be a soldier.

A 1949–1950 opera repeatedly describes her work as mobilising her fellow villagers in providing food, clothing and medical care for the front line.[69] However, this version also shows how she moves between hearth and home and the front lines. Hulan's spatial movement within the opera contrasts starkly with the other women in the play – her mother, sister and female neighbours stay literally around their stoves and on their *kangs* (a heated bed-*cum*-couch common in rural north China) sewing soldiers' shoes. It is Liu Hulan who carries these shoes to the front line for delivery – her feminine virtue is confirmed in her role as organiser of female activities such as spinning and sewing, healing and washing. But her radical devotion to the party is marked by her enthusiasm and courage in moving among the men on her multiple journeys to the front lines of action. The lyrics note numerous times that she is highly mobile in and out of the village: 'running east and west, coming and going through ice and snow' and the start of the play is replete with the lines like 'Is Liu Hulan home yet?' or 'Has Liu Hulan returned yet?' or 'Where is Liu Hulan?' – to which the reply is 'She's taken some supplies to the frontline.' While not unusual in today's terms, in China of the 1940s and 1950s the idea of a girl moving freely and on her own initiative out in public and away from the village would have been quite remarkable.

The Liang Xing 1952 novella had Hulan leaving her family home and walking for hours to get to the CCP's training camp. Her greatest fear during the whole journey was that her family would come and forcibly retrieve her. Leaving home is central to her successful participation in the war effort – and echoes the biographies of Zhao Yiman and Xie Bingying discussed in earlier chapters.[70] Similarly, the 1965 play version starts with Liu Hulan already fully mobilised and politicised for the war effort. She is checking on the progress of the village's quota for 'shoes and comfort gifts for the troops'. The women all gather around Hulan asking her to relay the latest news about the war's progress. Hulan explains recent battles, the CCP's desire for peace that led Mao Zedong to go to Chongqing despite Chiang Kai-shek's warmongering and the incitement of the USA to attack the liberated areas.[71] Hulan is the conduit for information about the front lines to the homes of ordinary villagers and the mediator between these two spaces.[72]

The 1977 Drum Song version of her life describes her as being initially designated to work on radicalising women in her home village to struggle against landlords and eradicate traitors and encourage them to be 'good warriors for the party'.[73] The poem established two militarised spaces for action – the front lines, where Mao's Eighth Route Army had victory after victory, and the rear, where the people unite to support the troops. Hulan mobilised her fellow village women into mass shoe sewing and made 200 pairs in record time; she struggled against selfish, reactionary elements; and as the fighting intensified, she formed a women's militia that not only nurtured wounded troops, but also took food, water and ammunition to the troops as fighting came close to Wenshui. Descriptions of her actions are interspersed with battle scenes of bombing, shooting, and explosions and her commentary and internal monologue place her right at the scene of the fighting. 'The great pity was that she didn't have a gun, so she gathered some nearby rocks to throw and joined the troops at the frontline only to be greeted by an incoming shell. The officer in charge shouted at her: "We're in the line of fire here, quick get down!"' She continued to work in the same location supporting the troops despite their repeated entreaties for her to go to safety.[74] Similarly, the Li Xueao and Meng Qingjiang comic book included a scene where she leads a group of villagers to the front lines 'facing a hail of bullets' and risking their lives to deliver basket after basket of food and box after box of ammunition to the troops.[75] Not surprisingly, the radical and militant Cultural Revolution years produced the most radical and actively violent version of Liu Hulan.

In the twenty-first-century versions, as China's leadership promoted domestic harmony and family stability, her movements are curtailed. In Xiao Bai's 2002 comic, she remains entirely within the confines of her natal village with the one exception of the forty days that she goes for CCP training in the county – walking distance from her village. Her actions focus around reporting to her 'uncles' on the actions of dubious characters or Japanese troops as they move in and out of the village. We never see or hear of her delivering supplies to the front lines or rescuing soldiers from the field. Instead, all the action is firmly within the village domestic space and her roles are those of 'reporting to responsible adults' rather than taking risks herself.[76] To sheltered, urban children of twenty-first-century China, her life is perhaps more believable in this rendition.

Taming the violent, rebellious daughter: changing relations with the family

Liu Hulan's dual capacity to invoke the battlefield and the home simultaneously is also evident in the way that she is discussed in relation to her family roles. The degrees of tension between her familial duties as a daughter and grand-daughter and her desire to serve the party vary considerably over time. In the more radical years prior to the 1980s Hulan is depicted as educating her elders in revolutionary thinking, rebelling against her conservative family members, disciplining those who are evil or backsliding (e.g. lazy landlords and widows) and yet simultaneously supportive of elderly women in need (e.g. one whose only son was away at war and another who donated a chicken to the troops despite obvious personal hardship). Hulan is a model of a new young person in a communist society – freed from old habits of obedience and respect for elders or elites simply because they are older or wealthier. She is respectful and supportive of those people who show the correct attitude to the war effort. Up to the 1980s these were the new social morals of new China and sometimes they conflict with her role as daughter.

In both the 1952 Liang Xing biography and the 1954 cartoon version of this biography drawn by Xu Hongda and Xu Zhengping, Liu Hulan's role as a daughter is to educate her elders and to rebel against them if they refuse to understand the correctness of the CCP's campaigns. In this 1952/1954 version of her story – targeting the child-reader – Hulan's grandmother repeatedly reprimands her for leaving the house to participate in party activities. But Hulan disobeys her and frequently evades her grandmother's scrutiny by sneaking out of the house to attend meetings of the CCP's women's groups. She even directly disobeys her grandmother's wishes and joins the CCP's month-long residential training camp. Her grandmother is so furious at Hulan's disobedience that she personally travels to the camp and shouts from the street for Hulan to return home. Knowing a friend had been tricked into going home on receiving false news that her father was ill, Hulan hides. Her grandmother is not depicted as being a 'bad' or 'counter revolutionary' person, but she is backward and conservative and Hulan's disobedience is 'good' in this moral framework.[77] In these years youth were frequently depicted as the political vanguards of the village – knowledgeable, courageous, forward-thinking and determined. Advocacy of the important role of youth in leading the revolution is declared at the outset of Liang Xing's novel. One of Hulan's earliest memories is witnessing the arrival in the village of the leader of the CCP's Eighth Route Army during one of its campaigns against the Japanese. The leader was a 19-year-old man and in response to the villagers' scepticism of his capacity readers are told that he is already a battle-hardened cadre and a young man whom they can depend upon to defend and lead them to victory.[78]

In the 1977 Drum Song version, Hulan's grandmother is instrumental in coaching Hulan's initial enthusiasm for the communist troops. The grandmother initially encourages Hulan to yearn for their arrival so that 'we poor people' will be fed and clothed and have something to rely upon.[79] However, she becomes the key obstacle to Hulan's further political education during the civil war. In answering Hulan's repeated requests to join the women's association training classes, her mother says 'I, your mother, agree that you should go, but I fear that your grandmother will cause a fuss. She's loved you the most since you were small and if a day goes by without seeing you, she'll just fret.'[80] But Hulan sneaks out to join the training camp – her desire to participate in the revolution overcoming the power of her family elders.

Hulan was also important in producing space in which 'girls could be leaders' within the CCP's policies of elevating their status by promoting women's engagement in public life and productive labour. In the 1949 opera version male characters explicitly support the leadership capacity of women. Agricultural Team Secretary, 50-year-old Li Laosi, described Hulan as 'extremely competent and no. 1 in the village' to which Hulan's mother replies: 'Everybody praises her like that but what can a young girl really do.' Li replies 'A competent girl can be stronger than a man.'[81] Later, as Hulan and Li go to the front lines with supplies they come across a wounded soldier, Zhao, and Hulan offers to carry him on her back so they can make faster progress. He rejects her offer saying, 'But you are a girl.' Li offers, but Zhao refuses again on the basis that he is an old man. So together Li and Liu support him between them as they hurry back to the village to get Zhao medical treatment. Although she does not carry this wounded soldier alone, it is evident that she thought she could physically manage the task. And the soldier's rejection appears to be derived from consideration for her.[82] At the end of the opera, as Hulan is being tortured she is repeatedly reminded that she is a young girl. Throughout the physical and psychological abuse she suffers, Hulan maintains a vehement and vocal attack on her interrogators – describing them as loathsome bandits, despicable running dogs of the warlord Yan Xishan and Nationalist Party leader Chiang Kai-shek. She concludes her tirades with assertions that the people and the party will prevail and deliver their stern justice. 'Everyone can see clearly with their own eyes who is good and who is evil.'[83] Liu Hulan's courage in the face of death is a match for any of the best village men.

This theme continued in the Yang Wei 1965 play. Within this version Hulan is an established authority figure within the village and has the right to criticise laggards and backsliders, such as the character known simply as 'Second Widow'. The latter is fined to make five pairs of shoes for her poor behaviour in the collective efforts to support the troops. Hulan's military-style discipline borders on officiousness during her criticism of the whinging widow. Hulan emerges as a young woman who is firm, resolute in her service to the party, and unflinching in the demands she places on herself and others. She demands that her views prevail. Coming soon after the establishment of the People's Communes and the allocation of a 'work points' system of reward for labour Hulan's 1965 exercise of bureaucratic power purportedly to ensure that everyone 'did their fair share' would have been close to audience's hearts. At no point in this play do we see Hulan engage with military action or even enter the battlefield. Her work in the village is political and managerial in its delivery of shoes and supplies to the communist troops. The military-style discipline that she applies to others is administered in more than equal portion to herself. On hearing that the enemy were about to enter the village she has the option to flee to the hills along with some other activists but she chooses to complete her mission of delivering to the communists the grain ration.[84] After the mission is complete she is captured, interrogated and executed. Maintaining throughout the anger and defiance she demonstrated to her elders (such as the laggard Second Widow) and her unflinching dedication to the CCP, she emerges as the icon of strong female leadership.

In 1964 Wenshui formed a branch of its People's Militia called the 'Liu Hulan People's Militia' invoking her role as a warrior-citizen who defended her nation with military skill and developed its productivity through her labour.[85] When Wenshui's Liu Hulan militia Production Brigade decided to start an experimental farming plot, Liu Hulan's leadership role was invoked to allay the fears of the 19-year-old selected to head the project: Liu Hulan's mother asked the young woman rhetorically 'Why can't a girl be the head?' – since under Mao Zedong men and women are equal. Liu Hulan's successful youthful leadership roles in the village and early martyrdom were invoked to stiffen the new leader's resolve to undertake her heavy responsibility.[86]

Liu Hulan images appeared in all the major labour campaigns of the 1950s–1970s designed to encourage women to extend their activities beyond the domestic realm – just as Zhao Yiman's were in these same years. She is regularly described as a 'labour hero and model worker'. Prior to the complete unification of the nation in autumn of 1949 the CCP promoted Liu Hulan as an exemplary worker who contributed to the collective productive work effort 'not subdued by force and unmoved by money'.[87] In the 1950s the CCP's land reform campaigns, the CCP's desire to increase productivity across the entire nation and its enthusiasm for expanding opportunities for women required female models for mass emulation, like Liu Hulan. The girl martyr/woman martyr was also used to retrain sex workers. A 1949 *People's Daily* report wrote that in a re-education session, Liu Hulan's diligence in her studies and desire for literacy used to encourage these young women to undertake 'productive labour'. The women sat under a banner declaring 'New Women must rely on labouring to eat' – confirming that in the new socialist order sex work was not 'labour'.[88]

From the 1980s onwards we see her role as a good daughter of a rural Chinese family return to prominence. The rebellious daughter from the radical years of Maoism does not sit comfortably with the domestic harmony deemed necessary for achieving the state's new 'harmonious society'. The tension between Hulan and her grandmother transforms into a dispute about Hulan attending school – a more age-appropriate activity than attending communist training classes in the eyes of a twenty-first-century audience. Moreover, other progressive adults mediate the dispute between the two family members rather than having Hulan wantonly disobey her granny's orders. In the 2004 *Biographies of Contemporary Heroic Models* series, Hulan's grandfather tries unsuccessfully to lobby her grandmother and it is only when the head of the Agricultural Cooperative intervenes – a man whose advice grandmother respects – that she relents.[89] Hulan, herself, did not act individually to openly defy her grandmother, but instead relied on respected, senior adults to lead a process of persuasion in which the old lady is drawn to make a harmonious compromise.

In 2002 the 'Old stories, new pictures' series of comic books updated Liu Hulan's story with now-fashionable Japanese-style *manga* artwork and frame layout. This version of the story also moderates her rebellion and dramatically reduces her connection to any soldiers. Her role as a good and supportive daughter of the family is demonstrated repeatedly through scenes of her working alongside her stepmother and in her care of her younger sister. Her dying mother exhorted Hulan to take care of her younger sister, Ailan, and readers are then treated to frames of Hulan playing with her sister, reassuring her and generally being a responsible, loving elder sister. In 2002 Hulan's grandmother is still a major block to her engagement in CCP activities and she had also attempted to stop Hulan's enrolment in school. This 2002 prohibition on school attendance is new to the Hulan story cycle. Hulan ultimately manages to go to school because her stepmother persuades grandmother that it will be good to have someone literate in the family. But, she still has to sneak away to join the longer CCP training camp and actively defy her grandmother's explicit demands that she return home. Although she tries to impede Hulan's progress, grandmother is described as being 'good natured and kind hearted' and as having worked her whole life for the small Liu family. Hulan's resistance to her grandmother is also moderated in tone and as her grandmother is dying she returns to the house to sit with her and continues her work from the house by spinning cotton that will eventually go to soldiers shoes. In the 'harmonious society' of twenty-first-century China, Hulan is a filial and respectful young girl and balances her family's expectations with those of the CCP as best she can.[90]

Hulan's stepmother recruits volunteers for the Korean War

The significance of Liu Hulan's stepmother in the propaganda life of Liu Hulan is important in understanding the way women are deployed in a militarising state. Nowhere is this more apparent that during the Korean War of 1950–1953. The campaign was officially called the 'resist the USA and support Korea' campaign and the memory of Liu Hulan and the real person of her stepmother became central to the mobilisation of women. China's mothers must encourage their sons to join the troops, the Chinese People's Volunteers, and march to Korea's battlefields. Liu Hulan's stepmother is routinely depicted as aiding her daughter's revolutionary actions and supports her decision to become a martyr. In many versions of her story, Hulan has the chance to escape capture – but she chooses to remain and face the enemy in full knowledge that she will suffer hardship and most likely, death, as a result. Her stepmother is unflinching in her support of this brave daughter. This aspect of the narrative is crucial to the spread of militarisation deep into the family home.

Liu Hulan's stepmother is invoked primarily as a symbol of a noble sacrificing mother. However in the midst of the war she also made direct pleas to other mothers to ensure that they remain firm in their resolve to support the war effort. On 23 April 1951, Liu Hulan's stepmother wrote an open letter to the mothers of China entreating them to:

Remember clearly the blood debt owed to us by the imperialists and the civil war reactionaries! For our murdered sons and daughters! So that our sons and daughters never again suffer this cruelty, please leap immediately to defend the manifesto of the world peace pact and sign your names and cast your votes, and vigorously take part in the movement to Resist America and Support Korea![91]

In July of 1951, at the peak of the recruitment drive to secure more volunteers for the Korean War, *People's Daily* published a letter by a certain Mother Zhou to her volunteer son at the front lines. Zhou writes that after reading a letter by Liu Hulan's stepmother to all the mothers of China, she was inspired to attend literacy classes – learning four characters a day until after three months 'I am able to take up a pen and write this letter to you.' Mother Zhou's letter is full of good wishes to him and reassurances about her health and livelihood and encouragement for him to fight with ferocity 'to protect the ancestral land and protect your mother'. She tells him about the U.S. forces using Japan to advance their attack on Korea and that he should avenge the deaths of martyrs gone before him.[92] A year later another report invoking Liu Hulan's stepmother ended with the cry: 'Beloved mother! Don't worry, we will attack the enemy with ferocity to protect our ancestral land and to protect our glorious mothers!'[93] As the icon of a sacrificing mother, Liu Hulan's stepmother is promoted to encourage women to support their sons' and, to a lesser extent, their daughters' enlistment in the volunteer troops.

In March 1952, a delegation of Koreans arrived to tour China with returning veterans of the Chinese People's Volunteers – they were taken to Mao's hometown and Liu Hulan's hometown. The delegation visited her execution ground and then told the gathered audience, who numbered over 1,000 strong, about the noble sacrifices being made by Chinese troops on the front lines in Korea. On hearing these stories the villagers were reported to have expressed their desire to 'increase production while practicing economies' in order to support the troops. The delegates then visited Hulan's family home where they met with her stepmother, father and grandfather, leaving gifts for the family – including parachutes, handkerchiefs and Korean coins. Hulan's step mother, Hu Wenxiu, declared 'We will definitely maintain glory and make as our (gift) in return to you our work in strengthening the struggle to resist the USA and support Korea.'[94]

A year after the war ended with the July 1953 Armistice Agreement, Korean delegates visited China to express their gratitude for China's contribution to the war effort. A Korean by the name of Cao Jing wrote an emotional piece for the *People's Daily* titled 'I met Liu Hulan's mother'. He explained that he was charged with singing a song from the 'Liu Hulan' opera in her hometown knowing that her stepmother was in the audience. His emotions were as follows:

Then I would have done justice to this heroic girl's place! Then I will have done justice to the mother that had raised this heroic daughter! Then I will have expressed our Korean people's respect towards this heroic model of the Chinese people! At that moment, the image of Liu Hulan appeared in front of my eyes! It was as if I heard Liu Hulan saying with passion and resolve: "Mama, learn from the CCP and the Eighth Route Army!" It was as if I saw Liu Hulan in the billowing snow taking shoes to the soldiers and it was also as if I saw the immortal image of Liu Hulan meeting her death like a hero in front of the bandits' hay-cutter.[95]

Conclusion

The commemoration of Liu Hulan, the girl martyr/woman martyr provides an excellent example of how militarisation within the Chinese communist propaganda system enters the family home steeped in emotion prompted by the execution of an innocent, noble girl. Proponents of militarisation promote both the ideal of youthful passion and the tragedy of early death as emotional hooks to draw the audience into sympathy with their militaristic 'People's War' ideology. But, her age becomes her undoing as the prosperity of the twenty-first century extends and communities seek harmony not revolution. The idea of children going to war and sacrificing themselves for that war is anathema to parents now and China's propagandists have reflected this sentiment in their recent reinventions of the girl martyr/woman martyr.

Liu Hulan's de-radicalisation is facilitated by another popular trend in liberalising China – the fascination with the 'intimate secrets' of communist heroes. Some of these are salacious tales of sex and depravity from 'insiders' and they circulate widely in the non-official sphere. Others, as is the case with Hulan, simply talk about the trials and tribulations of her love-life. In an ironic twist to the CCP's coaching of its population in 'seeking truth' the popular media in newly liberalised China presents documentary evidence of gossip that purports to have *the real* truth. These kinds of stories about Liu Hulan paint a more textured vision of our teenaged heroine.

In 2003 Hong Ni explained that Hulan once fell in love but because of the difficult, unstable times she and her beloved decided not to marry – instead they would wait until they were older and the times were more conducive to building a new family. The object of her affection was a certain Wang Bengu hailing from Hebei who was part of the Eighth Route Army that was operating in and around Hulan's village. Wang was injured and taken to Wenshui to recover and it was during this period of convalescence that he met Hulan. At the close of hostilities when he came back to marry Hulan, he was devastated to hear of her death. Hulan's mother returned Wang the items he had given the family during his convalescence – a pair of glasses, a blanket and a pen.[96] The young lovers' displacement of personal happiness for military duties added further weight to her sacrifice.

Although Wang's relationship with Hulan was described in Liang Xing's 1952 novel and confirmed as 'fact' in 1957 on the tenth anniversary of her death complete with interviews of Wang, it was still popular in the 1990s for journals to publish 'exposés' on Hulan's romantic life. One 1994 article published led with the sensational declaration that:

This is a small gap in the history. Everyone knows that Liu Hulan was heroically martyred on a blood-stained. Everyone knows that Liu Hulan was only 16 when she was martyred. . . . but not everyone knows that at 16 in the springtime of her youth she fell in love with a man, a hero, a courageous PLA cadre – by the name of Wang Bengu.[97]

Other articles link Hulan's romance with Wang to the CCP's program for free choice in marriage – also claiming to make a sensational scoop – these are 'very rarely discussed events'. For example, in 2002 Li Zemin outlined the three betrothals of Liu Hulan. The first was a parentally arranged betrothal between Hulan and a young neighbour, Chen Delin. Lin describes both young people as progressive thinkers and so they explained to both sets of parents that the union was against both their wishes because Hulan already had a romantic attachment to someone outside the village. The second suitor appeared pleasing to Hulan but when she discussed it with her party comrades they warned her that party members needed to consider the political status of their partners before committing – and because the CCP couldn't not be sure whether the young man had 'political problems' she rejected this second suitor.[98] The third betrothal was to Wang Bengu – the doomed revolutionary romance.

The artificial exaggeration of the 'previously unheard of' stories of Liu Hulan's romances serve important functions within the CCP's propaganda machinery – just as conspiracy stories allow people to feel a sense of control over their world (we know the *real* story; we can understand the *real* situation) the extensive interest in the personal lives of communist heroes allows people to feel they understand the truth behind the tightly controlled monochromatic stories of the CCP. The power of propaganda continues even as people read 'beneath' the story in the search for the kernels of truth they have been coached to seek. In the process of giving texture to Liu Hulan as a teenager looking for love, she becomes less dangerous to the twenty-first-century family-state that rejects radicalised youth who might engage in violent or militarised action of any sort. The militarisation of childhood and mothers that was the crux of Liu Hulan's propaganda life from the 1940s to the 1980s has morphed into a more complex story where Hulan is simultaneously warlike and childlike, a beacon of a girl's autonomy and a dutiful granddaughter, a wronged martyr deserving vengeance and a teenager looking for romance.

10 Women warriors and wartime spies as tools for 'total militarisation'

The Red Detachment of Women

There is a striking omission from the story of war presented in the narratives about the Chinese woman warriors and wartime spies – the question of whether the sacrifices required of people were 'worth it'. Jay Winter's study of European memories of the so-called Great War shows us the considerable extent to which the validity of the war project was repeatedly questioned in art, literature and film. Was all the sacrifice in vain? Were the promises of glory simply orchestrated deceit and lies? He identifies the 1914–1918 war as the point after which 'Slowly but surely, expressions of patriotism, or inhumanly idealised images of combat, suffering, and death as "glory", began to fade away.'[1] Soldiers, their families, journalists and medics queried the validity of the butchering they had just experienced. In China's twentieth and twenty-first centuries, there has never been such a point of public questioning. People may have expressed their doubts in private but the public record of art, literature, film, school texts and journalism remains mute about the possibility that any of the conflicts of the twentieth century were in vain or that those who lost their lives died in anything less than heroic glory. Those now governing the territory on which the blood of millions was spilt, the People's Republic of China (PRC), are invested in an unproblematised glorification of war. The glue that binds the nation to its communist state comprises a complex amalgam of narratives of imminent military threats to China's sovereign borders and threatened treacherous destabilisation by spies in foreign employ, as well as a sustained education about how the military weakness of the Qing court allowed foreigners and imperialists to 'carve up China like a melon'.

Since the mid-twentieth century these stories are bound together as 'national humiliation'. Militarisation in twentieth and twenty-first centuries' China is encased in teaching the PRC population that it has been shamed and degraded. Chinese leaders from both the Nationalist Party and the Chinese Communist Party (CCP) teach people who could otherwise have thought of themselves as glorious survivors of foreign aggression that they have been humiliated by the military aggression of others.[2] 'Never forget national humiliation' is a maxim all PRC citizens recognise. The narrative of humiliation undermines any moral high ground that could have been garnered from promoting China's victim-hood – an innocent victim of another nation's aggression. Humiliation and shame narratives also create a scenario that teaches collective culpability – the Chinese people are in some way responsible for their own humiliation because they allowed it to happen. The nation was let to degrade to such an extent that foreigners could bully China and the Chinese. Official stories of the 1842 Opium War, the 1894 Sino–Japanese War and the 1979 Sino–Vietnamese border war include discussion about how corrupt behaviour and incompetence led to China's defeat (or in the 1979 case, an inconclusive end). Corrupt Chinese officials and poor military industrial processes created scenarios where Chinese troops were fighting with inferior equipment and in impossible circumstances – weapons that fail to fire, bombs that fail to explode and canon with inadequate range are common tropes in film versions of these events.[3]

On this line of argument culpability lies in no small part with the Chinese for their poor preparations and lack of war-readiness when faced with foreign bullies. Usually the blame is shunted home to particular types of Chinese – such as the Manchu court or the Mao-era's 'Gang of Four' – but 'the Chinese people' still carry some modicum of culpability too. In promoting the narrative of 'One Hundred Years of Humiliation' the PRC's leaders call upon their citizens to ensure that it never happens again. Their support and celebration of a strong military force is the realised goal. In China, as elsewhere during the twentieth century, 'total war' becomes 'total militarisation' even in peacetime.

Roger Chickering and Stig Foster tell us that while the definition of 'total war' remains contested it has a number of key hallmarks: the massive size and scope of the war; a radicalisation of warfare that removes the 'last restraints on combat' such as law, moral codes and civility; the erasure of distinctions between soldiers and civilians making all people, regardless of age and gender, targets of militarised violence; and intense government involvement in garnering popular commitment to the war effort.[4] It is in the last two aspects that narratives of women warriors and wartime spies, such as those discussed throughout the book, have their impact. The romanticisation of these women's activities, the linking of their work to sex-equality rhetoric while simultaneously trumpeting their exceptionalism and the sexualisation of warfare in prurient ways are all made possible through recycling and reinventing narratives of women warriors. As we have seen in the preceding chapters, despite the apparent diversity in the roles and experience, and the sometimes contradictory ways they have been appraised, they are effectively handmaidens to total militarisation. In every instance, they fought to fight – against parents, against social norms, against their doubting comrades. In each case they were prepared to make the ultimate sacrifices should they be called upon to do so – sacrificing their lives, their children, their chastity. Women warriors and wartime spies have been created into the poster girls for war in ways that conscripted male soldier could never be. They make war sexy.

Sexualisation in the *Red Detachment of Women*

While the sex-appeal of the wartime spy is glaringly apparent in the depictions of her glamorous life adorned with beautiful clothes among powerful men, the sex appeal of the woman warrior is often less apparent. However, even in the hugely popular and still much-loved *Red Detachment of Women* produced during the stern first decades of the PRC the sexing up of women soldiers is apparent.[5] The story was performed and circulated in three main genres – the most famous being a 1961 film-drama, a 1964 ballet and modern Peking Opera (both had films produced of their stage productions in the 1970s).[6] Each served in different ways to harness the sexuality of women spies and soldiers. Rosemary Roberts's intensive study of the gender coding in the ballet, for example, argues that despite the asexual atmosphere of the strict and politically repressive 1960s and 1970s the public aesthetic display of the moving female body was sexually arousing to many viewers.[7] In this regard, the *Red Detachment*'s women spy brigade supported the daily pressure for women to be androgynous comrade sisters while their femaleness, sexuality and transgression of gender norms were integral to the success of the story. And, engendering militarised thinking among all China's citizens was a central concern during these, and later, years. As one review declared, *Red Detachment* shows that 'the Party and the army must rouse the people and rely on them to build and strengthen rural revolutionary bases and carry out a people's war'.[8] *Red Detachment of Women* helped militarise audiences and one of the devices it used was the sex appeal of the woman wartime warrior-spy.

Of the three main versions of the story, the film-drama and the ballet are the most clearly sexualised. Of all the performed genres the modern Peking Opera version achieves the closest approximation to the 1950s–1970s reality of androgynous, comrade sisters in its adoption of operatic forms of dance, narration and music. The ballet and the opera were included in the 'Model Works' promoted during the Cultural Revolution (1966–1976) to teach correct political attitudes to audiences and to encourage artists to produce similar works, or works with similar ideologies.[9] But, large segments of the audience were familiar with the film version and viewed the model ballet and opera through that lens. Barbara Mittler notes this in her research on the operations of Cultural Revolution propaganda and its capacity to harness the popularity of earlier works (such as the 1961 film-drama of *Red Detachment*). She explains 'alternate earlier versions are remembered – even relived – in watching the revised model [Cultural Revolution] version, and that revised versions can therefore play on this former knowledge'. Audiences preferred the film-drama version.[10]

The drama script's first version was as a play-script written in 1958 by Liang Xin, a People's Liberation Army cultural bureau writer and titled *Flower Hero of the Jade Island*. In 1960 the now-famous film director, Xie Jin, adapted it for a film with the new title *Red Detachment of Women*. Released in 1961 the film won four prizes at the 1962 National Film Awards (best picture, best director, best lead female actor and best supporting male actor).[11] The film is an excellent example of the Maoist principles of Socialist Realist literature and art discussed in Chapter 8. Negative characters (landlords, Nationalist Party military and their lackeys) are identified through dark lighting and deformed, grey faces, and positive characters (peasants, communists and their troops and followers) have bright lighting, beautiful faces and strong bodies. Its theme song, the 'Song of the Red Detachment of Women', would feature in all later versions and is still recognised today with its stirring lyrics and call to arms for all oppressed peoples, especially women: 'Forward! Forward! Important the soldier's task, deep the women's hatred'.

As the 1960s progressed China's artistic leaders continued to experiment with new, revolutionary art forms – the Beijing Ballet School was no exception. Closely linked to the USSR, the school needed to confirm its patriotic edge as the Sino-Soviet alliance crumbled in the early 1960s. They gave the *Red Detachment* a radical makeover and in 1964 adapted it to classic western ballet with a revolutionary socialist flare – raised fists and defiant glares are mixed with arabesques and pirouettes. Small elements of Peking Opera appear in the use of 'frozen poses' used to emphasise emotional charge. The song and music score draws on songs from Xie Jin's film and the PRC national anthem but also includes an original score to accompany the dances.[12] The ballet has no voice parts – the storyline is produced through dance action alone. The modern Peking Opera version, also produced in 1964, took traditional operatic stagecraft, stylised actions and the intermingling of aria and speech to reveal the story. It is recognisably Peking Opera in the musical score and high-pitched speech, the acrobatics and choreographing of the fight scenes. The costume and storyline, however, were distinctly revolutionary. Both the ballet and the opera were filmed and it is these cinematic versions that most audiences would have seen in public cinemas during the 1970s. The film of the ballet appeared in 1970 and the opera in 1972. There was little competition for audiences' time in this period of revolutionary culture and tight censorship so they both received wide viewing – writers like Ding Ling, as we saw in Chapter 8, were effectively silenced through jailing or reeducation. Nonetheless, the revolutionary aspects of the production continue to capture audience imagination and the ballet is still performed live within China and around the world.[13]

The story was based on real events that took place in the southern island of Hainan after the collapse of the First United Front in 1927 between the Communists and Nationalists – the same period of 'white terror' that sent Zhao Yiman and Xie Bingying into hiding. In 1931 a specialist communists women's spy brigade was established on the island called 'The Worker Peasant Red Soldier Second Independent Division, No. 3 Women's Spy Regiment'. It commenced with 104 women, and 19 had been killed in action by the time they ceased operations in 1933. Overwhelmed by the Nationalist troops the leadership were imprisoned, including their brigade leader, Long Qionghua. The women languished in a Guangzhou jail for six years until the Japanese invasion prompted the Second United Front and their release. While some joined the fight against the Japanese, others were forcibly married to Nationalist Party soldiers. In the 1950s those with Nationalist Party husbands faced criticism and in the 1960s even those who had been merely released from the Nationalist prison were accused of being traitors: 'Otherwise why would the Nationalist have released you?' ran the logic.[14] The women were gradually rehabilitated and by the 1980s were feted as 'old warriors' in their home province of Hainan. In 1984, the Hainan CCP identified sixty women from the original regiment still living but their numbers dwindled rapidly in the twenty-first century and in April 2014 the last of their troop passed away – Lu Yexiang was hundred years old.[15] Once rehabilitated, these remarkable women could be put to full propaganda use. In 1985 a 6.8-metre statue of a women soldier, complete with then national leader Hu Yaobang's calligraphy, was erected in Qionghai city to commemorate the role of 'women in the armed struggle' in establishing the nation.[16] In 2000 Qionghai City built a commemorative garden around the statue and in 2001 it became one of the PRC's key patriotic education sites where schools and workplaces visit to learn of PRC glories past.[17] The garden houses military relics such as tanks and cannon. A commemorative hall includes educational texts and photos about the women. The garden's grand entrance gate features a picture from the ballet with a female soldier performing a dramatic arabesque.

The plot of all the fictional versions revolves around the political awakening of a bondmaid, Wu Qinghua,[18] through the intervention of a local communist military cell. Qinghua becomes empowered to resist her oppression at the hands of sleazy and cruel landlord once she meets the male protagonist – disguised as a wealthy overseas Chinese merchant. She joins the women's guerrilla unit, engages in espionage and military battles and undergoes a political awakening and her troop succeeds in overcoming the landlords in their area – despite losing their heroic male commander, Comrade Hong, in the process.

The gendered nature of the war system is apparent throughout. Both the film and ballet use female vulnerability to amplify the righteousness of the communist guerrilla cause and the wounding of the female body is the key mechanism for achieving this amplification. The youthful beautiful bondmaid is repeatedly beaten and whipped at the hands of the evil landlord and the bruised and bleeding female body stands symbolic of oppression and the spur for revenge. Xie Jin's film commences with Qinghua being captured by the landlord's thugs, chained to a thick pole in a dungeon and whipped. She is chained with her hands above her head to display her body to best effect – chest and buttocks exaggerated by the arch in the back produced by her arms pulled up above her head and tied at the wrists. Likewise, the ballet's opening scene highlights the sexual appeal of Qinghua in a striking scene where the camera pans down Qinghua's body from her chained wrists stretched up over her head against the pole. The camera moves down along her naked arms and rests on her defiant face. Dressed in a red-coloured pyjama-style shirt and pants the curve of her breasts is amplified by her upstretched arms. As the camera draws out we see her standing on points in classic western ballet shoes with the arch of her back apparent despite loose fitting clothing. The ballet script book explains that she has been cruelly beaten after each of her many escape attempts and expresses her thoughts as follows: 'If only she could smash the bloody shackles which bind her and wreck the lair of these man-eating beasts.'[19]

In both the film and the ballet she escapes her prison only to be recaptured providing the audience with a chance to see her on-stage/screen whiplashing by the landlord's thugs and by his cane. They beat her until she is unconscious as a lesson for the other bondmaids who look upon the scene in distress.[20] The landlord leaves her 'lacerated and bruised'[21] body for dead. The Red Army Commander discovers her in a dazed state and is horrified at her injuries. Then he encourages her to join the women's brigade in the distant hills. From this moment her political and military training begins in earnest and she transforms from a defiant bondmaid to a first-rate guerrilla leader. In the film version, she displays her bruised throat and upper shoulders to the female troops as evidence of her resolve and sincerity. While modest by twenty-first century standards her actions drew attention to the eroticised throat and neck – a body part that was modestly covered in women's clothing of the first half of the twentieth century. She pulls open her collar and displays the hand marks bruising her neck with her chin pointed upwards to expose her throat – the eroticism of this display is amplified when, as a male commander walks over, she hurriedly covers her neck and throat from his eyes. In the ballet version she displays her bleeding and bruised arms, through torn sleeves, to the gathered troops as evidence of her suffering – the camera zooms in on their horrified faces. The brutalised female body sparks the desire for revenge.[22]

The woman soldier's clothing in both the film and ballet is central to the sexualisation of the war space by the differentiation of male bodies from female bodies. Dressed in thigh-length shorts, and long socks, their legs are bare

Figure 10.1 Modern Revolutionary Ballet – *The Red Detachment of Women*: Heroes under the trees, the red flag flies. China's Worker Peasant Red Soldier Women's Detachment is formed! Women soldiers of heroic bearing, wielding their rifles, in excellent form, diligently practicing their skills in fighting the enemy!

between calf and thigh – no other soldiers have their flesh exposed.[23] The women soldiers present an athletic image that is sexualised by the contrast with the male soldiers with their fully covered legs – the bare legs are markers of femininity. In Xie Jin's movie viewers are even treated to a classic erotic motif in an extended scene of the women soldiers bathing in a river. Displayed in various states of undress the women troops splash and play as they wash. The audience's invitation to be secret voyeurs to the scene is confirmed by the camera angle, which looks from the top of a riverbank down onto the river where the women are unknowingly being viewed amidst their ablutions. Displays of bare flesh among women soldiers are still apparent in the National Day military parades held each October to celebrate the foundation of the PRC. While male soldiers remain fully covered, women soldiers frequently have arms and/or legs bare – usually in mid-thigh length skirts. In one of the more controversial parades, that of the 2009 Sixtieth Anniversary, accusations circulated that real soldiers were replaced with fashion models in order to ensure the aesthetic and sexualised roles expected of women soldiers were performed 'properly'.

The women soldier-spies of the *Red Detachment* reveal another aspect of the gendered war realm – the importance of having women witness men's heroism. Just as the filming of sports events includes frequent close-ups of beautiful women in crowded stadiums at all-male sporting events today, the war system across the twentieth-century world uses the depiction of women looking at men's action to glamourise and sexualise the event. The admiring feminine gaze enhances the masculinity of the actions being undertaken. In the film version of *Red Detachment* the iconic scene demonstrating this aspect of the war system's gendered nature is on the death of the male commander, Hong. Qinghua rushes back to the battle ground where Hong was last seen fighting back the hoards of Nationalist troops in order that his comrades have time to retreat and regroup. Hidden behind a rock Qinghua sees him tied to a tree about to be burned to death. The feminine gaze enhances the masculinity of heroism.

Women soldiers and spies, in their proximity to male comrades during war, have become standard tools for the intensification of masculine power in multiple re-creations of war in art. In another scene Qinghua is kept awake as she ponders Hong's talent, courage and military skill. In yet another she prompts a conversation about his life by admiring his many books. Her admiration of his martial valour and capacities is only possible because she too is in the military space alongside him – women warriors become frequent additions to narratives that seek to enhance the masculinity of the male soldier. Women back at home cannot easily perform this role since they remain spatially distant from the actual battle. While not a feature of *Red Detachment,* depictions of female medical personnel frequently include their witnessing of male heroism or courage in the face of death and, in the process, increasing the masculinity of the 'our side' male soldier. Xie Bingying's diaries discussed in Chapter 4 includes repeated mention of her role and that of other women soldiers in standing as witness to men's heroism. Xie Jin's *Red Detachment* encapsulates this gendering pattern of the intimate feminine witness perfectly. The *Red Detachment of Women* is a model, not only of radical Maoist prescriptions for artistic works, but also of how gender operates within cultures of war and militarisation.

Conclusion

War does not sell itself. As a product it is patently unpleasant. It requires extensive decoration and constant makeovers to appear like a good idea. It gobbles resources, frequently bankrupting national economies even when their home territory is not invaded. It risks the destruction of roads, infrastructure and factories as well as homes, hospitals and schools. Whole systems of fabrication and elaboration are required to ensure that populations are complicit with war fighting and trust that their leaders are competent in its execution.[24] Stories of heroism, sacrifice, gallantry and honour intermingle with those of destroyed homes and mutilated bodies. Gender norms and sexuality are integral to the marketing of war and women warriors and wartime spies are central to its success.

By entrancing audiences with the breaking of gender norms operating in both peacetime and wartime they masquerade as women's liberation while relying on the 'exceptional woman' and 'crisis femininity' narratives to dampen any full-scale feminist revolution. By drawing women, in limited numbers, into war zones to face military danger they become crucial feminine witnesses to male heroism and sacrifice – first-hand ones, rather than the mediated witnesses of women grieving at home. China's use of narratives of women warriors is richer and more managed that most other nations but for efficacy they rely upon age-old gendered war systems that perpetuate violence around the world. Women warriors and wartime spies are the servants of militarisation and have unique and disturbing roles to play in perpetuating that system. And a state of war still continues in China today – officially there has been no peace declared between the Republic of China on Taiwan and the PRC on the mainland. Taiwanese jokingly refer to mainland women sex-workers arriving in Taiwan as 'Red Detachments of Women' in mock horror at the long-threatened invasion from the mainland. War humour needs women too.

Notes

1 Soldiering, war and gender in China

1. The most comprehensive examination of the connection between war and gender can be found in Joshua Goldstein, *War and Gender: How Gender Shapes the War System* (Cambridge: Cambridge University Press, 2001).
2. Jacklyn Cock, 'Women and the Military: Implications for Demilitarization in the 1990s in South Africa', *Gender and Society* 8, no. 2 (1994), 153.
3. Anuradha M. Chenoy, 'Militarization, Conflict, and Women in South Asia', in Jennifer Turpin (ed.), *The Women and War Reader* (New York: New York University Press, 1998), p. 101.
4. Cynthia Enloe, 'The Warriors behind the Women', *Women's Review of Books* 10, no. 5 (1993), 23.
5. See C.B. Otley, 'Militarism and Militarization in the Public Schools, 1900–1972', *British Journal of Sociology* 29, no. 3 (1978), 321–39; P.M. Regan, 'War Toys, War Movies, and the Militarization of the United States, 1900–85', *Journal of Peace Research* 31, no. 1 (1994), 45–58; Guy Westwell, *War Cinema: Hollywood on the Front Line* (London: Wallflower, 2006).
6. Cynthia Enloe, *Maneuvers: The International Politics of Militarizing Women's Lives* (Berkeley: University of California Press, 2000), p. 2.
7. Enloe, *Maneuvers*, p. 5. On Indonesia's militarisation, see Saraswati Sunindyo, 'When the Earth Is Female and the Nation Is Mother: Gender, the Armed Forces and Nationalism in Indonesia', *Feminist Review*, no. 58 (Spring 1998), 1–21.
8. Joshua Goldstein makes passing mention of Hua Mulan and other Chinese women's regiments in his study. Linda Grant de Pauw provides a brief history of some key historical figures but mentions only briefly twentieth-century women in *Battle Cries and Lullabies: Women in War from Prehistory to the Present* (Norman: University of Oklahoma Press, 1998), p. 206. The large number of women war fighters and commanders in China's lengthy documented history invites such summaries in books seeking global reach or broad historical coverage.
9. For book-length studies, see Lily Lee and Sue Wiles, *Women of the Long March* (Sydney: Allen and Unwin, 1999); Helen Praeger Young, *Choosing Revolution: Chinese Women Soldiers on the Long March* (Urbana: University of Illinois Press, 2001).
10. Nicole Ann Dombrowski, 'Soldiers, Saints or Sacrificial Lambs? Women's Relationship to Combat and the Fortification of the Home Front in the Twentieth

Century', in Ann Dombrowski (ed.), *Women and War in the Twentieth Century: Enlisted With or Without Consent* (New York: Routledge, 2004), p. 3.

11. I adopt Joshua Goldstein's definition of the 'war system'. He explains: 'I define the *war system* as the interrelated ways that societies organise themselves to participate in potential and actual wars. In this perspective, war is less a series of events than a system with continuity through time. The system includes, for example, military spending and attitudes about war, in addition to standing military forces and actual fighting'. Goldstein, *War and Gender*, p. 3.

12. Goldstein, *War and Gender*, p. 6.

13. There are ample excellent studies of war and espionage in China. Some of the most recent include Michael Schoenhals, *Spying for the People: Mao's Secret Agents 1949–1967* (Cambridge: Cambridge University Press, 2013); Odd Arne Westad, *Decisive Encounters: The Chinese Civil War, 1946–1950* (Stanford: Stanford University Press, 2003); Andrew Schobell, *China's Use of Military Force: Beyond the Great Wall and the Long March* (Cambridge: Cambridge University Press, 2003); Diana Lary and Stephen McKinnon (eds.), *Scars of War: The Impact of War on Modern China* (Vancouver: University of British Columbia Press, 2001); James Flath and Norman Smith (eds.), *Beyond Suffering: Recounting War in Modern China* (Vancouver: University of British Columbia Press, 2011).

14. Ishihara Koichiro, 'The Japanese Empire in the Balance: Critical Relations with the White Powers, The Ravages of Exploitation, The Task of the Saviour of Asia', *Peiping Chronicle* 6 January 1935, 5.

15. Goldstein, *War and Gender*, p. 356.

16. Lu Xun (Dong Hua), 'Xin "nüjiang"', *Beidou* (North Pole) 1, no. 3 (1931), 131–2.

17. On the dangers of hyper-masculinising the enemy in propaganda, see my article 'Drawing Sexual Violence in Wartime China: Anti-Japanese Propaganda Cartoons', *Journal of Asian Studies* 72, no. 3 (2013), 563–86.

18. Diana Lary reports that many women saw the wars of the 1930s and 1940s as 'opportunities' to take on new roles such as soldiering and providing military support. Diana Lary, 'War and Memory: Memories of China at War', in Flath and Smith (eds.), *Beyond Suffering*, p. 281.

19. Goldstein, *War and Gender*, p. 17.

20. Louise Edwards, 'Zhanzheng dui xiandai Zhongguo funü canzheng yundong de yinxiang: "weijinüxing" de wenti' (The impact of war on women's suffrage in China: the problem of 'crisis femininity'), in Wang Zheng and Chen Yan (eds.), *Bainian Zhongguo nüquan sichao yanjiu* (Research in one hundred years of Chinese feminist thought), (Shanghai: Fudan University Press, 2005), pp. 220–6.

21. The historical pattern of Chinese women becoming men in order to become soldiers differs from that of Vietnam where long tradition of women as war fighters exists. The Tru'ng Sisters (c. 40 CE) are the most famous example of Vietnam's women fighters. I am grateful to Bruce Lockhart for this point. For accounts of Vietnamese women soldiers' experiences, see Karen Turner-Gottschang and Thanh Hao Phan, *Even the Women Must Fight: Memories of War from North Vietnam* (New York: Wiley, 1998). For the most comprehensive overview of historical and contemporary women war fighters in the various nations of Southeast Asia, see Tobias Rettig and Vina Lanzona (eds.), *Women Warriors in Southeast Asia* (London: Routledge, 2016).

22. See Antonia Finnane, *Changing Clothes in China: Fashion, History, Nation* (New York: Columbia University Press, 2008). On military and school uniforms, see Louise Edwards, 'Dressing for Power: Scholars' Robes, School Uniforms and Military Attire in China', in M. Roces and L. Edwards (eds.), *The Politics of Dress in Asia and the Americas* (Brighton: Sussex Academic, 2007), pp. 42–64.

23. Lu Xun, 'Xin "nüjiang"', 132.

24. Tamara Jacka, 'Back to the Wok: Women and Employment in Chinese Industry in the 1980s', *Australian Journal of Chinese Affairs*, no. 24 (July 1990), 1–23.

25. This translation comes from Colin Green, 'Turning Bad Iron into Polished Steel: Whampoa and the Rehabilitation of the Chinese Soldier', in Flath and Smith (eds.), *Beyond Suffering*, pp. 153–4. For a nuanced discussion of the value placed on military skill in the Qing, see Joanna Waley-Cohen, *The Culture of War in China: Empire and the Military under the Qing Dynasty* (London: IB Tauris, 2006).

26. Green, 'Turning Bad Iron into Polished Steel', pp. 153–85.

27. On the increasing prestige of martial talent among men, see Lili Zhou, 'The Reconstruction of Masculinity in China', PhD diss., University of Technology, Sydney (2012); and on both women and men, see Louise Edwards and Lili Zhou, 'Gender and the "Virtue of Violence": Creating a New Vision of Political Engagement through the 1911 Revolution', *Frontiers of History in China* 6, no. 4 (2011), 485–504.

28. Robert Culp, 'Rethinking Governmentality: Training, Cultivation and Cultural Citizenship in Nationalist China', *Journal of Asian Studies* 65, no. 3 (2006), 529–54.

29. Edmund Fung, *Military Dimensions of the Chinese Revolution: The New Army and Its Role in the 1911 Revolution* (Canberra: Australian National University Press, 1981), p. 99.

30. Nicola Spakowski, 'Women's Military Participation in the Communist Movement of the 1930s and 1940s: Patterns of Inclusion and Exclusion', in Mechthild Leutner and Nicola Spakowski (eds.), *Women in China: The Republican Period in Historical Perspective* (Münster: LIT, 2005), pp. 129–71. However, in the twenty-first century the use of women for the public relations aspects of militarisation has opened the PRC government to charges of using women recruits as decorations only fit for the 'song and dance' acts of the People's Liberation Army's [PLA] cultural wings. See Sky Canaves, 'China's Military Women Hold Up Half the Sky (and Dance, and Sing, and…)', *Wall Street Journal: China Real Time Blog*, 30 November 2009, http://blogs.wsj.com/chinarealtime/2009/11/30/chinas-military-women-hold-up-half-the-sky-and-dance-and-sing-and.../

31. Laurie S. Stoff, *They Fought for the Motherland: Russia's Women Soldiers in World War I and the Revolution* (Lawrence: University of Kansas Press, 2006), p. 3.

32. See Yingjie Guo, *Cultural Nationalism in Contemporary China* (London: Routledge, 2004).

2   The archetypal woman warrior, Hua Mulan

1. Martial arts enthusiasts can now learn Mulan-style martial arts. Mass demonstrations of this form filled Shanghai's streets during International Women's Day in 2009.

'Healthy life balance', *Shanghai Daily* 9 March 2009, A3. Mulan's appearance in the 1998 Disney Classics Animation series, dubbed into multiple languages and globally marketed, propelled her story to international fame.

2. The two major collections of works on Hua Mulan are: Huang Canzhang and Li Shaoyi (eds.), *Hua Mulan kao* (Investigating Mulan), (Beijing: Zhongguo guangbo dianshi chubanshe, 1992); Ma Junhua and Su Lixiang (eds.), *Mulan wenxian daguan* (Overview of documents on Mulan), (Zhengzhou: Henan renmin chubanshe, 1993). There are literally hundreds of poems, epitaphs and inscriptions about Mulan from the Tang onwards and some are collected in these two volumes.

3. Wu Pei-Yi, 'Yang Miaozhen: A Woman Warrior in Thirteenth Century China', *Nan Nü: Men, Women and Gender in Early and Imperial China* 4, no. 2 (2002), 161. Wu contrasts Mulan's fame with the relative silence surrounding the story of Yang Miaozhen. The large corpus of historical material on the colourful Yang Miaozhen limits later redactors' scope to shape her into their fantasised form. Wu argues that Yang's adultery – she seduces a warlord for tactical purposes – renders her persona non grata.

4. See Joan Judge, 'Expanding the Feminine/National Imaginary: Social and Martial Heroines in Late Qing Women's Journals', *Jindai Zhongguo funü shi yanjiu* (Research on Modern China's women's history) 15 (December 2007), 16–17, 27.

5. For further discussion of this point and its more general applicability to other women warriors, see Louise Edwards, 'Women Warriors and Amazons of the Mid-Qing Texts *Jinghua yuan* and *Honglou meng*', *Modern Asian Studies* 29, no. 2 (1995), 225–55.

6. Shiamin Kwa and Wilt L. Idema have translated five versions of Mulan texts and provided plot summaries for a further few in their *Mulan: Five Versions of a Classic Chinese Legend with Related Texts* (Indianapolis: Hackett, 2010). Su Zheng discusses the immensely popular 1920 song by Bao Zhongwei that was based on the original poem. Other versions were promoted during the war against Japan. See Su Zheng, 'Female Heroes and Moonish Lovers: Women's Paradoxical Identities in Modern Chinese Songs', *Journal of Women's History* 8, no. 4 (1997), 91–125.

7. On Mulan's ethnicity, see Feng Lan, 'The Female Individual and the Empire: A Historicist Approach to Mulan and Kingston's Woman Warrior', *Comparative Literature* 55, no. 3 (2003), 229–45.

8. Despite the extensive range of tales narrating her adventures, historical evidence about Mulan's life is elusive. Details of her life are impossible to verify and most scholars regard her as a purely literary figure. Nonetheless, some contribute to the popular desire for the historical Mulan. For example, Huang and Liu's book includes sections titled 'Which era did Mulan live in?' and 'Where is Mulan from?' and, as if to remove any doubt about her existence, has a chapter grimly titled 'Mulan's death'. Huang and Liu, *Hua Mulan kao*, 3–9. Both Hubei and Henan provinces claim her as a native. The PRC's domestic tourism boom fuels these competing claims for ownership. In 1993, Henan's Yucheng County institutionalised its claim with a 'Mulan culture festival' celebrated annually on the eighth day of the fourth lunar month.

9. Translations are from Hans Frankel, *The Flowering Plum and the Palace Lady: Interpretations of Chinese Poetry* (New Haven: Yale University Press, 1976), pp. 68–70.

10. Xu Wei, 'Ci Mulan ti fu cong jun', in *Si sheng yuan* (Four cries of a Gibbon), (rpt. Shanghai: Shanghai guji chubanshe, 1995). For a translation of play, see Appendix III of Jeanette Louise Faurot, 'Four Cries of a Gibbon: A Tsa-chü Cycle by the Ming Dramatist Hsu Wei (1521–1593)', PhD diss., University of California, Berkeley (1972) and also in Kwa and Idema, *Mulan*. On Xu's life, see Anne-Marie Hsiung, 'A Feminist Re-vision of Xu Wei's *Ci Mulan* and *Nü zhuangyuan*', in Zhang Yingjin (ed.), *China in a Polycentric World: Essays in Chinese Comparative Literature* (Stanford: Stanford University Press, 1998), pp. 83–9.

11. Wilt Idema, 'Female Talent and Female Virtue: Xu Wei's *Nü Zhuangyuan* and Meng Chengshun's *Zhenwen ji*', in Hua Wei and Wang Ailing (eds.), *Ming Qing xiqu guoji yantaohui wenji* (Collected essays from the international symposium on Ming and Qing drama), (Taipei: Academia Sinica, Chinese Literature and Philosophy Research Institute, 1998), p. 563.

12. Xu Wei's play includes the following discussion among Mulan's comrades: 'It's very strange that Brother Hua [Mulan] never lets anyone see him urinate.' They explain this strange behaviour by presuming that Hua must be very refined and modest about bodily functions. Mulan deflects attention from her preference for private urination by telling her comrades about a 'far stranger story' of a Buddhist Guard statue in a temple near her village that suddenly turned into Chang'er, the beautiful Moon Goddess. R. Keith McMahon details the erotic trope of men viewing female urination in his *Causality and Containment in Seventeenth Century Chinese Fiction* (Leiden: E.J. Brill, 1988).

13. Idema explains that during the Ming there was an increasing trend for private household dramatic performance among literati families that generated demand for short, lively plays such as *Ci Mulan*. Idema, 'Female Talent and Female Virtue', p. 553.

14. Siu Leung Li, *Cross-dressing in Chinese Opera* (Hong Kong: Hong Kong University Press, 2006), p. 86. On the historical significance of footbinding, see Dorothy Ko, *Cinderella's Sisters: A Revisionist History of Footbinding* (Berkeley: University of California Press, 2005).

15. Chris Berry notes that the Disney version increased contemporary audience appeal by introducing anachronisms and geographic displacements. 'What these elements share is that they already signify "Chineseness" to people outside China.' Berry, 'Disney's Mulan, Disney's Feminism: Universal Appeal and Mutually Assured Destruction', *TAASA Review* 9 (2000), 6.

16. Qin Xiu avenged her parents' deaths by murdering their killers in complete disregard for her own safety. Ti Ying petitioned the emperor to seek a lighter sentence for her father. She offered herself as a slave in return.

17. Xu, 'Ci Mulan', p. 705.

18. Siu Leung Li notes that Xu Wei's play 'places more emphasis on filial piety and chastity than nationalism and patriotism'. Li, *Cross-dressing in Chinese Opera*, p. 85.

19. Xu, 'Ci Mulan', p. 708.

20. Mulan's chaste suicide is also a feature of Yingyuan jiuzhu's *Biography of an Extraordinary Woman, Mulan* (c. 1730–1830). For discussion of this novel, see the longer version of this chapter: Edwards, 'Transformations of the Woman Warrior, Hua Mulan', *Nan Nü: Men, Women and Gender in China* 12, no. 2 (2010), 190–3.

21. See Tien Ju-k'ang, *Male Anxiety and Female Chastity* (Leiden: E.J. Brill, 1988); Janet Theiss, *Disgraceful Matters: The Politics of Chastity in Eighteenth-Century China* (Berkeley: University of California Press, 2004).
22. Robert E. Hegel, *The Novel in Seventeenth Century China* (New York: Columbia University Press, 1981), p. 205.
23. Chu Renhuo, *Sui Tang yanyi* (Romance of the Sui and Tang), (1695 rpt. Shenyang: Changchun chubanshe, 2008), chapters 56–60.
24. Chu, *Sui Tang yanyi*, p. 430.
25. Chu, *Sui Tang yanyi*, p. 430.
26. Mulan also featured in official gazetteers. With the rising importance of female virtue as a signal-marker for local virtue in the Qing, Mulan's story was recreated within sections dedicated to virtuous women (*Lienü shang*) during the Yongzheng and Qianlong reigns. Her filial piety and sacrifice were evidence of the locality's virtue. The gazetteers include her suicide in response to the emperor's desire to make her his concubine. See 'Henan tongzhi', Yongzheng reign, Guide Prefecture, 67 juan, Lienü shang. Rpt. in Ma and Su, *Mulan wenxian daguan*, p. 52; 'Guide fuzhi', Qianlong reign, 26 juan, Lienü shang. Rpt. in Ma and Su, *Mulan wenxian daguan*, pp. 53–4.
27. Hegel, *The Novel in Seventeenth Century China*, p. 206.
28. Hegel, *The Novel in Seventeenth Century China*, p. 201.
29. Chu, *Sui Tang yanyi*, p. 396.
30. Chu, *Sui Tang yanyi*, pp. 396–7.
31. Chu, *Sui Tang yanyi*, p. 398.
32. David Faure, *Emperor and Ancestor: State and Lineage in China* (Stanford: Stanford University Press, 2007), pp. 2–15.
33. Judge notes that in one such book by Wei Xiyuan published in 1908 Mulan appears in the section on 'Filiality to Parents' and that several other such instructional texts also emphasise her 'daughterly dedication and upright feminine decorum'. Joan Judge, *The Precious Raft of History* (Stanford: Stanford University Press, 2008), p. 153. Their point of difference from the earlier Ming and Qing texts is that Mulan becomes for the first time a female citizen charged with the duty of defending her race/nation (*minzu*). See Judge, *The Precious Raft*, pp. 152, 154–55.
34. Judge, *The Precious Raft*, p. 152.
35. *Mulan congjun*, Bu Wancang dir., Emei dianying zhipian prod., b&w, 89 min, 1939, Film. Screen play by Ouyang Yuqian.
36. Poshek Fu, *Between Shanghai and Hong Kong: The Politics of Chinese Cinema* (Stanford: Stanford University Press, 2003), pp. 11–28.
37. The nationalist rhetoric of Bu's film is unrelenting. Mulan's father declares that he could not possibly contemplate eating the nation's grain if he was hiding at home while the country was in peril.
38. For detailed discussion of the impact of Hua Mulan plays and films, see Chang-tai Hung, *War and Popular Culture: Resistance in Modern China 1937–1945* (Berkeley: University of California Press, 1999), pp. 72–4.
39. Hung, *War and Popular Culture*, p. 74. See also, Edward Gunn, *The Unwelcome Muse: Chinese Literature in Shanghai and Peking* (New York: Columbia University Press, 1980) for discussion of the play and its reception. The play-script

was later reprinted in Hong Kong. Zhou Yibai, *Hua Mulan* (1941 rpt. Hong Kong: Jindai tushu, 1958).

40. Mao Zedong, 'Talks at the Yan'an Forum on Literature and Art', 2 and 23 May 1942, Web, https://www.marxists.org/reference/archive/mao/selected-works/volume-3/mswv3_08.htm.

41. Chang-Tai Hung, 'Female Symbols of Resistance in Chinese Wartime Spoken Drama', *Modern China* 15, no. 2 (1989), 166.

42. Zhou, *Hua Mulan*, pp. 10–11.

43. Zhou, *Hua Mulan*, p. 8.

44. Zhou, *Hua Mulan*, p. 15.

45. Zhou, *Hua Mulan*, p. 17.

46. Zhou, *Hua Mulan*, pp. 117–18.

47. *Hua Mulan*, Liu Guoquan and Zhang Xinshi dir., Changchun dianying prod., b&w, 1956, Film. Henan Opera.

48. Wong Hok-sing's 1961 film of a Cantonese Opera version includes a scene where Mulan is exposed as a woman and as a consequence faces certain death for her deceit. The opera concludes with Mulan's fellow soldiers entreating the emperor to spare her saying that her loyalty and filial piety are outstanding motivations for her transgression and therefore deserve praise not punishment. The twin loyalties, to family and to nation, are presented as highly compatible and their combination strengthens their power to save Mulan from execution. *Faa Muk Laan* (The Feminine General Far Mok Lan), Wong Hok-sing dir., Baak Daat prod., b&w, 97 min, 1961, Film. Cantonese Opera.

49. *Hua Mulan* (Lady General Hua Mu-lan), Yue Feng dir., Shaw Brothers prod., 106 min, 1964. Film. Huangmei Opera originated from Anhui province but became popular in Hong Kong's multilingual cultural scene in the 1950s and 1960s. The films of this dramatic form propelled Anhui's drama to international prominence. The Cantonese and Huangmei Opera versions gave Mulan's story wide circulation in Hong Kong and among the global Chinese diaspora. On this genre, see Tan See-Kam, 'Huangmei opera films, Shaw Brothers and Ling Bo: chaste love stories, genderless cross-dressers and sexless gender-plays?' *Jump Cut: A Review of Contemporary Media* 49 (2007), http://www.ejumpcut.org/archive/jc49.2007/Tan See-Kam/index.html

50. Bu Wancang's 1939 film includes a scene where two older soldiers spot the young and beautiful Mulan and assume him to be a boy. They agree that he is very 'fair' and decide to follow him/her. They bully Mulan and make sexually threatening comments such as 'You look like a flower.' Mulan repels them with her superior wit and strength. Later in the film, after Mulan is established as a great warrior, her comrades are sitting around discussing her attributes and one rather coyly declares that 'If she were a girl, I would not be able to resist her.' Wong Hok-sing's 1961 Cantonese Opera version also includes multiple jokes about the mysterious affinity that is developing between Mulan and one of her fellow soldiers. Wong's all-knowing audiences watch as their fellow soldiers spy on this 'strange romance' and pass salacious, voyeuristic comment.

51. *Hua Mulan*, Li Huiming and Lai Shuiqing dir., Young Pei Pei Studios and China TV prod., 44 episodes, 1999, Television Series.

52. Joseph Allen notes that in cartoon pictorial versions of her story she is often depicted as wearing trousers and standing with her legs spread. 'Here the reader's

gaze is ready to take advantage of that temporary immodesty and peel away the few layers of clothing that expose Mulan for what she is, a young woman with her legs spread wide.' Allen, 'Dressing and Undressing the Chinese Woman Warrior', *positions: East Asian Cultures Critique* 4 (1996), 359. Allen's examples are primarily from the late twentieth century. Susan Mann reproduces a 1908 picture of Mulan in a similar pose in her 'Myths of Asian Womanhood', *Journal of Asian Studies* 59, no. 4 (2000), 856.

53. *Mulan*, Jingle Ma Choh-hsing dir., Starlight International et al. prod., 114 min, 2009, Film.

3   Qiu Jin

1. Qiu Jin, 'Jinggao zimeimen' (Respectful note to my sisters), *Zhongguo nübao* (Chinese women's journal) 1 (1904), rpt. in Qiu Jin, *Qiu Jin ji* [Hereafter *QJJ*], (Shanghai: Guji chubanshe, 1962), p. 14.
2. Qiu, 'Jinggao zimeimen', p. 14.
3. See the many magical swordswomen of the Qing novel *Flowers in the Mirror* (*Jinghua yuan*) or the popular Thirteenth Sister from *The Tale of Romance and Heroism* (*Ernü yingxiong zhuan*). The latter has at least four film and television adaptations since 1959. On *Jinghua yuan*, see Edwards, 'Women Warriors and Amazons', 225–55.
4. Qiu, 'Jinggao zimeimen', pp. 14–5.
5. Chen Yiyi cited in Judge, 'Expanding the Feminine/National Imaginary', 16.
6. Hu Ying, 'Writing Qiu Jin's Life: Wu Zhiying and Her Family Learning', *Late Imperial China* 25, no. 2 (2004), 119. Her literary achievements are considerable. Qiu Jin produced 213 poems in the *chi* style, 39 in the *ci* style and an incomplete lengthy *tanci* prose poem. She wrote several essays and produced song lyrics aimed to rouse political action. See Kang-i Sun Chang and Haun Saussy (eds.), *Women Writers of Traditional China: An Anthology of Poetry and Criticism* (Stanford: Stanford University Press, 1999), p. 633.
7. Qiu Jin, 'Jinggao wo tongbao' (A respectful note to my country men and women), *Baihua* (The vernacular) nos 3–4 (1904), rpt. in *QJJ*, p. 8.
8. Changing literati attitudes to violence was a concomitant trend. See Edwards and Zhou, 'Gender and the "Virtue of Violence"', 485–504.
9. During her trial two documents were used as evidence of her involvement in the Guangfu army: 'Guangfu jun qiyi xigao' (Draft call to arms for the Guangfu uprising) and 'Guangfu jun junzhi gao' (Draft military regulations for the Guangfu army), rpt. in *QJJ*, pp. 21–6.
10. Qiu Jin, 'Tan Zhongguo' (Sighing over China), rpt. in *QJJ*, p. 114.
11. Qiu Jin, 'To the Melody of "Rivers and Mountains Like This"', in Wilt Idema and Beata Grant (eds.), *The Red Brush: Writing Women of Imperial China* (Cambridge: Harvard East Asia Centre, 2004), p. 786. Chinese version available in 'Ruci jiangshan', in *QJJ*, p. 109.
12. Qiu Jin, 'Tongbao ku' (My countrymen and women's bitterness), in *QJJ*, pp. 113–14.

13. This event would be immortalised in the 1963 movie *Fifty-five Days at Peking*, Nicholas Ray and Guy Green dir., Samuel Bronston prod., 154 min, 1963, Film. Starring Charlton Heston, Ava Gardner and David Niven.

14. Qiu Jin in Lingzhen Wang, *Personal Matters: Women's Autobiographical Practice in Twentieth-Century China* (Stanford: Stanford University Press, 2004), p. 38. Chinese version available in Qiu Jin, *QJJ*, p. 60.

15. Mary Backus Rankin, 'The Emergence of Women at the End of the Ch'ing: The Case of Ch'iu Chin', in Margery Wolf and Roxane Witke (eds.), *Women in Chinese Society* (Stanford: Stanford University Press, 1975), p. 46.

16. Her son became a journalist and teacher and remained in the PRC after 1949. He worked in the Hunan Office for Research on Written History. Her daughter studied aviation in New York and became known as China's first female aviator. After 1949 she lived in Taiwan and wrote frequently about her mother. Rankin, 'The Emergence of Women', p. 47.

17. Qiu Jin cited in Wang, *Personal Matters*, p. 35. Qiu Jin's letters to her brothers can be found in *QJJ*, pp. 33–46.

18. Qiu Jin cited in Wang, *Personal Matters*, p. 39.

19. Rankin, 'The Emergence of Women', p. 48.

20. Rankin, 'The Emergence of Women', p. 46.

21. Qiu Jin trans. in Wang, *Personal Matters,* p. 45. Chinese version available in 'You huai: you Riben shi zuo' (Regrets: lines written *en route* to Japan), in *QJJ*, p. 87.

22. On He Zhen, see Lydia Liu, Rebecca Karl and Dorothy Ko, *The Birth of Chinese Feminism* (New York: Columbia University Press, 2013). On Chen Xiefen, see Charlotte Beahan, 'Feminism and Nationalism in the Chinese Women's Press, 1902–1911', *Modern China* 1, no. 4 (1975), 379–416. On Tang Qunying, see David Strand, *An Unfinished Republic: Leading by Word and Deed in Modern China* (Berkeley: University of California Press, 2011).

23. Sun Yat-sen, 'Zhongguo Tongmenghui geming fanglüe' (General Plan for the Chinese Revolutionary Alliance revolution), in *Sun Zhongshan quanji: diyijuan* (Complete works of Sun Yat-sen, volume 1), (Guangzhou: Zhonghua shuju, 1981), p. 296. The General Plan goes into considerable detail including the rules for the military – specifying that troops found raping women would face capital punishment (p. 301).

24. Zheng Yunshan and Chen Dehe, *Qiu Jin pingzhuan* (Critical biography of Qiu Jin), (Zhengzhou: Henan jaioyu chubanshe, 1986), p. 127.

25. Helen Foster Snow, *Women of Modern China* (The Hague: Mouton, 1967), p. 98.

26. Wang, *Personal Matters*, p. 27.

27. Fonu, *Shenzhou nübao* (1907) cited in and trans. by Idema and Grant, *The Red Brush*, pp. 801–2.

28. Fonu, *Shenzhou nübao*, pp. 801–2.

29. Florence Ayscough, *Chinese Women: Yesterday and To-Day* (Boston: Houghton Mifflin, 1937), 174.

30. See Xia Xiaohong, *Wanqing shehui yu wenhua* (Late Qing society and culture), (Wuhan: Hubei jiaoyu chubanshe, 2000), p. 209. Xia provides detailed analysis of the media reporting on pp. 209–18.

31. Rankin, 'The Emergence of Women', p. 62.

32. 'Revolutionary Terms', *North China Herald* 26 July 1907, 203.

33. 'A Victim of a Governor's Panic', *North China Herald* 26 July 1907, 204–5.

34. Sabine Hieronymous, 'Qiu Jin (1875–1907): A Heroine for All Seasons', in Leutner and Spakowski (eds.), *Women in China*, p. 201.
35. For Wu Zhiying's biography and the significance of her role in commemorating Qiu Jin, see Hu, 'Writing Qiu Jin's Life', pp. 122–4.
36. Hu Ying, 'Gender and Modern Martyrology: Qiu Jin as *Lienü, Lieshi* or *Nülieshi*', in Joan Judge and Hu Ying (eds.), *Beyond Exemplar Tales: Women's Biography in Chinese History* (Berkeley: University of California Press, 2011), pp. 121–36; Hieronymous, 'Qiu Jin', pp. 194–207.
37. Hieronymous, 'Qiu Jin', p. 197.
38. Rankin, 'The Emergence of Women', p. 52.
39. Hu, 'Writing Qiu Jin's Life', 119–60.
40. James J.Y. Liu, *The Chinese Knight-Errant* (Chicago: Chicago University Press, 1967), pp. 4–7.
41. For a comprehensive study of female swordswomen in China's literary tradition, see Roland Altenburger, *The Sword or the Needle: The Female Knight-Errant (Xia) in Traditional Chinese Narrative* (Bern: Peter Lang, 2009). He explores major female *xia* figures from the Tang to the early republic.
42. Rankin, 'The Emergence of Women', p. 46.
43. Qiu Jin, 'To the Melody of "Full River Red"', in Idema and Grant, *The Red Brush*, p. 784. Chinese version available as 'Man Jiang hong' in *QJJ*, p. 108.
44. Xu Shuangyu, 'Qiu Jin ji' (Remembering Qiu Jin), cited in Eileen J. Cheng 'Gendered Spectacles: Lu Xun on Gazing at Women and Other Pleasures', *Modern Chinese Literature and Culture* 16, no. 1 (2004), 6. Original available in Guo Yanli (ed.), *Qiu Jin yanjiu ziliao* (Research materials on Qiu Jin), (Jinan: Shandong jiaoyu chubanshe, 1987), pp. 215–16.
45. Qiu Jin, 'Song of the Precious Sword', trans. in Idema and Grant, *The Red Brush*, pp. 774–5. Chinese version available as 'Bao dao ge', in *QJJ*, p. 82.
46. Qiu, 'Song of the Precious Sword', pp. 774–5.
47. Hu, 'Gender and Modern Martyrology', p. 122.
48. Qiu Jin cited in Hieronymus, 'Qiu Jin', p. 199. The obituary can be found in 'Diao Wu lieshi Yue', in *QJJ*, pp. 80–1.
49. See Peter Zarrow, *China in War and Revolution, 1895–1949* (London: Routledge, 2005), 54.
50. Qiu Jin, 'Zhi Wang Shize shu' (Letter to Wang Shize), in *QJJ*, pp. 46–7. See Zhang Yun, 'Nationalism and Beyond: Writings on *Nüjie* and the Emergence of a New Gendered Collective Identity in Modern China', *Nan nü: Men, Women and Gender in China* 17, no. 2 (2015) for a discussion of how women emerged as a collective political and social entity.
51. Qiu, 'Zhi Wang Shize shu', p. 47. Translation from 'Letter 13: From Qiu Jin to Wang Shize', by Marion Philips and Dorothea Martin in *Chinese Studies in History* 34, no. 2 (2000–2001), 73.
52. Qiu Jin, 'Letter to Qiu Yuzhang, Elder Brother – 12 September 1905', trans. by Marion Phillips and Dorothea Martin in *Chinese Studies in History* 34, no. 2 (2000–2001), 60. Chinese version available as 'Qi wu' (No. 5), in *QJJ*, p. 39.
53. Qiu Jin, 'Letter to Aunt Qinwen – 9 April 1901', trans. by Marion Phillips and Dorothea Martin in *Chinese Studies in History* 34, no. 2 (2000–2001), 51. Chinese version available as 'Zhi Qin Wen shu' (Letter to Qin Wen), in *QJJ*, pp. 31–2.

54. See Theiss, *Disgraceful Matters*.
55. Xu Zhihua cited in Hu, 'Writing Qiu Jin's Life', p. 130. Hu notes that this 'Garret for Mourning Qiu Jin' (*Bei Qiu ge*) was first printed in 1908 and later reprinted in 1912. Chinese version available in Wang Shaoji, *Qiu Jin nüshi yiji* (Mourning collection on Madam Qiu Jin) (Shanghai: Baiguang shudian, 1937), p. 66.
56. Xu Zhihua cited in Lionel Giles, *Ch'iu Chin: A Chinese Heroine* (London: East and West, 1917), p. 19. This is Giles's translation of Xu Zhihua's 'Garret for Mourning' published in a paper on Qiu Jin presented to London's China Society.
57. See Qiu, *QJJ*, pp. 87–90.
58. Zhang Binglin cited in Hu, 'Writing Qiu Jin's Life', 131. The Chinese version available in Wang, *Qiu Jin nüshi yiji*, pp. 67–8.
59. On how public speaking became important for women activists following Qiu Jin, see Chapter 3 of Strand, *An Unfinished Republic*.
60. Qiu Jin, 'Full River Red', in Idema and Grant, *The Red Brush*, p. 776. Chinese version available as 'Man jiang hong', in *QJJ*, p. 99.
61. Huang Chonggu, the cross-dressing official, is so successful that she wins an official government post and is invited to marry the prime minister's daughter. When her sex is revealed she escapes punishment because of her outstanding talents – but once discovered she returns to her life as a woman. Zhu Yingtai is the heroine of the famous 'Butterfly lovers' story. Zhu dresses as a boy to attend school and while there, falls in love with Liang Shanbo. Eventually she is called home from school to be married. Liang visits his school friend, discovers that 'he' is actually a woman and falls in love. Hearing of her impending marriage he dies of grief. On her wedding day Zhu visits Liang's grave, it opens with a thunderclap, she steps in to be united with him and two butterflies emerge. See Idema and Grant, *The Red Brush*, pp. 677–9. For discussion of cross-dressing, Zhu Yingtai and Hua Mulan, see Roland Altenburger, 'Is It Clothes That Make the Man?: Cross-Dressing, Gender, and Sex in Pre-Twentieth Century Zhu Yingtai Lore', *Asian Folklore Studies* 64, no. 2 (2005), 165–205.
62. Qiu Jin trans. in Jonathan Spence, *The Gate of Heavenly Peace: The Chinese and Their Revolution, 1895–1980* (New York: Penguin, 1982), p. 87. Chinese version available as 'Zi ti xiao zhao – nan zhuang' (Inscription on my photo – men's clothing), in *QJJ*, p. 78.
63. Rankin 'The Emergence of Women', p. 52.
64. Wang, *Personal Matters*, p. 44.
65. Qiu, 'Letter to Qiu Yuzhang', p. 61.
66. For a discussion of the 'Sick Man' epithet, see Xu Guoqi, *Olympic Dreams: China and Sports, 1895–2008* (Cambridge: Harvard University Press, 2008), pp. 17–20.
67. Qiu Jin in Idema and Grant, *The Red Brush*, p. 776. Chinese available in 'Ta suo xing', in *QJJ*, p. 108.
68. Qiu Jin wrote a eulogy to Qu Yuan. See 'Diao Qu Yuan' (Mourning Qu Yuan), in *QJJ*, p. 74.
69. Louise Edwards, 'Policing the Modern Woman in Republican China', *Modern China* 26, no. 2 (2000), 115–47.
70. Edwards, 'Zhanzheng dui xiandai Zhongguo', pp. 220–6.
71. Qiu Jin, 'Stones of the Jingwei Bird' (*Jingwei shi*), trans. in Idema and Grant, *The Red Brush*, pp. 786–94. More excerpts are available in Amy Dooling and Kristina

Torgeson, *Writing Women in Modern China: An Anthology of Women's Literature from the Early Twentieth Century* (New York: Columbia University Press, 1998), 39–78. Chinese version available in *QJJ*, 119–62.

72. Qiu, 'Stones of the Jingwei Bird', p. 790.

73. Qiu, 'Stones of the Jingwei Bird', p. 793.

74. Qiu Jin in Idema and Grant, *The Red Brush*, pp. 784–5. Chinese version available as 'Man jiang hong', in *QJJ*, p. 108.

75. Qiu Jin, 'On *Zhi kan ji*', cited in Wang, *Personal Matters*, pp. 32–3. The translations are Wang's. Chinese version available in *QJJ*, p.55. The *Zhikan ji* (Records of the Sesame Niche) is a fictional work in sixty chapters written in the mid Qing by Dong Rong. It narrates the fall of the Ming dynasty and extols classic Confucian virtues of filial piety and loyalty including the stories of Qin Liangyu and Shen Yunying. More controversially, it condemns the Ming officials and generals for their incompetence and praises the Manchu for their victory. See Tu Shu-min, '*Zhikan ji* chuanqi xulu' (Commentary on the *Zhikan ji*), *Tongshi jiaoyu xuebao* (General knowledge teaching journal) 8 (December 2005), 1–17.

76. See Louise Edwards, *Men and Women in Qing China: Gender in the Red Chamber Dream* (Leiden: E.J. Brill, 1994; Honolulu: Hawaii University Press, 2001).

77. On Lu Xun's critique of female spectacles, see Cheng 'Gendered Spectacles', 1–36. Lu Xun, 'Correspondence' cited in Cheng, 'Gendered Spectacles', 5.

78. Lu Xun, 'Yao' (Medicine), *Xin qingnian* (New youth) (May 1919), rpt. in *Lu Xun quanji, juan 1* (Complete works of Lu Xun), (Shanghai: Xinhua shuju, 1973), pp. 298–310.

79. Her use of vernacular rather than classical Chinese in her journals tempered this elitism. She wrote in her opening announcement for the *Chinese Women's Journal*: 'In this newspaper, in addition to the classical style, the colloquial will be used for the convenience of those who are not well versed in the classical language so that they too can read.' Translation from Yong Z. Volz, 'Going Public through Writing: Women Journalists and Gendered Journalistic Space in China, 1890s–1920s', *Media, Culture and Society* 29, no. 3 (2007), 477. Chinese original available as 'Zhongguo nübao fakan ci' (Inaugural introduction to the *Chinese Women's Journal*), in *QJJ*, pp. 12–13.

80. Xia Yan, *Ziyou hun* (The spirit of freedom), (Shanghai: Shenghuo shudian, 1937). It later became known as *Qiu Jin zhuan* (Biography of Qiu Jin) and underwent multiple rewritings and republications, the most significant written by Ke Ling. Ke's formed the basis of Xie Jin's 1983 film script. Xia Yan and Ke Ling, *Qiu Jin zhuan* (Biography of Qiu Jin) (1962; Shanghai: Shanghai wenyi chubanshe, 1979). See Xia Xiaohong on the evolution of the story. Xia Xiaohong, 'Qiu Jin wenxue xingxiang de shidai fengmao: cong Xia Yan de huaju dao Xie Jin de dianying' (Features of the times in Qiu Jin's literary imagery: from Xia Yan's play to Xie Jin's movie), *Zhongguo xiandai wenxue yanjiu congkan* (Research into modern Chinese literature) no. 4 (2009), 49–65.

81. Xia, *Ziyou hun*, pp. 81–2.

82. On changing ideals of female martyrdom, see Hu, 'Gender and Modern Martyrology', pp. 121–36.

83. There was some discontent about assassination as a technique. See He Qifang, 'Wu Yuzhang tongzhi geming gushi' (Comrade Wu Yuzhang's revolutionary story) *Renmin ribao* [Hereafter *RMRB*] 30 December 1948, 4.

84. Not all left-wing commentators objected to Qiu Jin's suicide. Soon-to-be PRC minister of culture, Guo Moruo, wrote in 1942 that Qiu Jin's actions were 'an answer to Nora'. By this he is referring to the intense debate that surrounded the translation of Henrik Ibsen's play 'The Dolls House'. The female protagonist, Nora, leaves home at the end of the play to forge her own life. After its circulation in China, Lu Xun wrote an essay provocatively titled 'What Happens after Nora Leaves Home?' in which he determines that she either becomes a prostitute or returns home. Guo Moruo is more optimistic. He wrote that Qiu Jin's revolutionary life was the ideal path for China's Noras. He found nothing problematic in her martyrdom. Guo Moruo, 'Nuola de da'an' (The solution for Nora), *Xinhua ribao* (New China daily) 19 July 1942, rpt. in Guo Yanli (ed.), *Qiu Jin yanjiu ziliao*, pp. 466–71.

85. Snow, *Women in Modern China*, p. 94.

86. Hu, 'Gender and Modern Martyrology', p. 122. He Qifang accused Xia Yan of presenting Qiu Jin as a 'reactionary' in her dismissive attitudes to the Boxer's attack on foreign imperialists. He Qifang, 'Xia Yan tongzhi zuopin zhong de zichanjieji sixiang' (The capitalist class thinking in Comrade Xia Yan's works), *RMRB* 1 April 1966, 5. In 1979, Xia Yan's rehabilitation was marked by his publication of an article on Qiu Jin in the official government newspaper, *People's Daily*. He explained his motives for writing the play and acknowledged other glorified CCP martyrs. 'Qiu Jin's blood did not flow in vain. In the past hundred years countless people of lofty ideals have also spilled their blood' and referred explicitly to Liu Hulan (see Chapter 9). Xia Yan 'Qiu Jin buxiu' (The eternal Qiu Jin), *RMRB* 5 December 1979, 6.

87. *Qiu Jin*, Xie Jin dir., Shanghai dianying prod., 144 min, 1983, Film.

88. *Jingxiong nüxia* (Woman knight of Mirror Lake), Herman Yau Lai-To dir., National Arts Film prod., 115 min, 2011, Film.

89. Qiu Jin secured an international film debut in the 2009 documentary drama *Autumn Gem: The True Story of China's first feminist*. The documentary reveals her deep female friendships and her commitment to feminism. Neither PRC biopic adequately recognises her feminist motivation. *Autumn Gem*, Rae Chang and Adam Tow dir., San Francisco Film Society prod., 56 min, 2009, Film.

4   Xie Bingying opening public spaces to women

1. On the literary-martial dichotomy as the operation of ideal Chinese masculinity, see Kam Louie, *Theorising Chinese Masculinity* (Cambridge: Cambridge University Press, 2002).

2. Xie Bingying, *Yi ge nübing de zizhuan* (A woman soldier's biography), (1936 rpt. Shanghai: Chenguang chuban, 1949), p. 248.

3. Xie Bingying, *Xin congjun riji* (New war diary) [Hereafter *XCJRJ*] (Hankou: Tianma chubanshe, 1938), p. 11. This book was also published in *Kangzhan riji* (Diary of the War of Resistance) (Taibei: Dongda tushu, 1981) and as *Chongshang zhengtu* (np: Zhongshe chubanshe, 1941). All references to this book come from the Tianma edition of 1938.

4. Xie Bingying, *Wo de huiyi* (My reminiscences) [Hereafter *WDHY*], (Taibei: Sanmin shuju, 1972), p. 8.

5. See her letter to her third brother in the Appendix to Xie Bingying, *Congjun riji* (War diary) [Hereafter *CJRJ*] (1928 rpt. Shanghai: Chunchao shuju, 1929), pp. 127–34.

6. *Girl Rebel*, trans. by Adet and Anor Lin (New York: John Day, 1940; New York: Da Capo Press, 1975); *Autobiography of a Chinese Girl*, trans by Tsui Chi (London: George Allen and Unwin, 1943); *The Struggle of a Girl*, trans. by Lin Rusi and Lin Wushuang (Adet and Tai-yi Lin) with parallel English and Chinese texts (n.p.: Shijie chubanshe, 1947); *A Woman Soldier's Own Story*, trans. Lily Chia Brissman and Barry Brissman (New York: Columbia University Press, 2001). This most recent translation was completed by her daughter and son-in-law and includes a timeline of key events and an engaging insight into her energetic later years.

7. Lin Yutang, *Letters of a Chinese Amazon and War-time Essays* (Shanghai: Commercial Press, 1934), pp. x–xi.

8. Xie, *XCJRJ*, p. 10.

9. Xie, *WDHY*, p. 43.

10. According to Lily Chia, her second daughter, Bingying would only see her first daughter briefly again. The daughter remained in China after 1949 died in 1966 in Beijing, well before her mother. Xie, *A Woman Soldier's Own Story*, p. 259.

11. Xie Bingying, *Nübing shinian* (Ten years a woman soldier), (Chongqing: Honglan chubanshe, 1947). This book includes excerpts from other previously published materials.

12. Xie, *Nübing shinian*, p. 186.

13. Xie Bingying, *Zai Riben yuzhong* (Inside a Japanese prison), (Shanghai: Gengyun chubanshe, 1940), pp. 1–3.

14. Xie, *Zai Riben yuzhong*, pp. 38–9.

15. Lin Yutang, *Letters of a Chinese Amazon and War-time Essays* (Shanghai: Commercial Press, 1934), p. ix.

16. Xie, *Nübing shinian,* p. 164.

17. Xie, *CJRJ*, pp. 90–1.

18. Xie, *Nübing shinian*, p. 165.

19. Xie, *WDHY*, p. 54.

20. Xie, *CJRJ*, p. 87.

21. Xie, *CJRJ*, p. 142.

22. Xie, *WDHY*, p. 56.

23. Xie, *WDHY*, p. 74.

24. Xie, *WDHY*, p. 55.

25. Xie, *WDHY*, p. 55.

26. Xie, *WDHY*, p. 53.

27. Xie, *WDHY*, p. 59.

28. Xie, *WDHY*, p. 58.

29. Xie, *CJRJ*, p. 153.

30. Xie, *XCJRJ*, p. 43.

31. Xie, *CJRJ*, pp. 91–2.

32. Xie, *CJRJ*, p. 46.

33. Xie, *CJRJ*, p. 47.

34. Xie, *A Woman Soldier's Own Story*, p. 275.
35. Xie, *XCJRJ*, p. 33.
36. Xie, *A Woman Soldier's Own Story*, p. 86.
37. Xie, *CJRJ*, p. 86.
38. Xie, *CJRJ*, p. 89.
39. Xie, *CJRJ*, p. 49. Translation adjusted from Lin Yutang's 'At Fengkow' p. 30. He translated *nübing* as 'girl cadets'.
40. Xie, *CJRJ*, pp. 44–5.
41. Xie, *CJRJ*, p. 44.
42. Xie, *CJRJ*, pp. 44–5.
43. Xie, *CJRJ*, p. 45.
44. Xie, *CJRJ*, p. 45.
45. Xie, *A Woman Soldier's Own Story*, p. 271.
46. Xie, *XCJRJ*, pp. 12–3.
47. Xie, *CJRJ*, p. 59.
48. Xie, *XCJRJ*, p. 24. The same scenario where women villagers hide until they see that the troops are women also can be found in *XCJRJ,* p. 40.
49. Xie, *CJRJ*, p. 22.
50. Xie, *CJRJ*, p. 20.
51. Xie, *CJRJ*, pp. 49–50.
52. Xie, *CJRJ*, p. 50.
53. Xie, *A Woman Soldier's Own Story*, p. 55.
54. Xie, *CJRJ*, pp. 61–2. Trans. by Lin, in *Letters of a Chinese Amazon*, pp. 43–4.
55. Xie, *WDHY*, p. 51.
56. Xie, *WDHY*, p. 51.
57. Xie, *WDHY*, p. 52.
58. Xie, *WDHY*, p. 143.
59. Xie, *WDHY*, p. 143.
60. Xie, *WDHY*, pp. 107–8.
61. Xie, *WDHY*, pp. 55–6.
62. Xie, *CJRJ*, p. 142.
63. Xie, *CJRJ*, p. 130.
64. Xie, *CJRJ*, p. 74.
65. Xie, *CJRJ*, p. 91.
66. Xie, *CJRJ*, p. 82.
67. Xie, *CJRJ*, p. 82.
68. She describes the initial march to their first base in 1927 as follows: 'Guanghui couldn't keep up with me. She had long since fallen behind. Her feet, like mine, had been bound, and hers were even a half-inch shorter than mine. Pitiful creature. At age five she had already become a sacrifice for her mother.' Xie Bingying, *A Woman Soldier's Own Story*, pp. 85–6.
69. Xie, *CJRJ*, p. 58. Altered trans. by Lin Yutang, in *Letters of a Chinese Amazon*, p. 38.
70. Xie, *CJRJ,* p. 58.
71. Bound feet were romantically called 'Three Inch Golden Lilies' so Xie is using this phrase metaphorically.
72. Xie, *CJRJ*, p. 48.

73. Xie, *CJRJ*, p. 48.
74. Xie, *WDHY*, pp. 64–6.
75. Xie, *WDHY*, p. 68.
76. Xie, *CJRJ*, pp. 114–15.
77. Xie, *CJRJ*, p. 124.
78. Xie, *CJRJ*, pp. 62–3.
79. Xie, *CJRJ*, p. 60.
80. Xie, *CJRJ*, p. 60.
81. Xie, *CJRJ*, p. 60.
82. Xie, *CJRJ*, pp. 36–7.
83. Xie, *A Woman Soldier's Own Story*, p. 174.
84. Xie, *WDHY*, pp. 24–6.
85. Xie, *A Woman Soldier's Own Story*, pp. 88–9.
86. Xie, *A Woman Soldier's Own Story*, p. 132.
87. Xie, *A Woman Soldier's Own Story*, p. 100.
88. Xie, *A Woman Soldier's Own Story*, p. 104.
89. See also Louise Edwards, 'International Women's Day in China: Feminism Meets Militarised Nationalism and Competing Political Party Programs', *Asian Studies Review* 40, no. 1 (2016).
90. Xie, *Nübing shinian*, pp. 127–9.
91. He Xiangning remained in China after 1949 and became a leader in the Communist government and was particularly influential in the women's movement.
92. Xie, *XCJRJ*, pp. 178–9.
93. Xie, *XCJRJ*, p. 181.

5   Aisin Gioro Xianyu

1. Publications narrating her adventures abound in multiple languages but most prolifically in Japanese. See Muramatsu Shofu, *Danso no reijin: Kawashima Yoshiko den* (A beauty dressed in male attire: a biography of Kawashima Yoshiko), (Ribaibaru gaichi bungaku senshu: Tokyo: Chuo koronsha, 1933; Reprint, Tokyo: Ozorasha, 1998); Umemoto Sutezo, *Yoka: Kawashima Yoshiko Den* (Evil flower: a biography of Kawashima Yoshiko), 1980, translated by Dan Dong as *Chuandao Fangzi qiren* (Chuangdao Fangzi the person) (Beijing: Shijie zhishi chubanshe, 1984); Watanabe Ryusaku, *Hiroku Kawashima Yoshiko* (Secret records of Kawashima Yoshiko), 1972, translated by Sun Wang as *Chuandao Fangzi* (Nanjing: Jiangsu renmin chubanshe, 1982); Kamisaka Fuyuko, *Danso no reijin: Kawashima Yoshiko den* (A beauty dressed in male attire: a biography of Kawashima Yoshiko), 1984, translated by Gong Changjin as *Nan zhuang nüdie – Chuandao Fangzi zhuan* (A female spy dressed in men's attire: a biography of Yoshiko Kawashima), (Beijing: Jiefangjun chubanshe, 1985). Two Japanese movies (2002 and 2006) generated attention among a new generation, cited in Li Gang and He Jingfang, *Chuandao Fangzi shengsi zhi mi xinzheng* (New evidence on the secrets of the life and death of Yoshiko Kawashima) (Changchun: Jinlin wenshi chubanshe, 2009), p. 2. In English, her life has been narrated in most detail in Phyllis Birnbaum, *Manchu Princess,*

Japanese Spy: The Story of Kawashima Yoshiko, the Cross-Dressing Spy Who Commanded Her Own Army (New York: Columbia University Press, 2015). Birnbaum's book came to my attention at the copyediting stage of this current book and too late for me to discuss its many interesting findings. It draws on rich Japanese sources that are not covered in my chapter.

2. Xianyu was not alone in her secessionist dreams. Rana Mitter shows that many Chinese helped build Manchukuo. Mitter, *The Manchurian Myth: Nationalism, Resistance and Collaboration in Modern China* (Berkeley: University of California Press, 2000).

3. Wang Qingxiang, *Chuandao fangzi shengsi dajie mi* (Revealing all the secrets of Yoshiko Kawashima's life and death) (Tianjin: Tianjin renmin chubanshe, 2010).

4. Carol Cohen, 'Women and Wars: Toward a Conceptual Framework', in Carol Cohen (ed.), *Women and Wars* (Cambridge: Polity Press, 2013), p. 23.

5. Dan Shao, 'Princess, Traitor, Soldier, Spy: Aisin Gioro Xianyu and the Dilemma of Manchu Identity', in Mariko Asano Tamanoi (ed.), *Crossed Histories: Manchuria in the Age of Empire* (Honolulu: University of Hawaii Press and Association for Asian Studies, 2005), p. 85.

6. Prasenjit Duara, *Sovereignty and Authenticity: Manchukuo and the East Asian Modern* (Lanham: Rowman & Littlefield, 2003), p. 9.

7. See Mariko Asano Tamanoi, 'Introduction', in Tamanoi, *Crossed Histories*, pp. 2–3 for a discussion of the Japanese names and the political implications of the Chinese terms.

8. Duara, *Sovereignty and Authenticity*, p. 41.

9. Louise Young, *Japan's Total Empire: Manchuria and the Culture of Wartime Imperialism* (Berkeley: University of California Press, 1998).

10. Thomas R. Gottschang, 'Economic Change, Disasters, and Migration: The Historical Case of Manchuria', *Economic Development and Cultural Change* 35, no. 3 (1987), 461.

11. Gavan McCormack, *Chang Tso-lin in Northeast China, 1911–1924: China, Japan and the Manchurian Idea* (Stanford: Stanford University Press, 1977).

12. Young, *Japan's Total Empire*, p. 4.

13. The 'nine' refers to the month of September and 'one eight' to the 18th day of that month. Wang Zheng, *Never Forget National Humiliation: Historical Memory in Chinese Politics and Foreign Relations* (New York: Columbia University Press, 2012).

14. Young, *Japan's Total Empire*, pp. 40–1.

15. Duara, *Sovereignty and Authenticity*, p. 50.

16. Aisin Gioro Puyi, *Wo de qianbansheng* (The first half of my life), (Beijing: Xinhua shudian, 1960). English translation by Paul Tsai, *The Last Manchu: The Autobiography of Henry Pu Yi, Last Emperor of China* (London: Weidenfeld and Nicolson, 1987).

17. Shao, 'Princess, Traitor', p. 85.

18. Li and He, *Chuandao Fangzi shengsi*, pp. 12–3.

19. 'Japan in Manchuria: Domination Extended', *Kalgoorlie Miner* (Kalgoorlie, Australia) 28 January 1932, 5.

20. '"The Lawrence of Manchuria": Romantic Figure in China: Move to Restore Monarch', *Sunday Mail* (Brisbane, Australia) 24 December 1933, 3.

21. Shao, 'Princess, Traitor', p. 87.

22. 'Daring Exploits of "Manchukuo's Joan of Arc"', *The Daily News* (Perth, Australia) 22 March 1934, 6.

23. Birnbaum, *Manchu Princess, Japanese Spy*, pp. 138–45.

24. Shao, 'Princess, Traitor', pp. 88–9. According to Saeki Chizuru, Muramatsu lived with Xianyu for two months while writing his novel. Saeki Chizuru, 'Yoshiko Kawashima: Politics and Gender in Sino-Japanese Relations', *Asian Journal of Women's Studies* 12, no. 3 (2006), 75–98, 125–6.

25. Willa Lou Woods, *Princess Jin: The Joan of Arc of the Orient* (Wenatchee,WA: World Publishing, 1937).

26. Woods, *Princess Jin,* inside front cover.

27. Woods, *Princess Jin,* p. 7.

28. Woods, *Princess Jin,* inside front cover.

29. 'Death of a Spy: Chinese Shoot "Eastern Mata Hari" and Display Body Outside the Jail', *Life* 26 April 1948, 39–40. An earlier *Life* article described her treatment in jail and among the many daring exploits listed also credited her with persuading Wang Jingwei to collaborate with the Japanese. Jim Burke, 'Japan's Mata Hari', *Life* 28 July 1947, 19–20.

30. Wang, *Chuandao fangzi shengsi dajie mi.*

31. Li and He, *Chuandao Fangzi shengsi.*

32. 'Chuandao fangzi shengsi dajie mi: 5 ji' (Thoroughly exposing the secrets of Yoshiko Kawashima's life and death: 5 parts), *Tansuo Faxian* (Explore discover), dir. by Hu Zhitang, Prod. China Central Television 10, Web,
Part 1: http://tv.sohu.com/20120423/n341331878.shtml;
Part 2: http://tv.sohu.com/20120423/n341386461.shtml;
Part 3: http://tv.sohu.com/20120424/n341513098.shtml;
Part 4: http://tv.sohu.com/20120425/n341626830.shtml;
Part 5: http://tv.sohu.com/20120426/n341715900.shtml.

33. Li Jun, 'Chuandao Fangzi: Ri zhengfu de zhuming nü mitan' (Yoshiko Kawashima: the Japanese government's most famous woman spy), *Linglong* 134 (1934), 526–7.

34. Li, 'Chuandao Fangzi', 527.

35. Bi Quan, 'Chuandao Fangzi de gushi' (The story of Kawashima Yoshiko), *Funü shenghuo* (Women's life) 4, no. 6 (1937), 35.

36. Bi, 'Chuandao Fangzi', 36.

37. This brief war was prompted by Japan's aggressive reaction to an incident in which a group of ultra-nationalist Japanese monks were attacked in the streets of Shanghai. There is some doubt about whether the attacks were instigated by the Japanese in order to prompt war – regardless, this war has become part of extension of Japan's militarised aggression in China. Donald Jordan, *China's Trial by Fire: The Shanghai War of 1932* (Ann Arbor: University of Michigan Press, 2001).

38. Xianyu cited in Bi, 'Chuandao Fangzi', 37.

39. Bi, 'Chuandao Fangzi', 37.

40. Yun Qiu, 'Tan geguo zhi nü jiandie' (Talking about women spies around the world), *Linglong* 248 (1936), 2295.

41. 'Guoji jian nü jiandie de huodong' (Activities of women spies in the international arena), *Linglong* 385 (1937), 386.

42. 'Guoji jian', 385.

43. 'Guoji jian', 385.

44. *Women's Life* also encouraged its readers to take up their patriotic duty because 'who knows how many imperialist and *Hanjian* spies are operating from the North East', in Ji Hong, 'Jieshao *Zhanzheng yu jiandie*' (Introducing *War and Spies*), *Funü shenghuo* (Women's life) 4, no. 1 (1937), 47. See also 'Nü jiandie Chuandao Fangzi zai Dongjing' (Woman spy Kawashima Yoshiko in Tokyo), *Linglong* 280 (1937), 983.

45. 'Jiandie de xunlian' (Spy training), *Linglong* 271 (1937), 303–5.

46. Wu Qun, 'Fandui ba funü tuo dao tewu xianshang' (Opposing putting women in the front lines of spying), *Zhongguo funü* (China's women) 2, no. 2 (10 July 1940), 18.

47. Wu, 'Fandui ba funü', 18.

48. Wang Pingling, 'Zhanshi funü de teshu renwu: ying xuexi nü jiandie de zhishi ji jiqiao' (The particular tasks of women in wartime: we ought to acquire the knowledge and skills of women spies), *Funü gongming* (Women's resonance) 7, no. 4 (1938), 12.

49. Wang, 'Zhanshi funü', 12.

50. Wang, 'Zhanshi funü', 12.

51. Shao, 'Princess, Traitor', p. 93.

52. Li and He, *Chuandao Fangzi shengsi,* pp. 106–7.

53. Shao's 'Princess Traitor', 87. Shao provides a riveting summary of the confusion about her identity and her changing views about herself on pp. 93–100 drawing on the reprint of documents of the trial edited by Niu Shanseng, (ed.), *Chuandao Fangzi de jingren miwen: Guomin zhengfu shenpan Jin Bihui mimi dang'an* (The shocking secrets of Yoshiko Kawashima: secret documents from the trial of Jin Bihui by the Nationalist government), (Hong Kong: Jinjian zixun jituan youxian gongsi, 1994).

54. 'Jin ni Bihui shenjie' (Traitor Jin Bihui's investigation complete), *Dagong bao* 17 September 1947, 3.

55. Shao, 'Princess, Traitor', p. 93.

56. 'Jin ni Bihui shenjie', 3; 'Jin ni Bihui zuo chen chu si' (Traitor Jin Bihui executed yesterday morning)', *Dagong bao* 26 March 1948, 3.

57. Shao, 'Princess, Traitor', p. 100.

58. The movie *Manmo kenkoku no reimi* was also known as *Liming zhi xiao* (Dawn of a bright morning) or *Manzhou jianguo zhi liming* (The bright dawn of the building of the Manchu nation).

59. 'Jin ni Bihui shenjie', 3.

60. 'Jin ni Bihui shenjie', 3.

61. 'Woman Spy to Die: Human Devil's Intrigues for Japan', *The West Australian* 24 October 1947, 13.

62. Hai Yi, 'Chuandao Fangzi: jie yu jiu shen de nü jiandie, Jin Siling eguan manying' (Yoshiko Kawashima: the woman spy exposed and on trial, the completely evil Commander Jin), *Haiguang* (Bright seas) 10 (1946), 4.

63. Ping Er, 'Nanxinghua de Riben nü jiandie' (A masculinised Japanese female spy), *Haichao zhoubao* (Ocean tide weekly) 26 (1946), 6.

64. 'Chinese Upset Trial of "Matahari of Far East"', *The Canberra Times* 17 October 1947, 1.

65. 'Manchu Mata Hari on Trial', *The Examiner* (Launceston, Australia) 18 October 1947, 4.

66. *Xinmin bao* 9 October 1947 cited in Xiong Xianjue, 'Wo muji shenpan nü jiandie Chuandao Fangzi' (I saw with my own eyes the trial of Kawashima Yoshiko), *Yan Huang chun qiu* (Yellow Emperor spring and autumn) 12 (1997), 66.

67. *Xinmin bao* 9 October 1947 cited in Xiong, 'Wo muji shenpan nü jiandie', 66.
68. Xiong, 'Wo muji shenpan nü jiandie', 66. *Life* includes a picture of her in this outfit in 'Death of a Spy', 40.
69. 'Jin ni Bihui zuo chen chu si' (Traitor Jin Bihui executed yesterday morning), *Dagong bao* 26 March 1948, 3.
70. 'Jin ni Bihui zuo chen chu si', 3.
71. 'Jin ni Bihui zuo chen chu si', 3. When the court ruled that only one journalist would be able to witness the execution, and that the journalist was an American from *Life* magazine, there was general uproar. 'Ping shi ji lianhui kangyi shu quan wen' (Complete text of the Beiping journalist association's protest), *Dagong bao* 26 March 1948, 3. The absence of a Chinese witness to her execution fuelled speculation that she escaped death. How could a foreigner who had never met Xianyu identify that it really was her who was executed? CCTV 10, 'Chuangdao fangzi shengsi dajie mi', Episode 1.
72. Wang, 'Zhanshi funü', 12.
73. Watanabe, *Hiroku Kawashima Yoshiko*, p. 34.
74. Watanabe, *Hiroku Kawashima Yoshiko*, p. 40.
75. Watanabe, *Hiroku Kawashima Yoshiko*, p. 42.
76. Umemoto, *Yoka: Kawashima Yoshiko den*, pp. 62–3.
77. Kamisaka, *Danso no reijin*, pp. 80–1.
78. Kamisaka, *Danso no reijin*, p. 82.
79. Li and He, *Chuandao Fangzi shengsi*, pp. 20–3.
80. Li and He, *Chuandao Fangzi shengsi*, pp. 20–3. Willa Lou Woods' 1937 narrative on her life makes no mention of any sexual assault. She describes her Japanese family as dedicated to giving her the best education possible 'Both as a boy and as a girl'. They disguised her as a boy to 'save her from the revolutionists who went to Japan to seek her life'. The tomboy of Woods's narrative is asexual except insofar as she worked as a taxi dancer for spy purposes. There was never a point that the tomboy behaviour was regarded as an abnormal reaction to trauma. To the contrary, it was a logical and strategic decision that continued to serve her well as she became a warrior and spy. Woods, *Princess Jin,* pp. 3, 9.
81. Li Yiming, *Chuandao Fangzi zhuan* (Biography of Chuandao Fangzi), (Changchun: Jilin daxue chubanshe, 2010), p. 16.
82. Li, *Chuandao Fangzi zhuan*, p. 18.
83. Li, *Chuandao Fangzi zhuan*, p. 19.
84. *Chuandao fangzi: The Last Princess of Manchuria*, Eddie Ling-Ching Fong, dir. Golden Harvest prod., 96 min, 1990, Film.
85. Lee Bik Wah (aka Lillian Lee, Lee Bihua), *Chuandao Fangzi: Manzhouguo de yaoyan* (Yoshiko Kawashima: The seductress from Manchukuo), (Hong Kong: Tiandi tushu youxian gongsi, 1990). Translated by Andrea Kelly as *The Last Princess of Manchuria* (New York: William Morrow, 1992).

6   Guerrilla resistance leader, Zhao Yiman

1. On China's propaganda system, see Anne-Marie Brady, *Marketing Dictatorship: Propaganda and Thought Work in Contemporary China*

(Lanham: Rowman & Littlefield, 2007). See also Brian DeMare, *Mao's Cultural Army: Drama Troupes in China's Rural Revolution* (Cambridge: Cambridge University Press, 2015).

2. Bai Yuan, 'Lao yingxiong Li Sheng de jingli' (The experience of an old hero, Li Sheng), *Renmin ribao* [Hereafter *RMRB*] 29 October 1951, 3.

3. On Zhao Yiman's memorial as a martyr and PRC martyrdom generally, see Kirk Denton, *Exhibiting the Past: Historical Memory and the Politics of Museums in Postsocialist* China (Honolulu: Hawaii University Press, 2014), p. 106.

4. Xu Guangrong, *Zhao Yiman* (Nanchang: Ershiyi shiji chubanshe, 2004, 2008), pp. 11–2.

5. Zhao Yiman (Yi Chao), 'Bei xiong sao boduo qiuxue quanli de wo' (Me, stripped of my rights to pursue an education by my brother and sister-in-law), *Funü zhoubao* (Women's weekly) 6 August 1924, 1–4.

6. Wen Ye and Zang Xiu, *Kang Ri yingxiong Zhao Yiman* (Anti-Japanese hero, Zhao Yiman), (Shenyang: Yanbian renmin chubanshe, 1959; Chengdu: Sichuan daxue chubanshe, 1989), p. 1.

7. See Andrea McElderry, 'Woman Revolutionary: Xiang Jingyu', *China Quarterly* 105 (March 1986), 95–122; Christina K. Gilmartin, *Engendering the Chinese Revolution: Radical Women, Communist Politics and Mass Movements in the 1920s* (Berkeley: University of California Press, 1995).

8. The Sun Yat-sen Communist University of the Toilers of China trained revolutionaries from both parties. Operating between 1925 and 1930 it disintegrated along with the United Front and as tensions between Trotsky and Stalin increased.

9. Yu Miin-ling, 'Sun Yat-sen University in Moscow, 1925–1930', PhD diss., New York University (1995), pp. 153–7.

10. Sheng Yueh, *Sun Yat-sen University in Moscow: A Personal Account* (Kansas: University of Kansas Center for East Asian Studies, 1971), p. 126.

11. Sheng, *Sun Yat-sen University*, p. 126.

12. Zhu He is part of present-day Shangzhi County.

13. See Rana Mitter, *China's War with Japan, 1937–1945: The Struggle for Survival* (London: Allen Lane, 2013).

14. Wen and Zang, *Kang Ri yingxiong Zhao Yiman*, p. 1.

15. Qiu He, 'Jinian nü yingxiong Zhao Yiman; wei yingpian 'Zhao Yiman' gongyan er zuo' (Commemorating the female hero, Zhao Yiman; written after the public screening of the movie *Zhao Yiman*), *RMRB* 1 July 1950, 4.

16. Lin Danqiu, 'Xin Zhongguo renmin dianying shiye de shengli' (Victory for new China's peoples' movie industry), *RMRB* 7 March 1951, 3. The screening of *Zhao Yiman* in India apparently elicited a positive appraisal. One Indian viewer was reported as having declared 'American movies are filled with pornography and crime and conspire to attract people's base, animal instincts. Chinese movies, in contrast, have ideological content and educational significance, so this inspires people.' So inspired were audiences in India that at the end of the movie, they shouted 'Long Live Zhao Yiman!' Xinhua she, 'Wo guo yingpian "Zhao Yiman" shoudao relie huanying' (Our country's film 'Zhao Yiman' receives a warm welcome in India), *RMRB* 11 April 1951, 4.

17. Paul Clark, *Chinese Cinema and Politics since 1949* (Cambridge: Cambridge University Press, 1987), p. 2.

18. *Zhao Yiman*. Sha Meng dir., Dongbei dianying, 92 min, 1950, Film.

19. Liu Heng, 'Jiefang qu de dianying shiye' (The film industry in the revolutionary areas), *RMRB* 24 June 1949, 4. The film was entered in the Prague International Film festival in June 1950. Xinhua she, '*Zhonghua nüer* deng shiwu bu yingpian canjia Bulage guoji dianying jingsai dahui' (Fifteen movies including *China's daughter* participate in the Prague International Film Festival), *RMRB* 8 July 1950, 3.

20. Zhao Hongben, *Dongbei nü yingxiong Zhao Yiman* (Woman hero of the North East, Zhao Yiman) (Shanghai: Jiaoyu chubanshe, 1950).

21. On 8 March 1951 the state-owned films of 1950 were screened simultaneously around sixty theatres in cities across the nation to demonstrate the success of the new government's film production capacities. Lin Danqiu, 'Xin Zhongguo renmin dianying', 3.

22. Zhao, *Dongbei nü*, p. 38.

23. Zhao, *Dongbei nü*, p. 128.

24. Zhao cited in Qiu He, 'Jinian nü yingxiong', 4.

25. Qiu, 'Jinian nü yingxiong', 4.

26. For more on Shi's pre-1949 career, see DeMare, *Mao's Cultural Army*.

27. Shi Lianxing, 'Zhongxin de ganxie – shiyan yingpian "Zhao Yiman" de yi xie weixiao de xinde' (Heartfelt gratitude – a few lessons from acting in the film 'Zhao Yiman'), *RMRB* 9 October 1951, 3.

28. Shi, 'Zhongxin de ganxie', 3.

29. Zhao Qi, 'Yinggai xuexi Shi Lianxing shiyan Zhao Yiman juese de jingshen' (We ought to learn from Shi Lianxing's spirit in her depiction of Zhao Yiman), *RMRB* 24 October 1951, 2.

30. Wang Xuanqiu, *Zhao Yiman* (Shanghai: Renmin meishu chubanshe, 1961), p. 209. Based on the text of Zhang Lin and Shu Yang from 1957.

31. Zhao, *Dongbei nü yingxiong*, p. 27.

32. Cao Mengjun, 'Jin yi bu jiefang funü ladongli wei duokuai haosheng di jianshe shehui zhuyi fuwu' (Advancing one step in the liberation of women's labour power in the service of achieving faster, better and more economical results in the service of building socialism), *RMRB* 2 June 1958, 2.

33. 'Funü ban biantian, shishi yao zhengxian, Hunan lishiwan nüjiang fenzhan luqian' (Women hold up half the sky, vying to be the first to do everything, in Hunan six million women generals bravely fight at the furnaces), *RMRB* 9 October 1958, 2; 'Zuguo wuqian yingxiong ernü shenglong huohu daxian shenshou' (Five thousand heroic sons and daughters of our ancestral land, full of vigour and vitality displaying their skill to the fullest), *RMRB* 25 November 1958, 1. The failure of these projects led to the 'three hard years' between 1958 and 1961 when millions of rural Chinese died of starvation. Zhao Yiman was used as a model of sacrifice with a new angle to her heroism in 1960 – her refusal to eat food that was due to others. The narrative ran that she and her troops faced acute food shortages when they were isolated from regular supply lines. Zhao went hungry alongside her troops. One night a young soldier brought her a bowl of millet gruel that was reserved for the sick and injured. Zhao was touched by the young soldier's solicitude but could not take the food. She slipped into the mess area and poured the gruel back into the communal pot. Only the cook witnessed her sacrifice – 'tears welled up in his eyes'.

Zhao's bowl has become a relic in the hagiography of Zhao Yiman and regularly appears in photographs and drawings of her life. Xiao Bai, 'Zhao Yiman de wan' (Zhao Yiman's bowl), *RMRB* 16 September 1960, 8. See the comic book by Zhao Huasheng, *Zhao Yiman* (Shenyang: Liaoning meishu chubanshe 1986).

34. See Beverley Hooper, '"Flower Vase and Housewife": Women in China's Consumer Society', in Krishna Sen and Maila Stivens (eds.), *Gender and Power in Affluent Asia* (London: Routledge, 1998), 167–93.

35. Ni Liangduan, 'Li Kunjie kuxun baomei Zhao Yiman' (Li Kunjie and the arduous search for younger sister Zhao Yiman), *Shiji* (Century) May (2007), 72.

36. Xu, *Zhao Yiman*. Other renditions of the discovery involve complicated stories of confirmation from Chen Dabang and Chen Yexian about Zhao's various pseudonyms. See Ni, *Li Kunjie*.

37. Zhang Lin and Shu Yang, *Zhao Yiman* (1957, rpt. Beijing: Zhongguo gongren chubanshe, 2006), p. 58.

38. Zhang and Shu, *Zhao Yiman*, p. 59.

39. Zhang and Shu, *Zhao Yiman*, p. 63.

40. Wen and Zang, *Kang Ri yingxiong*, p. 10.

41. Zeng Ke, 'Xian xue jiaoguan de hua' (Flowers irrigated with fresh blood), *RMRB* 5 October 1995, 10.

42. Zhao Yiman in Pan Yan, 'Xue sa baishan heishui jian' (Blood sprinkled between the white snow and the black water), *RMRB* 20 July 1993, 8.

43. Pan, 'Xue sa', 8.

44. Wen Ye, *Bi xue ying hun: Zhao Yiman zhuan* (The spirit of the hero that shed blood in a just cause: a biography of Zhao Yiman) (Harbin: Heilongjiang renmin chubanshe, 2005) pp. 165–6.

45. Zhu Yu and Bai Ruixue, 'Weichu hanchu de "baba mama": zhuming kangzhan yinglie houren de zhuiyi' (They have never called out 'father and mother': recalling the descendants of celebrated heroic martyrs from the war of resistance), *RMRB* 22 August 2005, 10.

46. Wen, *Bi xue ying hun*, p. 170.

47. Zhao cited in Huang Weilin and Li Yongmei (eds.), *Zuihou de tanhua* (Last words), (Guilin: Lijiang chubanshe, 1996), p. 153.

48. Wen, *Bi xue ying hun*, p. 166.

49. Zhu and Bai, 'Weichu hanchu de "baba mama"', p. 10.

50. *Wode muqin Zhao Yiman* (My mother Zhao Yiman), Sun Tie dir., Haixia shijie prod., 90 min, 2005, Film.

51. Wen, *Bi xue ying hun*.

52. Wen, *Bi xue ying hun*, pp. 69–72.

53. Wen, *Bi xue ying hun*, p. 72.

54. Sun Yaowen's book length study of Sun Yat-sen University confirms the narrative of her April marriage and the party's concern for her health in the cold USSR winter as the reason for her departure. The weather, combined with the party's need for more women cadre back in China, resulted in it allowing her to return early. She concurred with the party's recommendations and at four months' pregnant bid her husband farewell. The story is one of party's concern for women and babies. Sun Yaowen, *Feng yu wu zai: Mosike Zhongshan daxue shimo* (Records of tempestuous times: the rise and fall of Moscow's Sun Yat-sen University), (Beijing: Zhongyang

bianyi chubanshe 1996), pp. 268–9. Earlier in the book, Sun refers to another woman, Qian Ying, who, on discovering herself pregnant, tried to give herself an abortion by jumping up and down a lot. But the baby was born nonetheless so she sent it immediately to a nursery in Moscow to be raised so she could continue her studies undisturbed. See Sun, *Feng yu wu zai*, p. 202. This depiction of dedication to the cause makes no mention of the pressure women faced in these conditions as they were welcomed as sexual partners but had their health and welfare disregarded as soon as the consequences of any sexual intercourse appeared.

55. Wen, *Bi xue ying hun*, p. 76.
56. Wen, *Bi xue ying hun*, p. 76.
57. Wen, *Bi xue ying hun*, p. 169.
58. Yuan Baoshan, 'Zhao Yiman zhi zi de feichang rensheng' (The extraordinary life of Zhao Yiman's son), *Gongchandang yuan* (Communist Party members) 6 (2007), 18; Yuan Baoshan, 'Zhao Yiman lieshi zhi zi de feichang rensheng' (The extraordinary life of martyr Zhao Yiman's son), *Shiji tegao* (Century, special edition) 1 (2007), 9–13.
59. Yuan, 'Zhao Yiman lieshi'.
60. Wen, *Bi xue ying hun*, p. 171.

7   Negotiating sexual virtue

1. Zheng Huajun, 'Zheng Huajun wei Ding Mocun shahai Zheng Pingru zhi shoudu gaodeng fayuan han' (Case presented to the Capital high court by Zheng Huajun against Ding Mocun on the killing of Zheng Pingru), pp. 717–19 in Wang Chunnan (ed.), *Shenxun Wang wei hanjian bilü* (Record of the trials of traitors from the Wang Jingwei regime), (1946, rpt. Nanjing: Jiangsu guji chubanshe, 1992), p. 717.
2. Eileen Chang, *Lust Caution*, trans. by Julia Lovell (New York: Anchor Books, 2007). *Se, Jie* (Lust, Caution), Lee Ang, dir. Hai Shang prod., 157 min, 2007, Film. In 2004 Japanese author Tsujihara Noburo published a novel, *Jasmine*, in which Zheng Pingru featured significantly. Pingru is described as being alive in the 1990s and living with a Japanese spy in the cave houses of China's remote Loess Plateau. Tsujihara Noburo, *Jasmine*, trans. by Juliet Carpenter (London: Thames River Press, 2012).
3. Tammy M. Proctor, *Female Intelligence: Women and Espionage in the First World War* (New York: New York University Press, 2003), p. 149.
4. Allison Rottman, 'Crossing Enemy Lines: Shanghai and the Central China Base', in Christian Henriot and Wen-hsin Yeh (eds.), *In the Shadow of the Rising Sun: Shanghai under Japanese Occupation* (New York: Cambridge University Press, 2004), pp. 90–15.
5. Wu Qun, 'Fandui canhai muqin he haizi' (Opposing harming mothers and children), *Zhongguo funü* (China's women) 2, no. 4 (10 September 1940), 11.
6. Proctor, *Female Intelligence*, p. 149.
7. Frederic Wakeman, 'Hanjian (Traitor)! Collaboration and Retribution in Wartime Shanghai', in Wen-hsin Yeh (ed.), *Becoming Chinese: Passages to Modernity and Beyond* (Berkeley: University of California Press, 2000), p. 322.

8. For more detail, see Frederic Wakeman, *Spymaster: Dai Li and the Chinese Secret Service* (Berkeley: University of California Press, 2003), pp. 254–6.

9. Huang Meizhen, Jiang Yihua and Shi Yuanhua, *Wang wei 'no. 76' tegong zongbu* (The Wang regime's espionage HQ, No. 76), (Beijing: Tuanjie chubanshe, 2010), p. 106.

10. Wakeman, *Spymaster*, p. 90.

11. Rottman, *Crossing Enemy Lines*, p. 97.

12. Xiao Xu, 'Guan Lu: Beifu hanjian maming 43 nian' (Guan Lu: burdened with the infamous title of traitor for 43 years), *Xinwen tiandi* (News world) 12 (2009), 59–60.

13. Ma Zhendu, *Guomindang tewu huodong shi: shang, xia* (History of the Guomindang's espionage activities: 2 vols), (Beijing: Jiuzhou chubanshe, 2013), p. 217.

14. Frederic Wakeman, *The Shanghai Badlands: Wartime Terrorism and Urban Crime, 1937–1941* (New York: Cambridge University Press, 1996), p. 1.

15. Ding Mocun started his career in the CCP but switched to join the Nationalists and rose rapidly in their intelligence scene. In 1932 he was appointed to the Military Affairs Committee's Bureau of Investigation and in 1935 became one of its three heads. He fell out with senior members of the team and left for Shanghai to work with Wang Jingwei and the Japanese. Ding is regarded as one of the worst traitors of the war in both Nationalist and CCP accounts. For more detail of the Wang Jingwei regime's spies, see Brian Martin, 'Shield of Collaboration: The Wang Jingwei Regime's Security Service, 1939–1945', *Intelligence and National Security* 16, no. 4 (2001): 97–8.

16. Wakeman, *The Shanghai Badlands*, p. 11.

17. Wakeman, *The Shanghai Badlands*, p. 16.

18. Rottman, *Crossing Enemy Lines*, p. 100.

19. Wakeman, *The Shanghai Badlands*, p. 93.

20. *Liangyou huabao* (The young companion) 130, July (1937), Cover.

21. Xu Hongxin, *Yige nü jiandie* (A woman spy), (Shanghai: Shanghai cishu chubanshe 2009), pp. 23–5.

22. Huang et al., *Wang wei*, p. 125.

23. Huang et al., *Wang wei*, p. 106.

24. Huang et al., *Wang wei*, p. 109.

25. Ye Jiqing was the object of a fictionalised biography by Li Wei in 2008. The book presents Ye as No. 76's supreme female spy and an evil manipulator shadowing her husband, Li Shiqun. The book includes discussion of Zheng Pingru's activities, her capture and her execution. Li Wei, *76 hao moku nü jiandie* (The woman spy of the den of monsters at no. 76), (Wuhan: Hubei renmin chubanshe, 2008), pp. 157–67.

26. Zhang Zhenhua, 'Zhang Zhenhua wei Ding Mocun shahai Zheng Pingru zhi *Datong bao* han: 1946 nian 12 yue 27 ri' (Letter to *Datong bao* from Zhang Zhenhua on Ding Mocun's murder of Zheng Pingru: 27 December 1946), in Wang, *Shenxun Wang wei hanjian bilü*, pp. 768–9.

27. Zheng Nanyang, 'Shanghai gaodeng fayuan guanyu Zheng Pingru bei hai an xunwen bilü zhiyi: 1946 nian 12 yue 11 ri' (Part 1 of the hearing of the Shanghai high court into the harming of Zheng Pingru: 11 December 1946), pp. 746–9 in Wang, *Shenxun Wang wei hanjian bilü*, p. 747.

28. Huang et al., *Wang wei*, p. 110.
29. Zheng Huajun, 'Zheng Huajun wei Ding Mocun', pp. 717–19. See also Zheng Nanyang, 'Shanghai gaodeng', pp. 746–9.
30. Zheng Nanyang, 'Shanghai gaodeng', p. 747.
31. Zheng Huajun, 'Zheng Huajun wei Ding Mocun', p. 717.
32. Zheng Nanyang, 'Shanghai gaodeng', p. 134.
33. Zhang Zhenhua, 'Zhang Zhenhua wei Ding Mocun', p. 769.
34. Zhang Zhenhua goes to great length to describe the clothing that Pingru was wearing on the day of her execution – a horse-hair coat and gold jewelry. Zhang accuses Lin Zhijiang of keeping these items worth 300 yuan. See Zhang Zhenhua, 'Zhang Zhenhua wei Ding Mocun', p. 769. Pingru's mother's testimony also outlines the value of the clothing and jewels that Pingru's executioners kept.
35. Zhong diaoju, 'Zheng lieshi Pingru' (The martyr Zheng Pingru), 1964, rpt. in Xu, *Yige nü jiandie*, pp. 122–3.
36. Cai Dejin's study of the underground Nationalists agents working in the Wang Jingwei era depicts her as part of a noble band of patriots undertaking dangerous work. Cai Dejin, *Qishiliu hao: Wang wei tegong zongbu koushu mishi* (No. 76: the secret history of the oral recounting of the Wang regime's central spy branch), (Beijing: Tuanjie chubanshe, 2007).
37. Ding Mocun, 'Shoudu gaodeng fayuan shenpan Ding Mocun bilü:1946 nian, 11 yue, 19 ri' (Record of the Capital high court trial of Ding Mocun: 19 November 1946), pp. 719–42 rpt. in Wang, *Shenxun Wang wei hanjian bilü*, p. 731.
38. Ding Mocun, 'Shoudu gaodeng fayuan shenpan bilü: 1946 nian 12 yue 12 ri' (Record of the Capital high court trial: 12 December 1946), pp. 752–60, rpt. in Wang, *Shenxun Wang wei hanjian bilü*, p. 753.
39. Ding Mocun, 'Ding Mocun buchong da bian shu: 1947 nian 2 yue 3 ri' (Ding Mocun's supplementary reply: 3 February 1947), pp. 838–45, rpt. in Wang, *Shenxun Wang wei hanjian* bilü, p. 843.
40. Ding Mocun, 'Shoudu gaodeng fayuan shenpan Ding Mocun bilü: 1946 nian, 11 yue, 19 ri' (Record of the Capital high court trial of Ding Mocun: 19 November 1946), pp. 719–42, rpt. in Wang, *Shenxun Wang wei hanjian bilü*, p. 731.
41. Ding Mocun, 'Shoudu gaodeng fayuan shenpan bilü: 1947 nian 2 yue 1 ri' (Record of the Capital high court trial: 1 February 1947), pp. 769–90, rpt. in Wang, *Shenxun Wang wei hanjian bilü*, p. 775.
42. Ding Mocun, 'Shoudu gaodeng fayuan shenpan bilü: 1947 nian 2 yue 1 ri', p. 775.
43. 'Final Verdict' in 'Shoudu gaodeng fayuan tezhong xingshi panjue: 1947 nian 2 yue 8 ri' (Capital high court special criminal trial judgment: 8 February 1947), pp. 845–54, rpt. in Wang, *Shenxun Wang wei hanjian bilü*, p. 846.
44. In Ma and Wang's 1986 and 2010 books, their descriptions of Zheng are neutral and devoid of commentary about her sexual charms. Ma Xiaotian and Wang Manyun, *Wang wei tegong neimu: zhi qingren tan zhiqing shi* (The inside story on the Wang Jingwei regime's espionage work: Insiders talk about the inside facts), (1962 rpt. Zhengzhou: Henan renmin chubanshe, 1986), 108–14; Ma Xiaotian and Wang Manyun, *Wo suo zhidao de Wang wei tegong neimu* (What I know about behind the scenes of the Wang regime's spy operations), (Beijing: Dongfang chubanshe, 2010), pp. 111–15.

45. Ma Xiaotian and Wang Manyun, *Wang wei tegong zongbu: 76 hao* (The central spy agency of the Wang Jingwei regime: no. 76), 1960 circa, rpt. in Xu, *Yige nü jiandie*, p. 172.

46. Ma and Wang, *Wang wei tegong zongbu*, p. 177.

47. This pattern has centuries-old roots. Du Shiniang, a well-loved fictional figure from the Tang dynasty immortalised in the story 'Du Shiniang Sinks Her Jewel Box' is one such noble prostitute who symbolises a key virtue – loyalty. She secures the promise of marriage from her scholar lover regardless of his parents' opinions. But, on returning home he betrays his promise when told that his father will sever his access to family funds if he marries Du. On hearing of his betrayal Du throws herself and her jewel box into the river. The box contained treasures more than sufficient to cover the loss of his family's money.

48. Shengqing Wu, 'Gendering the Nation: The Proliferation of Images of Zhen Fei (1876–1900) and Sai Jinhua (1872–1936) in Late Qing and Republican China', *Nan Nü: Journal of Men, Women and Gender in China* 11, no. 1 (2009), 36.

49. This 1945 story would be reprinted at least twice more during 1946 as the trials of the traitors and collaborators commenced. Zheng Zhenfeng, 'Yi ge nü jiandie' (A woman spy), *Zhoubao* (The weekly) no. 5 (6 October 1945), 13; *Xiandai wenxian yuekan* (Modern literature monthly) 1, founding issue (1946), 108–10; *Wenxuan* (Literary selections) 1, founding issue (1946), 18–9.

50. Zheng, 'Yi ge nü jiandie', *Zhoubao*, 13.

51. On Mata Hari, see Pat Shipman *Femme Fatale: Love, Lies, and the Unknown Life of Mata Hari* (New York: Harper Perennial, 2008); Julie Wheelwright, *The Fatal Lover: Mata Hari and the Myth of Women in Espionage* (London: Trafalgar Square, 1993).

52. Zheng, 'Yi ge nü jiandie', *Zhoubao*, 13.

53. Zheng, 'Yi ge nü jiandie', *Zhoubao*, 13.

54. Jin Xiongbai, *Wang zhengquan shilu: yuanming 'Wang zhengquan de kaichang yu shouchang'* (Record of the Wang regime: originally titled *The commencement and conclusion of the Wang regime*) (Hong Kong: Chunqiu zazhishe, 1961), p. 58.

55. Jin, *Wang zhengquan*, pp. 58–9.

56. Jin, *Wang zhengquan*, p. 60.

57. Jin, *Wang zhengquan*, p. 60.

58. 'Shanghai gaodeng fayuan guanyu Zheng Pingru bei hai an xunwen bi lü zhi er: 1946 nian 12 yue 11 ri' (Part 2 of the hearing of the Shanghai high court into the harming of Zheng Pingru: 11 December 1946), rpt. in Wang, *Shenxun Wang wei hanjian bilü*, pp. 749–51.

59. Xia Yun, 'Engendering Contempt for Collaborators: Anti-*Hanjian* discourse following the Sino–Japanese War of 1937–1945', *Journal of Women's History* 25, no. 1 (2013), 111–34.

60. Jin, *Wang zhengquan*, p. 60.

61. Jin, *Wang zhengquan*, p. 60.

62. Yan Geling, *Jinling shisan chai* (Thirteen beauties of Jinling), (Nanjing: Jiangsu wenyi chubanshe, 2010).

63. Zhang Zailin, '"Se Jie" Wang Jiazhi yuanxing diaoxiang jiemu, liqiu wei yingxiong zhengming' (Unveiling the statue for Wang Jiazhi's prototype: striving to rectify the name of a hero), *Zhongguo xinwen wang* (China news web), 7 June 2009, Web http://www.chinanews.com/cul/news/2009/06-07/1723521.shtml
   Yu Yue, 'Meimei chengqing lishi zhenxiang Se Jie nüzhujue bushi Zheng Pingru' (Younger sister clarifies the historical fact that the lead female in Lust, Caution is not Zheng Pingru), 14 September 2007, Web, http://big5.china.com.cn/book/txt/2007-09/14/content_8875460.htm
64. Jane Macartney, 'Tang Wei blacklisted for "glorifying traitors"', *The Times* 11 March 2008, Web. http://www.thetimes.co.uk/tto/arts/film/article2426823.ece
65. Stephanie Hemelryk Donald, 'Tang Wei, Sex, the City and the Scapegoat in *Lust, Caution*', *Theory, Culture and Society* 27, no. 4 (2010), 46–68.
66. Xia, 'Engendering Contempt for Collaborators', 111–34.
67. Timothy Brook, *Collaboration: Japanese Agents and Local Elites in Wartime China* (Harvard: Harvard University Press, 2005).
68. Margherita Zanasi, 'New Perspectives on Chinese Collaborations', *The Asia-Pacific Journal: Japan Focus*, 24 July 2008, Web, http://japanfocus.org/-Margherita-Zanasi/2828; See also Margherita Zanasi, 'Globalizing the *Hanjian*: The Suzhou Trails and Post-World War II Discourse on Collaboration', *American Historical Review* 113, no. 3 (2008), 731–51.
69. Claire Duchen, 'Crime and Punishment in Liberated France: The Case of *les femmes tondues*', in Claire Duchen and Irene Bandhauer- Schöffmann (eds.), *When the War Was Over: Women, War and Peace in Europe, 1940–1956* (London: Leicester University Press, 2000), pp. 236–7. Duchen points out that sexual 'crimes' are most commonly represented in post-war cleansing because they are the most taboo.
70. Xia, 'Engendering Contempt'.
71. Barbara Barnouin and Yu Changgen, *Zhou Enlai: A Political Life* (Hong Kong: The Chinese University Press, 2006), pp. 81, 86.

8   Ding Ling and Zhenzhen

1. Wakeman, *Spymaster*, p. 216. On the Statistics Bureau see Wen-hsin Yeh, 'Dai Li and the Liu Geqing Affair', *Journal of Asian Studies* 48, no. 3 (1989), 545–62.
2. Matthew Sommer, *Sex, Law and Society in Late Imperial China* (Stanford: Stanford University Press, 2000), Chapter 1. He notes that illicit sex (*jian*) was linguistically linked to 'treacherous ministers' (*jianchen*) or 'treacherous factions' (*jiandang*).
3. Bill Jenner's translation of 'Xia Village' translates Zhenzhen's name as 'Purity' in order to alert the English reading audience to its significance. See Ding Ling, *Miss Sophie's Diary and Other Stories*, trans. By W.J.F. Jenner (Beijing: Panda Books, 1985), pp. 236–61. For discussion of how Ding Ling changed the way 'the woman problem' was conceived in communist thought, see Tani Barlow, *The Question of Women in Chinese Feminism* (Durham: Duke University Press, 2004).
4. Ding Ling, 'Wo zai Xiacun de shihou' (When I was in Xia Village), *Zhongguo wenhua* (Chinese culture) (20 June 1941), 24–31. This journal was published by Xinhua shudian and retailed for 3 *mao*. For another English translation see: Ding Ling, 'When I Was in Xia Village', trans. by Gary Bjorge, in Tani Barlow with Gary Bjorge (eds.), *I Myself Am a Woman: Selected Writings of Ding Ling* (Boston: Beacon, 1989), pp. 299–315.

5. Ding Ling, 'When I Was in Xia Village', p. 308 (Barlow and Bjorge edition).

6. Yi-tsi Feuerwerker, 'Ting Ling's When I Was in Sha chuan (Cloud Village)', *Signs* 2, no. 1 (1976), 275.

7. Ding Ling, 'When I Was in Xia Village', p. 308 of Barlow and Bjorge edition.

8. Tani Barlow, 'Forewords to "When I Was in Xia Village"', p. 298. Charles Alber wrote that 'Xia Village' was criticised in 1942 (specifically on March 31) but I failed to find evidence of this criticism. Alber, *Enduring the Revolution: Ding Ling and the Politics of Literature in Guomindang China* (Westport: Praeger 2002), p. 146. For a discussion of the debates, see Ellen Judd, 'Prelude to the "Yan'an Talks"', *Modern China* 11, no. 2 (1985), 377–408.

9. Ding Ling, 'Zai yiyuan zhong shi', *Guyu (Grain rains)* no. 1 (November 1941), np. Gary Bjorge notes that all original versions of this journal have been lost. Gary John Bjorge 'Ting Ling's Early Years: Her Life and Literature through 191942', The University of Wisconsin-Madison, unpublished PhD (1977), p. 127. Bjorge writes that Ding Ling was criticised for 'raising problems but not solving them' (p. 133). The criticism of 'In the hospital' appeared in Xue Wei, '"Zai yiyuan zhong shi" "maque" ji qita' ('In the Hospital', 'Sparrow' and other matters), *Jiefang ribao* (Liberation daily – hereafter *JFRB*) 5 December 1941, 4. The following year Ding Ling was criticised for 'holding stale class prejudices'. See Liao Ying [Wang Liaoying], "Ren … zai jianku zhong shengchang' – ping Ding Ling tongzhi de "Zai yiyuan zhong shi"' (People…develop in times of hardship – critiquing Comrade Ding Ling's 'In the Hospital'), *JFRB* 10 June 1942, 4. This translation comes from Bjorge, 'Ting Ling's Early Years', p. 154.

10. Ding Ling, 'Sanbajie yougan', *JFRB* 9 March 1942, 4. For an English translation, see Ding Ling, 'Thoughts on March 8th', trans. by Gregor Benton, in Barlow with Bjorge (eds.), *I Myself Am a Woman*, pp. 317–21.

11. For discussion of these criticism sessions, see Dai Qing, *Wang Shiwei and 'Wild Lilies'* (Armonk: ME Sharpe, 1994). Ding Ling survived the worst of the attacks by publishing a retraction of her earlier views on literature and art. Ding Ling, 'Bianzhe de hua' (Words from the editor), *JFRB* 12 March 1942, 4. Her retractions continued through June. See Ding Ling, 'Wenyijie dui Wang Shiwei yingyou de taidu ji fanxing' (The attitude and introspection that the literary and art world should adopt towards Wang Shiwei), *JFRB* 16 June 1942, 4.

12. Ding Ling, *Wo zai Xiacun de shihou* (When I was in Xia Village), (Guilin: Yuanfang shudian, 1944).

13. Luo Binji, 'Da fengbao zhong de renwu: ping Ding Ling de "Wo zai Xiacun de shihou"' (Characters from amidst a tempest: a critique of Ding Ling's 'When I was in Xia Village'), *Kangzhan wenyi (War literature and art)* 9, no. 5–6 (December 1944), 17–20.

14. Zhou Yang (ed.), *Jiefangqu duanpian xiaoshuo xuan (Collected short fiction from the liberated areas)* (Andong: Dongbei shudian, 1947), pp. 3–23.

15. Xue Feng [Feng Xuefeng], 'Cong "Meng Ke" dao "ye"' (From 'Meng Ke' to 'Night'), *Zhongguo zuojia* (China's authors) 2 (January 1948), 4. This essay also appeared as a postscript to *Ding Ling wenji* (Ding Ling's collected works) published in 1947 and has been republished in Feng Xuefeng's works under the title '*Ding Ling wenji* houji' (Postscript to Ding Ling's collected works).

16. Ding Ling, *Ding Ling ji* (Collected works of Ding Ling), (Beijing: Renmin wenxue chubanshe, 1954), pp. 71–87 for the story and p. 236 for the postscript.

17. See Ding Ling, *Yan'an ji* (The Yan'an collection), (Beijing: Renmin wenxue chubanshe, 1954), p. 85, 96.
18. These editions include essays as well as short fiction, so 'Thoughts on March Eighth' was not excluded on grounds of genre.
19. For discussion of the political campaigns and their impact on the literary and art worlds, see Merle Goldman, *Literary Dissent in Communist China* (New York: Atheneum, 1971) and Julia Andrews, 'Traditional Painting in New China: *Guohua* and the Anti-Rightist Campaign', *Journal of Asian Studies* 49, no. 3 (1990), 555–77.
20. Yang Guixin, *Ding Ling yu Zhou Yang de enyuan* (Gratitude and enmity between Ding Ling and Zhou Yang), (Wuhan: Hubei Renmin chubanshe, 2006), p. 47.
21. Zhou Yang, 'Wenyi zhanxian shang de yi chang dabianlun' (A great debate at the front lines of literature and art), *Renmin ribao* 28 February 1958, 2. Taken from a speech he gave in September 1957 to a meeting of the Writers' Association.
22. Guo Moruo, 'Nuli ba ziji gaizao chengwei wuchan jieji de wenhua gongren' (Strive to turn yourself into a proletarian literary worker), *Renmin ribao* 28 September 1957, 3.
23. Wang Liaoying, 'Kangzhan shiqi Ding Ling xiaoshuo de sixiang qingxiang' (The ideological trends in Ding Ling's wartime stories), *Wenxue yanjiu* (Literary research) 4 (1957), 93–110. *Literary Research* ceased publication at the end of 1959 and was superseded by *Wenxue pinglun* (Literary criticism).
24. Zhenzhen tried to escape an arranged marriage by becoming a nun and described her work for the CCP as 'important'.
25. Wang, 'Kangzhan shiqi Ding Ling xiaoshuo', p. 101.
26. Wang, 'Kangzhan shiqi Ding Ling xiaoshuo', p. 99. Wang does not use the term 'comfort woman' (*weian fu*) for any of the women and instead calls them 'camp following barrack prostitutes' (*suiying jinü*).
27. Wang, 'Kangzhan shiqi Ding Ling xiaoshuo', p. 99.
28. Lu Yaodong, 'Ping "Wo zai Xiacun de shihou"' (Critiquing 'When I was in Xia Village'), *Wenyi bao* (Literary news) 38 (1957), 4.
29. Lu, 'Ping "Wo zai Xiacun de shihou"', 4. Li Chi's 1963 comment that 'The traditional Chinese attitude towards the woman who has lost her chastity, whether voluntarily or otherwise, has always been contempt or pity, and that attitude has proved, among all the deeply imbedded false attitudes, the hardest for the Chinese to discard' appears to be upheld in Lu's attitudes. Li Chi, 'Communist War Stories', *China Quarterly* 13 (March 1963), 150.
30. Lu, 'Ping "Wo zai Xiacun de shihou"', 4.
31. The Barlow-Bjorge translation has a typographical error for this term and used 'evening goddess' instead of 'avenging goddess'. Ding Ling, 'When I Was in Xia Village', p. 311.
32. Hua Fu, 'Ding Ling de "Fuchou de nüshen": Ping "Wo zai Xiacun de shihou"' (Ding Ling's 'Avenging Goddess': critiquing 'When I was in Xia Village'), *Wenyi bao* (Literary news) 3 (1958), 22–5.
33. Liu Jie, 'Chongping "Wo zai Xiacun de shihou" zhong Zhenzhen de xingxiang' (Another critique of Zhenzhen from 'When I was in Xia Village'), *Gansu shida xuebao* (Gansu normal college journal) 1 (1981), 52.
34. Liu, 'Chongping "Wo zai Xiacun de shihou"', 53.

35. Liu, 'Chongping "Wo zai Xiacun de shihou"', 53.
36. Liu, 'Chongping "Wo zai Xiacun de shihou"', 55.
37. Yang Guixin, 'Chongdu Ding Ling de san ge duanpian' (Rereading three of Ding Ling's short pieces), *Qiqihaer shifan xueyuan xuebao* (Qiqihaer normal college journal) 4 (1982), 63.
38. Yang, 'Chongdu Ding Ling de san ge duanpian', 64.
39. Yang, 'Chongdu Ding Ling de san ge duanpian', 65.
40. See Wendy Larson, *Women and Writing in Modern China* (Stanford: Stanford University Press, 1998).
41. Zhang Mu, 'Ding Ling xiaoshuo zhong de san ge nüxing' (Three women from Ding Ling's short stories), *Wenyi zhengming* (Literary and arts debates) 5 (1993), 39–43. Zhang's essay is also among the first to explicitly describe Zhenzhen as being 'raped' (*qiangjian*), rather than euphemistically 'humiliated' or 'degraded'.
42. The first description of Zhenzhen as a 'comfort woman' came in a critique by Japanese scholar but the idea was not adopted in China until the early to mid-1990s when public awareness had developed. See Nakajima Midori, 'Ding Ling lun' (On Ding Ling), trans. by Yuan Yunhua and Pei Zheng in Yuan Liangjun (ed.), *Ding Ling yanjiu ziliao* (Research materials on Ding Ling), (Tianjin: Tianjin renmin chubanshe, 1982), p. 548.
43. See, for example, Liu Chuanxia, 'Ding Ling de 'Wo zai Xiacun de shihou' jieshou yu chanshi' (The reception and interpretation of Ding Ling's 'When I was in Xia Village'), *Yantai shifan xueyuan xuebao* (Yantai normal college journal) 21, no. 3 (2004), 52.
44. *Zhenzhen*, Qiao Liang dir., Beijing jizuhou tongying dianying prod., 90 min, 2003, Film.
45. Sommer, *Sex, Law and Society*.
46. See the conclusion in Edwards, *Gender, Politics and Democracy: Women's Suffrage in China* (Stanford: Stanford University Press, 2008).
47. Huang Wei, '"Hongse jiandie" Guan Lu zhi si' (The death of 'Red Spy' Guan Lu), *Zhuanji* (Legends) 1 (2010), 66–9, 15.

9   Mobilising and militarising rural China through the girl martyr/ woman martyr, Liu Hulan

1. Thomas C. Roberts, *The People's Militia and the Doctrine of the People's War* (Fort Lesley J. McNair, Washington DC: National Defense University Press, 1983), p. 15.
2. John Gittings, 'China's Militias', *China Quarterly* 18 (June 1964), 100.
3. Julian Schofield, *Militarization and War* (New York: Palgrave McMillan, 2007).
4. Ralph L. Powell, 'Maoist Military Doctrines', *Asian Survey* 8, no. 4 (1968), 239–62.
5. Ellis Joffe, '"People's War under Modern Conditions": A Doctrine for Modern War', *China Quarterly*, 112 (1987), 555–71. The professionalisation of the PLA in the post-Mao era has not entirely discarded Mao's philosophy – current policy evolved to incorporate the old rhetoric while emphasising that advanced weaponry required new styles of preparedness. Party philosophers adopted the neologism 'People's War under Modern Conditions' to manage this ambiguity. Joffe, 'People's War under Modern Conditions', 2.

6. Orna Naftali, 'Marketing War and the Military to Children and Youth in China: Little Red Soldiers in the Digital Age', *China Information* 28, no. 1 (2014), 3–25.

7. Mary Ann Farquhar, *Children's Literature in China: From Lu Xun to Mao Zedong* (Armonk: ME Sharpe, 1999); Stephanie Hemelryk Donald, *Little Friends: Children's Film and Media Culture in China* (Lanham: Rowman & Littlefield, 2005).

8. Orna Naftali, 'Chinese Childhood in Conflict: Children, Gender and Violence in China of the Cultural Revolution Period (1966–76)', *Oriens Extremus* 53 (2014), 85.

9. Lorraine Bayard de Volo, 'Mobilising Mothers for War: Cross-National Framing Strategies in Nicaragua's Contra War', *Gender and Society* 18, no. 6 (December 2004), 719.

10. Tiao Yang, 'Liu Hulan de shengqian shenhou' (The life and death of Liu Hulan), *Shanxi dang'an* (Shanxi archives) 4 (2001), 38.

11. The search for younger and earlier communist martyrs has also been part of the Liu Hulan's propaganda story. In 2000 two articles by Zhou Xun appeared promoting awareness of the 14- and 16-year-old sisters, Li Jie and Li Chang. These girls were executed in January of 1928 as part of the Nationalist Party's elimination of Communists in Hengshan, Hunan. Described by Zhou as 'Liu Hulan-style heroes', the sisters reportedly went to their execution shouting, 'Long Live the Communist Party!' Zhou Xun, 'Bei chenfeng 71 nian de Li Hulan shi de yingxiong jiemei' (The Liu Hulan style heroic sisters covered in dust for seventy-one years), *Dangshi tiandi* (Party history heaven and earth) 2 (2000), 8–11, and Zhou Xun, 'Bei chenfeng 72 nian de Liu Hulan shi de "Yingxiong jiemei"' (The Liu Hulan style heroic sisters buried in dust for 72 years), *Wenshi chunqiu* (Spring and Autumn literature and history) 2 (2000), 14–8.

12. Liu Ticfang, 'Xiang qi Liu Hulan' (Thinking of Liu Hulan), *Fujian luntan* (Fujian discussion platform) 10 (2005), 37–8.

13. 'Liu Hulan lieshi shilüe' (A brief history of martyr Liu Hulan), *Jin Sui ribao* (*Shanxi-Suiyuan daily*) [Hereafter *JSRB*] 13 February 1947, 4. For a discussion of the lives of women and girls in these years in north China, see Gail Hershatter's *The Gender of Memory: Rural Women and China's Collective Past* (Berkeley: University of California Press, 2011).

14. 'Nü yingxiong Liu Hulan benshi' (Female hero Liu Hulan's source material), *Renmin ribao* [Hereafter *RMRB*] 13 June 1949, 4.

15. 'Liu Hulan lieshi shilüe', 4.

16. Shi Shaochen, 'Jiujing shi shei chumaile Liu Hulan? Pantu 1963 nian bei zhengfu jiangjue' (Who actually betrayed Liu Hulan? The government executed the traitor in 1963), n.d. Web, http://it.sohu.com/20060116/n241448619.shtml

17. 'Da situ sha Wenshui renmin' (Massacre of people at Wenshui), *JSRB* 5 February 1947, 1.

18. Later versions of this narrative explain that her defiant cries included: 'Those who fear death are not CCP members!' and 'Long Live Chairman Mao!' In 'Nü yingxiong Liu Hulan benshi', 4.

19. 'Liu Hulan kangkai fuyi' (Liu Hulan, vehement and firm in her martyrdom), *JSRB* 6 February 1947, 1.

20. 'Xiang Liu Hulan tongzhi zhi jing' (Respects to Comrade Liu Hulan), *JSRB* 6 February 1947, 2.
21. 'Liu Hulan lieshi shilüe', 4.
22. Zhandou jushe, 'Nü yingxiong Liu Hulan ben shi' (The capabilities of the heroine Liu Hulan), *RMRB* 13 June 1949, 4.
23. Zhao Kai, 'Guanyu Mao Zedong wei Liu Hulan liang ci tici de kaozheng' (Researching the two times Mao Zedong penned his epithet on Liu Hulan), *Dang de wenxian* (Literature of the Chinese Communist Party) 6 (2005), 77.
24. 'Sheng de weida, si de guangrong' (A great life and a glorious death) *Taiyuan ribao* (Taiyuan daily) 12 January 2007, Web, www.tynews.com.cn/tyrbmap/2007-01/12/content_2958892.htm
25. Chinese title: *Xuexi Liu Hulan tongzhi*, produced for Jin Sui Cadres.
26. Chinese title: *Nüyingxiong Liu Hulan*. This Shaoxing (*Yue*) Opera was edited and published a year after it first appeared in 1949. Wang Pei and Zuo Xian, *Nü yingxiong Liu Hulan* (Woman hero Liu Hulan), (Shanghai: Laodong chubanshe, 1950). Re-editing of the Xibei zhandou jushe jiti chuangzuo 1948–49 original. For an excellent discussion of the genesis and impact of the opera, see Brian DeMare, *Mao's Cultural Army: Drama Troupes in China's Rural Revolution* (Cambridge: Cambridge University Press, 2015), Chapter 4.
27. 'Xibei yezhanjun zhengzhibu' (Military political bureau of the northwest field army), *RMRB* 11 March 1949, 1.
28. Mei Lingyi, 'Nüren bu zai shi "ruozhe"' (Women will no longer be the 'weak ones'), *RMRB* 7 March 1950, 6; Yu Cun, *Liu Hulan: simu qichang huaju* (Liu Hulan: a play in Four Mu and Seven Chang), (Beijing: Zuojia chubanshe, 1956).
29. 'Jing dier wenhua guan zhanlan' (The capital's No. 2 culture museum exhibition), *RMRB* 18 May 1950, 3.
30. Liang Xing, *Liu Hulan xiaozhuan* (A brief biography of Liu Hulan), (Beijing: Qingnian chubanshe, 1952).
31. *Liu Hulan*, Feng Bailu dir., Changchun dianying prod, 1950, Film.
32. He Guo, 'Shenyang shi beishi qu he Shenhe qu xiaoren shu yuedu qingkuang de diaocha' (An investigation into the reading materials for young people in Shenyang city's northern and river districts), *RMRB* 1 April 1951, 6.
33. Guo Moruo in Feng Xigang, '"Qiancheng saomu geng shengtang": Guo Moruo yong Liu Hulan' ('Devoutly paying respects on visiting the grave and ascending the hall': Guo Moruo's poem on Liu Hulan), *Dangshi wenhui* (Party history and culture) 3 (2000), 18.
34. The statue is reproduced in Chen Lüsheng, *Xin Zhongguo meishu tushi: 1949–1966* (The art history of new China), (Beijing: Zhongguo qingnian chubanshe, 2000), p. 288.
35. The picture is reproduced in Chen, *Xin Zhongguo meishu tushi*, p. 185. For a fascinating insight into the incorporation of artists into the CCP program after 1949, see Julia Andrews, *Painters and Politics in the People's Republic of China* (Berkeley: University of California Press, 1995).
36. Huo Zhanyue and Chen Xiangping, *Liu Hulan jinian guan* (Liu Hulan Memorial Hall), (Taiyuan: Shanxi jingji chubanshe, 1999), pp. 3–4. The museum displays calligraphy praising Liu penned by major CCP figures throughout the post-1949 years such as revolutionary era leaders Mao Zedong, General Zhu De and Hua Guofeng and post-1978 reformers Deng Xiaoping and Jiang Zemin. Sun Yutian

notes that the calligraphy of purged PLA commander, Lin Biao, is not on display even though he also penned a tribute to her. See Sun Yutian, 'Mao Zedong, Hua Guofeng, Lin Biao wei Liu Hulan tici beihou de gushi' (The story behind the poems penned by Mao Zedong, Hua Guofeng and Lin Biao on Liu Hulan), 23 August 2012, Web, http://blog.sina.com.cn/s/blog_4f030807010177g8.html.

37. Yang Wei, Guo Jian, Sun Wei, and Fang Yan, *Liu Hulan: bachang huaju* (Liu Hulan: a play in eight acts), (Beijing: Zhongguo xiju chubanshe, 1965).

38. Jin Qing, *Liu Hulan* (Hong Kong: Hong Kong zhaoyan chubanshe, 1972).

39. Yang Lanchun and Niu Guanli, *Liu Hulan: jiuchang Yuju* (Liu Hulan: a nine-act Yu opera), (Zhengzhou: Henan renmin chubanshe, 1979).

40. Li Xueao and Meng Qingjiang, *Liu Hulan* (n.p: Renmin meishu chubanshe, 1977).

41. Stefan Landsberger, 'Liu Hulan', 4 May 2014, Web, http://www.iisg.nl/~landsberger/lhl.html

42. Ma Feng, *Liu Hulan zhuan* (A biography of Liu Hulan), (Beijing: Zhongguo qingnian chubanshe, 1978), p. 405. The novella had been completed in draft format in 1964 but had been held back from publication by the leaders of the Cultural Revolution, the 'Gang of Four', according to Ma's postscript.

43. In Chinese the rhyme runs *Liu Hulan, shiba sui, Canjiale geming youji dui, Ta wei renmin xishengle, Mao Zhuxi shuo ta zuo de dui!*.

44. Shi Jun, 'Shenme shi zui baogui de? Kan "Liu Hulan" you gan' (What is the most precious: thoughts on watching 'Liu Hulan'), *Dazhong dianying* (Popular cinema) 5, no. 18 (1997), 18.

45. Huo and Chen, *Liu Hulan jinian guan*, pp. 81–2.

46. On 'red tourism' to these bases, see Denton, *Exhibiting the Past*, 214–42.

47. On Lei Feng and other male military models, see Louise Edwards, 'Military Celebrity in China: The Evolution of "Heroic and Model Servicemen"', in I. Edwards, E. Jeffreys (eds.), *Celebrity in China* (Hong Kong: Hong Kong University Press, 2010), pp. 21–44.

48. Zhandou jushe, 'Nü yingxiong Liu Hulan ben shi', 4.

49. Xu Jinsheng, '"1.12" da xue an kao lüe jiantan xuexi Liu Hulan jingsheng' (Overview of the double January 12 murder case and the learn from Liu Hulan spirit), *Lishi yanjiu* (History research) 5 (2004), 18.

50. 'Zhang Fei Quanbao' (The bandit Zhang Quanbao), *RMRB* 5 June 1951, 3.

51. For example, the aforementioned opera by the Northwest Combat Dramatic Society.

52. Wang Qinsheng, 'Shahai Liu Hulan de zhumou xiongfan zhi yi' (One of the main instigators in the murder of Liu Hulan), *RMRB* 22 June 1951, 3.

53. Xu, '"1.12" da xue', 16.

54. Yan Shujun's article on the ninetieth anniversary of the CCP includes photos of the 1951 trials with pictures of large crowds gathering around the stage and a close-up picture of one of the accused. Yan Shujun, 'Yingxiong chuanqi zhi Liu Hulan: Tanran miandui zhantou dao' (Tale of the heroic Liu Hulan: unperturbed in the face of the executioner's blade), 4 July 2011, Web, http://news.ifeng.com/mil/gundong/detail_2011_07/04/7425388_0.shtml

55. 'Zhang Fei Quanbao', 3.

56. Xu, '"1.12" da xue', 14.

57. Xu, '"1.12" da xue', 14.

58. Zhandou jushe, 'Nü yingxiong Liu Hulan ben shi'.

59. 'Xuexi Liu Hulan de geming yin gutou jingshen' (Learn from Liu Hulan's unyielding spirit), *RMRB* 8 December 1966, 2.

60. 'Sanwan duo ren zai Yunzhouxi cun ji hui jinian Liu Hulan lieshi jiuyi ershi zhounian' (Over 30,000 people gather at Yunzhouxi Village to commemorate the twentieth anniversary of the martyrdom of Liu Hulan), *RMRB* 15 January 1967, 2.

61. 'Renmin jundui ai renmin' (The people's military loves the people), *RMRB* 13 January 1974, 4.

62. Liu Shaoqi (1898–1969), leading CCP member, was president of the PRC from 1959–1968 but in an intra-party struggle lost out to Mao Zedong and was imprisoned as a 'capitalist roader'.

63. 'Xuexi Liu Hulan, yi bu pa ku, er bu pa si de geming jingsheng' (Learn from Lu Hulan's revolutionary spirit that has no fear of hardship or death), *RMRB* 14 January 1970, 1.

64. Ma, *Liu Hulan zhuan*, 405.

65. Wen Jianming, 'Wo de fuqin zhuazhu shahai Liu Hulan de xiongshou' (My father captured Liu Hulan's murderers), *Shanxi laonian* (Elders of Shanxi) 1 (2001), n.p.

66. Du Jie, 'Wo ceng yu Liu Hulan gongzuoguo bannian' (I worked with Liu Hulan for half a year), *Xianfeng dui* (The vanguard) 5 (2007), 53.

67. Hong Ni, 'Gaosu ni yi ge zhenshi de Liu Hulan' (I'll tell you about the real Liu Hulan), *Zongheng* (Traversing) 3 (2003), 26–30.

68. Hong, 'Gaosu ni yi ge zhenshi de Liu Hulan', 28.

69. Wang and Zuo, *Nü yingxiong Liu Hulan*.

70. Liang, *Liu Hulan xiaozhuan*, pp. 22–4.

71. Yang et al., *Liu Hulan: bachang huaju*, pp. 10–11.

72. Feng Baolu's 1950 film provides a brief glimpse of Hulan's transformation from support for the troops into an actual warrior, when in a brief scene before her capture she throws grenades at the enemy and picks up a rifle to shoot. Apart from this doomed, last ditch stand, Hulan of 1950 had focused on providing support in terms of food, clothing and medical care for soldiers and politicising the villagers.

73. Peng Huagao and Zhang Youluo, *Liu Hulan: Gu ci* (Liu Hulan Drum Song), (Taiyuan: Renmin chubanshe, 1977), pp. 75–6.

74. Peng and Zhang, *Liu Hulan*, p. 46.

75. Li and Meng, *Liu Hulan*, p. 18.

76. Xiao Bai et al., *Liu Hulan: lao gushi, xin manhua* (Liu Hulan: old stories, new cartoons) (Zhengzhou: Daxiang chubanshe, 2002).

77. Liang, *Liu Hulan xiaozhuan*, pp. 23–6.

78. Liang, *Liu Hulan xiaozhuan*, p. 7.

79. Peng and Zhang, *Gu ci,* pp. 7–11.

80. Peng and Zhang, *Gu ci,* pp. 33–4.

81. Wang and Zuo, *Nü yingxiong Liu Hulan*, p. 8.

82. Wang and Zuo, *Nü yingxiong Liu Hulan*, p. 22.

83. Wang and Zuo, *Nü yingxiong Liu Hulan*, p. 87.

84. Yang et al., *Liu Hulan: bachang huaju*, pp. 92–3.

85. See, for example, 'Jinggangshan de nüminbing' (Women's militia of Jinggangshan), *RMRB* 23 April 1960, 5; 'Jianjue zhichi woguo zhengfu dui

Meidi tichu de yanzheng jinggao' (Resolutely support my national government's serious warning to the American imperialists), *RMRB* 9 July 1966, 1.

86. 'Jiaoyu qingnian zou yu gong nong xiang jiehe de daolu' (Educating youth to go the united path of workers and peasants), *RMRB* 11 July 1974, 3. In 1992, twenty-seven years after it was established the Wenshui county Liu Hulan People's Militia had already received over thirty-one commendations from the party and army for its work in improved agricultural production. 'Liu Hulan minbingban duoci shou biaozhang' (The Liu Hulan People's Militia receives many commendations), *RMRB* 16 January 1992, 3.

87. 'Jiujing duanlian de funü yingxiongmen' (Well-trained and experienced heroes), *RMRB* 23 March 1949, 3.

88. Pei Lan, 'Tiaochu huokang de jiemeimen' (Sisters escaping a life of slavery), *RMRB* 26 December 1949, 6.

89. Bai Shu, *Dangdai yingmo xiaozhuan – Liu Hulan* (Biographies of contemporary heroic models – Liu Hulan), (Harbin: Heilongjiang renmin chubanshe, 2004), pp. 38–9.

90. Xiao et al., *Lao gushi*.

91. Ma Ming, 'Wei minzu jiefang benbo, wei guojia duli quanju' (Strive hard for the liberation of the people, sacrifice one's life for the independence of the country), *Dangshi wenhui* (Materials from CCP History), 1 (2007), 9–10.

92. 'Xie gei zhiyuan jun' (Letter to a volunteer), *RMRB* 25 July 1951, 4.

93. Zhang Lin, 'Fang kang Ri lian jun de mama' (Visiting the mother of the troops allied against the Japanese), *RMRB* 6 July 1952, 4.

94. 'Li Xuesan he Hong Chunzhe' (Li Xuesan and Hong Chunzhe), *RMRB* 22 March 1952, 1.

95. Cao Jing, 'Wo jiandaole Liu Hulan de muqin' (I met Liu Hulan's mother), *RMRB* 18 April 1954, 6.

96. Hong, 'Gaosu ni yi ge zhenshi de Liu Hulan', 26–30. Other articles fictionalise their romance in short story format complete with dialogue around their growing affection and blushing acknowledgement of their elders' approval. For one such story that takes Wang Bengu as the protagonist, see Shuang Song, 'Ta he lianren Liu Hulan' (He and his beloved Liu Hulan), *Laonian ren* (Elderly people) 6 (1994), 14–15.

97. Fang Jie, 'Lieshi Liu Hulan he ta de lianren' (The martyr Liu Hulan and her sweetheart), *Keji wencui* (Science and technology literature) 1 (1994), 78–81.

98. Li Zemin. 'Liu Hulan de yi duan lianqing' (Liu Hulan's love affair), *Hunan dang'an* (Hunan archives) no. 1 (2002), 42.

10   Women warriors and wartime spies as tools for 'total militarisation'

1. Jay Winter, *Sites of Memory, Sites of Mourning: The Great War in European Cultural History* (Cambridge: Cambridge University Press, 1995), p. 8.

2. On the education of ordinary people in the humiliation narrative, see Wang Zheng, *Never Forget National Humiliation* (New York: Columbia University Press, 2012).

3. See *Yapian zhanzheng* (Opium War), Xie Jin dir., Emei Film Studio, Xie Jin/Heng Tong Film and TV prod., 150 min, 1997, Film; *Gaoshanxia de huahuan* (Wreaths at the foot of the mountain), Xie Jin dir., Shanghai films prod., 80 min, 1984, Film;

Jiawu dahai zhan (The Great Sea Battle of 1894), Feng Xiaoning dir., CCTV 6 and China Film Group prod., 120 min, 2011, Film.

4. Roger Chickering and Stig Föster, 'Are We There Yet? World War II and the Theory of Total War', in Roger Chickering, Stig Föster and Bernd Greiner (eds.), *The World at Total War* (Cambridge: Cambridge University Press, 2004), p. 2.

5. On the importance of recognising the 'feminine' and the 'sexual' in Cultural Revolution cultural products, see Rosemary Roberts, 'Positive Women Characters in the Revolutionary Model Works of the Chinese Cultural Revolution: An Argument against the Theory of Erasure of Gender and Sexuality', *Asian Studies Review* 20, no. 4 (2004), 407–22.

6. For a comprehensive study of the various renditions of the story and especially its movement between stage and screen, see Kristine Harris, 'Re-makes/Re-models: *The Red Detachment of Women* between Stage and Screen', *The Opera Quarterly* 26, no. 2–3 (2010), 316–42.

7. Rosemary Roberts, 'Performing Gender in Maoist Ballet: Mutual Subversion of Genre and Ideology in *The Red Detachment of Women*', *Intersections: Gender and Sexuality in Asia and the Pacific* 16 (March 2008), Web, http://intersections.anu .edu.au/issue16/roberts.htm For her full study on this topic including other forms of Maoist theatre, see Rosemary Roberts, *Maoist Model Theatre: The Semiotics of Gender and Sexuality in the Chinese Cultural Revolution* (Leiden: E.J. Brill, 2010). Most recently she has written on the changing class status of the male protagonist in the 2006 TV Series remake as China's propagandists appeal to audiences' consumerism and middle-class aspirations. Rosemary Roberts, 'Reconfiguring Red: Class Discourses in the New Millennium TV adaptation of *The Red Detachment of Women*', *China Perspectives*, no. 2 (2015), 25–31.

8. 'Documents from China, *Red Detachment of Women*: A New Road for Chinese Ballet', *The Drama Review: TDR* 15, no. 2 (1971), 262.

9. Barbara Mittler explains the complex history of the Model Works and notes that it is commonplace for people to mistake the term 'eight model works' as a literal counting of their number. Barbara Mittler, *A Continuous Revolution: Making Sense of Cultural Revolution Culture* (Cambridge, MA: Harvard East Asia Centre, 2012), pp. 46–7. More model works were identified—the use of the number eight related to the CCP leadership's harnessing of its positive traditional associations as a 'lucky number'. The identification of the 'Gang of Four' as enemies of the people invokes similar superstition numerology, where 'four' is associated with death.

10. Mittler, *A Continuous Revolution*, p. 87.

11. *Hongse niangzi jun*, Xie Jin dir., Shanghai Tianma dianying prod., 90 min, 1961, Film. An excellent compendium of documents about the film, including the original Liang Xin script (*Qiong dao yingxiong hua*) can be found in Zhongguo dianying chubanshe, *Hongse niangzi jun: Congjuben dao yingpian* (The Red Detachment of Women: From drama script to film), (Beijing: Zhongguo dianying chubanshe, 1962). The book comprises 466 pages and includes the director's comments, main actors' analysis of the movie, its political agenda and Xie Jin's film script.

12. For the script and song sheets of the ballet, see *Geming xiandai wuju 'Hongse niangzi jun'* (Beijing: Renmin chubanshe, 1970). An English version is available at China Ballet Troup, *Red Detachment of Women: A Modern Revolutionary Ballet*

(May 1970 Script), (Beijing: Foreign Languages Press, 1972). Both have ample colour and black-and-white photos of the show.

13. See review of its performance in Paris in 2013 by Pierre Haski, 'Le *Détachement féminin rouge* à Paris, le maoïsme en dansant' (*The Red Detachment of Women*: Maoism in Dance), *Rue89* 2 October 2013, Web, http://rue89.nouvelobs.com/2013/10/02/detachement-feminin-rouge-a-paris-maoisme-dansant-246224

14. Mao Jianjie, 'Zuihou de Qionghua: Hongse niangzi jun de zhanhou rensheng fuchen' (The last immortal flower: The post-war life course of the Red Detachment of Women), n.d. Web, http://zhenhua.163.com/14/0420/16/9Q9OS4 RP000465DP.html During his presidency Jiang Zemin met with the surviving women to confirm their rehabilitation.

15. Zhou Huimin, 'Zuihou yiwei Hongse niangzi jun lao zhanshi qushi' (The passing of the last old warrior from the Red Detachment of Women), *Renmin ribao* [Hereafter *RMRB*] 20 April 2014, 4; Mao Jianjie, 'Zuihou de Qionghua'.

16. Cui Kaihong and Liu Lin, 'Hongse niangzi jun jinian xiang' (Commemorative statue for the Red Detachment of Women), *RMRB* 8 October 1985, 8.

17. 'Zhong xuanbu gongbu di er pi quango aiguo zhuyi jiaoyu shifan jidi' (The central propaganda bureau announces the second list of national patriotic education sites), *RMRB* 12 June 2001, 4.

18. Her name was Wu Qionghua in the Liang Xin story and Xie Jin film, but most people recognise the name Qinghua from the Operatic Ballet so I use this throughout.

19. China Ballet Troup, *Red Detachment of Women*, p. 1.

20. The sexual mutilation of women's bodies is a regular feature of war movies produced in China in the twenty-first century. The 2009 movie, *The Message*, narrates the final days of a CCP spy ring during the Sino-Japanese war after their cover is blown and they are captured. The female spy is dragged back and forth, straddled along a thick rope leaving her groin bleeding. Her male comrade, a CCP spy, is also tortured but the abuse has no sexual aspects. Another of the characters threatened with sexualised torture is an effeminate male collaborator – his torturer is seen sharpening a knife and instructing the jailors to 'remove his trousers'. Femininity is presented in this movie, and in many others of a similar kind, as an invitation to sexual mutilation. *Feng sheng* (The message), Chen Guofu and Gao Qunshu dir., Shanghai dianying jituan et al. prod., 118 min, 2009, Film.

21. China Ballet Troup, *Red Detachment of Women*, p. 11.

22. The ballet includes other scenes that reveal the vulnerability of the female physical form. Maidservants to the evil landlord are whipped, pushed and pulled by his thugs during an evening celebration. During Qinghua's first mission she is angered when she sees another maid being whipped and brutalised.

23. The opera version has the women soldiers in longer shorts than the ballet and film versions and with leg bindings so no flesh is exposed.

24. See John Dower on the myriad problems of wartime leadership in Japan's invasion of China and catastrophic expansion into war against the USA and its World War Two Allies and his comparison with the Gulf Wars and Afghanistan. John Dower, *Cultures of War: Pearl Harbor, Hiroshima, 9–11, Iraq* (New York: WW Norton and the New Press, 2010).

Bibliography

Translation and abbreviations of commonly featured newspapers

Renmin ribao – People's Daily – *RMRB*
Jiefang ribao – Liberation Daily – *JFRB*
Jin Sui ribao – Jin Sui Daily – *JSRB*
Qiu Jin, *Qiu Jin ji* – *QJJ*

'"The Lawrence of Manchuria": Romantic Figure in China: Move to Restore Monarch', *Sunday Mail* (Brisbane, Australia) 24 December 1933, 3.

'A Victim of a Governor's Panic', *North China Herald* 26 July 1907, 204–5.

Autumn Gem, Rae Chang and Adam Tow dir., San Francisco Film Society prod., 56 min, 2009, Film.

'Chinese Upset Trial of "Matahari of Far East"', *The Canberra Times* 17 October 1947, 1.

'Chuandao Fangzi shengsi dajie mi: 5 ji' (Thoroughly exposing the secrets of Yoshiko Kawashima's life and death: 5 Parts). *Tansuo Faxian* (Explore discover), Hu Zhitang, dir., China Central Television 10 prod. Web,

Part 1: http://tv.sohu.com/20120423/n341331878.shtml;

Part 2: http://tv.sohu.com/20120423/n341386461.shtml;

Part 3: http://tv.sohu.com/20120424/n341513098.shtml;

Part 4: http://tv.sohu.com/20120425/n341626830.shtml;

Part 5: http://tv.sohu.com/20120426/n341715900.shtml.

Chuandao fangzi: The Last Princess of Manchuria, Eddie Ling-Ching Fong, dir. Golden Harvest prod., 96 min, 1990, Film.

'Da situ sha Wenshui renmin' (Massacre of people at Wenshui), *JSRB* 5 February 1947, 1.

'Daring Exploits of "Manchukuo's Joan of Arc"', *The Daily News* (Perth, Australia) 22 March 1934, 6.

'Death of a Spy: Chinese Shoot "Eastern Mata Hari" and Display Body Outside the Jail', *Life* 26 April 1948, 39–40.

'Documents from China, *Red Detachment of Women*: A New Road for Chinese Ballet', *The Drama Review: TDR* 15, no. 2 (1971): 262–7.

Faa Muk Laan (The feminine general Far Mok Lan), Wong Hok-sing, dir., Baak Daat prod., 97 min, 1961, Film.

Feng sheng (The message). Chen Guofu and Gao Qunshu dir., Shanghai dianying jituan et al. prod., 118 min, 2009, Film.

Fifty-five Days at Peking. Nicholas Ray and Guy Green dir., Samuel Bronston prod., 154 min, 1963, Film.

'Funü ban biantian, shishi yao zhengxian, Hunan lishiwan nüjiang fenzhan luqian' (Women hold up half the sky, vying to be the first to do everything, in Hunan six million women generals bravely fight at the furnaces), *RMRB* 9 October 1958, 2.

Gaoshanxia de huahuan (Wreaths at the foot of the mountain). Xie Jin dir., Shanghai films prod., 80 min, 1984, Film.

'Guangfu jun qiyi xigao' (Draft call to arms for the Guangfu uprising) and 'Guangfu jun junzhi gao' (Draft military regulations for the Guangfu Army), *QJJ*, pp. 21–6.

'Guide fuzhi' Qianlong reign, 26 juan, Lienü shang. Rpt. in Ma and Su, *Mulan wenxian daguan*, pp. 53–4.

'Guoji jian nü jiandie de huodong' (Activities of women spies in the international arena), *Linglong* 385 (1937), 386.

'Healthy Life Balance', *Shanghai Daily* 9 March 2009, A3.

'Henan tongzhi', Yongzheng reign, Guide Prefecture, 67 juan, Lienü shang. Rpt. in Ma and Su, *Mulan wenxian daguan*, 52.

Hongse niangzi jun (Red Detachment of Women). Xie Jin dir., Shanghai Tianma dianying prod., 90 min, 1961, Film.

Hua Mulan. Liu Guoquan and Zhang Xinshi dir., Changchun dianying prod., b&w, 1956, Film.

Hua Mulan (Lady general Hua Mu-lan). Yue Feng dir., Shaw Brothers prod., 106 min, 1964, Film.

Hua Mulan. Li Huiming and Lai Shuiqing dir., Young Pei Pei Studios and China TV prod., 44 episodes, 1999, Television Series.

'Japan in Manchuria: Domination Extended', *Kalgoorlie Miner* (Kalgoorlie, Australia) 28 January 1932, 5.

Jiawu dahai zhan (The Great Sea Battle of 1894), Feng Xiaoning dir., CCTV 6 and China Film Group prod., 120 min, 2011, Film.

'Jiandie de xunlian' (Spy training), *Linglong* 271 (1937), 303–5.

'Jianjue zhichi woguo zhengfu dui Meidi tichu de yanzheng jinggao' (Resolutely support my national government's serious warning to the American imperialists), *RMRB* 9 July 1966, 1.

'Jiaoyu qingnian zou yu gong nong xiang jiehe de daolu' (Educating youth to go the united path of workers and peasants), *RMRB* 11 July 1974, 3.

'Jin ni Bihui shenjie' (Traitor Jin Bihui's investigation complete), *Dagong bao* 17 September 1947, 3.

'Jin ni Bihui zuo chen chu si' (Traitor Jin Bihui executed yesterday morning), *Dagong bao* 26 March 1948, 3.

'Jing dier wenhua guan zhanlan' (The capital's No. 2 culture museum exhibition), *RMRB* 18 May 1950, 3.

'Jinggangshan de nüminbing' (Women's militia of Jinggangshan), *RMRB* 23 April 1960, 5.

Jingxiong nüxia (Woman knight of Mirror Lake), Herman Yau Lai-To dir., National Arts Film prod., 115 min, 2011, Film.

'Jiujing duanlian de funü yingxiongmen' (Well-trained and experienced heroes), *RMRB* 23 March 1949, 3.

'Li Xuesan he Hong Chunzhe' (Li Xuesan and Hong Chunzhe), *RMRB* 22 March 1952, 1.

Liangyou huabao (The young companion) 130, July (1937), Cover.

Liu Hulan. Feng Bailu, dir., Changchun dianying prod., 1950, Film.

'Liu Hulan kangkai fuyi' (Liu Hulan, vehement and firm in her martyrdom), *JSRB* 6 February 1947, 1.

'Liu Hulan lieshi shilüe' (A brief history of Martyr Liu Hulan), *JSRB* 13 February 1947, 4.

'Liu Hulan minbingban duoci shou biaozhang' (The Liu Hulan People's Militia receives many commendations), *RMRB* 16 January 1992, 3.

'Manchu Mata Hari on Trial', *The Examiner* (Launceston, Australia) 18 October 1947, 4.

Mulan congjun (Mulan joins the army). Bu Wancang dir., Emei dianying zhipian prod., b&w, 89 min, 1939, Film.

Mulan. Jingle Ma Choh-hsing dir., Starlight International et al. prod., 114 min, 2009, Film.

'Nü jiandie Chuandao Fangzi zai Dongjing' (Woman spy Kawashima Yoshiko in Tokyo), *Linglong* 280 (1937), 983.

'Nü yingxiong Liu Hulan benshi' (Female hero Liu Hulan's source material), *RMRB* 13 June 1949, 4.

'Ping shi ji lianhui kangyi shu quan wen' (Complete text of the Beiping journalist association's protest), *Dagong bao* 26 March 1948, 3.

Qiu Jin. Xie Jin dir., Shanghai dianying prod., 144 min, 1983, Film.

'Renmin jundui ai renmin' (The people's military loves the people), *RMRB* 13 January 1974, 4.

'Revolutionary Terms', *North China Herald* 26 July 1907, 203.

'Sanwan duo ren zai Yunzhouxi cun ji hui jinian Liu Hulan lieshi jiuyi ershi zhounian' (Over 30,000 people gather at Yunzhouxi Village to commemorate the twentieth anniversary of the martyrdom of Liu Hulan), *RMRB* 15 January 1967, 2.

Se, Jie (Lust, caution). Lee Ang, dir. Hai Shang prod., 157 min, 2007, Film.

'Shanghai gaodeng fayuan guanyu Zheng Pingru bei hai an xunwen bi lü zhi er: 1946 nian 12 yue 11 ri' (Part 2 of the hearing of the Shanghai high court into the harming of Zheng Pingru: 11 December 1946), rpt. in Wang Chunnan (ed.), *Shenxun Wang wei hanjian bilü,* pp. 749–51.

'Sheng de weida, si de guangrong' (A great life and a glorious death), *Taiyuan ribao* (Taiyuan daily) 12 January 2007, Web, www.tynews.com.cn/tyrbmap/2007-01/12/con tent_2958892.htm

'Shoudu gaodeng fayuan tezhong xingshi panjue: 1947 nian 2 yue 8 ri' (Capital high court special criminal trial judgment: 8 February 1947), rpt. in Wang Chunnan (ed.), *Shenxun Wang wei hanjian bilü,* pp. 845–54.

The Feminine General Far Mok Lan. Wong Hok-sing dir., Baak Daat prod., b&w, 97 min, 1961, Film.

Wode muqin Zhao Yiman (My Mother Zhao Yiman). Sun Tie dir., Haixia shijie prod., 90 min, 2005, Film.

'Woman Spy to Die: Human Devil's Intrigues for Japan', *The West Australian* (Perth) 24 October 1947, 13.

'Xiang Liu Hulan tongzhi zhi jing' (Respects to Comrade Liu Hulan), *JSRB* 6 February 1947, 2.

'Xibei yezhanjun zhengzhibu' (Military political bureau of the northwest field army), *RMRB* 11 March 1949, 1.

'Xie gei zhiyuan jun' (Letter to a volunteer), *RMRB*, 25 July 1951, 4.

'Xuexi Liu Hulan de geming yin gutou jingshen' (Learn from Liu Hulan's unyielding spirit), *RMRB* 8 December 1966, 2.

'Xuexi Liu Hulan, yi bu pa ku, er bu pa si de geming jingsheng' (Learn from Lu Hulan's revolutionary spirit that has no fear of hardship or death), *RMRB* 14 January 1970, 1.

Yapian zhanzheng (Opium War). Xie Jin dir., Emei Film Studio, Xie Jin/Heng Tong Film and TV prod., 150 min, 1997, Film.

'Zhang Fei Quanbao' (The bandit Zhang Quanbao), *RMRB* 5 June 1951, 3.

Zhao Yiman. Sha Meng dir., Dongbei dianying, 92 min, 1950, Film.

Zhenzhen (Zhenzhen). Qiao Liang dir., Beijing jizuhou tongying dianying prod., 90 min, 2003, Film.

'Zhong xuanbu gongbu di er pi quango aiguo zhuyi jiaoyu shifan jidi' (The Central propaganda bureau announces the second list of national patriotic education sites), *RMRB* 12 June 2001, 4.

'Zhongguo nübao fakan ci' (Inaugural introduction to the *Chinese Women's Journal*), in Qiu Jin, *QJJ*, pp. 12–13.

'Zuguo wuqian yingxiong ernü shenglong huohu daxian shenshou' (Five thousand heroic sons and daughters of our ancestral land, full of vigor and vitality displaying their skill to the fullest), *RMRB* 25 November 1958, 1.

Aisin Gioro Puyi, *Wo de qian bansheng* (The first half of my life). Beijing: Xinhua shudian, 1960. English translation, *The Last Manchu: The Autobiography of Henry Pu Yi, Last Emperor of China* by Paul Tsai. London: Weidenfeld and Nicolson, 1987.

Alber, Charles, J. *Enduring the Revolution: Ding Ling and the Politics of Literature in Guomindang China*. Westport: Praeger, 2002.

Allen, Joseph R. 'Dressing and Undressing the Chinese Woman Warrior', *positions: East Asian Cultures Critique* 4 (1996), 343–79.

Altenburger, Roland. 'Is It Clothes That Make the Man?: Cross-Dressing, Gender, and Sex in Pre-Twentieth-Century Zhu Yingtai Lore', *Asian Folklore Studies* 64, no. 2 (2005), 165–205.

Altenburger, Roland. *The Sword or the Needle: The Female Knight-Errant (Xia) in Traditional Chinese Narrative*. Bern: Peter Lang, 2009.

Andrews, Julia. 'Traditional Painting in New China: *Guohua* and the Anti-Rightist Campaign', *Journal of Asian Studies* 49, no. 3 (1990), 555–77.

Andrews, Julia. *Painters and Politics in the People's Republic of China*. Berkeley: University of California Press, 1995.

Ayscough, Florence. *Chinese Women: Yesterday and To-Day*. Boston: Houghton Mifflin, 1937.

Bai Shu. *Dangdai yingmo xiaozhuan – Liu Hulan* (Biographies of contemporary heroic models – Liu Hulan). Harbin: Heilongjiang renmin chubanshe, 2004.

Bai Yuan. 'Lao yingxiong Li Sheng de jingli' (The experience of an old hero, Li Sheng), *RMRB* 29 October 1951, 3.

Barlow, Tani with Gary Bjorge (eds.). *I Myself Am a Woman: Selected Writings of Ding Ling*. Boston: Beacon, 1989.

Barlow, Tani. *The Question of Women in Chinese Feminism*. Durham: Duke University Press, 2004.

Barnouin, Barbara and Yu Changgen. *Zhou Enlai: A Political Life*. Hong Kong: The Chinese University Press, 2006.

Bayard de Volo, Lorraine. 'Mobilizing Mothers for War: Cross-National Framing Strategies in Nicaragua's Contra War', *Gender and Society* 18, no. 6 (2004), 715–34.

Beahan, Charlotte. 'Feminism and Nationalism in the Chinese Women's Press, 1902–1911', *Modern China* 1, no. 4 (1975), 379–416.

Berry, Chris. 'Disney's Mulan, Disney's Feminism: Universal Appeal and Mutually Assured Destruction', *TAASA Review* 9 (2000), 6–7.

Bi Quan. 'Chuandao Fangzi de gushi' (The story of Kawashima Yoshiko), *Funü shenghuo* (Women's life) 4, no. 6 (1937), 35.

Birnbaum, Phyllis. *Manchu Princess, Japanese Spy: The Story of Kawashima Yoshiko, the Cross-Dressing Spy Who Commanded Her Own Army.* New York: Columbia University Press, 2015.

Bjorge, Gary John. 'Ting Ling's Early Years: Her Life and Literature through 1942'. The University of Wisconsin-Madison, PhD 1977.

Brady, Anne-Marie. *Marketing Dictatorship: Propaganda and Thought Work in Contemporary China.* Lanham: Rowman & Littlefield, 2007.

Brook, Timothy. *Collaboration: Japanese Agents and Local Elites in Wartime China.* Harvard: Harvard University Press, 2005.

Burke, Jim. 'Japan's Mata Hari', *Life* 28 July 1947, 19–20.

Cai Dejin. *Qishiliu hao: Wang wei tegong zongbu koushu mishi* (No. 76: the secret history of the oral recounting of the Wang regime's central spy branch). Beijing: Tuanjie chubanshe, 2007.

Canaves, Sky. 'China's Military Women Hold up Half the Sky (and Dance, and Sing, and. . .)', *Wall Street Journal: China Real Time Blog*, 30 November 2009. http://blo gs.wsj.com/chinarealtime/2009/11/30/chinas-military-women-hold-up-half-the-sky-and-dance-and-sing-and. . ./

Cao Jing. 'Wo jiandaole Liu Hulan de muqin' (I met Liu Hulan's mother), *RMRB* 18 April 1954, 6.

Cao Mengjun. 'Jin yi bu jiefang funü ladongli wei duokuai haosheng di jianshe shehui zhuyi fuwu' (Advancing one step in the liberation of women's labour power in the service of achieving faster, better and more economical results in the service of building socialism), *RMRB* 2 June 1958, 2.

Chang, Eileen. *Lust Caution*, trans. by Julia Lovell. New York: Anchor Books, 2007.

Chang, Rae and Adam Tow dir. *Autumn Gem: The True Story of China's First Feminist*, 56 min, San Francisco Film Society, 2011, Film.

Chen Lüsheng. *Xin Zhongguo meishu tushi: 1949–1966* (The art history of new China). Beijing: Zhongguo qingnian chubanshe, 2000.

Cheng, Eileen J. 'Gendered Spectacles: Lu Xun on Gazing at Women and Other Pleasures', *Modern Chinese Literature and Culture* 16, no. 1 (2004), 1–30.

Chenoy, Anuradha M. 'Militarization, Conflict, and Women in South Asia', pp. 101–10 in Jennifer Turpin (ed.), *The Women and War Reader.* New York: New York University Press, 1998.

Chickering Roger and Stig Föster. 'Are We There Yet? World War II and the Theory of Total War', pp. 1–16 in Roger Chickering, Stig Föster and Bernd Greiner (eds.), *The World at Total War.* Cambridge: Cambridge University Press, 2004.

China Ballet Troup, *Red Detachment of Women: A Modern Revolutionary Ballet (May 1970 Script).* Beijing: Foreign Languages Press, 1972.

Chu Renhuo. *Sui Tang yanyi* (Romance of the Sui and Tang). 1695; rpt. Shenyang: Changchun chubanshe, 2008.

Clark, Paul. *Chinese Cinema and Politics since 1949*. Cambridge: Cambridge University Press, 1987.

Cock, Jacklyn. 'Women and the Military: Implications for Demilitarization in the 1990s in South Africa', *Gender and Society* 8, no. 2 (1994), 152–69.

Cohen, Carol. 'Women and Wars: Toward a Conceptual Framework', pp. 1–35 in Carol Cohen (ed.), *Women and Wars*. Cambridge: Polity Press, 2013.

Cui Kaihong and Liu Lin. 'Hongse niangzi jun jinian xiang' (Commemorative statue for the Red Detachment of Women), *RMRB* 8 October 1985, 8.

Culp, Robert. 'Rethinking Governmentality: Training, Cultivation and Cultural Citizenship in Nationalist China', *Journal of Asian Studies* 65, no. 3 (2006), 529–54.

Dai Qing. *Wang Shiwei and 'Wild Lilies'*. Armonk: ME Sharpe, 1994.

DeMare, Brian. *Mao's Cultural Army: Drama Troupes in China's Rural Revolution*. Cambridge: Cambridge University Press, 2015.

Denton, Kirk. *Exhibiting the Past: Historical Memory and the Politics of Museums in Postsocialist China*. Honolulu: Hawaii University Press, 2014.

Ding Ling. 'Bianzhe de hua' (Words from the editor), *JFRB* 12 March 1942, 4.

Ding Ling. 'Sanbajie yougan' (Thoughts on March eighth), *JFRB* 9 March 1942, 4. 'Thoughts on March 8th', trans. by Gregor Benton., in Barlow with Bjorge (eds.), *I Myself Am a Woman,* pp. 317–21.

Ding Ling. 'Wenyijie dui Wang Shiwei yingyou de taidu ji fanxing' (The attitude and introspection that the literary and art world should adopt towards Wang Shiwei), *JFRB* 16 June 1942, 4.

Ding Ling. 'When I Was in Xia Village', trans. by Gary Bjorge, in Barlow with Bjorge (eds.), *I Myself Am a Woman*, pp. 299–315.

Ding Ling. 'Wo zai Xiacun de shihou' (When I was in Xia Village), *Zhongguo wenhua* (Chinese culture) 20 June 1941, 24–31.

Ding Ling. 'Zai yiyuan zhong shi' (At the hospital), *Guyu* (Grain rains), no. 1 (November 1941), np.

Ding Ling. *Ding Ling ji* (Collected works of Ding Ling). Beijing: Renmin wenxue chubanshe, 1954.

Ding Ling. *Miss Sophie's Diary and Other Stories*, trans. By W.J.F. Jenner. Beijing: Chinese Literature, Panda Books, 1985.

Ding Ling. *Wo zai Xiacun de shihou* (When I was in Xia Village). Guilin: Yuanfang shudian, 1944.

Ding Ling. *Yan'an ji* (The Yan'an collection). Beijing: Renmin wenxue chubanshe, 1954.

Ding Mocun. 'Ding Mocun buchong da bian shu: 1947 nian 2 yue 3 ri' (Ding Mocun's supplementary reply: 3 February 1947), rpt. in Wang Chunnan (ed.), *Shenxun Wang wei hanjian bilü*, pp. 838–45.

Ding Mocun. 'Shoudu gaodeng fayuan shenpan bilü: 1946 nian 12 yue 12 ri' (Record of the Capital high court trial: 12 December 1946), rpt. in Wang Chunnan (ed.), *Shenxun Wang wei hanjian bilü,* pp. 752–60.

Ding Mocun. 'Shoudu gaodeng fayuan shenpan bilü: 1947 nian 2 yue 1 ri' (Record of the Capital high court trial: 1 February 1947), rpt. in Wang Chunnan (ed.), *Shenxun Wang wei hanjian bilü,* pp. 769–90.

Ding Mocun. 'Shoudu gaodeng fayuan shenpan Ding Mocun bilü: 1946 nian, 11 yue, 19 ri' (Record of the Capital high court trial of Ding Mocun: 19 November 1946), rpt. in Wang Chunnan (ed.), *Shenxun Wang wei hanjian bilü,* pp. 719–42.

Dombrowski, Nicole Ann. 'Soldiers, Saints or Sacrificial Lambs? Women's Relationship to Combat and the Fortification of the Home Front in the Twentieth Century', pp. 2–37 in Nicole Ann Dombrowski (ed.), *Women and War in the Twentieth Century: Enlisted with or without Consent.* New York: Routledge, 2004.

Donald, Stephanie Hemelryk. 'Tang Wei, Sex, the City and the Scapegoat in *Lust, Caution*', *Theory, Culture and Society* 27, no. 4 (2010), 46–68.

Donald, Stephanie Hemelryk. *Little Friends: Children's Film and Media Culture in China.* Lanham: Rowman & Littlefield, 2005.

Dooling, Amy and Kristina Torgeson. *Writing Women in Modern China: An Anthology of Women's Literature from the Early Twentieth Century.* New York: Columbia University Press, 1998.

Dower, John. *Cultures of War: Pearl Harbor, Hiroshima, 9–11, Iraq.* New York: WW Norton and the New Press, 2010.

Du Jie. 'Wo ceng yu Liu Hulan gongzuoguo bannian' (I worked with Liu Hulan for half a year), *Xianfeng dui* (The vanguard) 5 (2007), 53.

Duara, Prasenjit. *Sovereignty and Authenticity: Manchukuo and the East Asian Modern.* Lanham: Rowman & Littlefield, 2003.

Duchen, Claire. 'Crime and Punishment in Liberated France', pp. 233–51 in Claire Duchen and Irene Bandhauer-Schöffmann (eds.), *When the War Was Over: Women, War and Peace in Europe, 1940–1956.* London: Leicester University Press, 2000.

Edwards, Louise and Lili Zhou. 'Gender and the "Virtue of Violence": Creating a New Vision of Political Engagement through the 1911 Revolution', *Frontiers of History in China* 6, no. 4 (2011), 485–504.

Edwards, Louise. 'International Women's Day in China: Feminism Meets Militarised Nationalism and Competing Political Party Programs', *Asian Studies Review* 40, no. 1 (2016).

Edwards, Louise. 'Drawing Sexual Violence in Wartime China: Anti-Japanese Propaganda Cartoons', *Journal of Asian Studies* 72, no. 3 (2013), 563–86.

Edwards, Louise. 'Women Sex-Spies: Chastity, National Dignity, Legitimate Government and Ding Ling's "When I Was in Xia Village"', *China Quarterly* 212 (December 2012), 1059–78.

Edwards, Louise. 'Transformations of the Woman Warrior Hua Mulan: From Defender of the Family to Servant of the State', *Nan Nü: Men, Women and Gender in China* 12, no. 2 (2010), 175–214.

Edwards, Louise. 'Military Celebrity in China: The Evolution of "Heroic and Model Servicemen"', pp. 21–44 in Louise Edwards, Elaine Jeffreys (eds.), *Celebrity in China.* Hong Kong: Hong Kong University Press, 2010.

Edwards, Louise. *Gender, Politics and Democracy: Women's Suffrage in China.* Stanford: Stanford University Press, 2008.

Edwards, Louise. 'Dressing for Power: Scholars' Robes, School Uniforms and Military Attire in China', pp. 42–64 in M. Roces and L. Edwards (eds.), *The Politics of Dress in Asia and the Americas.* Brighton: Sussex Academic, 2007.

Edwards, Louise. 'Zhanzheng dui xiandai Zhongguo funü canzheng yundong de yinxiang: "weiji nüxing"; de wenti' (The impact of war on women's suffrage in

China: the problem of 'crisis femininity'), pp. 220–6 in Wang Zheng and Chen Yan (eds.), *Bainian Zhongguo nüquan sichao yanjiu* (Research in one hundred years of Chinese feminist thought). Shanghai: Fudan University 2005.

Edwards, Louise. 'Policing the Modern Woman in Republican China', *Modern China* 26, no. 2 (2000), 115–47.

Edwards, Louise. 'Women Warriors and Amazons of the Mid Qing Texts *Jinghua yuan* and *Honglou meng*', *Modern Asian Studies* 29, no. 2 (1995), 225–55.

Edwards, Louise. *Men and Women in Qing China: Gender in the Red Chamber Dream.* Leiden: E.J. Brill, 1994; Honolulu: Hawaii University Press, 2001.

Enloe, Cynthia. 'The Warriors behind the Women', *Women's Review of Books* 10, no. 5 (1993), 23–4.

Enloe, Cynthia. *Maneuvers: The International Politics of Militarizing Women's Lives.* Berkeley: University of California Press, 2000.

Fang Jie. 'Lieshi Liu Hulan he ta de lianren' (The martyr Liu Hulan and her sweetheart), *Keji wencui* (Science and technology literature) 1 (1994), 78–81.

Farquhar, Mary Ann. *Children's Literature in China: From Lu Xun to Mao Zedong.* Armonk: ME Sharpe, 1999.

Faure, David. *Emperor and Ancestor: State and Lineage in China.* Stanford: Stanford University Press, 2007.

Faurot, Jeanette Louise. *'Four Cries of a Gibbon: A Tsa-chü Cycle by the Ming Dramatist Hsu Wei (1521–1593)'*, PhD Diss., University of California, Berkeley, 1972.

Feng Lan. 'The Female Individual and the Empire: A Historicist Approach to Mulan and Kingston's Woman Warrior', *Comparative Literature* 55, no. 3 (2003), 229–45.

Feng Xigang. '"Qiancheng saomu geng shengtang": Guo Moruo yong Liu Hulan' ('Devoutly paying respects on visiting the grave and ascending the hall': Guo Moruo's poem on Liu Hulan), *Dangshi wenhui* (Party history and culture) 3 (2000), 18.

Feng Xuefeng [Xue Feng]. 'Cong "Meng Ke" dao "ye"' (From 'Meng Ke' to 'Night'), *Zhongguo zuojia* (China's Authors) 2 (January 1948), 4.

Feuerwerker, Yi-tsi. 'Ting Ling's When I Was in Sha chuan (Cloud Village)', *Signs* 2, no. 1 (1976), 255–79.

Finnane, Antonia. *Changing Clothes in China: Fashion, History, Nation.* New York: Columbia University Press, 2008.

Flath, James and Smith, Norman (eds.). *Beyond Suffering: Recounting War in Modern China.* Vancouver: University of British Columbia Press, 2011.

Frankel, Hans. *The Flowering Plum and the Palace Lady: Interpretations of Chinese Poetry.* New Haven: Yale University Press, 1976.

Fu, Poshek. *Between Shanghai and Hong Kong: The Politics of Chinese Cinema.* Stanford: Stanford University Press, 2003.

Fung, Edmund. *Military Dimensions of the Chinese Revolution: The New Army and Its Role in the 1911 Revolution.* Canberra: Australian National University Press, 1981.

Geming xiandai wuju 'Hongse niangzi jun' (Modern revolutionary ballet: 'Red Detachment of Women'). Beijing: Renmin chubanshe, 1970.

Geng Changjin. 'Yizhi de hua' (Words of the translator), in Kamisaka Fuyuko, *Danso no reijin*, pp. 1–4.

Giles, Lionel. *Ch'iu Chin: A Chinese Heroine.* London: East and West, 1917.

Gilmartin, Christina K. *Engendering the Chinese Revolution: Radical Women, Communist Politics and Mass Movements in the 1920s*. Berkeley: University of California Press, 1995.

Gittings, John. 'China's Militias', *China Quarterly* 18 (June 1964), 100–117.

Goldman, Merle. *Literary Dissent in Communist China*. New York: Atheneum, 1971.

Goldstein, Joshua. *War and Gender: How Gender Shapes the War System*. Cambridge: Cambridge University Press, 2001.

Gottschang, Thomas R. 'Economic Change, Disasters, and Migration: The Historical Case of Manchuria', *Economic Development and Cultural Change* 35, no. 3 (1987), 461.

Grant de Pauw, Linda. *Battle Cries and Lullabies: Women in War from Prehistory to the Present*. Norman: University of Oklahoma Press, 1998.

Green, Colin. 'Turning Bad Iron into Polished Steel: Whampoa and the Rehabilitation of the Chinese Soldier', in Flath and Smith (eds.) *Beyond Suffering*, pp. 153–85.

Gunn, Edward. *The Unwelcome Muse: Chinese Literature in Shanghai and Peking*. New York: Columbia University Press, 1980.

Guo Moruo. 'Nuli ba ziji gaizao chengwei wuchan jieji de wenhua gongren' (Strive to turn yourself into a proletarian literary worker), *RMRB* 28 September 1957, 3.

Guo Moruo. 'Nuola de da'an' (The solution for Nora), *Xinhua ribao* (New China daily) 19 July 1942, rpt. in Guo Yanli (ed.), *Qiu Jin yanjiu ziliao*, pp. 466–71.

Guo Yanli (ed.). *Qiu Jin yanjiu ziliao* (Research materials on Qiu Jin). Ji'nan: Shandong jiaoyu chubanshe, 1987.

Guo, Yingjie. *Cultural Nationalism in Contemporary China*. London: Routledge, 2004.

Hai Yi. 'Chuandao Fangzi: jie yu jiu shen de nü jiandie, Jin Siling eguan manying' (Yoshiko Kawashima: the woman spy exposed and on trial, the completely evil commander Jin), *Haiguang* 10 (1946), 4.

Harris, Kristine. 'Re-makes/Re-models: *The Red Detachment of Women* between Stage and Screen', *The Opera Quarterly* 26, no. 2–3 (2010), 316–42.

Haski, Pierre. 'Le *Détachement féminin rouge* à Paris, le maoïsme en dansant' (*The Red Detachment of Women*: Maoism in dance), *Rue89,* 2 October 2013, Web http://rue89 .nouvelobs.com/2013/10/02/detachement-feminin-rouge-a-paris-maoisme-dansant-246224

He Guo. 'Shenyang shi beishi qu he Shenhe qu xiaoren shu yuedu qingkuang de diaocha' (An investigation into the reading materials for young people in Shenyang city's northern and river districts), *RMRB* 1 April 1951, 6.

He Qifang. 'Xia Yan tongzhi zuopin zhong de zichanjieji sixiang' (The capitalist class thinking in Comrade Xia Yan's works), *RMRB* 1 April 1966, 5.

He Qifang. 'Wu Yuzhang tongzhi geming gushi' (Comrade Wu Yuzhang's revolutionary story), *RMRB* 30 December 1948, 4.

Hegel, Robert E. *The Novel in Seventeenth Century China*. New York: Columbia University Press, 1981.

Hershatter, Gail. *The Gender of Memory: Women and China's Collective Past*. Berkeley: University of California Press, 2011.

Hieronymous, Sabine. 'Qiu Jin (1875–1907): A Heroine for All Seasons', in Leutner and Spakowski (eds.), *Women in China*, pp. 194–207.

Hong Ni. 'Gaosu ni yi ge zhenshi de Liu Hulan' (I'll tell you about the real Liu Hulan), *Zongheng* (Traversing) 3 (2003), 26–30.

Hooper, Beverley. '"Flower Vase and Housewife": Women in China's Consumer Society', pp. 167–93 in Krishna Sen and Maila Stivens (eds.), *Gender and Power in Affluent Asia*. London: Routledge, 1998.

Hsiung, Anne-Marie. 'A feminist Re-Vision of Xu Wei's Ci Mulan and Nü zhuangyuan', pp. 73–89 in Zhang Yingjin (ed.), *China in a Polycentric World: Essays in Chinese Comparative Literature*. Stanford: Stanford University Press, 1998.

Hu Ying. 'Gender and Modern Martyrology: Qiu Jin as Lienü, Lieshi or Nülieshi', pp. 121–36 in Joan Judge and Hu Ying (eds.), *Beyond Exemplar Tales: Women's Biography in Chinese History*. Berkeley: University of California Press, 2011.

Hu Ying. 'Writing Qiu Jin's Life: Wu Zhiying and Her Family Learning', *Late Imperial China* 25, no. 2 (2004), 119–60.

Hua Fu. 'Ding Ling de "Fuchou de nüshen": Ping "Wo zai Xiacun de shihou"' (Ding Ling's 'Avenging Goddess': critiquing 'When I was in Xia Village'), *Wenyi bao* (Literary News) 3 (1958), 22–5.

Huang Canzhang and Li Shaoyi (eds.). *Hua Mulan kao* (Investigating Mulan). Beijing: Zhongguo guangbo dianshi chubanshe, 1992.

Huang Meizhen, Jiang Yihua and Shi Yuanhua. *Wang wei "no. 76"; tegong zongbu* (The Wang regime's espionage HQ, No. 76). Beijing: Tuanjie chubanshe, 2010.

Huang Wei. '"Hongse jiandie"; Guan Lu zhi si' (The death of 'Red Spy' Guan Lu), *Zhuanji* (Legends) 1 (2010), 66–9, 15.

Huang Weilin and Li Yongmei (eds.). *Zuihou de tanhua* (Last Words). Guilin: Lijiang chubanshe, 1996.

Hung, Chang-Tai. 'Female Symbols of Resistance in Chinese Wartime Spoken Drama', *Modern China* 15, no. 2 (1989), 149–77.

Hung, Chang-Tai. *War and Popular Culture: Resistance in Modern China 1937–1945*. Berkeley: University of California Press, 1999.

Huo Zhanyue and Chen Xiangping. *Liu Hulan jinian guan* (Liu Hulan Memorial Hall). Taiyuan: Shanxi jingji chubanshe, 1999.

Idema, Wilt and Beata Grant. *The Red Brush: Writing Women of Imperial China*. Cambridge: Harvard East Asia Centre, 2004.

Idema, Wilt. 'Female Talent and Female Virtue: Xu Wei's Nü Zhuangyuan and Meng Chengshun's Zhenwen ji', pp. 549–71 in Hua Wei and Wang Ailing (eds.), *Ming Qing xiqu guoji yantaohui wenji* (Collected essays from the international symposium on Ming and Qing drama). Taipei: Academia Sinica, Chinese Literature and Philosophy Research Institute, 1998.

Ishihara Koichiro. 'The Japanese Empire in the Balance: Critical Relations with the White Powers, the Ravages of Exploitation, the Task of the Saviour of Asia', *Peiping Chronicle* 6 January 1935, 5.

Jacka, Tamara. 'Back to the Wok: Women and Employment in Chinese Industry in the 1980s', *Australian Journal of Chinese Affairs* no. 24 (July 1990), 1–23.

Ji Hong. 'Jieshao Zhanzheng yu jiandie' (Introducing War and Spies), *Funü shenghuo* (Women's life) 4, no. 1 (1937), 47.

Jin Qing. *Liu Hulan*. Hong Kong: Hong Kong zhaoyan chubanshe, 1972.

Jin Xiongbai. *Wang zhengquan shilu: yuanming 'Wang zhengquan de kaichang yu shouchang'* (Record of the Wang Regime: originally titled *The commencement and conclusion of the Wang Regime*). Hong Kong: Chunqiu zazhishe, 1961.

Joffe, Ellis. '"People's War under Modern Conditions": A Doctrine for Modern War', *China Quarterly* 112 (1987), 555–71.

Jordan, Donald A. *China's Trial by Fire: The Shanghai War of 1932*. Ann Arbor: University of Michigan Press, 2001.

Judd, Ellen. 'Prelude to the "Yan'an Talks"', *Modern China* 11, no. 2 (1985), 377–408.

Judge, Joan. 'Expanding the Feminine/National Imaginary: Social and Martial Heroines in Late Qing Women's Journals', *Jindai Zhongguo funü shi yanjiu* (Research on Modern China's women's history) 15 (December 2007), 1–33.

Judge, Joan. *The Precious Raft of History: The Past, the West and the Woman Question in China*. Stanford: Stanford University Press, 2008.

Kamisaka Fuyuko. *Danso no reijin: Kawashima Yoshiko den* (A beauty dressed in male attire: a biography of Kawashima Yoshiko), 1984, trans. by Gong Changjin, *Nan zhuang nüdie – Chuandao Fangzi zhuan* (A female spy dressed in men's attire: a biography of Yoshiko Kawashima). Beijing: Jiefangjun chubanshe, 1985.

Ko, Dorothy. *Cinderella's Sisters: A Revisionist History of Footbinding*. Berkeley: University of California Press, 2005.

Kwa, Shiamin and Idema, Wilt L. (eds. & trans.). *Mulan: Five Versions of a Classic Chinese Legend with Related Texts*. Indianapolis: Hackett, 2010.

Landsberger, Stefan. 'Liu Hulan', 4 May 2014, Web, www.iisg.nl/~landsberger/lhl .html

Larson, Wendy. *Women and Writing in Modern China*. Stanford: Stanford University Press, 1998.

Lary, Diana and McKinnon, Stephen (eds.). *Scars of War: The Impact of War on Modern China*. Vancouver: University of British Columbia Press, 2001.

Lary, Diana. 'War and Memory: Memories of China at War', in James Flath and Norman Smith (eds.), *Beyond Suffering*, pp. 262–87.

Lee Bik Wah (aka Lillian Lee, Lee Bihua). *Chuandao Fangzi: Manzhouguo de yaoyan* (Yoshiko Kawashima: the seductress from Manchukuo). Hong Kong: Tiandi tushu youxian gongsi, 1990. Rpt. as *The Last Princess of Manchuria*, trans. by Andrea Kelly. New York: William Morrow, 1992.

Lee, Lily and Wiles, Sue. *Women of the Long March*. Sydney: Allen and Unwin, 1999.

Leutner, Mechthild and Nicola Spakowski (eds.). *Women in China: The Republican Period in Historical Perspective*. Münster: LIT, 2005.

Li Chi. 'Communist War Stories', *China Quarterly* 13 (March 1963), 139–57.

Li Gang and He Jingfang, *Chuandao Fangzi shengsi zhi mi xinzheng* (New evidence on the secrets of the life and death of Yoshiko Kawashima). Changchun: Jinlin wenshi chubanshe, 2009.

Li Jun. 'Chuandao Fangzi: Ri zhengfu de zhuming nü mitan' (Yoshiko Kawashima: the Japanese government's most famous woman spy), *Linglong* 134 (1934), 526–27.

Li Wei. *76 hao moku nü jiandie* (The woman spy of the den of monsters at no. 76). Wuhan: Hubei renmin chubanshe, 2008.

Li Xueao and Meng Qingjiang. *Liu Hulan*. n.p.: Renmin meishu chubanshe, 1977.

Li Yiming. *Chuandao Fangzi zhuan* (Biography of Chuandao Fangzi). Changchun: Jilin daxue chubanshe, 2010.

Li Zemin. 'Liu Hulan de yi duan lianqing' (Liu Hulan's love affair), *Hunan dang'an* (Hunan archives) no. 1 (January 2002), p. 42.

Li, Siu Leung. *Cross-dressing in Chinese Opera*. Hong Kong: Hong Kong University Press, 2006.

Liang Xing. *Liu Hulan xiaozhuan* (A brief biography of Liu Hulan). Beijing: Qingnian chubanshe, 1952.

Lin Danqiu. 'Xin Zhongguo renmin dianying shiye de shengli' (Victory for new China's peoples' movie industry), *RMRB* 7 (March 1951), 3.

Lin Yutang. *Letters of a Chinese Amazon and War-time Essays*. Shanghai: Commercial Press, 1934.

Liu Chuanxia. 'Ding Ling de "Wo zai Xiacun de shihou" jieshou yu chanshi' (The reception and interpretation of Ding Ling's 'When I was in Xia Village'), *Yantai shifan xueyuan xuebao* (Yantai normal college journal) 21, no. 3 (2004), 51–4.

Liu Heng. 'Jiefang qu de dianying shiye' (The film industry in the revolutionary areas), *RMRB* 24 (June 1949), 4.

Liu Jie. 'Chongping "Wo zai Xiacun de shihou" zhong Zhenzhen de xingxiang' (Another critique of Zhenzhen from 'When I was in Xia Village'), *Gansu shida xuebao* (Gansu Normal College Journal) 1 (1981), 53–5.

Liu Tiefang. 'Xiang qi Liu Hulan' (Thinking of Liu Hulan), *Fujian luntan* (Fujian Discussion Platform) 10 (2005), 37–8.

Liu, James J.Y. *The Chinese Knight-Errant*. Chicago: Chicago University Press, 1967.

Liu, Lydia H., Rebecca Karl and Dorothy Ko. *The Birth of Chinese Feminism*. New York: Columbia University Press, 2013.

Louie, Kam. *Theorising Chinese Masculinity*. Cambridge: Cambridge University Press, 2002.

Lu Xun [Dong Hua]. 'Xin "nüjiang"'; (New 'women generals'), *Beidou* (North Pole) 1, no. 3 (1931), 131–2.

Lu Xun. 'Yao' (Medicine), *Xin qingnian* (New youth) (May 1919), rpt. in pp. 298–310 *Lu Xun quanji, juan 1* (Complete works of Lu Xun). Shanghai: Xinhua shuju, 1973.

Lu Yaodong. 'Ping "Wo zai Xiacun de shihou"' (Critiquing 'When I was in Xia Village'), *Wenyi bao* (Literary news) 38 (1957), 4–5.

Luo Binji. 'Da fengbao zhong de renwu: Ping Ding Ling de "Wo zai Xiacun de shihou"'; (Characters from amidst a tempest: a critique of Ding Ling's 'When I was in Xia Village'), *Kangzhan wenyi* (War Literature and Art) 9, no. 5–6 (December 1944), 17–20.

Ma Choh-hsing, Jingle, dir. *Mulan*, Panorama Entertainment, 221 min, 2009, Film.

Ma Feng. *Liu Hulan zhuan* (A biography of Liu Hulan). Beijing: Zhongguo qingnian chubanshe, 1978.

Ma Junhua and Su Lixiang (eds). *Mulan wenxian daguan* (Overview of documents on Mulan). Zhengzhou: Henan renmin chubanshe, 1993.

Ma Ming. 'Wei minzu jiefang benbo, wei guojia duli quanju' (Strive hard for the liberation of the people, sacrifice one's life for the independence of the country), *Dangshi wenhui* (Materials from CCP History), 1 (2007), 9–10.

Ma Xiaotian and Wang Manyun. *Wang wei tegong neimu: zhi qingren tan zhiqing shi* (The inside story on the Wang Jingwei regime's espionage work: insiders talk about the inside facts). Zhengzhou: Henan renmin chubanshe, 1986.

Ma Xiaotian and Wang Manyun. *Wang wei tegong zongbu: 76 hao* (The central spy agency of the Wang Jingwei regime: no. 76), 1960 circa, rpt. in Xu Hongxin, *Yige nü jiandie,* pp. 171–8.

Ma Xiaotian and Wang Manyun. *Wo suo zhidao de Wang wei tegong neimu* (What I know about behind the scenes of the Wang regime's spy operations). Beijing: Dongfang chubanshe, 2010.

Ma Zhendu. *Guomindang tewu huodong shi: shang, xia* (History of the Guomindang's espionage activities: 2 vols). Beijing: Jiuzhou chubanshe, 2013.

Macartney, Jane. 'Tang Wei Blacklisted for "Glorifying Traitors"', *The Times* 11 March 2008, Web, www.thetimes.co.uk/tto/arts/film/article2426823.ece

Mann, Susan. 'Myths of Asian Womanhood', *Journal of Asian Studies* 59, no. 4 (2000), 835–62.

Mao Jianjie. 'Zuihou de Qionghua: Hongse niangzi jun de zhanhou rensheng fuchen' (The last immortal flower: the post-war life course of the Red Detachment of Women), n.d. Web http://zhenhua.163.com/14/0420/16/9Q9OS4RP000465DP.html

Mao Zedong. 'Talks at the Yan'an Forum on Literature and Art', 2 and 23 May 1942, Web, www.marxists.org/reference/archive/mao/selected-works/volume-3/msw v3_08.htm

Martin, Brian. 'Shield of Collaboration: The Wang Jingwei Regime's Security Service, 1939–1945', *Intelligence and National Security* 16, no. 4 (2001), 89–148.

McCormack, Gavan. *Chang Tso-lin in Northeast China, 1911–1924: China, Japan and the Manchurian Idea.* Stanford: Stanford University Press, 1977.

McElderry, Andrea. 'Woman Revolutionary: Xiang Jingyu', *China Quarterly* 105 (March 1986), 95–122.

McMahon, R. Keith. *Causality and Containment in Seventeenth Century Chinese Fiction.* Leiden: E.J. Brill, 1988.

Mei Lingyi. 'Nüren bu zai shi "ruozhe"; (Women will no longer be the 'weak ones') *RMRB* 7 (March 1950), 6.

Mitter, Rana. *China's War with Japan, 1937–1945: The Struggle for Survival.* London: Allen Lane, 2013.

Mitter, Rana. *The Manchurian Myth: Nationalism, Resistance and Collaboration in Modern China.* Berkeley: University of California Press, 2000.

Mittler, Barbara. *A Continuous Revolution: Making Sense of Cultural Revolution Culture.* Cambridge: Harvard East Asia Centre, 2012.

Muramatsu Shofu. *Danso no reijin: Kawashima Yoshiko den* (A beauty dressed in male attire: a biography of Kawashima Yoshiko). Ribaibaru gaichi bungaku senshu: Tokyo: Chuo koronsha, 1933; rpt. Tokyo: Ozorasha, 1998.

Naftali, Orna. 'Chinese Childhood in Conflict: Children, Gender and Violence in China of the Cultural Revolution Period (1966–1976)', *Oriens Extremus* 53 (2014), 85–110.

Naftali, Orna. 'Marketing War and the Military to Children and Youth in China: Little Red Soldiers in the Digital Age', *China Information* 28, no. 1 (2014), 3–25.

Nakajima, Midori. 'Ding Ling lun' (On Ding Ling), trans. by Yuan Yunhua and Pei Zheng pp. 526–554 in Yuan Liangjun (ed.), *Ding Ling yanjiu ziliao* (Research materials on Ding Ling). Tianjin: Tianjin renmin chubanshe, 1982.

Ni Liangduan. 'Li Kunjie kuxun baomei Zhao Yiman' (Li Kunjie and the arduous search for younger sister Zhao Yiman), *Shiji* (Century) May (2007), 72–4.

Niu Shanseng (ed.). *Chuandao Fangzi de jingren miwen: Guomin zhengfu shenpan Jin Bihui mimi dang'an* (The shocking secrets of Yoshiko Kawashima: secret documents from the trial of Jin Bihui by the Nationalist government). Hong Kong: Jinjian zixun jituan youxian gongsi, 1994.

Otley, C.B. 'Militarism and Militarization in the Public Schools, 1900–1972', *British Journal of Sociology* 29, no. 3 (1978), 321–39.

Pan Yan. 'Xue sa baishan heishui jian' (Blood sprinkled between the white snow and the black water), *RMRB* 20 (July 1993), 8.

Pei Lan. 'Tiaochu huokang de jiemeimen' (Sisters escaping a life of slavery), *RMRB* 26 (December 1949), 6.

Peng Huagao and Zhang Youluo. *Liu Hulan: Gu ci* (Liu Hulan drum song). Taiyuan: Renmin chubanshe, 1977.

Ping Er. 'Nanxinghua de Riben nü jiandie' (A masculinized Japanese female spy), *Haichao zhoubao* (Ocean tide weekly) 26 (1946), 6.

Powell, Ralph L. 'Maoist Military Doctrines', *Asian Survey* 8, no. 4 (1968), 239–62.

Proctor, Tammy M. *Female Intelligence: Women and Espionage in the First World War*. New York: New York University Press, 2003.

Qiu He. 'Jinian nü yingxiong Zhao Yiman; wei yingpian "Zhao Yiman" gongyan er zuo' (Commemorating the female hero, Zhao Yiman; written after the public screening of the movie 'Zhao Yiman'), *RMRB* 1 (July 1950), 4.

Qiu Jin. 'Diao Qu Yuan' (Mourning Qu Yuan), *QJJ*, p. 74.

Qiu Jin. 'Full River Red', in Idema and Grant, *The Red Brush*, p. 776. Chinese version 'Man jiang hong', *QJJ*, p. 99.

Qiu Jin. 'Jinggao wo tongbao' (A respectful note to my country men and women), *Baihua* (Vernacular) nos 3–4 (1904), *QJJ*, pp. 7–8.

Qiu Jin. 'Jinggao zimeimen' (Respectful note to my sisters), *Zhongguo nübao* (China's Women's Journal) 1 (1904), *QJJ*, pp. 13–6.

Qiu Jin. 'Letter to Aunt Qinwen – 9 April 1901', trans. by Marion Phillips and Dorothea Martin in *Chinese Studies in History* 34, no. 2 (2000–2001), 51. Chinese version 'Zhi Qin Wen shu' (Letter to Qin Wen), *QJJ*, pp. 31–2.

Qiu Jin. 'Letter to Qiu Yuzhang, Elder Brother – 12 September 1905', trans. by Marion Phillips and Dorothea Martin in *Chinese Studies in History* 34, no. 2 (2000–2001), 60. Chinese version 'Qi wu' (No. 5), *QJJ*, p. 39.

Qiu Jin. 'Song of the Precious Sword', in Idema and Grant, *The Red Brush*, pp. 774–75. Chinese version 'Bao dao ge', *QJJ*, p. 82.

Qiu Jin. 'Stones of the Jingwei Bird' (*Jingwei shi*), in Idema and Grant, *The Red Brush*, pp. 786–94.

Qiu Jin. 'Tan Zhongguo' (Sighing over China), *QJJ*, p. 114.

Qiu Jin. 'To the Melody of "Full River Red"', in Idema and Grant, *The Red Brush*, p. 784. Chinese version 'Man Jiang hong', *QJJ*, p. 108.

Qiu Jin. 'To the Melody of "Rivers and Mountains Like This"', in Idema and Grant, *The Red Brush*, p. 786. Chinese version 'Ruci jiangshan', *QJJ*, p. 109.

Qiu Jin. 'Tongbao ku' (My countrymen and women's bitterness), *QJJ*, pp. 113–14.

Qiu Jin. 'Zhi Wang Shize shu' (Letter to Wang Shize), *QJJ*, pp. 46–7.

Qiu Jin. 'Zhi Wang Shize shu', p. 47. Trans. as 'Letter 13: From Qiu Jin to Wang Shize', by Marion Philips and Dorothea Martin in *Chinese Studies in History* 34, no. 2 (2000–2001), 73.

Qiu Jin. *Qi Jin ji* (Collected Works of Qiu Jin). Shanghai: Guji chubanshe, 1962.

Rankin, Mary Backus. 'The Emergence of Women at the End of the Ch'ing: The Case of Ch'iu Chin', pp. 39–66 in Margery Wolf and Roxane Witke (eds.), *Women in Chinese Society*. Stanford: Stanford University Press, 1975.

Regan, P.M. 'War Toys, War Movies, and the Militarization of the United States, 1900–85', *Journal of Peace Research* 31, no. 1 (1994), 45–58.

Rettig, Tobias and Vina Lanzona (eds.), *Women Warriors in Southeast Asia*. London: Routledge, 2016.

Roberts, Rosemary. 'Positive Women Characters in the Revolutionary Model Works of the Chinese Cultural Revolution: An Argument against the Theory of Erasure of Gender and Sexuality', *Asian Studies Review* 20, no. 4 (2004), 407–22.

Roberts, Rosemary. 'Performing Gender in Maoist Ballet: Mutual Subversion of Genre and Ideology in *The Red Detachment of Women*', *Intersections: Gender and Sexuality in Asia and the Pacific* 16 (March 2008), Web, http://intersections.anu.edu.au/issu e16/roberts.htm

Roberts, Rosemary. *Maoist Model Theatre: The Semiotics of Gender and Sexuality in the Chinese Cultural Revolution*. Leiden: E.J. Brill, 2010.

Roberts, Rosemary. 'Reconfiguring Red: Class Discourses in the New Millennium TV adaptation of *The Red Detachment of Women*', *China Perspectives*, no. 2 (2015), 25–31.

Roberts, Thomas C. *The People's Militia and the Doctrine of the People's War*. Fort Lesley J. McNair Washington, DC: National Defense University Press, 1983.

Rottman, Allison. 'Crossing Enemy Lines: Shanghai and the Central China Base', pp. 90–115 in Christian Henriot and Wen-hsin Yeh (eds.), *In the Shadow of the Rising Sun: Shanghai under Japanese Occupation*. New York: Cambridge University Press, 2004.

Saeki Chizuru. 'Yoshiko Kawashima: Politics and Gender in Sino–Japanese Relations', *Asian Journal of Women's Studies* 12, no. 3 (2006), 75–98, 125–6.

Schobell, Andrew. *China's Use of Military Force: Beyond the Great Wall and the Long March*. Cambridge: Cambridge University Press, 2003.

Schoenhals, Michael. *Spying for the People: Mao's Secret Agents 1949–1967*. Cambridge: Cambridge University Press, 2013.

Schofield, Julian. *Militarization and War*. New York: Palgrave McMillan, 2007.

Shao, Dan. 'Princess, Traitor, Soldier, Spy: Aisin Gioro Xianyu and the Dilemma of Manchu Identity', in Tamanoi (ed.) *Crossed Histories*, pp. 83–118.

Sheng Yueh. *Sun Yat-sen University in Moscow: A Personal Account*. Kansas: University of Kansas Center for East Asian Studies, 1971.

Shi Jun. 'Shenme shi zui baogui de? Kan "Liu Hulan" you gan' (What is the most precious: thoughts on watching 'Liu Hulan'), *Dazhong dianying* (Popular cinema) 5, no. 18 (1997), 18.

Shi Lianxing. 'Zhongxin de ganxie – shiyan yingpian "Zhao Yiman" de yi xie weixiao de xinde' (Heartfelt gratitude – a few lessons from acting in the film 'Zhao Yiman'), *RMRB* 9 (October 1951), 3.

Shi Shaochen. 'Jiujing shi shei chumaile Liu Hulan? Pantu 1963 nian bei zhengfu jiangjue' (Who actually betrayed Liu Hulan? The traitor was executed by the government in 1963), n.d., Web http://it.sohu.com/20060116/n241448619.shtml

Shipman, Pat. *Femme Fatale: Love, Lies, and the Unknown Life of Mata Hari*. New York: Harper Perennial, 2008.

Shuang Song. 'Ta he lianren Liu Hulan' (He and his beloved Liu Hulan), *Laonian ren* (Elderly people) 6 (1994), 14–15.

Snow, Helen Foster. *Women in Modern China*. The Hague: Mouton, 1967.

Sommer, Matthew. *Sex, Law and Society in Late Imperial China*. Stanford: Stanford University Press, 2000.

Spakowski, Nicola. 'Women's Military Participation in the Communist Movement of the 1930s and 1940s: Patterns of Inclusion and Exclusion', in Leutner and Spakowski (eds.), *Women in China*, pp. 129–71.

Spence, Jonathan D. *The Gate of Heavenly Peace: The Chinese and Their Revolution, 1895–1980*. New York: Penguin, 1982.

Stoff, Laurie S. *They Fought for the Motherland: Russia Women Soldiers in World War 1 and the Revolution*. Lawrence: University of Kansas Press, 2006.

Strand, David. *An Unfinished Republic: Leading by Word and Deed in Modern China*. Berkeley: University of California Press, 2011.

Sun Chang, Kang-i and Haun Saussy (eds.), *Women Writers of Traditional China: An Anthology of Poetry and Criticism*. Stanford: Stanford University Press, 1999.

Sun Yaowen. *Feng yu wu zai: Mosike Zhongshan daxue shimo* (Records of tempestuous times: the rise and fall of Moscow's Sun Yat-sen University). Beijing: Zhongyang bianyi chubanshe, 1996.

Sun Yat-sen. 'Zhongguo Tongmenghui geming fanglüe' (General plan for the Chinese Revolutionary Alliance revolution), pp. 296–318 in *Sun Zhongshan quanji: di yijuan* (Complete works of Sun Yat-sen, volume 1). Guangzhou: Zhonghua shuju, 1981.

Sun Yutian. 'Mao Zedong, Hua Guofeng, Lin Biao wei Liu Hulan tici beihou de gushi' (The story behind the poems penned by Mao Zedong, Hua Guofeng and Lin Biao on Liu Hulan), 23 August 2012, Web, http://blog.sina.com.cn/s/blog_4f030807010177 g8.html

Sunindyo, Saraswati. 'When the Earth Is Female and the Nation Is Mother: Gender, the Armed Forces and Nationalism in Indonesia', *Feminist Review* no. 58 (Spring 1998), 1–21.

Tamanoi, Mariko Asano (ed.). *Crossed Histories: Manchuria in the Age of Empire*. Honolulu: University of Hawaii Press and Association for Asian Studies, 2005.

Tan See-Kam. 'Huangmei Opera Films, Shaw Brothers and Ling Bo: Chaste Love Stories, Genderless Cross-dressers and Sexless Gender-plays?', *Jump Cut: A Review of Contemporary Media* 49 (2007), www.ejumpcut.org/archive/jc49.2007/TanSee-Kam/index.html

Theiss, Janet. *Disgraceful Matters: The Politics of Chastity in Eighteenth-Century China*. Berkeley: University of California Press, 2004.

Tiao Yang. 'Liu Hulan de shengqian shenhou' (The life and death of Liu Hulan), *Shanxi dang'an* (Shanxi archives) 4 (2001), 38–9.

Tien Ju-k'ang. *Male Anxiety and Female Chastity*. Leiden: E.J. Brill, 1988.

Tsujihara Noboru. *Jasmine*, trans. by Juliet Carpenter. London: Thames River Press, 2012.

Tu Shu-min. '*Zhikan ji* chuanqi xulu' (Commentary on the *Zhikan ji*), *Tongshi jiaoyu xuebao* (General knowledge teaching journal) 8 (December 2005), 1–17.

Turner-Gottschang, Karen and Thanh Hao Phan, *Even the Women Must Fight: Memories of War from North Vietnam*. New York: Wiley, 1998.

Umemoto Sutezo. *Yoka: Kawashima Yoshiko Den* (Evil flower: a biography of Kawashima Yoshiko), 1980, trans. by Dan Dong as *Chuandao Fangzi qiren* (Kawashima Yoshiko the person). Beijing: Shijie zhishi chubanshe, 1984.

Volz, Yong Z. 'Going Public through Writing: Women Journalists and Gendered Journalistic Space in China, 1890s–1920s', *Media, Culture and Society* 29, no. 3 (2007), 469–89.

Wakeman, Frederic. 'Hanjian (Traitor)! Collaboration and Retribution in Wartime Shanghai', pp. 298–341 in Wen-hsin Yeh (ed.), *Becoming Chinese: Passages to Modernity and Beyond*. Berkeley: University of California Press, 2000.

Wakeman, Frederic. *Spymaster: Dai Li and the Chinese Secret Service*. Berkeley: University of California Press, 2003.

Wakeman, Frederic. *The Shanghai Badlands: Wartime Terrorism and Urban Crime, 1937–1941*. New York: Cambridge University Press, 1996.

Waley-Cohen, Joanna. *The Culture of War in China: Empire and the Military under the Qing Dynasty*. London: IB Tauris, 2006.

Wang Chunnan (ed.). *Shenxun Wang wei hanjian bilü* (Record of the trials of traitors from the Wang Jingwei regime). 1946, rpt. Nanjing: Jiangsu guji chubanshe, 1992.

Wang Liaoying [Liao Ying]. '"Ren. . . zai jianku zhong shengchang" – ping Ding Ling tongzhi de "Zai yiyuan zhong shi"' (People. . .develop in times of hardship – critiquing Comrade Ding Ling's 'In the hospital'), *JFRB* 10 June 1942, 4.

Wang Liaoying. 'Kangzhan shiqi Ding Ling xiaoshuo de sixiang qingxiang' (The ideological trends in Ding Ling's wartime stories), *Wenxue yanjiu* (Literary research) 4 (1957), 93–110.

Wang Pei and Zuo Xian. *Nü yingxiong Liu Hulan* (Woman hero Liu Hulan). Shanghai: Laodong chubanshe, 1950.

Wang Pingling. 'Zhanshi funü de teshu renwu: ying xuexi nü jiandie de zhishi ji jiqiao' (The particular tasks of women in wartime: we ought to acquire the knowledge and skills of women spies), *Funü gongming* (Women's resonance) 7, no. 4 (1938), 12.

Wang Qingxiang. *Chuandao Fangzi shengsi dajie mi* (Revealing all the secrets of Yoshiko Kawashima's life and death). Tianjin: Tianjin renmin chubanshe, 2010.

Wang Qinsheng. 'Shahai Liu Hulan de zhumou xiongfan zhi yi' (One of the main instigators in the murder of Liu Hulan), *RMRB* 22 (June 1951), 3.

Wang Shaoji. *Qiu Jin nüshi yiji* (Mourning collection on Madam Qiu Jin). Shanghai: Baiguang shudian, 1937.

Wang Xuanqiu. *Zhao Yiman*. Shanghai: Renmin meishu chubanshe, 1961.

Wang, Lingzhen. *Personal Matters: Women's Autobiographical Practice in Twentieth-Century China*. Stanford: Stanford University Press, 2004.

Wang, Zheng. *Never Forget National Humiliation: Historical Memory in Chinese Politics and Foreign Relations*. New York: Columbia University Press, 2012.

Watanabe Ryusaku, *Hiroku Kawashima Yoshiko* (Secret records of Kawashima Yoshiko), 1972, trans. by Sun Wang as *Chuandao Fangzi*. Nanjing: Jiangsu renmin chubanshe, 1982.

Wen Jianming. 'Wo de fuqin zhuazhu shahai Liu Hulan de xiongshou' (My father captured Liu Hulan's murderers), *Shanxi laonian* (Elders of Shanxi) 1 (2001), n.p.

Wen Ye and Zang Xiu. *Kang Ri yingxiong Zhao Yiman* (Anti-Japanese hero, Zhao Yiman). Shenyang: Yanbian renmin chubanshe, 1959; rpt. Chengdu: Sichuan daxue chubanshe, 1989.

Wen Ye. *Bi xue ying hun: Zhao Yiman zhuan* (The spirit of the hero that shed blood in a just cause: a biography of Zhao Yiman). Harbin: Heilongjiang renmin chubanshe, 2005.

Westad, Odd Arne. *Decisive Encounters: The Chinese Civil War, 1946–1950*. Stanford: Stanford University Press, 2003.

Westwell, Guy. *War Cinema: Hollywood on the Front Line*. London: Wallflower, 2006.

Wheelwright, Julie. *The Fatal Lover: Mata Hari and the Myth of Women in Espionage*. London: Trafalgar Square, 1993.

Winter, Jay. *Sites of Memory, Sites of Mourning: The Great War in European Cultural History*. Cambridge: Cambridge University Press, 1995.

Woods, Willa Lou. *Princess Jin: The Joan of Arc of the Orient*. Wenatchee: World Publishing, 1937.

Wu Pei-Yi. 'Yang Miaozhen: A Woman Warrior in Thirteenth Century China', *Nan nü: Men, Women and Gender in China* 4, no. 2 (2002), 137–69.

Wu Qun. 'Fandui ba funü tuo dao tewu xianshang' (Opposing putting women in the frontlines of spying), *Zhongguo funü* (China's women) 2, no. 2 (10 July 1940), 18.

Wu Qun. 'Fandui canhai muqin he haizi' (Opposing harming mothers and children), *Zhongguo funü* (China's women) 2, no. 4 (10 September 1940), 11.

Wu Shengqin. 'Gendering the Nation: The Proliferation of Images of Zhen Fei (1876–1900) and Sai Jinhua (1872–1936) in Late Qing and Republican China', *Nan Nü: Men, Women and Gender in China* 11, no. 1 (2009), 1–64.

Xia Xiaohong. 'Qiu Jin wenxue xingxiang de shidai fengmao: cong Xia Yan de huaju dao Xie Jin de dianying' (Features of the times in Qiu Jin's literary imagery: From Xia Yan's play to Xie Jin's movie), *Zhongguo xiandai wenxue yanjiu congkan* (Research into modern Chinese literature) no. 4 (2009), 49–65.

Xia Xiaohong. *Wanqing shehui yu wenhua* (Late Qing society and culture). Wuhan: Hubei jiaoyu chubanshe, 2000.

Xia Yan and Ke Ling. *Qiu Jin zhuan* (Biography of Qiu Jin). 1962 rpt. Shanghai: Shanghai wenyi chubanshe, 1979.

Xia Yan. 'Qiu Jin buxiu' (The eternal Qiu Jin), *RMRB* 5 (December 1979), 6.

Xia Yan. *Ziyou hun* (The spirit of freedom). Shanghai: Shenghuo shudian, 1937.

Xia Yun. 'Engendering Contempt for Collaborators: Anti-*Hanjian* Discourse Following the Sino-Japanese War of 1937–1945', *Journal of Women's History* 25, no. 1 (2013), 111–34.

Xiao Bai et al. *Liu Hulan: Lao gushi, xin manhua* (Liu Hulan: old stories new cartoons). Zhengzhou: Daxiang chubanshe, 2002.

Xiao Bai. 'Zhao Yiman de wan' (Zhao Yiman's bowl), *RMRB* 16 (September 1960), 8.

Xiao Xu. 'Guan Lu: Beifu hanjian maming 43 nian' (Guan Lu: burdened with the infamous title of traitor for 43 years), *Xinwen tiandi* (News world) 12 (2009), 59–60.

Xie Bingying. *Congjun riji* (War diary). 1928 rpt. Shanghai: Chunchao shuju, 1929.

Xie Bingying. *Nübing shinian* (Ten years a woman soldier). Chongqing: Honglan chubanshe, 1947.

Xie Bingying. *Wo de huiyi* (My reminiscences). Taibei: Sanmin shuju, 1972.

Xie Bingying. *Xin congjun riji* (New war diary). Hankou: Tianma chubanshe, 1938. Republished as *Kangzhan riji* (Diary of the War of Resistance). Taibei: Dongda tushu,

1981. And as *Chongshang zhengtu* (On a journey once more). np: Zhongshe chubanshe, 1941.

Xie Bingying. *Yi ge nübing de zizhuan* (A woman soldier's biography). 1936 rpt. Shanghai: Chenguang chuban, 1949. The English translations of this book include: *Girl Rebel*, trans. by Adet and Anor Lin. New York: John Day, 1940; New York: Da Capo Press, 1975; *Autobiography of a Chinese Girl*, trans. by Tsui Chi. London: George Allen and Unwin, 1943; *The Struggle of a Girl*, trans. by Lin Rusi and Lin Wushuang (Adet and Tai-yi Lin) with parallel English and Chinese texts. n. p.: Shijie chubanshe, 1947; *A Woman Soldier's Own Story*, trans. Lily Chia Brissman and Barry Brissman. New York: Columbia University Press, 2001.

Xie Bingying. *Zai Riben yuzhong* (Inside a Japanese prison). Shanghai: Gengyun chubanshe, 1940.

Xinhua she. 'Wo guo yingpian "Zhao Yiman" shoudao relie huanying' (Our country's film 'Zhao Yiman' receives a warm welcome in India), *RMRB* 11 (April 1951), 4.

Xinhua she. '*Zhonghua nüer* deng shiwu bu yingpian canjia Bulage guoji dianying jingsai dahui' (Fifteen movies including *China's daughter* participate in the Prague International Film Festival), *RMRB* 8 (July 1950), 3.

Xiong Xianjue. 'Wo muji shenpan nü jiandie Chuandao Fangzi' (I saw with my own eyes the trial of Kawashima Yoshiko), *Yan Huang chun qiu* (Yellow Emperor spring and autumn) 12 (1997), 66.

Xu Guangrong. *Zhao Yiman*. Nanchang: Ershiyi shiji chubanshe, 2004, 2008.

Xu Guoqi, *Olympic Dreams: China and Sports, 1895–2008*. Cambridge: Harvard University Press, 2008.

Xu Hongxin. *Yige nü jiandie* (A woman spy). Shanghai: Shanghai cishu chubanshe, 2009.

Xu Jinsheng. '"1.12" da xue an kao lüe jiantan xuexi Liu Hulan jingsheng' (Overview of the double January 12 murder case and the learn from Liu Hulan spirit), *Lishi yanjiu* (History research) 5 (2004), 14–8.

Xu Shuangyu. 'Qiu Jin ji' (Remembering Qiu Jin), in Guo Yanli (ed.), *Qiu Jin yanjiu ziliao*, pp. 215–16.

Xu Wei. *Si sheng yuan* (Four cries of a Gibbon). rpt. Shanghai: Shanghai guji chubanshe, 1995.

Xue Wei. '"Zai yiyuan zhong shi", "Maque" ji qita' ('In the hospital', 'sparrow' and other matters), *JFRB* 5 (December 1941), 4.

Yan Geling. *Jinling shisan chai* (Thirteen beauties of Jinling). Nanjing: Jiangsu wenyi chubanshe, 2010.

Yan Shujun. 'Yingxiong chuanqi zhi Liu Hulan: Tanran miandui zhantou dao' (Tale of the heroic Liu Hulan: unperturbed in the face of the executioners blade), 4 July 2011, Web, http://news.ifeng.com/mil/gundong/detail_2011_07/04/7425388_0.shtml

Yang Guixin. 'Chongdu Ding Ling de san ge duanpian' (Rereading three of Ding Ling's short pieces), *Qiqihaer shifan xueyuan xuebao* (Qiqihaer normal college journal) 4 (1982), 63–5.

Yang Guixin. *Ding Ling yu Zhou Yang de enyuan* (Gratitude and enmity between Ding Ling and Zhou Yang). Wuhan: Hubei renmin chubanshe, 2006.

Yang Lanchun and Niu Guanli. *Liu Hulan: jiuchang Yuju* (Liu Hulan: a nine act Yu opera). Zhengzhou: Henan renmin chubanshe, 1979.

Yang Wei, Guo Jian, Sun Wei, and Fang Yan. *Liu Hulan: bachang huaju* (Liu Hulan: a play in eight acts). Beijing: Zhongguo xiju chubanshe, 1965.

Yeh, Wen-hsin. 'Dai Li and the Liu Geqing Affair', *Journal of Asian Studies* 48, no. 3 (1989), 545–62.

Young, Helen Praeger. *Choosing Revolution: Chinese Women Soldiers on the Long March*. Urbana: University of Illinois Press, 2001.

Young, Louise. *Japan's Total Empire: Manchuria and the Culture of Wartime Imperialism*. Berkeley: University of California Press, 1998.

Yu Cun. *Liu Hulan: simu qichang huaju* (Liu Hulan: a play in Four Mu and Seven Chang). Beijing: Zuojia chubanshe, 1956.

Yu Miin-ling. 'Sun Yat-sen University in Moscow, 1925–1930', PhD diss., New York University, 1995.

Yu Yue. 'Meimei chengqing lishi zhenxiang Se Jie nüzhujue bushi Zheng Pingru' (Younger sister clarifies the historical fact that the lead female in Lust, Caution is not Zheng Pingru), 14 September 2007, Web, http://big5.china.com.cn/book/txt/2007-09/14/content_8875460.htm

Yuan Baoshan. 'Zhao Yiman lieshi zhi zi de feichang rensheng' (The extraordinary life of Martyr Zhao Yiman's son), *Shiji tegao* (Century Special Edition) 1 (2007), 9–13.

Yuan Baoshan. 'Zhao Yiman zhi zi de feichang rensheng' (The extraordinary life of Zhao Yiman's son), *Gongchandang yuan* (Communist Party members) 6 (2007), 18.

Yun Qiu. 'Tan geguo zhi nü jiandie' (Talking about women spies around the world), *Linglong* 248 (1936), 2295.

Zanasi, Margherita. 'Globalizing the *Hanjian*: The Suzhou Trails and Post-World War II Discourse on Collaboration', *American Historical Review* 113, no. 3 (2008), 731–51.

Zanasi, Margherita. 'New Perspectives on Chinese Collaborations', *The Asia-Pacific Journal: Japan Focus,* 4 July 2008, Web http://japanfocus.org/-Margherita-Zanasi/2828

Zarrow, Peter. *China in War and Revolution, 1895–1949*. London: Routledge, 2005.

Zeng Ke. 'Xian xue jiaoguan de hua' (Flowers irrigated with fresh blood), *RMRB* 5 October 1995, 10.

Zhandou jushe. 'Nü yingxiong Liu Hulan ben shi' (The capabilities of the heroine Liu Hulan), *RMRB* 13 June 1949, 4.

Zhang Lin and Shu Yang. *Zhao Yiman*. 1957, rpt. Beijing: Zhongguo gongren chubanshe, 2006.

Zhang Lin. 'Fang kang Ri lian jun de mama' (Visiting the mother of the troops allied against the Japanese), *RMRB* 6 (July 1952), 4.

Zhang Mu. 'Ding Ling xiaoshuo zhong de san ge nüxing' (Three women from Ding Ling's short stories), *Wenyi zhengming* (Literary and arts debates) 5 (1993), 39–43.

Zhang Yun. 'Nationalism and Beyond: Writings on Nüjie and the Emergence of a New Gendered Collective Identity in Modern China', *Nan nü: Men, Women and Gender in China* 17, no. 2 (2015).

Zhang Zailin. '"Se Jie"; Wang Jiazhi yuanxing diaoxiang jiemu, liqiu wei yingxiong zhengming' (Unveiling the statue for Wang Jiazhi's prototype: striving to rectify the name of a hero), *Zhongguo xinwen wang* (China news web), 7 June 2009, Web www.chinanews.com/cul/news/2009/06-07/1723521.shtml

Zhang Zhenhua. 'Zhang Zhenhua wei Ding Mocun shahai Zheng Pingru zhi *Datong bao* han: 1946 nian 12 yue 27 ri' (Letter to *Datong bao* from Zhang Zhenhua on Ding

Mocun's murder of Zheng Pingru: 27 December 1946), in Wang Chunnan (ed.), *Shenxun Wang wei hanjian bilü*, pp. 768–9.

Zhao Hongben. *Dongbei nü yingxiong Zhao Yiman* (Woman hero of the northeast, Zhao Yiman). Shanghai: Jiaoyu chubanshe, 1950.

Zhao Huasheng. *Zhao Yiman*. Shenyang: Liaoning meishu chubanshe 1986.

Zhao Kai. 'Guanyu Mao Zedong wei Liu Hulan liang ci tici de kaozheng' (Researching the two times Mao Zedong penned his epithet on Liu Hulan), *Dang de wenxian* (Literature of the Chinese Communist Party) 6 (2005), 77–8.

Zhao Qi. 'Yinggai xuexi Shi Lianxing shiyan Zhao Yiman juese de jingshen' (We ought to learn from Shi Lianxing's spirit in her depiction of Zhao Yiman), *RMRB* 24 (October 1951), 2.

Zhao Yiman (Yi Chao). 'Bei xiong sao boduo qiuxue quanli de wo' (Me, stripped of my rights to pursue an education by my brother and sister-in-law), *Funü zhoubao* (Women's weekly) 6 August 1924, 1–4.

Zheng Huajun. 'Zheng Huajun wei Ding Mocun shahai Zheng Pingru zhi shoudu gaodeng fayuan han' (Case presented to the Capital high court by Zheng Huajun against Ding Mocun on the killing of Zheng Pingru), in Wang Chunnan (ed.), *Shenxun Wang wei hanjian bilü,* pp. 717–19.

Zheng Nanyang. 'Shanghai gaodeng fayuan guanyu Zheng Pingru bei hai an xunwen bilü zhiyi: 1946 nian 12 yue 11 ri' (Part 1 of the hearing of the Shanghai high court into the harming of Zheng Pingru: 11 December 1946), in Wang Chunnan (ed.), *Shenxun Wang wei hanjian bilü,* pp. 746–9.

Zheng Yunshan and Chen Dehe. *Qiu Jin pingzhuan* (Critical biography of Qiu Jin). Zhengzhou: Henan jaioyu chubanshe, 1986.

Zheng Zhenfeng. 'Yi ge nü jiandie' (A woman spy), *Wenxuan* (Literary selections) 1: founding issue (1946), 18–19.

Zheng Zhenfeng. 'Yi ge nü jiandie' (A woman spy), *Xiandai wenxian yuekan* (Modern literature monthly) 1: founding issue (1946), 108–10.

Zheng Zhenfeng. 'Yi ge nü jiandie' (A woman spy), *Zhoubao* (The weekly) no. 5 (6 October 1945), 13.

Zheng, Su. 'Female Heroes and Moonish Lovers: Women's Paradoxical Identities in Modern Chinese Songs', *Journal of Women's History* 8, no. 4 (1997), 91–125.

Zhong diaoju. 'Zheng lieshi Pingru' (The martyr Zheng Pingru), 1964, rpt. in Xu Hongxin, *Yige nü jiandie,* pp. 122–3.

Zhongguo dianying chubanshe. *Hongse niangzi jun: Congjuben dao yingpian* (The Red Detachment of Women: from drama script to film). Beijing: Zhongguo dianying chubanshe, 1962.

Zhou Huimin. 'Zuihou yiwei Hongse niangzi jun lao zhanshi qushi' (The passing of the last old warrior from the Red Detachment of Women), *RMRB* 20 (April 2014), 4.

Zhou Xun. 'Bei chenfeng 71 nian de Li Hulan shi de yingxiong jiemei' (The Liu Hulan style heroic sisters covered in dust for 71 years), *Dangshi tiandi* (Party history heaven and earth) 2 (2000), 8–11.

Zhou Xun. 'Bei chenfeng 72 nian de Liu Hulan shi de "Yingxiong jiemei"' (The Liu Hulan style heroic sisters covered in dust for 72 years), *Wenshi chunqiu* (Spring and Autumn literature and history) 2 (2000), 14–8.

Zhou Yang (ed.). *Jiefangqu duanpian xiaoshuo xuan* (Collected short fiction from the liberated areas). Andong: Dongbei shudian, 1947.

Zhou Yang. 'Wenyi zhanxian shang de yi chang dabianlun' (A great debate at the front lines of literature and art), *RMRB* 28 (February 1958), 2.

Zhou Yibai. *Hua Mulan*. 1941 rpt. Hong Kong: Jindai tushu, 1958.

Zhou, Lili. 'The Reconstruction of Masculinity in China', PhD diss., University of Technology, Sydney, 2012.

Zhu Yu and Bai Ruixue. 'Weichu hanchu de "baba mama": zhuming kangzhan yinglie houren de zhuiyi' (They have never called 'father and mother': recalling the descendants of celebrated heroic martyrs from the war of resistance), *RMRB* 22 August 2005, 10.

Index